EVERYMAN, I will go with thee,
and be thy guide,

In thy most need to go by thy side

D1205979

LUCY HUTCHINSON
(*née* Apsley)

Born on 29th January 1620 in the Tower of London, the daughter of Sir Allen Apsley, Lieutenant-Governor of the Tower. Married John Hutchinson 1638 (who died at Sandown Castle, Kent, in 1664). Wrote the memoirs between 1664 and 1671. Date of death not known, but it was after 1675.

LUCY HUTCHINSON

Memoirs of the Life of Colonel Hutchinson

EDITED WITH A PREFACE BY
THE REV. JULIUS HUTCHINSON

INTRODUCTION BY
MARGARET BOTTRALL, M.A.

DENT: LONDON
EVERYMAN'S LIBRARY
DUTTON: NEW YORK

All rights reserved
Made in Great Britain
at the
Aldine Press · Letchworth · Herts
for
J. M. DENT & SONS LTD
Aldine House · Bedford Street · London
First included in Everyman's Library 1908
Last reprinted 1968

No. 1317   ISBN: 0 460 01317 3

CONTENTS

CONTENTS

HUTCHINSON OF OWTHORPE

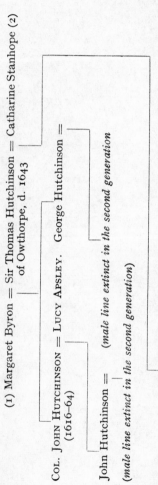

(1) Margaret Byron = Sir Thomas Hutchinson = Catharine Stanhope (2)
of Owthorpe, d. 1643

COL. JOHN HUTCHINSON = LUCY APSLEY. George Hutchinson =
(1616–64)

John Hutchinson =   (male line extinct in the second generation)
(male line extinct in the second generation)

Charles Hutchinson = a daughter and co-heiress of Sir F. Boteler of Hatfield Woodhall
(purchased Owthorpe after the
death of Col. Hutchinson

Julius Hutchinson = Betty Norton

Thomas Hutchinson, d.s.p.   a younger son =

THE REV. JULIUS HUTCHINSON
(editor of the memoirs)

INTRODUCTION

LUCY HUTCHINSON's Memoirs of her husband is a book that
no student of seventeenth-century English history can afford
to ignore. The upheavals of the Civil War gave rise to a good
many informal memoirs, which have been preserved in
private archives. This one was first published in 1806. Ever
since then social historians have recognized its value and
lovers of biography its charm.

Mrs Hutchinson wrote for the benefit of her children and to
moderate her own grief at her husband's untimely death; but
we have only to compare this biography with that written by
her Royalist contemporary, Ann Fanshawe, to perceive how
much more ambitious an effort it represents. Lady Fanshawe's delightfully intimate double portrait of her husband
and herself is not connected in any systematic way with a
survey of the general political scene. She recounts the adventures forced upon her by the troublous times, but does not
comment or moralize about public affairs. Lucy Hutchinson,
however, had her husband's reputation to vindicate. He had
died in prison, untried and ignored. She was very conscious of
the part he had played both in war and politics. Nothing less
than a 'Life and Times' type of biography could commemorate him fitly, even though it was not meant for the
eyes of strangers.

Mrs Hutchinson was not only a woman of outstanding
intelligence, admirably well educated; she had a strongly
developed historical sense. Even when she began to write her
autobiography, summing up 'some few things for my own
use', she was not content simply to trace her descent, describe
her parents, recall her childhood. To illustrate the particular
providence that had made her an Englishwoman, she included
a survey of English history, as if to suggest that no individual
life makes sense unless it is seen in a longer perspective.
Similarly in the Memoirs, she did not confine her account of
the Civil War to what she saw of it from her vantage-point as
wife of the governor of Nottingham Castle and town. She

incorporated material from May's *History of the Parliament of England* and referred to other contemporary records. When she felt that local incidents could not be properly understood without reference to the larger scene, she inserted a purposeful digression.

Mrs Hutchinson seems to have spent several years on the composition of these Memoirs. Certainly they represent much careful effort. No edition has yet appeared which systematically traces the relation between the biography in its final form and the draft which preceded it, fragments of which are in the British Museum.[1] Julius Hutchinson, her first editor,[2] called this 'a kind of diary', but it was not a record kept while the story was unfolding itself; rather, it was a notebook, fuller in some respects and more particularized, which Mrs Hutchinson used as a basis for the Memoirs. Sir Charles Firth refers frequently to this notebook in his footnotes and prints excerpts as appendices to his edition.[3] He also mentions the fact that Mrs Hutchinson incorporated in her narrative part of the account which the colonel himself wrote, and had printed, of his arrest and imprisonment in the Tower.,

Lucy Hutchinson included in her chronicle an immense amount of local detail. Her readers are made to feel the immediacy of the Civil War—the suspicions, the fears, the machinations, the occasional magnanimities. After a lapse of three centuries, the ins and outs of military and political manœuvres are sometimes tedious. Her first-hand impressions, however, can be extremely striking; e.g. her description of the routed cavaliers, who

> for two miles left a great track of blood, which froze as it fell upon the snow, for it was such bitter weather that the foot had waded almost to the middle in snow as they came, and were so numbed with cold when they came into the town that they were fain to be rubbed to get life into them, and in that condition were more eager for fires and warm meat than for plunder . . . (p. 164).

The personalities, seen at close range and depicted without fear or favour, are also very much alive. As a delineator of 'Characters', Lucy Hutchinson is less subtle and elaborate than Clarendon, but she had a real gift for epitomizing a

[1] B.M. Add. MS. 25901, Add. MS. 39779 ff. 42–47 and Add. MS. 46172N.
[2] *Memoirs of the Life of Colonel Hutchinson, Governor of Nottingham Castle and Town*, with preface and footnotes, 1806, 1808, 1810 and 1822.
[3] Revised edition, with additional notes, 1906.

man's disposition and manners; witness her presentation of the detestable Sir John Gell (p. 101) and the even more odious Humphrey Chadwick (p. 107). Her impressions of Oliver Cromwell, whom both she and her husband distrusted, and of the sober Henry Ireton, are of historic value; her sketches of James I and Charles I, though hostile, are shrewd and incisive. Those whom she whole-heartedly admired she could also picture convincingly; e.g. the valiant Colonel Thornhagh (p. 255) or, in the autobiographical fragment, her own father.

But it was the character and deeds of her adored husband that Lucy Hutchinson primarily aimed to describe and celebrate. He was a man worth praising; sincerely religious, a valiant soldier, a cultivated gentleman, good-looking and elegant. He was also hot-tempered and not much liked by the citizens of Nottingham, though his widow naturally dwelt only on his virtues. She exaggerated the importance of the part he played in national affairs, and also suppressed certain incidents that were to his discredit. The most signal instance of this is her handling of his attempts, at the Restoration, to escape the consequences of having signed the death-warrant of King Charles I. From the story Lucy Hutchinson tells of the letter of contrition that she sent to the Speaker of the House of Commons, counterfeiting her husband's signature, we gather that the colonel knew nothing of the enterprise, and that he was angered at what she evidently regarded as a proof of her devotion and cleverness. He may indeed have regretted his wife's intervention, but he did not repudiate the letter, which was phrased in terms of abject repentance. It alleged that men 'of seeming sanctity and subtle arts' had perverted his judgment by their 'pernicious snares'. It also promised that, if he were granted liberty on parole for the sake of his family, he would dedicate them and himself to the service of Charles II. Far from disowning this appeal, Colonel Hutchin- followed it up with a petition to the House of Lords, dated some six weeks after the Commons had acceded to his request for liberty, asking that the safety of his family and possessions might be assured and making 'humble and sorrowful acknow- ledgement of those crimes whereunto seduced judgment and not malice nor any other self-respect unfortunately betrayed him'.[1] Both petitions were backed up by recommendations

[1] Both letters are printed as appendices to the 1906 edition of the Memoirs by Sir C. H. Firth.

from Royalist friends and connections, and they were successful; but it is evident from the Memoirs that the colonel paid
for his liberty by forfeiting the regard of his parliamentarian
friends and by the loss of his own peace of mind.

Sir Charles Firth has pointed out two or three minor
incidents recorded by Mrs Hutchinson in her notebook, but
suppressed in the final version of the Memoirs because they
reflected adversely on her husband. But this editor, who was
not at all disposed to favour the colonel or his widow, stated
in his introduction that her accounts of the war as it affected
Nottingham are accurate, 'confirmed in almost every point
by the evidence of newspapers, letters and State papers'. He
also acknowledged that her character-sketches of people
involved in the conduct of affairs are factually sound, though
often passionately prejudiced.

As a historian, then, Lucy Hutchinson is to be taken
seriously, and as a biographer she was no mere eulogist. If
these Memoirs are compared with *The Life of William Cavendish, Duke of Newcastle,* written by the duchess and published
in 1667, the difference in tone and method is striking. The
duke was still alive when his wife's extravagant tribute was
printed. His exploits as a Royalist general and his life in exile
are duly chronicled, but the whole of the third book of
Margaret Cavendish's biography is a descriptive catalogue of
the duke's attributes. His personal appearance, his natural
humours, his pedigree, habits, diet, exercise, are methodically
chronicled; his misfortunes are also itemized. Lucy Hutchinson, though she prefaces her Memoirs with an eloquent address
to her children and an introductory account of her husband's
appearance, temperament and virtues, builds up her portrait
of him gradually as she proceeds with the story of his life. She
reveals her hero in action, reports his sayings, conveys to the
reader his development from a romantic youth, through a
strenuous career as soldier and statesman, to a man careworn,
disillusioned, patient in adversity and not unwilling to die.

Although she adopts a formal style for her narrative,
referring to herself as Mrs Hutchinson and trying to sustain a
judicious tone, the author herself emerges as vividly from the
pages of this biography as the colonel does. It is not only
through reading of episodes in which she actually participated
that we gain the impression of a woman with passionate
feelings, strong convictions and remarkable honesty. Her

whole endeavour to relate private to public issues betokens
an exceptional powerfulness of mind. Her autobiography
shows what a precocious little girl she was, and what an avid
bookworm. In the Memoirs we first meet her as a blue-
stocking, careless of the impression she made on others. It
was because she had 'sense above the rest' that young John
Hutchinson was attracted to Lucy Apsley before he ever met
her. She did not abandon her love of learning or her practice
of writing when she married. Her translation of Lucretius was
undertaken, she says, 'out of youthful curiosity to understand things I heard so much of at second-hand'. It was
carried out under conditions that might have deterred anyone
less resolute:

> I turned it into English in a room where my children practised
> the several qualities they were taught by their tutors, and I
> numbered the syllables of my translation by the threads of the
> canvas I wrought in, and set them down with a pen and ink that
> stood by me . . . How superficially it must needs be done in this
> manner, the thing itself will show . . .[1]

The verses included at the end of the present volume, in the
Beatus ille vein so fashionable in the mid seventeenth century,
may belong to a later period in her married life. Later still,
widowed and far from prosperous, she composed for her
daughter Mrs Orgill a treatise, *On the Principles of the Christian
Religion*, and another *On Theology*, which testify to her
continued vigour of mind.[2]

The variation of pace and tone is an attractive feature of
the Memoirs. Some of the effects were certainly contrived;
others give the effect of spontaneity. Quite often Mrs Hutchinson uses a sermonizing style, or employs heightened rhetoric.
The preliminary address to her children, a tissue of meta-
phors, is as elaborate a monument as any erected by her St
John uncle in the church of Lydiard Tregoze. She can, however, recount adventures with speed and verve, and enlivens
episodes with dialogue. Mrs Hutchinson's sense of humour
manifests itself from time to time, and her comments can be
either fiercely or demurely ironic. Sometimes she breaks into
the historic present. Occasionally, in spite of her attempted
impersonality, her feelings overcome her. 'We' and even 'I'

---

[1] Dedication to the Earl of Anglesey, 1675: reprinted in Firth's 1906
edition of the Memoirs, p. 452.
[2] Published by Julius Hutchinson, 1817.

supersede the distancing third person singular. There are inadvertent touches, too, which betray her close involvement. Describing the wretched room in Sandown Castle in which her husband was confined, she exclaims:

> The air made the chamber so unwholesome and damp, that even in the summer time the colonel's hat-case and trunks, and everything of leather, would be every day all covered over with mould—wipe them as clean as you could one morning, by the next day they would be mouldy again . . . (p. 371).

The punctuation of the original manuscript was regularized by its first editor, who thereby increased the coherence and slowed down the apparent tempo of the story. He did not modernize the spelling, though some subsequent editors did. H. Child (1904) (Dryden House Memoirs) preferred the seventeenth-century orthography. The Everyman's Library text is in the main a reprint of the fifth edition (Bohn, 1846). It now, however, contains as an appendix the original ending to the manuscript, which Julius Hutchinson rejected. He no doubt had artistic reasons to justify this high-handed piece of editing, but it is of great interest to have the final pages that Lucy Hutchinson wrote, so melancholy in her uncertainty as to what had really caused her husband's death. Worth preserving, too, is the strange little ghost story; why should the apparition of Mrs Hutchinson, still living at Owthorpe, have haunted the warders of Sandown Castle, rather than that of her husband, who died there?

Sydney Race exposed other editorial idiosyncrasies of Julius Hutchinson in two articles in *Notes and Queries*, April and May 1954. Not only did he choose to omit the second, elaborated Character which Mrs Hutchinson composed to commemorate her husband; even from the first description he left out, inexplicably, one vivid sentence:

> His eyes had an excellencie of beauty, vigor and cheerefulnesse, especially when he was well pleased, that conveyed delight to all that beheld them, and if he were angry darted a becoming fire as terrible as bright.

Julius Hutchinson also curtailed the account of the colonel's election to the 1660 parliament, cut out a long recital of his religious beliefs, together with a series of biblical quotations, and considerably shortened the narrative of the final months at Sandown Castle.

The original manuscript of the Memoirs is now in the possession of the City of Nottingham Museum and Art Gallery, which stands on the site of the castle defended by Colonel Hutchinson. Notes on the manuscript of Mrs Hutchinson's various works were contributed by Sydney Race to *Notes and Queries* at intervals from 1923; they are listed in the article referred to, April 1954; Mr Race's transcript of the original rejected ending of the Memoirs is reproduced from the May 1954 issue by permission of the Oxford University Press.

François Guizot's *Monk: chute de la République* (1851) contains an essay on the Hutchinson Memoirs. An anonymous translation of this was prefixed as an Introduction to the original Everyman edition of the Memoirs (1908–36). The possible influence of the Duchess of Newcastle's *Life* on Lucy Hutchinson's Memoirs is discussed by A. P. Upham in *Anglia*, vol. xxxvi, 1912, and by B. G. MacCarthy in *Women Writers: their contribution to the English Novel*, 1944. D. A. Stauffer includes a good appreciation of Lucy Hutchinson in Chapter V of his *English Biography before 1700*, 1930, and there is an interesting account of Lucy Hutchinson and her writings in Lady Stenton's *The English Woman in History*, 1957. The Memoirs are a source-book for historians of seventeenth-century Puritanism.

MARGARET BOTTRALL.

BIBLIOGRAPHY

Lucy Hutchinson's *Memoirs of the Life of Colonel Hutchinson, Governor of Nottingham Castle and Town* was edited with preface and footnotes by the Rev. Julius Hutchinson, who published them, together with the autobiographical fragment (pages 1–15 of the present volume), in 1806. With minor alterations this edition was reprinted in 1808, 1810 and 1822. The fifth edition (Bohn), 1846, included an account of the siege of Lathom House by another hand. Everyman's Library reprints the Bohn edition, omitting the account of Lathom House. The present, revised edition includes the original conclusion to the Memoirs, omitted by Julius Hutchinson. Other editions include Sir C. H. Firth (with a collection of Colonel Hutchinson's letters and extracts from an earlier account of the Civil War in Nottinghamshire, by Mrs Hutchinson), 1885, revised 1906; H. Child (Dryden House Memoirs), 1904.

The following works are referred to, but insufficiently or inaccurately identified, in Julius Hutchinson's footnotes to the present text:

Besse, J., *A Collection of the Sufferings of the People called Quakers from 1650 to 1689*, 1753. Burnet, G., *Bishop Burnet's History of His Own Time*, 1724 and 1734; ed. M. J. Routh, 7 vols., 1823. Clarendon, Edward Hyde, Earl of, *The History of the Rebellion and Civil Wars in England, Begun in the Year 1641*, 3 vols., 1702–4 (ed. D. W. Macray, 1888); *State Papers collected by Edward, Earl of Clarendon*, ed. R. Scroge and T. Monkhouse, 3 vols., 1767–86. Fox, G., *A Journal of Historical Account of the Life, Travels, Sufferings, Christian Experiences, and Labours of Love in the Work of the Ministry of that Ancient Eminent and Faithful Servant of Jesus Christ, George Fox*, ed. T. Ellwood and other, 1694; ed. N. Penney and T. E. Harvey, 2 vols., 1911; abridged version, ed. N. Penney, 1924 (Everyman's Library, No. 754). Granger, J., *A Bibliographical History of England, from Egbert the Great to the Revolution*, 2 vols. and supplement, 1769–74. Hamilton, A., *Mémoires de la vie du Comte de Grammont*, 1713; trans. A. Boyer, 1714. Heylin, P., *Aerius Redivivus; or, the History of the Presbyterians*, 1670. Ludlow, E., *Memoirs*, 3 vols. (bowdlerized), 1698–9; ed. Sir C. H. Firth, 2 vols. (unexpurgated), 1894. May, T., *The History of the Parliament of England: Which began November the third M.DC.XL, 1647*; ed. F. Maseres, 1812; reprinted, 1854; [May's History comes down to Sept. 1643]. Rapin de Thoyras, P., *Histoire de l'Angleterre*, 13 vols., 1724–36; trans. N. Tindal, 15 vols., 1725–31. Rushworth, J., *Historical Collections of Private Passages of State* [1618–49], 7 vols., 1659–1701. Sewel, W., *The History of the Rise*,

Increase and Progress of the Christian People called Quakers, 1722.
Sprigge, J., *Anglia rediviva; England's Recovery: Being the History of the Army under Sir Thomas Fairfax*, 1647; reprinted 1854. Thoroton, R., *The Antiquities of Nottinghamshire*, 1677; ed. J. Thoresby (as *A History of Nottinghamshire*), 3 vols., 1790. [Thurloe, J.], *A Collection of State Papers of John Thurloe*, ed. T. Birch, 7 vols., 1742. Walker, C., *History of Independency*, 2 vols., 1648–9. Warwick, Sir Philip, *Memoires of the Reigne of King Charles I*, 1701; ed. Sir Walter Scott, 1813. Whitelock, B., *Memorials of the English Affairs: from the beginning of the reign of King Charles the First, to King Charles the Second his happy restauration*, 1682; reprinted 1853.

EDITOR'S PREFACE

IT is conceived to be necessary, for the satisfaction of the public, to prefix to this work some account of the manuscripts from which it has been printed, and of the manner in which they came into the hands of the editor; which we shall accordingly do, interweaving therewith such subsequent information as we have been able to collect respecting the families and descendants of Colonel and Mrs. Hutchinson.

The memoirs of the Life of Colonel Hutchinson had been seen by many persons, as well as the editor, in the possession of the late Thomas Hutchinson, Esq., of Owthorpe, in Nottinghamshire, and of Hatfield Woodhall, in Hertfordshire; and he had been frequently solicited to permit them to be published, particularly by the late Mrs. Catharine Maccaulay, but had uniformly refused. This gentleman dying without issue, the editor, his nephew, inherited some part of his estates which were left unsold, including his mansion-house of Hatfield Woodhall. In the library he found the following books, written by Mrs. Lucy Hutchinson. First. The Life of Colonel Hutchinson. Second. A book without a title, but which appears to have been a kind of diary made use of when she came to write the Life of Colonel Hutchinson. Third. A Fragment giving an account of the early part of her own life. This book clearly appears to have been Mrs. Hutchinson's first essay at composition, and contains, besides the story of her life and family, several short copies of verses, some finished, some unfinished, many of which are above mediocrity. And, Fourth. Two books treating entirely of religious subjects; in which, although the fancy may be rather too much indulged, the judgment still maintains the ascendency, and sentiments of exalted piety, liberality, and benevolence, are delivered in terms apposite, dignified, and perspicuous.

These works had all been read, and marked in several places with his initials, by Julius Hutchinson, Esq., of Owthorpe, the father of the late Thomas Hutchinson, Esq., just mentioned, and son of Charles Hutchinson, Esq., of Owthorpe, only son of Sir Thomas Hutchinson by his second wife, the Lady Catharine Stanhope. Lady Catharine Hutchinson lived to the age of 102, and is reported to have retained her faculties to the end of her life. Some remarks made by the above-mentioned Julius Hutchinson, which will be found in their proper places in the body of the work, are declared by him to have been communicated by his grandmother Lady Catharine; and as this lady dwelt in splendour at Nottingham, and had ample means of information; as there is only one instance wherein the veracity of the biographer is at all called in question, and even in this, it does not appear to the editor, and probably may not to the reader, that there was sufficient ground for objection; the opposition and the acquiescence of her grandson and herself seem alike to confirm the authenticity and faithfulness of the narrative.

Colonel Hutchinson left four sons, of which the youngest only, John, left issue, two sons; and there is a tradition in the family, that these two last descendants of Colonel Hutchinson emigrated, the one to the West Indies or America, the other to Russia; the latter is said to have gone out with the command of a ship of war given by Queen Anne to the Czar Peter, and to have been lost at sea. One of the female descendants of the former the editor once met with by accident at Portsmouth, and she spoke with great warmth of the veneration in which his descendants in the new world held the memory of their ancestor Colonel Hutchinson. Of the daughters little more is known than that Mrs. Hutchinson, addressing one of her books of devotion to her daughter, Mrs. Orgill, ascertains that one of them was married to a gentleman of that name.

The family of Mr. George Hutchinson likewise became extinct in the second generation.

Charles Hutchinson, only son of Sir Thomas Hutchinson by Lady Catharine Stanhope, married one of the daughters and co-heiresses of Sir Francis Boteler, of Hatfield Woodhall, Herts; which family being zealous royalists, and he solicitous to gain their favour (which he did so effectually, as in the end to obtain nearly their whole inheritance), it is probable that he gave small encouragement or assistance to the elder branch of the family while they suffered for their republican sentiments; on the contrary, it is certain that he purchased of Mrs. Hutchinson and her son, after the death of Colonel Hutchinson, their estate at Owthorpe, which, joined to what his father had given him, and what he obtained by his marriage, raised him to more opulence than his father had ever possessed; and he seems not to have fallen short of him in popularity, for he represented the town of Nottingham in parliament from the year 1690 (being the first general election after the accession of King William) till his death.

His son Julius returned into that line of conduct and connexions which was most natural for one of his descent, for he married Betty, daughter of Colonel Norton, of Wellow, of the well-known patriotic family of that name in Hampshire, and whose mother was a Fiennes. He seems to have bestowed a very rational and well-deserved attention upon the writings of Mrs. Hutchinson, and there is a tradition in the family, that although he had many children of his own, he treated with kindness and liberality the last descendants of his uncle, and assisted them with money to fit them out for their emigration. The editor has seen a written memorandum of his, expressing his regret at hearing no more of them after their departure.

From the circumstance of these, the only grandchildren of Colonel Hutchinson, standing in need of this pecuniary assistance, from the mention Mrs. Hutchinson makes of her husband's debts, and from an expression contained in that book which she addresses to her daughter, Mrs. Orgill, desiring her not to despise her advice though she sees her in adversity, it is highly probable that, even after selling her husband's estates, the sum to be divided left each member of the family in strait circumstances.

The affection and well-merited esteem with which Mrs. Hutchinson speaks of her brother Sir Allen Apsley, will excite an interest in the reader to know what became of him and his posterity. By two marriages, and by the death of his grandson in his minority, the family of Apsley entirely merged in the noble family of Bathurst, who have adopted the name Apsley as their second title; there are five or six of the family of Apsley entombed in Westminster Abbey, near to the entrance of Henry the Seventh's Chapel.

Having traced the manuscript from the hands of the writer to those of the editor, in such a manner as to establish its authenticity beyond all doubt; the next, and that not a less important point, is to remove those objections which may be raised against the tendency of a work of this nature, and to show that the assumption of any evil tendency is groundless.

That avowed predilection for a republican government, which is conspicuous in this history, as it was in the lives of the persons who are the principal subjects of it, may perhaps give a momentary alarm; but a little reflection will dissipate it. At the time when Colonel Hutchinson first entered on the great theatre of life, the contest was just begun between the partisans of the divine right of the sovereign, and the indispensable obligation of the subject to a passive obedience and nonresistance, on one side; and the assertors of the claims of the people to command, through their representatives, the public purse, the freedom of debate in parliament, and the responsibility of ministers, on the other. When the sword, the *ratio ultima regum,* the *last appeal of kings,* was resorted to by the former, and the latter gained the victory, they very naturally adopted the republican system, as concluding, that persons holding such opinions as the princes of the House of Stuart and their adherents did, would never concede to them their franchises, but with a full intention to resume them, whenever they should recover power enough to attempt it with success. The event fully justified this conclusion,[1] and it is now evident to all, that the only thing which could ever give this nation permanent tranquillity, and put an end to those heartburnings which either openly or covertly had existed even from the time of the Norman conquest, was an explicit compact between king and people, which took its date indeed from the revolution in 1688, but obtained its consummation at the fortunate accession of the house of Brunswick, when the title of the monarch, and the rights of the people, became identified and established on one common basis. Of this truly may be said,

> Quod optanti Divum permittere nemo
> Auderet, volvenda dies en attulit ultrò.—*Virg. Æn.* ix. 6, 7.

> What to his vot'ry not a God dared promise,
> Revolving years spontaneously produced.

---

[1] In the reigns of Charles II. and James II.

No one will pretend that such an occasion was within the reach of human foresight; of course the only remedy then attainable was applied to the disorder of the state. Upon a fair review of the contest it will be seen, that what the tory and the courtier of the present day, the friend or even the flatterer of kingly power admits as axioms, were the grand desiderata of the whig and the patriot of those times; and that what were then cried out upon as daring encroachments, now pass as the most moderate and unquestioned claims. Not to deceive ourselves then with words, nor attach our minds to names instead of things, although the government under which we prosper be termed Imperial; yet the greater part of the legislative power resting with the people, and the executive being vested in a chief magistrate, who is under so many limitations that he seems placed in that situation very much more for the common weal, the public benefit, than his own ease or advantage, it must be allowed to come up to Colonel Hutchinson's favourite idea of a republic for all beneficial purposes, and would assuredly be not less acceptable to him, for that the hereditary succession would be found to repress that effervescence of individual ambition which was the study and the labour of his life to keep down. Possessing himself, but finding not in others, the virtue worthy of and essential to a republic, he would gladly have taken shelter under a well-limited monarchy, and of such a one he would unquestionably have been a loyal subject, a vigorous assertor.

The Puritanism which appears in the story, and actuated the conduct of Colonel Hutchinson all through life, may be accounted for on almost a similar ground with his predilection for a republic.

The puritanic turn of thought and style of expression had been adopted by the vindicators of religious freedom and right of inquiry, with whom the champions of civil liberty naturally made common cause. Divinity as a science was a study then in vogue, and seems to have tinctured the conversation and writings of the greater part of society.[1] In

---

[1] From the practice of dragging religion or religious phraseology into the service of politics, none, not even the king, was exempt, who, making a speech to his small army in the year 1642, to animate them, tells them they will have none to encounter but rebels, most of them *Brownists, Anabaptists,* and *Atheists!* who would destroy both church and commonwealth.

this Mr. Hutchinson had been encouraged by his father, whose library subsisted at his family seat of Owthorpe till about the year 1775, and contained a vast number of folio volumes of polemical divinity. A study environed with many dangers! and which led Colonel Hutchinson into whatever errors he was guilty of. On another hand, the ministers of the established church in those times preached up the prerogative in all its extravagance, and endeavoured to establish, jointly and inseparably, implicit faith in, and unqualified obedience to, the church and king (still giving the church the precedency); whilst the laymen of their party practised, and even professed, a total dissoluteness of life; so that those who were slaves in principle were libertines in practice, while those who were deemed rebels by the court, and latitudinarians by the hierarchy, were rigorists in religion and morality.

This contrariety produced a constant and incessant opposition, augmented the vehemence of antipathy, fortified prejudice, and seemed almost to justify bigotry.[1] But from this (bigotry) we are bound to exculpate Colonel Hutchinson. The Independents, to whose party, if a man of so much candour and liberality can be said to be of any party, he belonged, proceeded upon that principle, which, however general soever it ought to be, is however unfortunately very uncommon, of allowing to all that liberty of conscience they demanded for themselves. Accordingly, they began by desiring only an act[2] to be passed "for taking away all coercive power, authority, and jurisdiction, from bishops, extending to civil penalties," etc. It was not till after they saw the extreme pertinaciousness of the king to retain the bishops as instruments at a future opportunity for remounting his system of arbitrary sway, and that "the prelatical party about him prevailed with him to refuse an accommodation, and hazard his crown and life, rather than diminish their greatness and power to persecute others," that they insisted on the abolition of the order.[3] It was quite a

---

[1] The flower of the French democrats avoided all such inconsistency and paradox, by discarding at once their king, their God, and their morality.

[2] Articles of the army, Rushworth, vol. vii. p. 731.

[3] The words of Whitelocke, p. 340, where he regrets that the king's chaplains prevailed with him beyond the parliament's commissioners or his own judgment.

different party, that of the rigid Presbyterians, and peculiarly their ministers, " who cried out against the tyranny of the bishops only that they might get the power into their own hands, and, without the name, might exercise the authority [1] of popes." That instead of this power being irrevocably and immovably established over us, we are now governed by the mildest church discipline in the universe, we owe to these Independents! Colonel Hutchinson in particular, if he had lived in times like ours, " when bishops and ministers desire only to be helpers,[2] not lords over the consciences of God's people," would either have been a conforming member of the church of England, or at most have only dissented from it in few things, and that with modesty and moderation. For it is well worthy of notice, that after having suffered provocation and persecution from catholic, episcopalian, and presbyterian, when power came into his own hands he treated all with lenity, and to the worthy persons of all sects and parties extended his protection.

We have next to consider a part of the conduct of Colonel Hutchinson, which will be the most generally blamed, and is the least capable of defence, the condemnation of Charles the First. To speak of the justice of such a measure in a legal point of view would be a mockery; nothing but the breaking up of the very foundations of the state, and a war of its elements, could let in the possibility of such a procedure. Amidst the tempest and darkness which then involved the whole political horizon, it savours of presumption to decide what measures were right, expedient, or even necessary: this much alone may safely be asserted, that the king and his friends during the contest, and still more after it was virtually ended by the battle of Naseby, maintained such a conduct as rendered his destruction inevitable: but the remark of Whitelocke, p. 363, seems no less just than ingenious: " that such an irregular and unheard of business should have been left to that irregular set of men—the army, who urged it on." They, however, were determined to throw the odium on others, or at least draw others in to share it.

Be it as it may, though some may blame, many more will pity a man such as Colonel Hutchinson, who found or con-

[1] *Vide* Letter of Irving, laird of Drum, and his appeal to Colonel Overton: Whitelocke, p. 526.

[2] Words of Cromwell in his letter to the Scots ministers: Whitelocke p. 473.

ceived himself reduced to the cruel alternative of permitting all that system of liberty, civil and religious, to the establishment of which he had devoted all his faculties, and was ready to sacrifice his existence, to be risked upon the good faith of a man whose misfortune it was, to say no worse, to be environed by designing and ambitious persons, who rendered all his virtues abortive, and made all afraid to trust him, or of signing a sentence which has since been called a murder, and the undergoing it a martyrdom! at any rate, it would be highly ungracious and ungrateful in us, while we enjoy in our well-balanced constitution, the benefits derived to us from the virtue, the energy, the sufferings, and even the faults of our ancestors, to pass a severe censure on their conduct; for it will hardly be denied, that the remembrance of his father's fate influenced James the Second to yield so easy and bloodless a victory to his opponents, and leave them to settle the constitution amidst calm and sober councils.   On the contrary, we are bound to ascribe many of the oversights of those first founders of our liberties, to a precipitancy forced on them by urgent circumstances, to cast a veil over their imperfections, and cherish their memory with thankfulness.

So much having been said for the purpose of obviating misapprehension as to the effect of this work, it may be further expected that some merit or utility should be shown, to justify the editor in presenting it to the public notice. Being not the child of his brain and fancy, but of his adoption and judgment, he may be supposed to view it with so much the less partiality, and allowed to speak of it with so much the more freedom.

The only ends for which any book can reasonably be published are to inform, to amuse, or to improve: but unless many persons of highly reputed judgment are mistaken as well as ourselves, this work will be found to attain all three of them. In point of amusement, perhaps novelty or curiosity holds the foremost rank; and surely we risk little in saying that a history of a period the most remarkable in the British annals, written one hundred and fifty years ago by a lady of elevated birth, of a most comprehensive and highly cultivated mind, herself a witness of many of the scenes she describes, and active in several of them, is a literary curiosity of no mean sort.

As to information, although there are many histories of the same period, there is not one that is generally considered satisfactory; most of them carry evident marks of prejudice or partiality; nor were any of those which are now read written at or near the time, or by persons who had an opportunity of being well acquainted with what was passing, except that of Clarendon. But any one who should take the pains, which the editor has done, to examine Clarendon's *State Papers*, would find therein documents much better calculated to support Mrs. Hutchinson's representation of affairs than that which he himself has given. Mrs. Hutchinson writing from a motive which will very seldom be found to induce any one to take so much trouble, that of giving her children, and especially her eldest son, then about to enter on the stage of life, a true notion of those eventful scenes which had just been passing before her eyes, and which she well judged must be followed by others not less interesting to the same cause and persons, will surely be thought to have possessed both the means and the inclination to paint with truth and correctness: in effect, she will be seen to exhibit such a faithful, natural, and lively picture of the public mind and manners, taken sometimes in larger, sometimes in smaller groups, as will give a more satisfactory idea to an observant reader than he will anywhere else discover. He will be further pleased to see avoided the most common error of historians, that of displaying the paradoxical and the marvellous, both in persons and things. But surely the use of history being to instruct the present and future ages by the experience of the past, nothing can be more absurd than a wish to excite and leave the reader in astonishment, which instead of assisting, can only confound his judgment. Mrs. Hutchinson, on the contrary, has made it her business, and that very successfully, to account by common and easy causes for many of those actions and effects which others have left unaccounted for, and only to be gazed at in unmeaning wonder; or, in attempting to account for them, have employed vain subtlety or groundless conjecture. She has likewise not merely described the parties in the state by their general character, but delineated them in *their minute ramifications*, and thus enabled us to trace the springs, and discover the reasonableness of many of those proceedings which had hitherto seemed incongruous and inconsistent.

Many of these instances will be pointed out in the notes as the passages arise.

But the greater merit shall appear in this work as a history, the greater will be the regret that the writer did not dedicate more of her attention to render it complete and full, instead of summary.

However, the most numerous class of readers are the lovers of biography, and to these it has of late been the practice of historians to address themselves, as Lyttleton in his *Life of Henry the Second*, Robinson of *Charles the Fifth*, Roscoe of *Leo the Tenth*, and many minor writers. Perhaps the prevalence of this predilection may be traced to the circumstance of the reader's thus feeling himself to be, as it were, a party in the transactions which are recounted. A person of this taste will, it is hoped, here have his wishes completely gratified; for he will, in fancy, have lived in times, and witnessed scenes the most interesting that can be imagined to the human mind, especially the mind of an Englishman; he will have conversed with persons the most celebrated and extraordinary, whom one party represent as heroes and demi-gods, the other as demons, but whom, having had opportunity to view close at hand, he will judge to have been truly great men, and to have carried at once to a high degree of perfection the characters of the warrior, the politician, the legislator, and the philosopher; yet to have had their great qualifications alloyed by such failings, and principally the want of moderation, as defeated their grand designs. He will have accompanied the hero of the tale, not only through all the ages of life, but through almost every situation in society, from the lowest that can become noticeable, which Mrs. Hutchinson calls the *even ground of a gentleman*, to the highest which his principles permitted him to aspire to, that of a counsellor of state, in a large and flourishing republic; he will have seen him mark each with the exercise of its appropriate grace and virtue, and so completely to have adapted himself to each department, as to appear always to move in the sphere most natural to him: and, finally, to have maintained so steady a course through all the vicissitudes of prosperity and adversity, as enabled him, though he could neither control the conduct of his coadjutors, nor stem the fluctuating tides of fortune or popular opinion, yet to preserve for himself not only the great and inexhaustible resource of a good conscience, but even the unanimous esteem of the great assembly of the nation, when they agreed in no other thing; he will no doubt be sensible that such a character is rare, but he will perceive such a consistency and harmony of parts as to make him deem the whole easy of belief, and conclude that such an one would be even more difficult to feign than to find; he will hence be led to concur with us in asserting, that it is much more efficacious and conducive to improvement and to the advancement of morality thus to hold forth a great example in real life, and to elicit principle from practice, than first to feign a sentiment, and then actions and events to support it, as has been done both by ancients and moderns, from the *Hercules* of Prodicus to the *Grandison* of Richardson. Nor has the skill and attention of our author been confined to the portraying of her principal character, she has equally succeeded in the delineation of the subordinate ones; so that whenever their speeches or actions are brought afresh before our view, we need not that they should be named in order to recognise the personage; and both in this department, and in that of the development of the intrigues which she occasionally lays open to us, we shall acknowledge the advantage of her adding to the vigour of a masculine understanding, the nice feeling and discrimination, the delicate touch of the pencil of a female.

As to the style and phraseology, there are so few prose writings of a prior or coeval date now read, that we should be at a loss to point out any which could have served her for models, or us for a standard of comparison; nor does it so much appear to us to bear the stamp of any particular age, as by its simplicity, significancy, and propriety, to be worthy of imitation in all times. Some expressions will be found that are uncommon, or used in an uncommon sense, but they are such as are justified by classical propriety, and, had her book been published, would probably have been adopted and brought into general use.

We conclude with expressing a confident hope, that the public will find this memoir to be such as we first announced it,—a faithful image of the mode of thinking in those days of which it treats, an interesting and new specimen of private and public character, of general and individual biography; and that recommended as it comes by clearness of discern-

ment, strength and candour of judgment, simplicity, and
perspicuity of narrative, pure, amiable, and Christian
morality, sentiments at once tender and elevated, conveyed
in language elegant, expressive, and classical, occasionally
embellished with apposite, impressive, and well-supported
figures, it will be found to afford pleasure and instruction to
every class of readers.

The ladies will feel that it carries with it all the interest of
a novel, strengthened with the authenticity of real history;
they will no doubt feel an additional satisfaction in learning,
that though the author added to the erudition of the scholar,
the research of the philosopher, the politician, and even the
divine, the zeal and magnanimity of a patriot; yet she descended from all these elevations to perform, in the most
exemplary manner, the functions of a wife, a mother, and
mistress of a family.

THE LIFE OF

MRS. LUCY HUTCHINSON

WRITTEN BY HERSELF

A FRAGMENT

THE Almighty Author of all beings,[1] in his various providences, whereby he conducts the lives of men from the cradle to the tomb, exercises no less wisdom and goodness than he manifests power and greatness, in their creation; but such is the stupidity of blind mortals, that instead of employing their studies in these admirable books of providence, wherein God daily exhibits to us glorious characters of his love, kindness, wisdom, and justice, they ungratefully regard them not, and call the most wonderful operations of the great God the common accidents of human life, especially if they be such as are usual, and exercised towards them in ages wherein they are not very capable of observation, and whereon they seldom employ any reflection; for in things great and extraordinary, some, perhaps, will take notice of God's working, who either forget or believe not that he takes as well a care and account of their smallest concernments, even the hairs of their heads.

Finding myself in some kind guilty of this general neglect, I thought it might be a means to stir up my thankfulness for

---

[1] That noble turn of thought which led Mrs. Hutchinson to open her work with thanks to her Maker, instead of apologies to the readers, besides the claim it has to their respect instead of their indulgence, will probably by its originality recommend itself, and prevent the distaste which the air of religion it wears might give to many, in times when it is so little in fashion. It should be borne in mind that the usage of the times in which it was written was so very different from the present, that those who wish to read with pleasure the works then written, will do well to set their taste according to that standard.

Through the whole of both these works, moral and religious reflections will be seen to abound, but so as neither to confuse nor fetter, but rather elevate the mind.

things past, and to encourage my faith for the future, if I recollected as much as I have heard or can remember of the passages of my youth, and the general and particular providences exercised to me, both in the entrance and progress of my life. Herein I meet with so many special indulgences as require a distinct consideration, they being all of them to be regarded as talents intrusted to my improvement for God's glory. The parents by whom I received my life, the places where I began and continued it, the time when I was brought forth to be a witness of God's wonderful workings in the earth, the rank that was given me in my generation, and the advantages I received in my person, each of them carries along with it many mercies which are above my utterance, and as they give me infinite cause of glorifying God's goodness, so I cannot reflect on them without deep humiliation for the small improvement I have made of so rich a stock; which, that I may yet by God's grace better employ, I shall recall and seriously ponder: and, first, as far as I have since learnt, set down the condition of things in the place of my nativity, at that time when I was sent into the world. It was on the 29th day of January, in the year of our Lord 1619-20, that in the Tower of London, the principal city of the English Isle, I was, about four of the clock in the morning, brought forth to behold the ensuing light. My father was Sir Allen Apsley, lieutenant of the Tower of London; my mother, his third wife, was Lucy, the youngest daughter of Sir John St. John, of Lidiard Tregooze, in Wiltshire, by his second wife. My father had then living a son and a daughter by his former wives, and by my mother three sons, I being her eldest daughter. The land was then at peace (it being towards the latter end of the reign of King James), if that quietness may be called a peace, which was rather like the calm and smooth surface of the sea, whose dark womb is already impregnated with a horrid tempest.

Whoever considers England will find it no small favour of God to have been made one of its natives, both upon spiritual and outward accounts. The happiness of the soil and air contribute all things that are necessary to the use or delight of man's life. The celebrated glory of this isle's inhabitants, ever since they received a mention in history, confers some honour upon every one of her children, and with it an obligation to continue in that magnanimity and virtue, which hath famed this island, and raised her head in glory higher than the great kingdoms of the neighbouring continent. Britain hath been as a garden enclosed, wherein all things that man can wish, to make a pleasant life, are planted and grow in her own soil, and whatsoever foreign countries yield, to increase admiration and delight, are brought in by her fleets. The people, by the plenty of their country, not being forced to toil for bread, have ever addicted themselves to more generous employments, and been reckoned, almost in all ages, as valiant warriors as any part of the world sent forth: insomuch, that the greatest Roman captains thought it not unworthy of their expeditions, and took great glory in triumphs for imperfect conquests. Lucan upbraids Julius Cæsar for returning hence with a repulse, and it was two hundred years before the land could be reduced into a Roman province, which at length was done, and such of the nation, then called Picts, as scorned servitude, were driven into the barren country of Scotland, where they have ever since remained a perpetual trouble to the successive inhabitants of this place. The Britons, that thought it better to work for their conquerors in a good land, than to have the freedom to starve in a cold or barren quarter, were by degrees fetched away, and wasted in the civil broils of these Roman lords, till the land, almost depopulated, lay open to the incursions of every borderer, and were forced to call a stout warlike people, the Saxons, out of Germany, to their assistance. These willingly came at their call, but were not so easily sent out again, nor persuaded to let their hosts inhabit with them, for they drove the Britons into the mountains of Wales, and seated themselves in those pleasant countries which from the new masters received a new name, and ever since retained it, being called England; and on which the warlike Dane made many attempts, with various success, but after about two or three hundred years' vain contest, they were for ever driven out, with shame and loss, and the Saxon Heptarchy melted into a monarchy, which continued till the superstitious prince, who was sainted for his ungodly chastity, left an empty throne to him that could seize it. He who first set up his standard in it, could not hold it, but with his life left it again for the Norman usurper, who partly by violence, partly by falsehood, laid here the foundation of his monarchy, in the people's blood, in which it hath swam about five hundred years, till the flood that bore it was ploughed into such deep furrows as had almost sunk the proud vessel. Of those Saxons that remained subjects to the Norman conqueror, my father's family descended; of those Normans that came in with him, my mother's was derived; both of them, as all the rest in England, contracting such affinity, by mutual marriages, that the distinction remained but a short space; Normans and Saxons becoming one people, who by their valour grew terrible to all the neighbouring princes, and have not only bravely acquitted themselves in their own defence, but have showed abroad how easily they could subdue the world, if they did not prefer the quiet enjoyment of their own part above the conquest of the whole.

Better laws and a happier constitution of government no nation ever enjoyed, it being a mixture of monarchy, aristocracy, and democracy, with sufficient fences against the pest of every one of those forms—tyranny, faction, and confusion; yet is it not possible for man to devise such just and excellent bounds, as will keep in wild ambition, when prince's flatterers encourage that beast to break his fence, which it hath often done, with miserable consequences both to the prince and people; but could never in any age so tread down popular liberty, but that it arose again with renewed vigour, till at length it trod on those that trampled it before. And in the just bounds, wherein our kings were so well hedged in, the surrounding princes have with terror seen the reproof of their usurpations over their free brethren, whom they rule rather as slaves than subjects, and are only served for fear, but not for love; whereas this people have ever been as affectionate to good, as unpliable to bad sovereigns.

Nor is it only valour and generosity that renown this nation; in arts we have advanced equal to our neighbours, and in those that are most excellent, exceeded them. The world hath not yielded men more famous in navigation, nor ships better built or furnished. Agriculture is as ingeniously practised; the English archers were the terror of Christendom, and their clothes the ornament; but these low things bounded not their great spirits, in all ages it hath yielded men as famous in all kinds of learning, as Greece or Italy can boast of.

And to complete the crown of all their glory, reflected from the lustre of their ingenuity, valour, wit, learning, justice, wealth, and bounty, their piety and devotion to God, and his worship, hath made them one of the most truly noble nations in the Christian world. God having as it were enclosed a people here, out of the waste common of the world, to serve him with a pure and undefiled worship. Lucius the British king was one of the first monarchs of the earth that received the faith of Christ into his heart and kingdom; Henry the Eighth, the first prince that broke the antichristian yoke off from his own and his subjects' necks. Here it was that the first Christian emperor received his crown; here began the early dawn of Gospel light, by Wickliffe and other faithful witnesses, whom God raised up after the black and horrid midnight of antichristianism; and a more plentiful harvest of devout confessors, constant martyrs, and holy worshippers of God, hath not grown in any field of the church, throughout all ages, than those whom God hath here glorified his name and gospel by. Yet hath not this wheat been without its tares; God in comparison with other countries hath made this as a paradise, so, to complete the parallel, the serpent hath in all times been busy to seduce, and not unsuccessful; ever stirring up opposers to the infant truths of Christ.

No sooner was the faith of Christ embraced in this nation, but the neighbouring heathens invaded the innocent Christians, and slaughtered multitudes of them; and when, by the mercy of God, the conquering Pagans were afterwards converted, and there were none left to oppose the name of Christ with open hostility, then the subtle serpent put off his own horrid appearance, and comes out in a Christian dress, to persecute Christ in his poor prophets, that bore witness against the corruption of the times. This intestine quarrel hath been more successful to the devil, and more afflictive to the church, than all open wars; and, I fear, will never happily be decided, till the Prince of Peace come to conclude the controversy, which at the time of my birth was working up into that tempest, wherein I have shared many perils, many fears, and many sorrows; and many more mercies, consolations, and preservations, which I shall have occasion to mention in other places.

From the place of my birth I shall only desire to remember the goodness of the Lord, who hath caused my lot to fall in a good ground; who hath fed me in a pleasant pasture, where the well-springs of life flow to all that desire to drink of them. And this is no small favour, if I consider how many poor people perish among the heathen, where they never hear the name of Christ; how many poor Christians spring up in countries enslaved by Turkish and antichristian tyrants, whose souls and bodies languish under miserable slavery. None know what mercy it is to live under a good and wholesome law, that have not considered the sad condition of being subject to the will of an unlimited man; and surely it is too universal a sin in this nation, that the common mercies of God to the whole land are so slightly regarded, and so inconsiderately passed over; certainly these are circumstances which much magnify God's loving-kindness and his special favour to all that are of English birth, and call for a greater return of duty from us than from all other people of the world.

Nor is the place only, but the time of my coming into the world, a considerable mercy to me. It was not in the midnight of popery, nor in the dawn of the gospel's restored day, when light and shades were blended and almost undistinguished, but when the Sun of truth was exalted in his progress, and hastening towards a meridian glory. It was, indeed, early in the morning, God being pleased to allow me the privilege of beholding the admirable growth of gospel light in my days: and oh! that my soul may never forget to bless and praise his name for the wonders of power and goodness, wisdom and truth, which have been manifested in this my time.

The next blessing I have to consider in my nativity is my parents, both of them pious and virtuous in their own conversation, and careful instructors of my youth, not only by precept but example; which, if I had leisure and ability, I should have transmitted to my posterity, both to give them the honour due from me in such a grateful memorial, and to increase my children's improvement of the patterns they set them; but since I shall detract from those I would celebrate, by my imperfect commemorations, I shall content myself to sum up some few things for my own use, and let the rest alone, which I either knew not, or have forgotten, or cannot worthily express.

My grandfather by the father's side was a gentleman of a competent estate, about £700 or £800 a year, in Sussex. He being descended of a younger house, had his residence at a place called Pulborough; the family out of which he came was an Apsley of Apsley, a town where they had been seated before the conquest, and ever since continued, till of late the last heir male of that eldest house, being the son of Sir Edward Apsley, died without issue, and his estate went with his sister's daughters into other families. Particularities concerning my father's kindred or country I never knew much of, by reason of my youth at the time of his death, and my education in far distant places; only in general I have heard, that my grandfather was a man well reputed and beloved in his country, and that it had been such a continued custom for my ancestors to take wives at home, that there was scarce a family of any note in Sussex to which they were not by intermarriages nearly related; but I was myself a stranger to them all, except my Lord Goring, who living at court, I have seen with my father, and heard of him, because he was appointed one of my father's executors, though he declined the trouble. My grandfather had seven sons, of which my father was the youngest; to the eldest he gave his whole estate, and to the rest, according to the custom of those times, slight annuities. The eldest brother married to a gentlewoman of a good family, and by her had only one son, whose mother dying, my uncle married himself again to one of his own maids, and by her had three more sons, whom, with their mother, my cousin William Apsley, the son of the first wife, held in such contempt, that a great while after, dying without children, he gave his estate of inheritance to my father, and two of my brothers, except about £100 a year to the eldest of his half brothers, and annuities of £30 a piece to the three for their lives. He died before I was born, but I have heard very honourable mention of him in our family. The rest of my father's brothers went into the wars in Ireland and the Low Countries, and there remained none of them, nor their issues, when I was born, but only three daughters who bestowed themselves meanly, and their generations are worn out, except two or three unregarded children. My father, at the death of my grandfather, being but a youth at school, had not patience to stay the perfecting of his studies, but put himself into present action, sold his annuity, bought himself good clothes, put some money in his purse, and came to London; and by means of a relation at court, got a place in the household of Queen Elizabeth, where he behaved himself so that he won the love of many of the court; but being young, took an affection to gaming, and spent most of the money he had in his purse. About that time, the Earl of Essex was setting forth on a voyage to Cadiz, and my father, that had a mind to quit his idle court life, procured an employment from the victualler of the navy, to go along with that fleet. In which voyage he demeaned himself with so much courage and prudence, that after his return he was honoured with a very noble and profitable employment in Ireland. There a rich widow, that had many children, cast her affections upon him, and he married her; but she not living many years with him, and having no children by him, after her death he distributed all her estate among her children, for whom he ever preserved a fatherly kindness, and some of her grand-children were brought up in his house after I was born. He, by God's blessing, and his fidelity and industry, growing in estate and honour, received a knighthood from king James soon after his coming to the crown, for some eminent service done to him in Ireland, which, having only heard in my childhood, I cannot perfectly set down. After that, growing into a familiarity with Sir George Carew, made now by the king Earl of Totness, a niece of this earl's, the daughter of Sir Peter Carew, who lived a young widow in her uncle's house, fell in love with him, which her uncle perceiving, procured a marriage between them. She had divers children by my father, but only two of them, a son and daughter, survived her, who died whilst my father was absent from her in Ireland. He led, all the time of his widowhood, a very disconsolate life, careful for nothing in the world but to educate and advance the son and daughter, the dear pledges she had left him, for whose sake he quitted himself of his employments abroad, and procured himself the office of Victualler of the Navy, a place then both of credit and great revenue. His friends, considering his solitude, had procured him a match of a very rich widow, who was a lady of as much discretion as wealth; but while he was upon this design he chanced to see my mother, at the house of Sir William St. John, who had married her eldest sister; and though he went on his journey, yet something in her person and behaviour, which he carried along with him, would not let him accomplish it, but brought him back to my mother. She was of a noble family, being the youngest daughter of Sir John St. John, of Liddiard Tregooze in the county of Wilts; her father and mother died when she was not above five years of age, and yet at her nurse's, from whence she was carried to be brought up in the house of the Lord Grandison, her father's younger brother; an honourable and excellent person, but married to a lady so jealous of him, and so ill-natured in her jealous fits, to anything that was related to him, that her cruelties to my mother exceeded the stories of step-mothers. The rest of my aunts, my mother's sisters, were dispersed to several places, where they grew up till my uncle, Sir John St. John, being married to the daughter of Sir Thomas Laten, they were all again brought home to their brother's house. There were not in those days so many beautiful women found in any family as these, but my mother was by the most judgments preferred before all her elder sisters, who, something envious at it, used her unkindly. Yet all the suitors that came to them still turned their addresses to her, which she in her youthful innocency neglected, till one of greater name, estate, and reputation than the rest, happened to fall deeply in love with her, and to manage it so discreetly, that my mother could not but entertain him. My uncle's wife, who had a mother's kindness for her, persuaded her to remove herself from her sisters' envy, by going along with her to the Isle of Jersey, where her father was governor; which she did, and there went into the town, and boarded in a French minister's house, to learn the language, that minister having been, by the persecution in France, driven to seek his shelter there. Contracting a dear friendship with this holy man and his wife, she was instructed in their Geneva discipline, which she liked so much better than our more superstitious service, that she could have been contented to have lived there, had not a powerful passion in her heart drawn her back. But at her return she met with many afflictions; the gentleman who had professed so much love to her, in her absence had been, by most vile practices and treacheries, drawn out of his senses, and into the marriage of a person, whom, when he recovered his reason, he hated. But that served only to augment his misfortune, and the circumstances of that story not being necessary to be here inserted, I shall only add that my mother lived in my uncle's house, secretly discontented at this accident, but was comforted by the kindness of my uncle's wife, who had contracted such an intimate friendship with her, that they seemed to have but one soul. And in this kindness she had some time a great solace, till some malicious persons had wrought some jealousies, which were very groundless, in my uncle concerning his wife; but his nature being inclinable to that passion, which was fomented in him by subtle wicked persons, and my mother endeavouring to vindicate injured innocence, she was herself not well treated by my uncle, whereupon she left his house, with a resolution to withdraw herself into the island, where the good minister was, and there to wear out her life in the service of God. While she was deliberating, and had fixed upon it in her own thoughts, resolving to impart it to none, she was with Sir William St. John, who had married my aunt, when my father accidentally came in there, and fell so heartily in love with her, that he persuaded her to marry him, which she did, and her melancholy made her conform cheerfully to that gravity of habit and conversation, which was becoming the wife of such a person, who was then forty-eight years of age, and she not above sixteen. The first year of their marriage was crowned with a son, called after my father's name, and born at East Smithfield, in that house of the king's which belonged to my father's employment in the navy. The next year they removed to the tower of London, whereof my father was made lieutenant, and there had two sons more before me, and four daughters, and two sons after; of all which only three sons and two daughters survived him at the time of his death, which was in the sixty-third year of his age, after he had three years before languished of a consumption, that succeeded a fever which he got in the unfortunate voyage to the Isle of Rhee.

He died in the month of May, 1630, sadly bewailed by not only all his dependants and relations, but by all that were acquainted with him; for he never conversed with any to whom he was not at some time or in some way beneficial; and his nature was so delighted in doing good, that it won him the love of all men, even his enemies, whose envy and malice it was his custom to overcome with obligations. He had great natural parts, but was too active in his youth to stay the heightening of them by study of dead writings; but in the living books of men's conversations he soon became so skilful that he was never mistaken, but where his own good would not let him give credit to the evil he discerned in others. He was a most indulgent husband, and no less kind to his children; a most noble master, who thought it not enough to maintain his servants honourably while they were with him, but, for all that deserved it, provided offices or settlements, as for children. He was a father to all his prisoners, sweetening with such compassionate kindness their restraint, that the affliction of a prison was not felt in his days. He had a singular kindness for all persons that were eminent either in learning or arms, and when, through the ingratitude and vice of that age, many of the wives and children of Queen Elizabeth's glorious captains were reduced to poverty, his purse was their common treasury, and they knew not the inconvenience of decayed fortunes till he was dead: many of those valiant seamen he maintained in prison, many he redeemed out of prison, and cherished with an extraordinary bounty. If among his excellencies one outshined the rest, it was the generous liberality of his mind, wherein goodness and greatness were so equally distributed that they mutually embellished each other. Pride and covetousness had not the least place in his breast. As he was in love with true honour, so he contemned vain titles; and though in his youth he accepted an addition to his birth, in his riper years he refused a baronetcy, which the king offered him. He was severe in the regulating of his family, especially would not endure the least immodest behaviour or dress in any woman under his roof. There was nothing he hated more than an insignificant gallant, that could only make his legs and prune himself, and court a lady, but had not brains to employ himself in things more suitable to man's nobler sex. Fidelity in his trust, love and loyalty to his prince, were not the least of his virtues, but those wherein he was not excelled by any of his own or succeeding times. The large estate he reaped by his happy industry, he did many times over as freely resign again to the king's service, till he left the greatest part of it at his death in the king's hands. All his virtues wanted not the crown of all virtue, piety and true devotion to God. As his life was a continued exercise of faith and charity, it concluded with prayers and blessings, which were the only consolations his desolate family could receive in his death. Never did any two better agree in mag-

nanimity and bounty than he and my mother, who seemed
to be actuated by the same soul, so little did she grudge any
of his liberalities to strangers, or he contradict any of her
kindness to all her relations; her house being a common
home for all of them, and a nursery to their children. He
gave her a noble allowance of £300 a year for her own private
expense, and had given her all her own portion to dispose of
how she pleased, as soon as she was married; which she
suffered to increase in her friend's hands; and what my
father allowed her she spent not in vanities, although she had
what was rich and requisite upon occasions, but she laid
most of it out in pious and charitable uses. Sir Walter
Raleigh and Mr. Ruthin being prisoners in the Tower, and
addicting themselves to chemistry, she suffered them to
make their rare experiments at her cost, partly to comfort
and divert the poor prisoners, and partly to gain the knowledge of their experiments, and the medicines to help such
poor people as were not able to seek physicians. By these
means she acquired a great deal of skill, which was very
profitable to many all her life.[1] She was not only to these,
but to all the other prisoners that came into the Tower, as a
mother. All the time she dwelt in the Tower, if any were
sick she made them broths and restoratives with her own
hands, visited and took care of them, and provided them all
necessaries; if any were afflicted she comforted them, so
that they felt not the inconvenience of a prison who were in
that place. She was not less bountiful to many poor widows
and orphans, whom officers of higher and lower rank had
left behind them as objects of charity. Her own house was
filled with distressed families of her relations, whom she
supplied and maintained in a noble way. The worship and
service of God, both in her soul and her house, and the

---

[1] This anecdote of Sir Walter Raleigh will no doubt attract the notice
of the observant reader: it merits to be borne in mind, as it will account for a passage in the memoirs, where Mrs. Hutchinson is represented as acting the part of a surgeon in the siege of Nottingham
Castle; and as the treatment Sir Allen Apsley and his lady gave their
prisoners forms a striking contrast with that which it will appear at
the end of the history was practised by some of his successors, at a
time when mildness seemed most requisite, and was most professed.
Perhaps prejudice will render it incredible, that in the Bastile of Paris,
which has become a proverbial expression to signify cruel durance,
the conduct of the murdered governor resembled that of Sir Allen
Apsley; it is nevertheless true.

education of her children, were her principal care. She was a constant frequenter of week-day lectures, and a great lover and encourager of good ministers, and most diligent in her private reading and devotions.

When my father was sick she was not satisfied with the attendance of all that were about him, but made herself his nurse, and cook, and physician, and, through the blessing of God, and her indefatigable labours and watching, preserved him a great while longer than the physicians thought it possible for his nature to hold out. At length, when the Lord took him to rest, she showed as much humility and patience, under that great change, as moderation and bounty in her more plentiful and prosperous condition, and died in my house at Owthorpe, in the county of Nottingham, in the year 1659. The privilege of being born of, and educated by, such excellent parents, I have often revolved with great thankfulness for the mercy, and humiliation that I did no more improve it. After my mother had had three sons, she was very desirous of a daughter, and when the women at my birth told her I was one, she received me with a great deal of joy; and the nurses fancying, because I had more complexion and favour than is usual in so young children, that I should not live, my mother became fonder of me, and more endeavoured to nurse me. As soon as I was weaned a French woman was taken to be my dry-nurse, and I was taught to speak French and English together. My mother, while she was with child of me, dreamed that she was walking in the garden with my father, and that a star came down into her hand, with other circumstances, which, though I have often heard, I minded not enough to remember perfectly; only my father told her, her dream signified she should have a daughter of some extraordinary eminency; which thing, like such vain prophecies, wrought as far as it could its own accomplishment: [1] for my father and mother fancying me

---

[1] This is an ingenious way of accounting for the fulfilment of superstitious predictions and expectations, which might frequently with close attention be traced to their source, as is here done. It is clear that in the present case it occasioned a peculiar care to be taken of her education; and this again caused her mind and disposition to take that singular stamp which attracted the notice of Mr. Hutchinson, and led her to the highest situation that she could wish for, that of the lady of a counsellor of state in her beloved, but short-lived, republic. When the reader shall have followed her to the end of her labours, let him judge whether there could be any situation to which she was not adequate.

then beautiful, and more than ordinarily apprehensive, applied all their cares, and spared no cost to improve me in my education, which procured me the admiration of those that flattered my parents. By the time I was four years old I read English perfectly, and having a great memory, I was carried to sermons; and while I was very young could remember and repeat them exactly, and being caressed, the love of praise tickled me, and made me attend more heedfully. When I was about seven years of age, I remember I had at one time eight tutors in several qualities, languages, music, dancing, writing, and needlework; but my genius was quite averse from all but my book, and that I was so eager of, that my mother thinking it prejudiced my health, would moderate me in it; yet this rather animated me than kept me back, and every moment I could steal from my play I would employ in any book I could find, when my own were locked up from me. After dinner and supper I still had an hour allowed me to play, and then I would steal into some hole or other to read. My father would have me learn Latin, and I was so apt that I outstripped my brothers who were at school, although my father's chaplain, that was my tutor, was a pitiful dull fellow. My brothers, who had a great deal of wit, had some emulation at the progress I made in my learning, which very well pleased my father; though my mother would have been contented if I had not so wholly addicted myself to that as to neglect my other qualities. As for music and dancing, I profited very little in them, and would never practise my lute or harpsichords but when my masters were with me; and for my needle I absolutely hated it. Play among other children I despised, and when I was forced to entertain such as came to visit me, I tired them with more grave instructions than their mothers, and plucked all their babies to pieces, and kept the children in such awe, that they were glad when I entertained myself with elder company; to whom I was very acceptable, and living in the house with many persons that had a great deal of wit, and very profitable serious discourses being frequent at my father's table and in my mother's drawing-room, I was very attentive to all, and gathered up things that I would utter again, to great admiration of many that took my memory and imitation for wit. It pleased God that, through the good instructions of my mother, and the sermons she carried me to, I was convinced that the knowledge of God was the most excellent study, and accordingly applied myself to it, and to practise as I was taught. I used to exhort my mother's maids much, and to turn their idle discourses to good subjects; but I thought, when I had done this on the Lord's day, and every day performed my due tasks of reading and praying, that then I was free to anything that was not sin; for I was not at that time convinced of the vanity of conversation which was not scandalously wicked. I thought it no sin to learn or hear witty songs and amorous sonnets or poems, and twenty things of that kind, wherein I was so apt that I became the confidant in all the loves that were managed among my mother's young women; and there was none of them but had many lovers, and some particular friends beloved above the rest. Among these I have [1] . . . Five years after me my mother had a daughter that she nursed at her own breast, and was infinitely fond of above all the rest; and I being of too serious a temper was not so pleasing to my [2] . . .

[1] At this place is a great chasm, many leaves being torn out, apparently by the writer herself.
[2] Here the story of herself abruptly ends.

MRS. HUTCHINSON TO HER CHILDREN
CONCERNING THEIR FATHER

"TO MY CHILDREN"

THEY who dote on mortal excellencies, when by the inevitable fate of all things frail, their adored idols are taken from them, may let loose the winds of passion to bring in a flood of sorrow; whose ebbing tides carry away the dear memory of what they have lost; and when comfort is essayed to such mourners, commonly all objects are removed out of their view, which may with their remembrance renew the grief; and in time these remedies succeed, and oblivion's curtain is by degrees drawn over the dead face, and things less lovely are liked, while they are not viewed together with that which was most excellent. But I that am under a command not to grieve at the common rate of desolate women,[1] while I am studying which way to moderate my woe, and if it were possible to augment my love, can for the present find out none more just to your dear father nor consolatory to myself than the preservation of his memory; which I need not gild with such flattering commendations as the hired preachers do equally give to the truly and titularly honourable. A naked, undressed narrative, speaking the simple truth of him, will deck him with more substantial glory, than all the panegyrics the best pens could ever consecrate to the virtues of the best men.

Indeed, that resplendent body of light, which the beginning and ending of his life made up, to discover the deformi-

---

[1] The command of her husband at his death. It will be readily admitted that she does indeed not grieve after any common rate, but with that noble sorrow which raises instead of depressing the soul: it would be an affront to the reader's taste to point out the beauties of this dirge; but it is only a just commendation of our authoress's judgment and modesty to observe, that having shown her ability to ornament and embellish, she confines herself to such occasions as are most suitable, and employs the greatest simplicity in her narrative.

ties of this wicked age, and to instruct the erring children of
this generation, will, through my apprehension and expression, shine as under a very thick cloud, which will obscure
much of their lustre; but there is need of this medium to
this world's weak eyes, which I fear hath but few people in
it so virtuous as can believe (because they find themselves
so short), that any other could make so large a progress in the
race of piety, honour, and virtue: but I am almost stopped
before I set forth to trace his steps; finding the number of
them, by which he still outwent himself, more than my imperfect arithmetic can count, and the exact figure of them
such as my unskilful pen cannot describe. I fear to injure
that memory which I would honour, and to disgrace his
name with a poor monument; but when I have beforehand
laid this necessary caution, and ingenuously confessed that
through my inability either to receive or administer much of
that wealthy stock of his glory that I was intrusted with for
the benefit of all, and particularly his own posterity, I must
withhold a great part from them, I hope I shall be pardoned
for drawing an imperfect image of him; especially when even
the rudest draft that endeavours to counterfeit him, will
have much delightful loveliness in it.

Let not excess of love and delight in the stream make us
forget the fountain; he and all his excellencies came from
God, and flowed back into their own spring: there let us
seek them, thither let us hasten after him; there having
found him, let us cease to bewail among the dead that which
is risen, or rather was immortal. His soul conversed with
God so much when he was here, that it rejoices to be now
eternally freed from interruption in that blessed exercise; his
virtues were recorded in heaven's annals, and can never
perish; by them he yet teaches us and all those to whose
knowledge they shall arrive. It is only his fetters, his sins,
his infirmities, his diseases, that are dead never to revive
again, nor would we have them; they were his enemies and
ours; by faith in Christ he vanquished them. Our conjunction, if we had any with him, was indissoluble; if we were
knit together by one spirit into one body of Christ, we are so
still; if we were mutually united in one love of God, good
men, and goodness, we are so still. What is it then we wail
in his remove? the distance? Faithless fools! sorrow only
makes it. Let us but ascend to God in holy joy for the

great grace given his poor servant, and he is there with us. He is only removed from the malice of his enemies, for which, in being afflicted, we should not express our love to him we may mourn for ourselves that we come so tardily after him; that we want his guide and assistance in our way; and yet if our tears did not put out our eyes we should see him even in heaven, holding forth his flaming lamp of virtuous examples and precepts, to light us through the dark world. It is time that I let in to your knowledge that splendour which, while it cheers and enlightens your heavy senses, should make us remember to give all his and all our glory to God alone, who is the father and fountain of all light and excellence.

Desiring, if my treacherous memory have not lost the dearest treasure that ever I committed to its trust, to relate to you his holy, virtuous, honourable life, I would put his picture in the front of his book, but my unskilful hand will injure him. Yet to such of you as have not seen him to remember his person, I leave this—

HIS DESCRIPTION

He was of a middle stature, of a slender and exactly well-proportioned shape in all parts, his complexion fair, his hair of light brown, very thick set in his youth, softer than the finest silk, and curling into loose great rings at the ends; his eyes of a lively grey, well-shaped and full of life and vigour, graced with many becoming motions; his visage thin, his mouth well made, and his lips very ruddy and graceful, although the nether chap shut over the upper, yet it was in such a manner as was not unbecoming; his teeth were even and white as the purest ivory; his chin was something long, and the mould of his face; his forehead was not very high; his nose was raised and sharp; but withal he had a most amiable countenance, which carried in it something of magnanimity and majesty mixed with sweetness, that at the same time bespoke love and awe in all that saw him; his skin was smooth and white, his legs and feet excellently well-made; he was quick in his pace and turns, nimble and active and graceful in all his motions; he was apt for any bodily exercise, and any that he did became him; he could dance

admirably well, but neither in youth nor riper years made
any practice of it; he had skill in fencing, such as became a
gentleman; he had a great love of music, and often diverted
himself with a viol, on which he played masterly; and he
had an exact ear and judgment in other music; he shot
excellently in bows and guns, and much used them for his
exercise; he had great judgment in paintings, graving,
sculpture, and all liberal arts, and had many curiosities of
value in all kinds; he took great delight in perspective
glasses, and for his other rarities was not so much affected
with the antiquity as the merit of the work; he took much
pleasure in improvement of grounds, in planting groves, and
walks, and fruit-trees, in opening springs and making fish-
ponds; of country recreations he loved none but hawking,
and in that was very eager and much delighted for the time
he used it, but soon left it off; he was wonderfully neat,
cleanly, and genteel in his habit, and had a very good fancy
in it, but he left off very early the wearing of anything that
was costly, yet in his plainest negligent habit appeared very
much a gentleman; he had more address than force of body,
yet the courage of his soul so supplied his members that he
never wanted strength when he found occasion to employ it;
his conversation was very pleasant, for he was naturally
cheerful, had a ready wit and apprehension; he was eager in
everything he did, earnest in dispute, but withal very rational,
so that he was seldom overcome; everything that it was
necessary for him to do he did with delight, free and uncon-
strained; he hated ceremonious compliment, but yet had a
natural civility and complaisance to all people; he was of a
tender constitution, but through the vivacity of his spirit
could undergo labours, watchings, and journeys, as well as
any of stronger compositions; he was rheumatic, and had a
long sickness and distemper occasioned thereby, two or three
years after the war ended, but else, for the latter half of his
life, was healthy though tender; in his youth and childhood
he was sickly, much troubled with weakness and toothaches,
but then his spirits carried him through them; he was very
patient under sickness or pain, or any common accidents,
but yet, upon occasions, though never without just ones, he
would be very angry, and had even in that such a grace as
made him to be feared, yet he was never outrageous in
passion; he had a very good faculty in persuading, and

would speak very well, pertinently, and effectually without premeditation upon the greatest occasions that could be offered, for indeed, his judgment was so nice, that he could never frame any speech beforehand to please himself; but his invention was so ready, and wisdom so habitual in all his speeches, that he never had reason to repent himself of speaking at any time without ranking the words beforehand; he was not talkative, yet free of discourse; of a very spare diet, not given to sleep, and an early riser when in health; he never was at any time idle, and hated to see any one else so; in all his natural and ordinary inclinations and composure, there was something extraordinary and tending to virtue, beyond what I can describe, or can be gathered from a bare dead description; there was a life of spirit and power in him that is not to be found in any copy drawn from him. To sum up, therefore, all that can be said of his outward frame and disposition, we must truly conclude, that it was a very handsome and well furnished lodging prepared for the reception of that prince, who in the administration of all excellent virtues reigned there a while, till he was called back to the palace of the universal emperor.

HIS VIRTUES

To number his virtues is to give the epitome of his life, which was nothing else but a progress from one degree of virtue to another, till in a short time he arrived to that height which many longer lives could never reach; and had I but the power of rightly disposing and relating them, his single example would be more instructive than all the rules of the best moralists, for his practice was of a more divine extraction, drawn from the word of God, and wrought up by the assistance of his Spirit; therefore in the head of all his virtues I shall set that which was the head and spring of them all, his Christianity—for this alone is the true royal blood that runs through the whole body of virtue, and every pretender to that glorious family, who hath no tincture of it, is an impostor and a spurious brat. This is that sacred fountain which baptiseth all the gentle virtues that so immortalise the names of Cicero, Plutarch, Seneca, and all the old philosophers; herein they are regenerated, and take a new name and nature. Dug up in the wilderness of nature, and dipped in this living spring, they are planted and flourish in the paradise of God.

By Christianity I intend that universal habit of grace which is wrought in a soul by the regenerating Spirit of God, whereby the whole creature is resigned up into the divine will and love, and all its actions directed to the obedience and glory of its Maker. As soon as he had improved his natural understanding with the acquisition of learning, the first studies in which he exercised himself were the principles of religion, and the first knowledge he laboured for was a knowledge of God, which by a diligent examination of the Scripture, and the several doctrines of great men pretending that ground, he at length obtained. Afterwards, when he had laid a sure and orthodox foundation in the doctrine of the free grace of God given us by Jesus Christ, he began to survey the superstructures, and to discover much of the hay and stubble of men's inventions in God's worship, which his spirit burned up in the day of their trial. His faith being established in the truth, he was full of love to God and all his saints.[1] He hated persecution for religion, and was always a champion for all religious people against all their great oppressors. He detested all scoffs at any practice of worship, though such a one as he was not persuaded of it. Whatever he practised in religion was neither for faction nor advantage, but contrary to it, and purely for conscience' sake. As he hated outsides in religion, so could he worse endure those apostacies and those denials of the Lord and base compliances of his adversaries, which timorous men practise under the name of prudent and just condescensions to avoid persecution. Christianity being in him as the fountain of all his virtues, and diffusing itself in every stream, that of his prudence falls into the next mention. He from a child was wise, and sought to by many that might have been his fathers for counsel, which he could excellently give to himself and others; and whatever cross event in any of his affairs may give occasion to fools to overlook the wisdom of the design, yet he had as great a foresight, as strong a judgment, as clear an apprehension of men and things as any man. He had rather a firm impression than a great memory, yet he

[1] Saints. An expression commonly used in that time to signify good and religious people.

was forgetful of nothing but injuries. His own integrity
made him credulous of other men's, till reason and experience
convinced him; and he was as unapt to believe cautions
which could not be received without entertaining ill opinions
of men; yet he had wisdom enough never to commit himself
to a traitor, though he was once wickedly betrayed by friends
whom necessity and not mistake forced him to trust.[1] He
was as ready to hear as to give counsel, and never pertinacious in his will when his reason was convinced. There was
no opinion which he was most settled in, either concerning
divine or human things, but he would patiently and impartially hear it debated. In matters of faith his reason always
submitted to the Word of God, and what he could not com-
prehend, he would believe because it was written; but in all
other things, the greatest names in the world could never
lead him without reason: he would deliberate when there
was time, but never, by tedious dispute, lost an opportunity
of anything that was to be done. He would hear as well as
speak, and yet never spoke impertinently or unseasonably.
He very well understood his own advantages, natural parts,
gifts, and acquirements, yet so as neither to glory of them to
others, nor overvalue himself for them; for he had an excellent virtuous modesty, which shut out all vanity of mind,
and yet admitted that true understanding of himself which
was requisite for the best improvement of all his talents.
He no less understood and was more heedful to remark his
defects, imperfections, and disadvantages, but that too only
to excite his circumspection concerning them, not to damp
his spirit in any noble enterprise. He had a noble spirit of
government, both in civil, military, and domestic adminis-
trations, which forced even from unwilling subjects a love and
reverence of him, and endeared him to the souls of those who
rejoiced to be governed by him. He had a native majesty
that struck an awe of him into the hearts of men, and a sweet
greatness that commanded love. He had a clear discerning
of men's spirits, and knew how to give every one their just
weight. He contemned none that were not wicked, in whatever low degree of nature or fortune they were otherwise:

[1] It is not known what peculiar transaction this refers to, though it
may be conjectured to refer to the false protestations of Monk and Sir
Ashley Cooper at the Restoration; whom he and many others trusted
much against their will.

wherever he saw wisdom, learning, or other virtues in men, he honoured them highly, and admired them to their full rate, but never gave himself blindly up to the conduct of the greatest master. Love itself, which was as powerful in his as in any soul, rather quickened than blinded the eyes of his judgment in discerning the imperfections of those that were most dear to him. His soul ever reigned as king in the internal throne, and never was captive to his sense; religion and reason, its two favoured counsellors, took order that all the passions kept within their own just bounds, did him good service there, and furthered the public weal. He found such felicity in that proportion of wisdom that he enjoyed, as he was a great lover of that which advanced it—learning and the arts; which he not only honoured in others, but had by his industry arrived to be himself a far greater scholar than is absolutely requisite for a gentleman. He had many excellent attainments, but he no less evidenced his wisdom in knowing how to rank and use them, than in gaining them. He had wit enough to have been subtle and cunning, but he so abhorred dissimulation that I cannot say he was either. Greatness of courage would not suffer him to put on a vizor, to secure him from any; to retire into the shadow of privacy and silence was all his prudence could effect in him. It will be as hard to say which was the predominant virtue in him, as which is so in its own nature. He was as excellent in justice as in wsidom; nor could the greatest advantage, or the greatest danger, or the dearest interest or friend in the world, prevail on him to pervert justice even to an enemy. He never professed the thing he intended not, nor promised what he believed out of his own power, nor failed the performance of anything that was in his power to fulfil. Never fearing anything he could suffer for the truth, he never at any time would refrain a true or give a false witness; he loved truth so much that he hated even sportive lies and gulleries. He was so just to his own honour that he many times forbore things lawful and delightful to him, rather than he would give any one occasion of scandal. Of all lies he most hated hypocrisy in religion; either to comply with changing governments or persons, without a real persuasion of conscience, or to practise holy things to get the applause of men or any advantage. As in religion so in friendship, he never professed love when he had it not, nor disguised hate or aversion, which indeed he never had to any party or person, but to their sins: and he loved even his bitterest enemies so well, that I am witness how his soul mourned for them, and how heartily he desired their conversion. If he were defective in any part of justice, it was when it was in his power to punish those who had injured him; whom I have so often known him to recompense with favours instead of revenge, that his friends used to tell him, if they had any occasion to make him favourably partial to them, they would provoke him by an injury. He was as faithful and constant to his friends as merciful to his enemies: nothing grieved him more than to be obliged where he could not hope to return it. He that was a rock to all assaults of might and violence, was the gentlest, easiest soul to kindness, of which the least warm spark melted him into anything that was not sinful. There never was a man more exactly just in the performance of duties to all relations and all persons. Honour, obedience, and love to his father, were so natural and so lasting in him, that it is impossible to imagine a better son than he was; and whoever would pray for a blessing in children to any one, could but wish them such a son as he.[1] He never repined at his father's will in anything, how much soever it were to his prejudice, nor would endure to hear any one say his father was not so kind to him as he might have been; but to his dying day preserved his father's memory with such tender affection and reverence as was admirable, and had that high regard for his mother-in-law and the children she brought his father, that he could not have been more dearly concerned in all their interest if she had been his own mother—which, all things considered, although they were deserving persons, was an example of piety and goodness that will not easily be matched. For conjugal affection to his wife, it was such in him, as whosoever would draw out a rule of honour, kindness, and religion, to be practised in that estate, need no more, but exactly draw out his example; never man had a greater passion for a woman, nor a more honourable esteem of a wife; yet he was not uxorious, nor remitted he that just rule which it was her honour to obey, but managed the reins of government with such prudence and affection that she who would not delight in such an honourable and advantageable sub-

[1] This we shall find called in question by his mother-in-law, and will be discussed in the course of the history.

jection, must have wanted a reasonable soul. He governed by persuasion, which he never employed but to things honourable and profitable for herself; he loved her soul and her honour more than her outside, and yet he had even for her person a constant indulgence, exceeding the common temporary passions of the most uxorious fools. If he esteemed her at a higher rate than she in herself could have deserved, he was the author of that virtue he doted on, while she only reflected his own glories upon him; all that she was, was *him*, while he was here, and all that she is now at best is but his pale shade. So liberal was he to her, and of so generous a temper, that he hated the mention of severed purses; his estate being so much at her disposal, that he never would receive an account of anything she expended; so constant was he in his love, that when she ceased to be young and lovely, he began to show most fondness; he loved her at such a kind and generous rate as words cannot express; yet even this, which was the highest love he or any man could have, was yet bounded by a superior, he loved her in the Lord as his fellow-creature, not his idol, but in such a manner as showed that an affection, bounded in the just rules of duty, far exceeds every way all the irregular passions in the world. He loved God above her, and all the other dear pledges of his heart, and at his command and for his glory cheerfully resigned them. He was as kind a father, as dear a brother, as good a master, and as faithful a friend as the world had, yet in all these relations, the greatest indulgence he could have in the world never prevailed on him to indulge vice in the dearest person; but the more dear any were to him, the more was he offended at anything that might take off the lustre of their glory. As he had great severity against errors and follies pertinaciously pursued, so had he the most merciful, gentle, and compassionate frame of spirit that can be imagined to those who became sensible of their errors and frailties, although they had been ever so injurious to himself.

Nor was his soul less shining in honour than in love. Piety being still the bond of all his other virtues, there was nothing he durst not do or suffer, but sin against God; and therefore, as he never regarded his life in any noble and just enterprise, so he never staked it in any rash or unwarrantable hazard. He was never surprised, amazed, nor confounded, with great difficulties or dangers, which rather served to ani-

mate than distract his spirits; he had made up his accounts
with life and death, and fixed his purpose to entertain both
honourably, so that no accident ever dismayed him, but he
rather rejoiced in such troublesome conflicts as might signalise his generosity. A truer or more lively valour there
never was in any man, but in all his actions it ever marched
in the same file with wisdom. He understood well, and as
well performed when he undertook it, the military art in all
parts of it; he naturally loved the employment, as it suited
with his active temper more than any, conceiving a mutual
delight in leading those men that loved his conduct; and
when he commanded soldiers, never was man more loved and
reverenced by all that were under him; for he would never
condescend to them in anything they mutinously sought, nor
suffer them to seek what it was fit for him to provide, but
prevented them by his loving care; and while he exercised
his authority no way but in keeping them to their just duty,
they joyed as much in his commands as he in their obedience.
He was very liberal to them, but ever chose just times and
occasions to exercise it. I cannot say whether he were more
truly magnanimous or less proud; he never disdained the
meanest person, nor flattered the greatest; he had a loving
and sweet courtesy to the poorest, and would often employ
many spare hours with the commonest soldiers and poorest
labourers, but still so ordering his familiarity as it never
raised them to a contempt, but entertained still at the same
time a reverence with love of him; he ever preserved himself
in his own rank, neither being proud of it so as to despise any
inferior, nor letting fall that just decorum which his honour
obliged him to keep up. He was as far from envy of superiors
as from contemning them that were under him; he was above
the ambition of vain titles, and so well contented with the
even ground of a gentleman, that no invitation could have
prevailed upon him to advance one step that way; he loved
substantial not airy honour. As he was above seeking or
delighting in empty titles for himself, so he neither denied nor
envied any man's due precedency, but pitied those that took
a glory in that which had no foundation of virtue. As little
did he seek after popular applause, or pride himself in it, if
at any time it cried up his just deserts; he more delighted
to do well than to be praised, and never set vulgar commendations at such a rate, as to act contrary to his own

conscience or reason for the obtaining them; nor would he forbear a good action which he was bound to, though all the world disliked it, for he ever looked on things as they were in themselves, not through the dim spectacles of vulgar estimation. As he was far from a vain affectation of popularity, so he never neglected that just care that an honest man ought to have of his reputation, and was as careful to avoid the appearances of evil as evil itself; but if he were evil spoken of for truth or righteousness' sake, he rejoiced in taking up the reproach; which all good men that dare bear their testimony against an evil generation must suffer. Though his zeal for truth and virtue caused the wicked, with the sharp edges of their malicious tongues, to shave off the glories from his head, yet his honour springing from the fast root of virtue, did but grow the thicker and more beautiful for all their endeavours to cut it off.[1] He was as free from avarice as from ambition and pride. Never had any man a more contented and thankful heart for the estate that God had given, but it was a very narrow compass for the exercise of his great heart. He loved hospitality as much as he hated riot; he could contentedly be without things beyond his reach, though he took very much pleasure in all those noble delights that exceeded not his faculties. In those things that were of mere pleasure, he loved not to aim at that he could not attain; he would rather wear clothes absolutely plain, than pretend to gallantry; and would rather choose to have none than mean jewels or pictures, and such other things as were not of absolute necessity. He would rather give nothing than a base reward or present, and upon that score he lived very much retired, though his nature was very sociable, and delighted in going into and receiving company; because his fortune would not allow him to do it in such a noble manner as suited with his mind. He was so truly magnanimous, that prosperity could never lift him up in the least, nor give him any tincture of pride or vain-glory, nor diminish a general affability, courtesy, and civility, that he always showed to all persons. When he was most exalted, he was most merciful and compassionate to those that were humbled. At the same time that he vanquished any enemy, he cast away all his ill-will to him, and entertained thoughts of love and kindness as soon as he ceased to be in a posture of opposition. He was as far

[1] Samson and Delilah.

from meanness as from pride, as truly generous as humble, and showed his noble spirit more in adversity than in his prosperous condition; he vanquished all the spite of his enemies by his manly suffering, and all the contempts they could cast at him were their shame not his.

His whole life was the rule of temperance in meat, drink, apparel, pleasure, and all those things that may be lawfully enjoyed; and herein his temperance was more excellent than in others, in whom it is not so much a virtue, but proceeds from want of appetite or gust of pleasure; in him it was a true, wise, and religious government of the desire and delight he took in the things he enjoyed. He had a certain activity of spirit which could never endure idleness either in himself or others, and that made him eager, for the time he indulged it, as well in pleasure as in business; indeed, though in youth he exercised innocent sports a little while, yet afterwards his business was his pleasure. But how intent soever he were in anything, how much soever it delighted him, he could freely and easily cast it away when God called him to something else. He had as much modesty as could consist with a true virtuous assurance, and hated an impudent person. Neither in youth nor riper age could the most fair or enticing women ever draw him into unnecessary familiarity or vain converse or dalliance with them, yet he despised nothing of the female sex but their follies and vanities; wise and virtuous women he loved, and delighted in all pure, holy, and unblamable conversation with them, but so as never to excite scandal or temptation. Scurrilous discourse even among men he abhorred; and though he sometimes took pleasure in wit and mirth, yet that which was mixed with impurity he never would endure. The heat of his youth a little inclined him to the passion of anger, and the goodness of his nature to those of love and grief, but reason was never dethroned by them, but continued governor and moderator in his soul.[1]

---

[1] In this place Mrs. Hutchinson has written, " All this and more is true, but I so much dislike the manner of relating it, that I will make another essay." And accordingly she proceeds to write his character over again, but it has the appearance of being much *more laboured*, and much *less characteristic*, and therefore the former is preferred.

At the same place is written: " This book was written by Lucy, the widow and relict of Col. John Hutchinson, of Owthorpe." J.H.

(Julius Hutchinson, grandfather of the Editor).

THE
LIFE OF JOHN HUTCHINSON

OF OWTHORPE, IN THE COUNTY OF NOTTINGHAM, ESQUIRE

HE was the eldest surviving son of Sir Thomas Hutchinson,
and the Lady Margaret, his first wife, one of the daughters
of Sir John Biron, of Newstead, in the same county, two
persons so eminently virtuous and pious in their generations,
that to descend from them was to set up in the world upon
a good stock of honour, which obliged their posterity to improve it, as much as it was their privilege to inherit their
parents' glories. Sir Thomas was he that removed his dwelling to Owthorpe; his father, though he was possessor of that
lordship, having dwelt at Cropwell, another town, within
two miles of which he had an inheritance, which, if I mistake
not, was the place where those of the family that began to
settle the name in this county, first fixed their habitation.
The family for many generations past have been of good
repute in Yorkshire, and there is yet a gentleman in that
county, descendant of the elder house, that possesses a fair
estate and reputation in his father's ancient inheritance.[1]
They have been in Nottinghamshire for generations; wherein
I observe that as if there had been an Agrarian law in the
family, as soon as they arrived to any considerable fortune
beyond his who was first transplanted hither, they began
other houses, of which one is soon decayed and worn out
in an unworthy branch, (he of Basford,) another began to
flourish, and long may it prosper.[2] It is further observable
in their descent that though none of them before Sir Thomas
Hutchinson advanced beyond an esquire, yet they successively matched into all the most eminent and noble families

[1] At Wykeham Abbey, in the county of York, where it is believed
they still reside.

[2] It stood only two generations; the last possessor, who was the great
grandson of Sir Thomas Hutchinson, directing by his will the estate to
be sold, and the produce given to strangers.

in the country; which shows that it was the unambitious
genius of the family rather than their want of merit, which
made them keep upon so even a ground, after their first
achievements had set them on a stage elevated enough from
the vulgar, to perform any honourable and virtuous actions.
I spoke with one old man who had known five generations of
them in these parts, where their hospitality, their love to
their country, their plain and honest conversation with all
men, their generous and unambitious inclinations, had made
the family continue as well beloved and reputed as any of
the prouder houses in the country.[1]   Although they changed
not their titles, yet every succession increased the real honour
of their house.   One disadvantage they had, that few of them
were so long lived as to prevent their sons from the bondage
of wardship, whereby they fell into the hands of wicked
guardians, that defaced instead of cultivating their seats, and
made every heir a new planter.   Sir Thomas Hutchinson, as
I have heard, was not above eight years of age when his
father died, and his wardship fell into the hands of an unworthy person, Sir Germaine Poole, who did him so many
injuries, that he was fain, after he came of age, to have suits
with him.   This so raised the malice of the wicked man that
he watched an opportunity to assassinate him unawares, and
as Sir Thomas was landing out of a boat at the Temple stairs
in London, Poole having on a private coat, with some wicked
assistants, before he was aware, gave him some cuts on the
head and his left hand that was upon the boat; but he full
of courage drew his sword, run at Poole and broke his weapon,
which could not enter his false armour; whereupon he run in
to him, resolved not to be murdered without leaving some
mark on the villain, and bit off his nose; and then, by the
assistance God sent him of an honest waterman, being
rescued, he was carried away so sorely wounded that his life
was in some danger: but the fact being made public, his
honourable carriage in it procured him a great deal of glory,
and his adversary carried the mark of his shame to the grave.[2]

[1] Sir Thomas Hutchinson's son and grandson fell no way short of
him in this.

[2] This is a singular tale, and savours almost too much of the ridiculous for the gravity of an historian: however Rushworth recites a
story of this same man not a little resembling it, in the appendix to his
2nd vol.   " Sir German Poole vowed revenge against a Mr. Bright-
house, shot two pistols at him out of a window, set two servants on

After this, returning into the country, he there lived with very much love, honour, and repute; but having been tossed up and down in his youth, and interrupted in his studies, he grew into such an excessive humour for books, that he wholly addicted himself to them; and deeply engaging in school divinity, spent even his hours of meat and sleep among his books, with such eagerness, that though he himself attained a high reputation of learning thereby, and indeed a great improvement in wisdom and piety, yet he too much deprived his dear friends and relations of his conversation. When he was entered into this studious life, God took from him his dear wife, who left him only two weak children; and then being extremely afflicted for so deplorable a loss, he entertained his melancholy among the old fathers and school-men, instead of diverting it; and having furnished himself with the choicest library in that part of England, it drew to him all the learned and religious men thereabouts, who found better resolutions from him than from any of his books. Living constantly in the country, he could not be exempted from administering justice among them, which he did with such equity and wisdom, and was such a defender of the country's interest, that, without affecting it at all, he grew the most popular and most beloved man in the country, even to the envy of those prouder great ones that despised the common interest. What others sought, he could not shun, being still sought by the whole country, to be their representative, to which he was several times elected,[1] and ever faithful to his trust and his country's interest, though never approving violence and faction. He was a man of a most moderate and wise spirit, but still so inclined to favour the oppressed saints and honest people of those times, that, though he conformed to the government, the licentious and profane encroachers upon common native rights branded him with the reproach of the world, though the glory of good

him with swords, who ran him through the cloak between the arm and body, but killed him not, he defending himself effectually till Sir German came on, who wounded him, and for which he and another were committed to the Fleet, fined £1100. etc." This does not seem to have cured him; perhaps the mark set on him by Sir Thomas H. succeeded better. Did Charles the Second take the hint from this when he set assassins to slit Mr. Coventry's nose, which caused the Coventry act to pass?

[1] He was omitted only in that parliament which was chosen at a time when he and other patriots were imprisoned to prevent their being re-elected. See note, page 38.

men—Puritanism; yet notwithstanding he continued constant to the best interest, and died at London in the year 1643, a sitting member of that glorious Parliament that so generously attempted, and had almost effected, England's perfect liberty. He was a person of great beauty and comeliness in all ages,[1] of a bounteous and noble nature, of clear courage, sweet and affable conversation, of a public spirit, of great prudence and reputation, a true lover of all pious learned persons, and no less of honest plain people; of a most tender conscience, and therefore declaring much for and endeavouring moderation, if it had been possible in the beginning of our wars that the greatest wisdom could have cast on any drops of healing counsel, to have allayed the furious rage of both parties. Though never man was a deeper nor truer mourner than he for his first wife, yet that long dropping grief did but soften his heart for the impression of a second love, which he conceived for a very honourable and beautiful lady, who was Katherine, the youngest daughter of Sir John Stanhope, of Elvaston, a noble family in Derbyshire, by whom he had a son and two daughters surviving him, not unworthy of their family.

Mr. John Hutchinson, the eldest of his surviving sons, by his first wife, was born at Nottingham in the month of September, in the year 1616. That year there had been a great drought, by reason of which the country would not afford his father any provision for his stables, so that he was forced to remove from Owthorpe to winter in the town of Nottingham, somewhat before his lady's time of account. She being in the coach on her way thither, and seeing her husband in some danger by reason of a mettled horse he rode upon, took a fright, and was brought to bed the next day, as they imagined some three weeks before her time, and they were confirmed in that opinion by the weakness of the child, which continued all his infancy. When he was born there was an elder brother in the family, but he died a child. Two years

[1] His picture remained at Owthorpe, and very well justified this description, and is now in the editor's possession in high preservation. For the bounty and nobleness of his nature take this instance from Thoroton's *History of Notts.* "Henry Sacheverell, Esq., being dissatisfied with his only daughter for an improper marriage, left the whole estate at Ratcliff upon Soar to Sir Thomas Hutchinson, his sister's son, who willingly divided it with the disinherited lady." His moiety came afterwards to Alderman Ireton, being sacrificed to him through necessity by Col. Hutchinson, as will hereafter be shown.

and a half after this Mr. George Hutchinson, his younger brother, was born at Owthorpe; and half a year after his birth the two children lost their mother, who died of a cold she had taken, and was buried at Owthorpe. She was a lady of as noble a family as any in the county, of an incomparable shape and beauty, embellished with the best education those days afforded; and above all had such a generous virtue joined with attractive sweetness, that she captivated the hearts of all that knew her. She was pious, liberal, courteous, patient, kind above an ordinary degree, ingenuous to all things she would apply herself to; and notwithstanding she had had her education at court, was delighted in her own country habitation, and managed all her family affairs better than any of the homespun housewives, that had been brought up to nothing else. She was a most affectionate wife, a great lover of her father's house, showing that true honour to parents is the leading virtue, which seldom wants the concomitancy of all the rest of honour's train. She was a wise and bountiful mistress in her family, a blessing to her tenants and neighbourhood, and had an indulgent tenderness to her infants; but death veiled all her mortal glories in the 26th year of her age. The stories I have received of her have been but scanty epitaphs of those things which were worthy of a large chronicle, and a better recorder than I can be. I shall therefore draw again the sable curtain before that image which I have ventured to look at a little, but dare not undertake to discover to others. One that was present at her death told me that she had an admirable voice, and skill to manage it; and that she went away singing a psalm, which this maid apprehended she sung with so much more than usual sweetness, as if her soul had already ascended into the celestial choir.

There is a story of her father and mother so memorable that though it be not altogether pertinent to their grandchild's affairs, which I only intend to record, yet I shall here put it in, since the third generation, for whom I make this collection, is not altogether unconcerned in the great grandfather. He (the great grandfather) was not the eldest son of his father Sir John Biron, but he had an elder brother who had married a private gentleman's daughter in the country, and so displeased his father in that match, that he intended an equal part of his estate to this Sir John Biron, his younger

son, and thereupon married him to a young lady who was
one of the daughters of my lord Fitzwilliam, that had been
deputy of Ireland in the reign of Queen Elizabeth, and lived
as a prince in that country.[1] This daughter of his having an
honourable aspiring to all things excellent, and being assisted
by the great education her father gave her, attained to a high
degree of learning and language, and to such an excellency
in music and poetry, that she made rare compositions in both
kinds; and there was not any of those extraordinary qualities,
which are therefore more glorious because more rare in the
female sex, but she was excellent in them; and besides all
these ornaments of soul, she had a body of as admirable a
form and beauty, which justly made her husband so infinitely
enamoured of her as never man was more. She could not set
too high a value on herself if she compared herself with other
women of those times; yet it was an alloy to her glories that
she was a little grieved that a less woman, the elder brother's
wife, was superior to her in regard of her husband, though
inferior in regard of her birth and person; but that grief was
soon removed by a sad accident. That marriage wherein the
father had not been obeyed was fruitless, and the young
gentleman himself being given to youthful vanity, as he was
one day to go out a hunting with his father, had commanded
something to be put under the saddle of a young serving man,
that was to go out with them, to make sport at his affright
when his horse should prove unquiet. The thing succeeded
as it was designed, and made them such sport, that the young
gentleman, in the passion of laughter, died, and turned their
mirth into mourning; leaving a sad caveat by his example,
to take heed of hazarding men's precious lives for a little
sport. The younger brother by this means became the heir
of the family, and was father of a numerous and hopeful
issue. But while the incomparable mother shined in all the
human glory she wished, and had the crown of all outward
felicity to the full, in the enjoyment of the mutual love of her
most beloved husband, God in one moment took it away,

[1] By mistake Mrs. Hutchinson calls him lord. The person here
meant was Sir William Fitzwilliam, appointed governor of Ireland
seven times with the different titles of Lord Justice and Lord Deputy,
by that distinguishing and judicious princess. A sufficient eulogy!
From him descends in a direct line the present Earl Fitzwilliam.
Fortes creantur, fortibus et bonis. The reader will most likely find this
episode too beautiful and affecting to think it needs the apology the
writer makes.

and alienated her most excellent understanding in a difficult child-birth; wherein she brought forth two daughters which lived to be married, and one more that died I think as soon or before it was born.[1]   But after that, all the art of the best physicians in England could never restore her understanding: yet she was not frantic, but had such a pretty deliration, that her ravings were more delightful than other women's most rational conversations.   Upon this occasion her husband gave himself up to live retired with her, as became her condition, and made haste to marry his son; which he did so young that I have heard say when the first child was born, the father, mother, and child, could not make one-and-thirty years old.   The daughters and the rest of the children as soon as they grew up were married and dispersed.   I think I have heard she had some children after that child-birth which distempered her, and then my lady Hutchinson must have been one of them, for she was the youngest daughter, and at nine years old so taking, and of such an amiable conversation, that the lady Arabella[2] would needs take her from her parents, along with her to the court; where she minded nothing but her lady, and grew up so intimate in all her counsels, that the princess was more delighted in her than in any of the women about her; but when she (the princess) was carried away from them to prison, my lady's brother fetched her home to his house.   There, although his wife, a most prudent and virtuous lady, laboured to comfort her with all imaginable kindness, yet so constant was her friendship to the unfortunate princess, that I have heard her servants say, she would steal many melancholy hours to sit and weep in remembrance of her, even after her marriage. Meanwhile her parents were driving on their age, in no less constancy of love to each other; for even that distemper which had estranged her mind in all things else, had left her love and obedience entire to her husband, and he retained the same fondness and respect for her, after she was distempered, as when she was the glory of her age.   He had two beds in

[1] The twins here mentioned as daughters are said by Thoroton to have been sons, viz. Sir John, presently herein spoken of as the brother-in-law of Sir Thomas Hutchinson, and Sir Nicholas, who served Charles the First with the same zeal as the rest of that family.

[2] By the lady Arabella is here meant the lady Arabella Stuart, whose romantic and melancholy story is told by Rapin, vol. ii. p. 161 and 189, in the reign of James the First.   That mean-souled tyrant shut her up in the Tower, where she died, not without suspicion of poison.

one chamber, and she being a little sick, two women watched by her, some time before she died. It was his custom, as soon as ever he unclosed his eyes, to ask how she did; but one night, he being as they thought in a deep sleep, she quietly departed towards the morning. He was that day to have gone a hunting, his usual exercise for his health, and it was his custom to have his chaplain pray with him before he went out; and the women, fearful to surprise him with the ill news, knowing his dear affection to her, had stolen out and acquainted the chaplain, desiring him to inform him of it. Sir John waking, did not on that day, as was his custom, ask for her, but called the chaplain to prayers, and joining with him, in the midst of the prayer, expired, and both of them were buried together in the same grave. Whether he perceived her death, and would not take notice, or whether some strange sympathy in love or nature, tied up their lives in one, or whether God was pleased to exercise an unusual providence towards them, preventing them both from that bitter sorrow which such separations cause, it can be but conjectured; but the thing being not ordinary, and having received it from the relation of one of his daughters and his grandchild, I thought it not impertinent here to insert it. I shall now proceed to our own story.

As soon as my lady Hutchinson [1] was dead, her brother, Sir John Biron, came over and found the most desolate afflicted widower that ever was beheld, and one of his sisters, the lady Ratcliffe, who was the dear sister of the dead lady, scarce alive for sorrow; and indeed such a universal lamentation in the house and neighbourhood, that the protraction of their griefs for such a funeral as was intended her, might possibly have made them all as she: Sir John therefore the next morning privately, unknown to her husband, with only her own family, carried her to the church, which was but the next door, and interred her without further ceremony. It booted not Sir Thomas to be angry at her brother's care of him; who pursued it so far, that the next day he carried away Sir Thomas, lady Ratcliffe, and Mr. John Hutchinson, towards his own house at Bulwell, leaving Mr. George at his nurse's. But the horses of the coach being mettled, in the halfway between Owthorpe and Nottingham they ran away, overthrew it, and slightly hurt all that were in the coach;

[1] The mother of Col. Hutchinson, see page 33.

who all got out, one by one, except the maid that had the
child in her arms, and she stayed as long as there was any
hope of preventing the coach from being torn to pieces: but
when she saw no stop could be given to the mad horses, she
lapped him as close as she could in the mantle, and flung him
as far as she could from the coach into the ploughed lands,
whose furrows were at that time very soft; and by the good
providence of God the child, reserved to a more glorious
death, had no apparent hurt. He was taken up and carried
to Bulwell, where his aunt had such a motherly tenderness
for him that he grew and prospered in her care. As the fresh
memory and excessive love they bore the mother, endeared
the young child to all her relations at the first; so as he grew,
he discovered so much growing wisdom, agility, and pretty
sprightfulness, had such a natural gravity without sullenness,
and such sweet innocence, that every child of the family
loved him better than their own brothers and sisters, and
Sir John Biron and my lady were not half so fond of any of
their own. When it was time for them to go to school, both
the brothers were sent to board with Mr. Theobalds, the
master of the free school at Nottingham, who was an excellent
scholar; but having no children, some wealth, and a little
living that kept his house, he first grew lazy, and afterwards
left off his school. Sir Thomas then removed his sons to the
free school at Lincoln, where there was a master very famous
for learning and piety, Mr. Clarke; but he was such a supercilious pedant, and so conceited of his own pedantic forms,
that he gave Mr. Hutchinson a disgust of him, and he profited
very little there. At this place it was that God began early
to exercise him with affliction and temptation; he was deprived of the attendance and care he had been used to, and
met with many inconveniences unsuitable to his tender and
nice constitution; but this was little, for he had such discretion in his childhood that he understood what was fit for him
to require, and governed wherever he lived; for he would not
be denied what was reasonable, and he would not ask other
things. He was as a father over his brother, and having
some advantage of years, took upon him to be the guide of
his youth, yet with such love, that never were children more
commendable and happy in mutual affections. But it
pleased God to strike his brother with a sad disease, the falling
sickness, wherein Mr. Hutchinson most carefully attended

him while he continued at Lincoln; which his father permitted him to do, for the opportunity of Dr. Pridgeon, one of the best physicians in those parts. When he had in vain exercised all his art on the young gentleman, and found no success in it, he advised he should return to his father's house, and be entertained with all the sports that could be found to delight his mind or exercise his body. Accordingly he was carried home, and had a pack of hounds, huntsmen, and horses kept for him, and was something recreated, but not cured thereby; till afterwards it pleased God to effect that cure by a young practitioner, which the ablest physicians of the country could not work. This separation from his brother, to whom he had such an entire affection, considered with the sad occasion of it, was a great affliction to the elder brother; who remained in a place where he had little to delight him, having an aversion to his austere, pedantic master, increased by an opinion that his severity had been the cause of his dear brother's distemper.

The great encouragement Sir Thomas had to trust his sons in this town was, because at that time a gentleman inhabited it who had married his uncle's widow, and had been his fellow-sufferer in a confinement in Kent, when King Charles the First had broken up a parliament to the disgust of the people, and durst not trust those gentlemen that had been most faithful defenders of their country's interest, to return for some time to their own counties, for which they served.[1] Of these worthy patriots, Sir Thomas Hutchinson and Sir Thomas Grantham, the gentleman of whom I am speaking, were confined from Nottingham and Lincolnshire to the house of one Sir Adam Newton in Kent; the good father little thinking then, that in that fatal country his son should suffer an imprisonment upon the same account, to the destruction of his life and family. Sir Thomas Grantham was a gentleman of great repute in his country, and kept up all his life the old hospitality of England, having a great retinue and a noble table, and a resort for all the nobility and gentry in those

---

[1] This piece of history is mentioned by Rapin; Sir Thomas Grantham is named, but Sir Thomas Hutchinson and many others not named. It appears, in Thoroton's *History of Nottingham*, edited by Throsby, that this confinement so far answered the purpose of Charles the First, that it caused another to be chosen instead of Sir Thomas Hutchinson, knight of the shire; but as soon as Sir Thomas got free he was again chosen, and continued to represent the county till his death.

parts. He had only two sons, whereof the eldest was a fine gentleman, bred beyond the seas, according to the best education of those times; the other was a foolish youth, schoolfellow with Mr. Hutchinson, who every Saturday night was fetched from school to Sir Thomas Grantham's, and returned again the Monday morning. Upon the intimate friendship between Sir Thomas Hutchinson and this gentleman, Sir Thomas Hutchinson had a lodging always kept for him at Lincoln, and was very often there. My Lady Grantham had with her a very pretty young gentlewoman, whom she brought with her out of Kent, the daughter of Sir Adam Newton; my lady's design was to begin an early acquaintance, which might afterwards draw on a marriage between her and Mr. Hutchinson, and it took such effect that there was a great inclination in the young gentlewoman to him; and there was so much good nature on his side, as amounted to a mutual respect, and to such a friendship as their youth was capable of, which the parents and others that wished so, interpreted to be a passion of love; but if it were so, death quenched the flame, and ravished the young lady from him in the sweet blooming of her youth. That night she died, he lay in his father's chamber, and by accident being very sick, it was imputed to that cause; but he himself least perceived he had any more of love for her than gratitude for her kindness to him, upon which account her death was an affliction to him, and made that house which had been his relief from his hated school less pleasant to him; especially when he met there continual solicitations to sin by the travelled gentleman, who, living in all seeming sobriety before his father, was in his own chamber not only vicious himself, but full of endeavour to corrupt Mr. Hutchinson, who by the grace of God resisted, and detested his frequent temptations of all kinds. An advantage he had at this school was that there being very many gentlemen's sons there, an old Low-country soldier was entertained to train them in arms, and they all bought themselves weapons; and, instead of childish sports, when they were not at their books, they were exercised in all their military postures, and in assaults and defences; which instruction was not useless a few years after, to some of them. Colonel Thornhagh, who was now trained in this sportive militia, with Colonel Hutchinson, afterwards was his fellow soldier in earnest, when the great cause of God's and

England's rights came to be disputed with swords against encroaching princes. Sir Thomas Grantham dying, Mr. Hutchinson was removed from Lincoln to the free-school at Nottingham, where his father married a second wife, and for a while went up to London with her; leaving his son at board in a very religious house, where new superstitions and pharisaical holiness, straining at gnats and swallowing camels, gave him a little disgust, and was for a while a stumbling-block in his way of purer profession, when he saw among professors such unsuitable miscarriages. There was now a change in the condition and contentment of his life; he was old enough to be sensible that his father's second love and marriage to a person of such quality, as required a settlement for her son, must needs be a lessening to his expectation; but he was so affectionate to his father that he received it very contentedly, and rejoiced in his removal, coming from a supercilious pedant to a very honest man, who using him with respect, advanced him more in one month than the other did in a year. This tied him to no observation, and restrained him from no pleasure, and needed not, for he was so moderate when he was left at his liberty, that he needed no regulation. The familiar kindness of his master made him now begin to love that which the other's austerity made him loathe; and in a year's time he advanced exceedingly in learning, and was sent to Cambridge. He was made a fellow-commoner of Peter House, under the tuition of one Mr. Norwich, an admirable scholar, who by his civil demeanour to him won so much upon his good nature, that he loved and reverenced him as a father, and betook himself with such delight to his studies that he attained to a great height of learning, performed public exercises in his college with much applause, and upon their importunity took a degree in the university; whereof he was at that time the grace, there not being any gentleman in the town that lived with such regularity in himself, and such general love and good esteem of all persons as he did. He kept not company with any of the vain young persons, but with the graver men, and those by whose conversation he might gain improvement. He was constant at their chapel, where he began to take notice of their stretching superstition to idolatry; and was courted much into a more solemn practice of it than he could admit, though as yet he considered not the emptiness and carnality, to say no more, of that public service which was then in use. For his exercise he practised tennis, and played admirably well at it; for his diversion, he chose music, and got a very good hand, which afterwards he improved to a great mastery on the viol. There were masters that taught to dance and vault, whom he practised with, being very agile and apt for all such becoming exercises. His father stinted not his expense, which the bounty of his mind made pretty large, for he was very liberal to his tutors and servitors, and to the meaner officers of the house. He was enticed to bow to their great idol, learning, and had a higher veneration for it a long time than can strictly be allowed; yet he then looked upon it as a handmaid to devotion, and as the great improver of natural reason. His tutor and the masters that governed the college while he was there, were of Arminian principles, and that college was noted above all for popish superstitious practises; yet through the grace of God, notwithstanding the mutual kindness the whole household had for him and he for them, he came away, after five years' study there, untainted with those principles or practices, though not yet enlightened to discern the spring of them in the rites and usages of the English church.

When he came from the university, he was about twenty years of age, and returned to his father's house, who had now settled his habitation at Nottingham; but he there enjoyed no great delight, another brood of children springing up in the house, and the servants endeavouring with tales and flatteries to sow dissension on both sides. Therefore, having a great reverence for his father, and being not willing to disturb him with complaints, as soon as he could obtain his leave he went to London. In the meantime the best company the town afforded him was a gentleman of as exquisite breeding and parts as England's court ever enjoyed, one that was now married, and retired into this town; one of such admirable power of language and persuasion as was not anywhere else to be found; but after all this, discontents, or the debaucheries of the times, had so infected him, that he would not only debauch himself, but make a delight to corrupt others for his sport. Some he would commend into such a vain-glorious humour, that they became pleasantly ridiculous; some he would teach apish postures, and make them believe themselves rare men; some he would encourage to be poets, and laugh at their ridiculous rhymes; some young preachers he would make stage-players in their pulpits; and several ways sported himself with the follies of most of the young men that he conversed with. There was not any way which he left unpractised upon Mr. Hutchinson; but when with all his art and industry he found he could not prevail, then he turned seriously to give him such excellent advice and instructions for living in the world, as were not afterwards unuseful to him.[1] There was besides this gentleman, a young physician, who was a good scholar and had a great deal of wit, but withal a professed atheist, and so proud, insolent, and scurrilous a fellow, daring to abuse all persons how much soever above him, that he was thrown out of familiarity with the great people of the country, though his excellency in his profession made him to be taken in again. There was also an old man, who had been Mr. Hutchinson's first schoolmaster, a person once of great learning, but afterwards becoming a cynic, yet so pleasantly maintaining that kind of humour, that his conversation was sometimes a good diversion. These were Mr. Hutchinson's companions, yet, through the grace of God, they had not power to infect him, who, like the bee, sucked a great deal of honey from these bitter flowers. At that time there was in the town a young maid, beautiful, and esteemed to be very rich, but of base parentage and penurious education, though else ingenuous enough. She was the grandchild of an old physician, and from her childhood having been acquainted with Mr. Hutchinson, who used to visit her grandmother, she had conceived a kindness for him, which though he civilly resented,[2] his great heart could never stoop to think of marrying into so mean a stock; yet by reason of some liking he showed for her company, and the melancholy he had, with some discontents at home, she was willing to flatter herself it was love for her, wherein, when she discovered her mistake, it was a great grief. However, she was, without much love on either side, married to an earl's son, and both of them, wanting the ground of happiness in marriage, mutual love, enjoyed but

<hr />

[1] Who the first gentleman was does not appear. The physician here meant is Dr. Plumtre, of whom much more will be said in this work.

[2] Resent, in English, never used but in a bad sense; in French, *ressentir* is used to signify a reciprocal sentiment of kindness as well as unkindness.

little felicity, either in their great fortunes or in one another.[1]

In the house with Mr. Hutchinson there was a young gentlewoman of such admirable tempting beauty, and such excellent good nature, as would have thawed a rock of ice, yet even she could never get an acquaintance with him. Wealth and beauty thus in vain tempted him, for it was not yet his time of love; but it was not far off. He was now sent to London, and admitted of Lincoln's Inn, where he was soon coveted into the acquaintance of some gentlemen of the house; but he found them so frothy and so vain, and could so ill centre with them in their delights, that the town began to be tedious to him, who was neither taken with wine, nor gaming, nor the converse of wicked or vain women; to all which he wanted not powerful tempters, had not the power of God's grace in him been above them. He tried a little the study of the law, but finding it unpleasant and contrary to his genius, and the plague that spring beginning to drive people out of the town, he began to think of leaving it, but had no inclination to return home, finding his father's heart so set upon his second family, that his presence was but disturbance: yet his father was wonderfully free and noble to him in allowance, at all places, as large as any of his quality had made to them; and it was very well bestowed on him, who consumed nothing in vain expense, but lived to the honour of his friends and family. For his diversion he exercised himself in those qualities he had not had such good opportunities for in the country, as dancing, fencing, and music, wherein he had great aptness and address; and entertaining the best tutors, was at some expense that way, and loth to leave them off before he had perfected himself. However, many things putting him into thoughts of quitting the town, while he was in deliberation how to dispose of himself, and had some reflections upon travel, a cousin-german of his, a French merchant, came to visit him one morning, and told him he was immediately going into France, and understand-

[1] It is written in the margin by Julius Hutchinson, Esq., probably from the information given him by Lady Catharine Hutchinson, that this lady's name was Martin, and the gentleman who married her Mr. Pierrepont. It would not have been thought worth while to inform the reader of these minute particulars in a note, but for the sake of pointing out the accuracy with which Mr. Julius Hutchinson read and remarked upon this history, and the full knowledge he had of all the circumstances of Colonel Hutchinson's life.

ing Mr. Hutchinson had some such inclination, had almost persuaded him to go along with him. The only obstacle in the way was that his father could not be acquainted with it time enough to receive his answer before they went. While he was in this deliberation, his music-master came in, to whom he communicated his thoughts; and the man told him it was better to go into France at the latter end than the beginning of summer, and that if he pleased, in the meantime, to go to Richmond, where the Prince's court was, he had a house there, where he might be accommodated; and there was very good company and recreations, the king's hawks being kept near the place, and several other conveniences. Mr. Hutchinson considering this, resolved to accept his offer; and that day telling a gentleman of the house whither he was going, the gentleman bid him take heed of the place, for it was so fatal for love, that never any young disengaged person went thither, who returned again free. Mr. Hutchinson laughed at him, but he to confirm it told him a very true story of a gentleman who not long before had come for some time to lodge there, and found all the people he came in company with, bewailing the death of a gentlewoman that had lived there. Hearing her so much deplored, he made inquiry after her, and grew so in love with the description that no other discourse could at first please him, nor could he at last endure any other; he grew desperately melancholy, and would go to a mount where the print of her foot was cut, and lie there pining and kissing of it all the day long, till at length death, in some months' space, concluded his languishment. This story was very true; but Mr. Hutchinson was neither easy to believe it, nor frighted at the example, thinking himself not likely to make another. He therefore went to Richmond, where he found a great deal of good young company, and many ingenuous persons that, by reason of the court, where the young princes were bred, entertained themselves in that place, and had frequent resort to the house where Mr. Hutchinson tabled. The man being a skilful composer in music, the rest of the king's musicians often met at his house to practise new airs and prepare them for the king; and divers of the gentlemen and ladies that were affected with music, came thither to hear; others that were not, took that pretence to entertain themselves with the company. Mr. Hutchinson was soon courted into their acquaintance, and invited to their houses, where he was nobly treated, with all the attractive arts that young women and their parents use to procure them lovers; but though some of them were very handsome, others wealthy, witty, and well qualified, and all of them set out with all the gaiety and bravery that vain women put on to set themselves off, yet Mr. Hutchinson could not be entangled in any of their fine snares; but without any taint of incivility, he in such a way of handsome raillery reproved their pride and vanity, as made them ashamed of their glory, and vexed that he alone, of all the young gentlemen that belonged to the court or neighbourhood, should be insensible of their charms. In the same house with him there was a younger daughter of Sir Allen Apsley, late lieutenant of the Tower, tabled for the practice of her lute, staying till the return of her mother; who was gone into Wiltshire for the accomplishment of a treaty that had been made some progress in, about the marriage of her elder daughter with a gentleman of that country, out of which my lady herself came, and where her brothers, Sir John St. John and Sir Edward Hungerford, living in great honour and reputation, had invited her to visit them. This gentlewoman, that was left in the house with Mr. Hutchinson, was a very child, her elder sister being at that time scarcely passed it; but a child of such pleasantness and vivacity of spirit, and ingenuity in the quality she practised, that Mr. Hutchinson took pleasure in hearing her practise, and would fall in discourse with her. She having the keys of her mother's house, some half a mile distant, would sometimes ask Mr. Hutchinson, when she went over, to walk along with her. One day when he was there, looking upon an odd by-shelf in her sister's closet, he found a few Latin books; asking whose they were, he was told they were her elder sister's; whereupon, inquiring more after her, he began first to be sorry she was gone, before he had seen her, and gone upon such an account that he was not likely to see her. Then he grew to love to hear mention of her, and the other gentlewomen who had been her companions used to talk much to him of her, telling him how reserved and studious she was, and other things which they esteemed no advantage. But it so much inflamed Mr. Hutchinson's desire of seeing her, that he began to wonder at himself, that his heart, which had ever entertained so much indifference for the most excellent of womankind, should have such strong impulses towards a stranger he never saw; and certainly it was of the Lord (though he perceived it not), who had ordained him, through so many various providences, to be yoked with her in whom he found so much satisfaction. There scarcely passed any day but some accident or some discourse still kept alive his desire of seeing this gentlewoman; although the mention of her, for the most part, was inquiries whether she had yet accomplished the marriage that was in treaty. One day there was a great deal of company at Mr. Coleman's, the gentleman's house where he tabled, to hear the music; and a certain song was sung, which had been lately set, and gave occasion to some of the company to mention an answer to it, which was in the house, and upon some of their desires, read. A gentleman saying it was believed that a woman in the neighbourhood had made it, it was presently inquired who; whereupon a gentleman, then present, who had made the first song, said, there were but two women that could be guilty of it, whereof one was a lady then among them, the other Mrs. Apsley. Mr. Hutchinson, fancying something of rationality in the sonnet beyond the customary reach of a she-wit, although, to speak truth, it signified very little, addressed himself to the gentleman, and told him he could scarcely believe it was a woman's; whereupon this gentleman, who was a man of good understanding and expression, and inspired with some passion for her himself, which made him regard all her perfections through a multiplying-glass, told Mr. Hutchinson, that though, for civility to the rest, he entitled another lady to the song, yet he was confident it was Mrs. Apsley's only, for she had sense above all the rest; and fell into such high praises of her, as might well have begotten those vehement desires of her acquaintance, which a strange sympathy in nature had before produced. Another gentleman, that sat by, seconded this commendation with such additions of praise as he would not have given if he had known her. Mr. Hutchinson hearing all this, said to the first gentleman, " I cannot be at rest till this lady's return, that I may be acquainted with her." The gentleman replied, " Sir, you must not expect that, for she is of a humour she will not be acquainted with any of mankind; and however this song is stolen forth, she is the nicest creature in the world of suffering her perfections to be known; she shuns the converse of men as the plague; she only lives in the enjoyment of herself, and had not the humanity to communicate that happiness to any of our sex." "Well," said Mr. Hutchinson, "but I will be acquainted with her:" and indeed the information of this reserved humour pleased him more than all else he had heard, and filled him now with thoughts how he should attain the sight and knowledge of her. While he was exercised in this, many days passed not, but a footboy of my lady her mother's came to young Mrs. Apsley [1] as they were at dinner, bringing news that her mother and sister would in a few days return; and when they inquired of him, whether Mrs. Apsley was married; having before been instructed to make them believe it, he smiled, and pulled out some bride laces, which were given at a wedding, in the house where she was, and gave them to the young gentlewoman and the gentleman's daughter of the house, and told them Mrs. Apsley bade him tell no news, but give them those tokens, and carried the matter so, that all the company believed she had been married. Mr. Hutchinson immediately turned pale as ashes, and felt a fainting to seize his spirits in that extraordinary manner, that, finding himself ready to sink at table, he was fain to pretend something had offended his stomach, and to retire from the table into the garden; where the gentleman of the house going with him, it was not necessary for him to feign sickness, for the distemper of his mind had infected his body with a cold sweat, and such a depression of spirit, that all the courage he could at present collect, was little enough to keep him alive. His host was very troublesome to him, and to be quit of him he went to his chamber, saying he would lie down. Little did any of the company suspect the true cause of his sudden qualm, and they were all so troubled at it, that the boy then passed without further examination. When Mr. Hutchinson was alone he began to recollect his wisdom and his reason, and to wonder at himself, why he should be so concerned in an unknown person; he then remembered the story that was told him when he came down, and began to believe there was some magic in the place, which enchanted men out of their right senses; but it booted him not to be angry at himself, nor to set wisdom in her reproving chair, nor reason in her throne of council, the sick

[1] It was the custom at that time to call young ladies Mistress, not Miss. Shakespeare calls Ann Page, Mrs. Ann.

heart could not be chid nor advised into health. This anxiety
of mind affected him so, that it sent him to his bed that afternoon, which indeed he took to entertain his thoughts alone
that night, and having fortified himself with resolution, he
got up the next day; but yet could not quit himself of an
extravagant perplexity of soul concerning this unknown
gentlewoman, which had not been remarkable in another
light person, but in him, who was from his childhood so
serious and so rational in all his considerations, it was the
effect of a miraculous power of Providence, leading him to her
that was destined to make his future joy. While she so ran
in his thoughts, meeting the boy again, he found out, upon a
little stricter examination of him, that she was not married,
and pleased himself in the hopes of her speedy return; when
one day, having been invited by one of the ladies of that
neighbourhood to a noble treatment at Sion Garden, which
a courtier, that was her servant, had made for her and whom
she would bring, Mr. Hutchinson, Mrs. Apsley, and Mr.
Coleman's daughter were of the party, and having spent the
day in several pleasant divertisements, at evening when they
were at supper, a messenger came to tell Mrs. Apsley her
mother was come. She would immediately have gone, but
Mr. Hutchinson, pretending civility to conduct her home,
made her stay till the supper was ended, of which he ate no
more, now only longing for that sight which he had with
such perplexity expected. This at length he obtained; but
his heart, being prepossessed with his own fancy, was not
free to discern how little there was in her to answer so great
an expectation. She was not ugly in a careless riding-habit,
she had a melancholy negligence both of herself and others,
as if she neither affected to please others, nor took notice of
anything before her; yet, in spite of all her indifference, she
was surprised with some unusual liking in her soul when she
saw this gentleman, who had hair, eyes, shape, and countenance enough to beget love in any one at the first, and these
set off with a graceful and generous mien, which promised
an extraordinary person. He was at that time, and indeed
always very neatly habited, for he wore good and rich
clothes, and had a variety of them, and had them well suited
and every way answerable; in that little thing, showing both
good judgment and great generosity, he equally becoming
them and they him, which he wore with such equal un-

affectedness and such neatness as we do not often meet in one. Although he had but an evening sight of her he had so long desired, and that at disadvantage enough for her; yet the prevailing sympathy of his soul made him think all his pains well paid, and this first did whet his desire to a second sight, which he had by accident the next day, and to his joy found that she was wholly disengaged from that treaty, which he so much feared had been accomplished; he found withal, that though she was modest, she was accostable, and willing to entertain his acquaintance. This soon passed into a mutual friendship between them, and though she innocently thought nothing of love, yet was she glad to have acquired such a friend, who had wisdom and virtue enough to be trusted with her councils, for she was then much perplexed in mind. Her mother and friends had a great desire she should marry, and were displeased that she refused many offers which they thought advantageous enough; she was obedient, loth to displease them, but more herself, in marrying such as she could find no inclination to. The troublesome pretensions of some of the courtiers, had made her willing to try whether she could bring her heart to her mother's desire; but being, by a secret working which she then understood not, averted, she was troubled to return, lest some might believe it was a secret liking for them which had caused her dislike for others; and being a little disturbed with these things and melancholy, Mr. Hutchinson, appearing, as he was, a person of virtue and honour, who might be safely and advantageously conversed with, she thought God had sent her a happy relief. Mr. Hutchinson, on the other side, having been told, and seeing how she shunned all other men, and how civilly she entertained him, believed that a secret power had wrought a mutual inclination between them; and he daily frequented her mother's house, and had the opportunity of conversing with her in those pleasant walks, which, at that sweet season of the spring, invited all the neighbouring inhabitants to seek their joys; where, though they were never alone, yet they had every day opportunity for converse with each other, which the rest shared not in, while every one minded their own delights.

They had not six weeks enjoyed this peace, but the young men and women, who saw them allow each other that kindness which they did not afford commonly to others, first

began to grow jealous and envious at it, and afterwards to
use all the malicious practices they could invent to break the
friendship. Among the rest, that gentleman who at the first
had so highly commended her to Mr. Hutchinson, now began
to caution him against her, and to disparage her, with such
subtle insinuations, as would have ruined any love less constant and honourable than his. The women, with witty
spite, represented all her faults to him, which chiefly ter-
minated in the negligence of her dress and habit, and
all womanish ornaments, giving herself wholly up to study
and writing. Mr. Hutchinson, who had a very sharp and
pleasant wit, retorted all their malice with such just reproofs
of their idleness and vanity, as made them hate her, who,
without affecting it, had so engaged such a person in her protection, as they with all their arts could not catch. He, in
the meanwhile, prosecuted his love with so much discretion,
duty, and honour, that at the length, through many difficulties, he accomplished his design. I shall pass by all the
little amorous relations, which, if I would take the pains to
relate, would make a true history of a more handsome
management of love than the best romances describe; but
these are to be forgotten as the vanities of youth, not worthy
of mention among the greater transactions of his life. There
is this only to be recorded, that never was there a passion
more ardent and less idolatrous; he loved her better than his
life, with inexpressible tenderness and kindness, had a most
high obliging esteem of her, yet still considered honour,
religion, and duty above her, nor ever suffered the intrusion
of such a dotage as should blind him from marking her imperfections; these he looked upon with such an indulgent eye
as did not abate his love and esteem of her, while it augmented
his care to blot out all those spots which might make her
appear less worthy of that respect he paid her; and thus
indeed he soon made her more equal to him than he found
her; for she was a very faithful mirror, reflecting truly,
though but dimly, his own glories upon him, so long as he
was present; but she, that was nothing before his inspection
gave her a fair figure, when he was removed, was only filled
with a dark mist, and never could again take in any delightful object, nor return any shining representation. The
greatest excellency she had was the power of apprehending
and the virtue of loving his; so as his shadow she waited on

him everywhere, till he was taken into that region of light which admits of none, and then she vanished into nothing. It was not her face he loved, her honour and her virtue were his mistresses; and these (like Pygmalion's) images of his own making, for he polished and gave form to what he found with all the roughness of the quarry about it; but meeting with a compliant subject for his own wise government, he found as much satisfaction as he gave, and never had occasion to number his marriage among his infelicities. That day that the friends on both sides met to conclude the marriage, she fell sick of the small pox, which was in many ways a great trial upon him. First, her life was almost in desperate hazard, and then the disease, for the present, made her the most deformed person that could be seen, for a great while after she recovered; yet he was nothing troubled at it, but married her as soon as she was able to quit the chamber, when the priest and all that saw her were affrighted to look on her; but God recompensed his justice and constancy by restoring her, though she was longer than ordinary before she recovered to be as well as before. One thing is very observable, and worthy imitation in him: although he had as strong and violent affections for her, as ever any man had, yet he declared it not to her till he had acquainted first his father; and afterwards he never would make any engagement but what his love and honour bound him in; wherein he was more firm and just than all the promissory oaths and ties in the world could have made him, notwithstanding many powerful temptations of wealth and beauty, and other interests, that were laid before him. For his father had concluded another treaty, before he knew his son's inclinations were this way fixed, with a party in many things much more advantageous for his family, and more worthy of his liking; but his father was no less honourably indulgent to his son's affection, than the son was strict in the observance of his duty; and at length, to the full content of all, the thing was accomplished, and on the third day of July, in the year 1638, he was married to Mrs. Lucy Apsley, the second daughter of Sir Allen Apsley, late lieutenant of the Tower of London, at St. Andrew's church in Holborn. He lived some time in this neighbourhood with her mother, but four months were scarcely past after their marriage before he was in great danger of losing her, when she lost two children she had conceived by him.

Soon after conceiving again she grew so sickly, that her indulgent mother and husband, for the advantage of her health, removed their dwelling out of the city, to a house they took in Enfield Chace, called the Blue House, where, upon the third of September, 1639, she was brought to bed of two sons, whereof the elder he named after his own father, Thomas, the younger was called Edward, who both survived him. September, 1641, she brought him another son, called by his own name, John, who lived scarce six years, and was a very hopeful child, full of his father's vigour and spirit, but death soon nipped that blossom.

Mr. Hutchinson, after about fourteen months' various exercise of his mind, in the pursuit of his love, being now at rest in the enjoyment of his wife, his next design was to draw her into his own country; but he would not set upon it too roughly, and therefore let her rest awhile, when he had drawn her ten miles nearer it, out of the city where she had her birth and education, and where all her relations were most conversant, and which she could not suddenly resolve to quit altogether, to betake herself to the north, which was a formidable name among the London ladies. While she was weaning from the friends and places she had so long conversed in, Mr. Hutchinson employed his time in making an entrance upon the study of school divinity, wherein his father was the most eminent scholar of any gentleman in England, and had a most choice library,[1] valued at a thousand pounds; which Mr. Hutchinson, mistakingly expecting to be part of his inheritance, thought it would be very inglorious for him not to understand how to make use of his father's books. Having therefore gotten into the house with him an excellent scholar in that kind of learning, he for two years made it the whole employment of his time. The gentleman that assisted him he converted to a right belief in that great point of predestination, he having been before of the Arminian judgment, till, upon the serious examination of both principles, and comparing them with the Scriptures,

---

[1] This is spoken of in the preface, and did in fact remain at Owthorpe, but probably was placed there by Charles, the son of Sir Thomas Hutchinson by his second wife: it was of excessively small value when taken possession of in the year 1776.

It is apparent, from Sir Thomas Hutchinson being upon all the committees for religion, as may be seen in Rushworth's collection, that he was in repute for this kind of knowledge.

Mr. Hutchinson convinced him of the truth, and he grew so well instructed in this principle, that he was able to maintain it against any man. At that time, this great doctrine grew much out of fashion with the prelates, but was generally embraced by all religious and holy persons in the land. Mr. Hutchinson being desirous to inform himself thoroughly of it, when he was able to manage the question, offered it to his father; but Sir Thomas would not declare himself on the point to him, nor indeed in any other, as we conceived, lest a father's authority should sway against his children's light, who he thought ought to discern things with their own eyes, and not with his. Mr. Hutchinson, taking delight in the study of divinity, presently left off all foolish nice points, that tended to nothing but vain brangling, and employed his whole study in laying a foundation of sound and necessary principles, among which he gave the first place to this of God's absolute decrees. This was so far from producing a carelessness of life in him, a thing generally objected against this faith,[1] that, on the other side, it excited him to a more strict and holy walking in thankfulness to God, who had been pleased to choose him out of the corrupted mass of lost mankind, to fix his love upon him, and give him the knowledge of himself by his ever-blessed Son. This principle of love and life in God, which had been given him when he discerned not what it was in himself, had from a child preserved him from wallowing in the mire of sin and wickedness, wherein most of the gentry of those times were miserably plunged, except a few, that were therefore the scorn of mankind; and there were but few of those few, that had not natural and superstitious follies, that were in some kind justly ridiculous and contemptible. It was a remarkable providence of God

[1] Mrs. Hutchinson, in exculpating her husband, goes no part of the way towards showing that the natural tendency of this principle differs from that which is objected against it, but merely that he resisted this bias from another consideration. This is certainly not a suitable place to discuss such a subject; and it is therefore dismissed with this remark, that the partisans of the two opposite, or supposed opposite, principles of predestination and free will, while they endeavour to implicate each other in absurdity and irreligion, agree in practice, and, guiding their actions by the best discretion they are masters of, end with referring the event to Providence, and praying to God for a blessing on their endeavours—much more rational in so doing than farther exposing the weakness of human understanding by disquisitions far too refined for its reach. The conduct of modern times is in this respect more commendable than that of the past.

in his life, that must not be passed over without special notice, that he gave him these two years' leisure, and a heart so to employ it, before the noise of war and tumult came upon him. Yet about the year 1639, the thunder was heard afar off rattling in the troubled air, and even the most obscured woods were penetrated with some flashes, the forerunners of the dreadful storm which the next year was more apparent; but Mr. Hutchinson was not yet awakened till it pleased God to deliver him from a danger into which he had run himself, had not mercy prevented him. His wife having already two sons, and being again with child, considered that it would be necessary to seek an augmentation of revenue, or retire into a cheaper country; and more inclining to the first, than to leave at once her mother, and all the rest of her dear relations, she had propounded to him to buy an office, which he was not of himself very inclinable to; but, to give her and her mother satisfaction, he hearkened to a motion that was made him in that kind. Sir William Pennyman, who had married his cousin-german, a very worthy gentleman, who had great respect both for and from his father, had purchased the chief office in the Star-chamber; the gentleman who held the next to him was careless and debauched, and thereby a great hindrance of Sir William's profits, who apprehended that if he could get an honest man into that place, they might mutually much advantage each other; whereupon he persuaded Mr. Hutchinson to buy the place, and offered him any terms, to go any share with him, or any way he could desire. Mr. Hutchinson treated with the gentleman, came to a conclusion, went down into the country, provided the money, and came up again, thinking presently to enter into the office; but the gentleman that should have sold it, being of an uncertain humour, thought to make the benefit of another term before he sold his place; and it pleased God, in the meantime, that arbitrary court was, by the parliament then sitting, taken away. Mr. Hutchinson was very sensible of a peculiar providence to him herein, and resolved to adventure no more such hazards; but to retire to that place whither God seemed to have called him by giving him so good an interest there, and to study how he was to improve that talent. His wife, convinced by this kind check which God had given to her desires, that she ought to follow her husband where the Lord seemed to call him, went along with him, and

about October 1641, they came to their house at Owthorpe.
Here Mr. George Hutchinson (Sir Thomas being then chosen
knight for Nottinghamshire, and sitting in the parliament at
London) came and gave a glad entertainment of his brother
and sister into the country, by his good company; and they
were, for a few months, peaceful and happy in their own
house, till the kingdom began to blaze out with the long-
conceived flame of civil war.   But here I must make a short
digression from our particular actions, to sum up the state
of the kingdom at that time, which though I cannot do
exactly, yet I can truly relate what I was then able to take
notice of; and if any one have a desire of more particular
information, there were so many books then written, as will
sufficiently give it them.   And although those of our enemies
are all fraught with abominable lies, yet if all ours were
suppressed, even their own writings, impartially considered,
would be a sufficient chronicle of their injustice and oppression; but I shall only mention what is necessary to be
remembered, for the better carrying on of my purpose.[1]

When the dawn of the gospel began to break upon this
isle, after the dark midnight of papacy, the morning was
more cloudy here than in other places by reason of the state-
interest, which was mixing and working itself into the
interest of religion, and which in the end quite wrought it
out.   King Henry the Eighth, who, by his royal authority,
cast out the pope, did not intend the people of the land
should have any ease of oppression; but only changed their
foreign yoke for home-bred fetters, dividing the pope's spoils
between himself and his bishops, who cared not for their
father at Rome, so long as they enjoyed their patrimony and
their honours here under another head: so that I cannot
subscribe to those who entitle that king to the honour of the
reformation.   But even then there wanted not many who
discerned the corruptions that were retained in the church,

[1] In a small book, entitled, a Parallel of Clarendon and Whitelock,
this is set in the clearest light possible, and in a variety of instances
the unfaithfulness of Clarendon's testimony made evident by the pro-
duction of palpable self-contradictions. Most of those who read the
summary account Mrs. Hutchinson gives of the public transactions,
will extremely regret that she was not much more full in it, seeing the
candour and perspicuity with which she writes: short as it is, however,
it will be found to throw light upon many obscure points; and, from
being so much concentrated, will be useful and acceptable to many, as
serving to fix a general and just idea of the public mind, as well as
transactions, in the times of which she treats.

and eagerly applied their endeavours to obtain a purer reformation; against whom, those who saw no need of further reformation, either through excess of joy for that which was already brought forth, or else through a secret love of superstition rooted in their hearts thought this too much,— were bitterly incensed, and, hating that light which reproved their darkness, everywhere stirred up spirits of envy and persecution against them. Upon the great revolution which took place at the accession of Queen Elizabeth to the crown, the nation became divided into three great factions, the papists, the state protestants, and the more religious zealots, who afterwards were branded with the name of Puritans. In vain it was for these to address the queen and the parliament; for the bishops, under the specious pretences of uniformity and obedience, procured severe punishments to be inflicted on such as durst gainsay their determinations in all things concerning worship, whereupon some even in those godly days lost their lives.

The papists had a most inveterate hatred to all the protestants, but especially to those who were godly;[1] and they again many of them suffered their zeal to run out into bitter personal hate. Between these two extremes, the common protestants were in the middle, though I cannot reckon them as a virtuous medium; for of them the more profane and ignorant only left popery because it grew out of fashion, but in their hearts inclined that way; those who were peaceable, conscientious, or moral persons, inclined to the puritans, of whom there were many that unwillingly bore the burden of the ceremonies, for quietness' sake, and through false doctrine of their unfaithful teachers, as well as some that discerned the base and carnal minds of those seducers, and would not be persuaded by them to defile their consciences. The former sort of these, in zeal to reduce the whole land from their idolatrous practices, procured laws and invented oaths to suppress popery, which they little thought, but we now sadly find, are the bitterest engines to batter down the pure worship and destroy the pure worshippers of God; which I have often looked upon as an evidence that God is not pleased with the conversions that are enforced by men's

---

[1] Godly. The name always given by the puritans to those of their own party, and not unfrequently so used by different sectaries at the present day.

laws. We have spiritual weapons given us for spiritual combats, and those who go about to conquer subjects for Christ with swords of steel, shall find the base metal break to shivers when it is used, and hurtfully fly in their own faces.

About the time of the reformation, there was a great change in the civil interest of all that part of the world which had long lain under the bondage of the Roman prelate and his tyrannical clergy. These had by degrees so encroached upon all the secular princes, that they were nothing but vassals and hangmen to the proud insolent priest. Obtaining his empire by fraud, false doctrine, lies, and hypocrisy, he maintained it by blood and rapine, till it pleased God to cause that light to break forth about Luther's time, which hath ever since been increasing; and, notwithstanding all the attempts of Satan and his ministers, it will in the end grow up to a glorious flame and quite devour that bloody city. When the wrath of princes and priests was in vain at first blown up against the professors of the gospel, and their blood and ashes became fruitful seed in God's field, then the old fox comes into the fold as a lamb, and seduces some of them that saw the approach of Christ's kingdom, to set it up irregularly; and, indeed (though I know not whether they perceived their own delusion), to set up themselves in Christ's throne, casting down the thrones of all other magistrates, and destroying the properties of men, and ruling by their own arbitrary lust, which they brought forth in the name of God's law.[1] This example was so threatening to all mankind, that the gospel itself, from the adversaries thereof, suffered much reproach upon this miscarriage; whereupon the protestants, in all places, to clear themselves from the just aspersions which the Munster anabaptists and others had occasioned, fell into an error on the other hand, not much less hurtful in the consequence; for to flatter the princes of the world, whether popish or protestant, they invested them with God's prerogative, and preached to them and the people such doctrines as only changed the idol, but left the idolatry still in practice.[2]

[1] A description of the principles of the most extravagant of those whom in history they call Fifth Monarchy Men, from their affecting to set up the empire of Christ as the fifth; the Assyrian, Persian, Grecian, and Roman, being the first four.

[2] This could hardly be carried further anywhere than in England,

The popes of Rome had for many ages challenged and practised a power to dethrone princes, to give away their realms, to interdict whole kingdoms and provinces, and devote them to slaughter, to loose subjects from all bonds and oaths of allegiance to their sovereigns, and to stir up both princes and people to the mutual murder of each other; which abominable courses, had been justly cast upon them as reproach, they pretending to do all these things for the propagation of the true worship and the advance of God's glory. This reproach they retorted when some protestants, upon the same pretence, did maintain that idolatrous princes were to be removed, and such magistrates set up as feared God, who were guardians of both tables, and were bound to compel all their people to the right religion. This confusion was there among the sons of darkness at the first appearance of gospel light.

About this time in the kingdom of Scotland there was a wicked queen, daughter of a mother that came out of the bloody house of Guise,[1] and brought up in the popish religion, which she zealously persevered in, as most suitable to her bloody lustful temper; she being guilty of murders and adulteries, and hateful for them to the honestest of the people, was deposed, imprisoned, and forced to fly for her life; but her son was received upon the throne, and educated after the strictest way of the protestant religion according to Calvin's form. Those who were chiefly active and instrumental in the justice executed on this wicked queen, were the reformers of religion in Scotland, which made the neighbouring idolatrous princes fear them of the same faith. About the same time likewise, the provinces of the Netherlands united themselves in a resistance against the king of Spain,

where in all cases passive, in most cases active, obedience was indiscriminately inculcated; where two divines stating in their discourses, one, " that it was the king's duty to make laws, and the subject's to obey them; " another, that " the king is not bound to observe the laws of the realm, but that his royal will and command in imposing taxes and loans without consent of parliament, doth oblige the subject's conscience, upon pain of eternal damnation." For refusing to license the publication of the first sermon, the good Archbishop Abbot was banished, and confined to a bad and unhealthy country-house. For the latter, the preacher, though sentenced by the lords to be fined and imprisoned, was by the king pardoned, and promoted to a bishoprick. After this, let it be decided whether Charles reverenced episcopacy as a divine institution, or valued it as an engine of state? and in what light he caused his subjects to view it?

[1] Mary, Queen of Scots.

and cast off that yoke wherewith he had most barbarously galled them. The king of France, persecuting his protestant subjects with much inhuman violence, forced them to defend themselves against his unsanctified league, and much blood was shed in those civil wars; till at length those who had had so much experience of God's providence in delivering them from their cruel princes, were persuaded to make up an alliance with the enemies of God and religion, and by the treacherous foe drawn into his snares, where they were most wickedly and barbarously massacred.[1] Now, although religion was the main ground of those bloody quarrels, yet there were, in all these countries, many disputes of civil right, which for the most part were borne on the face of the wars, whereat I have only hinted, in this survey of the condition of other states, and their interests in those days and since; which is something necessary to be known for the better understanding of our own, with which I shall now proceed.

The civil government of England, from the time called the Conquest, had been administered by a King, Lords, and Commons, in a way of Parliaments; the parliament entrusted with the legislative, and the king with the executive power; but several of the kings, not satisfied with their bounded monarchy, made attempts to convert it into an absolute sovereignty, attempts fatal both to themselves and their people, and ever unsuccessful. For the generous people of England, as they were the most free and obsequious subjects in the world to those princes that managed them with a kind and tender hand, commanding them as freemen, not as slaves, so were they the most untameable, invincible people, in defence of their freedoms against all those usurping lords that scorned to allow them liberty. The nobility of the realm having at first the great balance of the lands, and retaining some of that free honourable virtue, for which they were exalted above the vulgar, ever stood up in the people's defence and curbed the wild ambition of the tyrants, whom they sometimes reduced to moderation, and sometimes deposed for their misgovernments; till, at length the kings, eager to break this yoke, had insensibly worn out the interest of the nobility, by drawing them to their courts, where luxuries melted away the great estates of some, others were

[1] The famous massacre on St. Bartholomew's day at Paris.

destroyed by confiscations in divers civil wars, and others otherwise mouldered with time. While the kings were glad to see the abatement of that power, which had been such a check to their exorbitancies, they perceived not the growing of another more dangerous to them; and that when the nobility shrunk into empty names, the throne lost its supporters, and had no more but a little puff of wind to bear it up, when the full body of the people came rolling in upon it.[1] The interest of the people, which had been many years growing, made an extraordinary progress in the days of King Henry the Eighth, who returning the vast revenues of the church into the body of the people, cast the balance clear on their side, and left them now only to expect [2] an opportunity to resume their power into their own hands; and had not differences in religion divided them among themselves, and thereby prolonged the last gasps of expiring monarchy, they had long since exercised it in a free commonwealth.

England was not an idle spectator of the great contest between the papist and protestant, in which all Christendom seemed to be engaged. During the reign of Queen Elizabeth, the protestant interest, being her peculiar interest, that princess became not only glorious in the defence of her own realm, but in the protection she gave to the whole protestant cause in all the neighbouring kingdoms; wherefore, as if it had been devolved upon her person, the pope shot all his arrows at her head, and set on many desperate assassinations against her, which, by the good providence of God, were all frustrated, and she, not only miraculously delivered from those wretches, but renowned at home and abroad for successes against her rebellious subjects in England and Ireland, and for the assistance of her distressed neighbours; but,

---

[1] It is wonderful that the experience of so many ages and so many other states had not been sufficient to warn the princes of the house of Bourbon of this fatal error! From the moment of Cardinal Richelieu's coming into power under Louis XIII. to Neckar's return to power after his rustication under Louis XVI. the plan of lowering the power of the noblesse of France had been systematically pursued. The last stroke was given to it when this delusive and deluded minister advised that unfortunate monarch to give to the commons a double number of representatives in the states general, and to blend the noblesse with them. It was in vain that the Prince of Conti gave him a short note of admonition, written on the spur of the occasion upon his hat:— " Sire, the moment you sign this arret your throne is overturned." He rejected the advice, and betrayed the author.

[2] Expect, a Latinism; expectare, to wait for; or, Italian, aspettare, id.

above all, for the mercy which it pleased God to afford her
and this realm in the year 1588, when the invading Spaniard
had devoured us in his proud hopes, and by the mighty hand
of God was scattered as a mist before the morning beams.
That which kept alive the hopes of the papists, most part of
her reign, was the expectation of the Queen of Scots, who,
entering into confederacy with them, lost her head for the
forfeit, wherein the duke of Norfolk suffered also for her the
loss of his. The Queen of England was very loath to execute
this necessary justice; but the true-hearted protestants of
her council, foreseeing the sad effects that might be expected
if ever she arrived to the crown, urged it on;[1] and after the
death of Queen Elizabeth, the wiser of them much opposed
the admission of her son. But he, dissembling the resentment of his mother's death, by bribes and greater promises,
managed a faction in the court of the declining queen,
which prevailed on her dotage to destroy the Earl of Essex,
the only person who would have had the courage to keep
out him they thought it dangerous to let in.[2] So subtlely
brought they their purpose about, that wise counsel was in
vain to a blinded and betrayed people. The anti-prelatical
party hoping that, with a king bred up among the Calvinists,
they should now be freed from the episcopal yoke, were
greedy of entertaining him, but soon cured of their mistake;
when, immediately after his entry into the kingdom, himself
being moderator at a dispute between both parties, the
nonconformists were cast out of doors, and the offensive
ceremonies, instead of being removed, were more strictly
imposed; the penalties against papists were relaxed, and
many of them taken into favour; whilst those families who
suffered for his mother were graced and restored as far as the

[1] The signing and expediting the warrant for the execution of Mary
Queen of Scots is an enigma which has employed the wits of many to
solve—perhaps this may be the true solution of it; it is at least clear,
that it thus appeared to well-informed persons, living in times when
the thing was recent, and accounts for it more naturally than the mean
jealousy attributed to Queen Elizabeth, which would in fact have been
a better reason for putting her to death many years sooner.

[2] In Heylin's *History of the Presbyterians*, it is said that the Earl of
Essex was much courted by the puritans, and in return caressed them;
that a title to the crown was drawn out for him, and he began to look up
to it; that he encouraged an opinion, that inferior magistrates might
curb and control their sovereign; that he was outwitted and brought
to the scaffold by Cecil and Raleigh, very opportunely for king James,
whose entrance might have been opposed and his title questioned.

times would bear, and those who consented any way to the justice done upon her, disfavoured. A progress was made suitable to this beginning, the protestant interest abroad was deserted and betrayed, the prelates at home daily exalted in pride and pomp, and declining in virtue and godliness. Arminianism [1] crept in to the corruption of sound doctrine, till at length they had the impudence to forbid the preaching of those great and necessary truths concerning the decrees of God; secret treaties were entertained with the court of Rome; [2] and, notwithstanding that hellish powder plot, the papists lost not their credit at court, where they now wrought no longer by open and direct ways, but humouring the king and queen in their lusts and excesses, they found the most ready way to destroy the doctrine of the gospel was to debauch the professors. The court of this king was a nursery of lust and intemperance; he had brought in with him a company of poor Scots, who, coming into this plentiful kingdom, were surfeited with riot and debaucheries, and got all the riches of the land only to cast away. The honour, wealth, and glory of the nation, wherein Queen Elizabeth left it, were soon prodigally wasted by this thriftless heir; and the nobility of the land was utterly debased by setting honours to public sale, and conferring them on persons that had neither blood nor merit fit to wear, nor estates to bear up their titles, but were fain to invent projects to pill [3] the people, and pick their purses for the maintenance of vice and lewdness. The generality of the gentry of the land soon learned the court fashion, and every great house in the country became a sty of uncleanness. To keep the people in their deplorable security, till vengeance overtook them, they were entertained with masks, stage plays, and various sorts of ruder sports. Then began murder, incest, adultery, drunkenness, swearing, fornication, and all sort of ribaldry, to be no concealed but countenanced vices, because they held such conformity with the court example. Next to this, a great cause of these abominations was the mixed marriages of papist and protestant families, which, no question, was a design of the popish party to compass and procure; and so successful, that I have observed that there was not one house

[1] James, however, professed himself a great enemy to it.
[2] The first volume of Clarendon's *State Papers* is half filled with them.
[3] Pill—pillage, plunder.

in ten, where such a marriage was made, but the better party
was corrupted, the children's souls were sacrificed to devils,
the worship of God was laid aside in that family, for fear of
distasting the idolater; the kindred, tenants, and neighbours,
either quite turned from it, or cooled in their zeal for religion.
As the fire is most fervent in a frosty season, so the general
apostacy from holiness, if I may so call it, and defection to
lewdness, stirred up sorrow, indignation, and fear, in all that
retained any love of God in the land, whether ministers or
people; the ministers warned the people of the approaching
judgments of God, which could not be expected but to follow
such high provocations; God in his mercy sent his prophets
into all corners of the land, to preach repentance, and cry
out against the ingratitude of England, who thus requited
so many rich mercies that no nation could ever boast of
more; and by these a few were everywhere converted and
established in faith and holiness; but at court they were
hated, disgraced, and reviled, and in scorn had the name
of Puritan [1] fixed upon them.   And now the ready way to
preferment there was to declare an opposition to the power
of godliness, under that name; so that their pulpits might
justly be called the scorner's chair, those sermons only
pleasing that flattered them in their vices, and told the poor
king that he was Solomon, and that his sloth and cowardice,
by which he betrayed the cause of God and honour of the
nation, was gospel meekness and peaceableness; for which
they raised him up above the heavens, while he lay wallowing
like a swine in the mire of his lust.   He had a little learning,
and this they called the spirit of wisdom, and so magnified

---

[1] This artifice of affixing a name of reproach on those of an opposite
party, in order indiscriminately to subject them to hatred or ridicule,
could hardly be better exposed than it is here. That Mrs. Hutchinson
is guilty of no exaggeration, may well be conjectured from some
speeches in parliament preserved by Rushworth, peculiarly one of Sir
Benjamin Rudyard, at least a moderate man, if not a favourer of the
king, complaining of the very same thing.   Rushworth, vol. ii. 1355,
" It is the artifice of the favourers of the catholic and of the prelatical
party to call all who are sticklers for the constitution in church or state,
or would square their actions by any rule, human or divine, Puritans."
In the petition and remonstrance this is stated nearly in the same
manner.   It was no way inconsistent with the other injustices of the
French revolutionists to invent the term of Aristocrat, and mark out
by it every one whom the populace or their demagogues designed to
plunder or destroy; it would not be so excusable if in this country we
should suffer cant terms or nicknames to pass for reasoning or proof.
For the rest, the name of Puritan should have no bad meaning.

him, so falsely flattered him, that he could not endure the words of truth and soundness, but rewarded these base, wicked, unfaithful fawners with rich preferments, attended with pomps and titles, which heaped them up above a human height. With their pride, their envy swelled against the people of God, whom they began to project how they might root out of the land; and when they had once given them a name, whatever was odious or dreadful to the king, they fixed upon the puritan, who, according to their character, was nothing but a factious hypocrite.

The king had upon his heart the dealings both of England and Scotland with his mother, and harboured a secret desire of revenge upon the godly in both nations, yet had not courage enough to assert his resentment like a prince, but employed a wicked cunning he was master of, and called king-craft, to undermine what he durst not openly oppose,— the true religion; this was fenced with the liberty of the people, and so linked togther, that it was impossible to make them slaves, till they were brought to be idolaters of royalty and glorious lust; and as impossible to make them adore these gods, while they continued loyal to the government of Jesus Christ. The payment of civil obedience to the king and the laws of the land satisfied not; if any durst dispute his impositions in the worship of God, he was presently reckoned among the seditious and disturbers of the public peace, and accordingly persecuted; if any were grieved at the dishonour of the kingdom, or the griping of the poor, or the unjust oppressions of the subject, by a thousand ways, invented to maintain the riots of the courtiers, and the swarms of needy Scots the king had brought in to devour like locusts the plenty of this land, he was a puritan; if any, out of mere morality and civil honesty, discountenanced the abominations of those days, he was a puritan, however he conformed to their superstitious worship; if any showed favour to any godly honest persons, kept them company, relieved them in want, or protected them against violent or unjust oppression, he was a puritan; if any gentleman in his country maintained the good laws of the land, or stood up for any public interest, for good order or government, he was a puritan: in short, all that crossed the views of the needy courtiers, the proud encroaching priests, the thievish projectors, the lewd nobility and gentry —whoever was zealous for God's glory or worship, could not endure blasphemous oaths, ribald conversation, profane scoffs, sabbath breaking, derision of the word of God, and the like—whoever could endure a sermon, modest habit or conversation, or anything good,—all these were puritans; and if puritans, then enemies to the king and his government, seditious, factious, hypocrites, ambitious disturbers of the public peace, and finally, the pest of the kingdom. Such false logic did the children of darkness use to argue with against the hated children of light, whom they branded besides as an illiterate, morose, melancholy, discontented, crazed sort of men, not fit for human conversation;[1] as such they made them not only the sport of the pulpit, which was become but a more solemn sort of stage, but every stage, and every table, and every puppet-play, belched forth profane scoffs upon them, the drunkards made them their songs, and all fiddlers and mimics learned to abuse them, as finding it the most gameful way of fooling. Thus the two factions in those days grew up to great heights and enmities one against the other; while the papist wanted not industry and subtlety to blow the coals between them, and was so successful that, unless the mercy of God confound them by their own imaginations, we may justly fear they will at last obtain their full wish.

But to deal impartially, we must, with sadness enough, confess, that the wolf came into the fold in a sheep's clothing, and wrought more slaughter that way among the lambs than he could have done in his own skin; for it is true that many of wit and parts, discontented when they could not obtain the preferments their ambition gaped at, would declare themselves of the puritan party. And such were either bought off, or, if the adversary would not give their price, seduced their devout hearers sometimes into indiscreet opposition to work out their own revenge; others, that had neither learning, nor friends, nor opportunities to arrive to any preferments, would put on a form of godliness, finding devout people that way so liberal to them, that they could

---

[1] Such is the idea entertained of them in general even at this day; whoever shall read these memoirs will be well convinced that not one of these qualities needs or does by any natural consequence accompany the character. It is a great misfortune that many of the zealous professors of piety should give it so austere an aspect, and this can never be better contrasted than by the cheerful and amiable tone this professed puritan gives it.

not hope to enrich themselves so much in any other way. Some that had greater art and parts, finding there was no inconsiderable gain to be made of the simple devotion of men and women, applied their wits to it, and collected great sums for the advancement of the religious interest, of which they converted much to their own private uses. Such as these tempted the people of God to endeavour to shelter themselves in human policies, and found out ways, by bribes and other not less indirect courses, to procure patrons at court, and to set up against the prelates with countermines and other engines, which, being of man's framing, were all at last broken.

The puritan party being weak and oppressed, had not faith enough to disown all that adhered to them for worldly interests, and indeed it required more than human wisdom to discern at the least all of them; wherefore they, in their low condition, gladly accepted any that would come over to them, or incline towards them; and their enemies, through envy at them, augmented much their party, while, with injuries and reproaches, they drove many, that never intended it, to take that party; which in the end got nothing but confusion by those additions. While these parties were thus counter-working, the treasure of the kingdom being wasted by court-caterpillars, the parliaments were called to re-supply the royal coffers, and therein there wanted not some, that retained so much of the English spirit as to represent the public grievances, and desire to call the corrupt ministers of state to an account. But the king, grudging that his people should dare to gainsay his pleasure, and correct his misgovernment in his favourites, broke up parliaments, violated their privileges, imprisoned their members for things spoken in the house, and grew disaffected to them, and entertained projects of supply by other grievances of the people. The prelates, in the meantime, finding they lost ground, meditated reunion with the popish faction, who began to be at a pretty agreement with them;[1] and now there was no more endeavour in their public sermons to confute the errors of that church, but to reduce our doctrines and theirs to an accommodation. The king, to bring it about, was deluded[2]

[1] The first volume of Clarendon's State Papers abounds with instances.

[2] It is very rare to see a delusion so long and successfully carried on as this appears to have been, at the expense of this modern Solomon, in the State Papers just mentioned.

into the treaty of a match for his son with the Infanta of Spain; and the prince, with the Duke of Buckingham, was privately sent into Spain, from whence he came back with difficulty, but to the great rejoicing of the whole people in general, who were much afflicted at his going thither. During this treaty the papists got many advantages of the king, to the prejudice of the protestant interest at home and abroad, and the hearts of all but the papists were very much saddened; and the people loath to lay the miscarriages of things at the king's own door, began to entertain a universal hatred of the Duke of Buckingham, raised from a knight's fourth son to that pitch of glory, and enjoying great possessions, acquired by the favour of the king, upon no merit but that of his beauty and his prostitution. The parliament had drawn up a charge against him, and though the king seemed to protect him, yet knowing the fearfulness of his nature, and doubting his constancy, it was believed he added some help to an ague that killed that king; however the king died, and the duke continued as high in the favour of the next succeeding as of the deceased prince; whereupon one, not unaptly, says of him, " he seemed as an unhappy exhalation, drawn up from the earth, not only to cloud the setting, but the rising sun." [1]

The face of the court was much changed in the change of the king, for King Charles was temperate, chaste, and serious; so that the fools and bawds, mimics and catamites, of the former court, grew out of fashion; and the nobility and courtiers, who did not quite abandon their debaucheries, yet so reverenced the king as to retire into corners to practise them. Men of learning and ingenuity in all arts were in esteem, and received encouragement from the king, who was a most excellent judge and a great lover of paintings, carvings, gravings, and many other ingenuities, less offensive than the bawdry and profane abusive wit which was the only exercise of the other court. But, as in the primitive times, it is observed that the best emperors were some of them stirred up by Satan to be the bitterest persecutors of the church, so this king was a worse encroacher upon the civil and spiritual liberties of his people by far than his father.

[1] The justice of the character here given of James, as well as the candour of that about to be given to Charles, will, it is hoped, be recognised by every reader.

He married a papist, a French lady, of a haughty spirit, and a great wit and beauty, to whom he became a most uxorious husband. By this means the court was replenished with papists, and many who hoped to advance themselves by the change, turned to that religion. All the papists in the kingdom were favoured, and, by the king's example, matched into the best families; the puritans were more than ever discountenanced and persecuted, insomuch that many of them chose to abandon their native country, and leave their dearest relations, to retire into any foreign soil or plantation, where they might, amidst all outward inconveniences, enjoy the free exercise of God's worship. Such as could not flee were tormented in the bishops' courts, fined, whipped, pilloried, imprisoned, and suffered to enjoy no rest, so that death was better than life to them; and notwithstanding their patient sufferance of all these things, yet was not the king satisfied till the whole land was reduced to perfect slavery. The example of the French king was propounded to him, and he thought himself no monarch so long as his will was confined to the bounds of any law; but knowing that the people of England were not pliable to an arbitrary rule, he plotted to subdue them to his yoke by a foreign force, and till he could effect it, made no conscience of granting anything to the people, which he resolved should not oblige him longer than it served his turn; for he was a prince that had nothing of faith or truth, justice or generosity, in him. He was the most obstinate person in his self-will that ever was, and so bent upon being an absolute, uncontrollable sovereign, that he was resolved either to be such a king or none. His firm adherence to prelacy was not for conscience of one religion more than another, for it was his principle that an honest man might be saved in any profession; but he had a mistaken principle that kingly government in the state could not stand without episcopal government in the church; and, therefore, as the bishops flattered him with preaching up his sovereign prerogative, and inveighing against the puritans as factious and disloyal, so he protected them in their pomp and pride, and insolent practices against all the godly and sober people of the land.[1] In the first

[1] In note, page 57, it has been shown that their political, not their religious principles, were the criterion whereby the king judged the prelates of the church of England. That the same served for the

parliament after he came to the crown, the Duke of Buckingham was impeached concerning the death of King James, and other misdemeanours; but the present king, who had received him into the same degree of favour that he was with the former, would not endure the question of his favourite, and, to deliver him from it, broke up the parliament, which gave too just a suspicion that he favoured the practice; for it is true that the duke's mother, without the consent of the physicians, had made an application to the wrists of the king for his ague, after which he died in his next fit. Some other parliaments there were, but still abruptly broken up when they put forth any endeavour to redress grievances. The protestants abroad were all looked upon as puritans, and their interests, instead of being protected, sadly betrayed; ships were let out to the French king to serve against them; and all the flower of the English gentry were lost in an ill-managed expedition to the Isle of Rhee, under pretence of helping them, but so ordered that it proved the loss of Rochelle, the strong fort and best defence of all the protestants in France. Those in Germany were no less neglected in all treaties, although his own sister and her children were so highly concerned. The whole people were sadly grieved at these misgovernments, and, loath to impute them to the king, cast all the odium upon the Duke of Buckingham, whom at length a discontented person stabbed, believing he did God and his country good service by it. All the kingdom, except the duke's own dependents and kindred, rejoiced in the death of this duke; but they found little cause, for after it the king still persisted in his design of enslaving them, and found other ministers ready to serve his self-willed ambition, such as were Noy, his attorney-general, who set on foot that hateful tax of ship-money, and many more illegal exactions; and ten of the judges, who perverted

church of Rome is shown pretty clearly in the first volume of Clarendon's State Papers, where Mr. Courtenay having refused some compliances against conscience, and giving as his reason that " the king was not the law-maker, but the king and parliament, and that the king has not a dispensing power; " and father Scudamore, alias Leander, asserting that he has, Courtenay is committed to prison, held there, and a trial refused him; Leander protected, encouraged, and rewarded; and it is stated that " Laud was at the helm of the king's counsel in these matters." This opinion of the king's candour, or even indifference, as to the mode of religion, is stated in nearly the same manner in Rushworth, but it is not said on what authority. The Stuarts sported with and ruined all religions, and in turn were ruined by them.

judgment in the cause of those who refused the illegal imposition; although there were, even in that time, found two honest judges, who durst judge rightly against the king, although he had changed the words usual in their commissions, which were *Quamdiù bene se gesserint*,[1] into another form, *Durante bene placito*. Besides these, and a great rascally company of flatterers and projectors, there were all the corrupted, tottering bishops, and others of the proud, profane clergy of the land, who, by their insolencies, grown odious to the people, bent their strong endeavours to disaffect the prince to his honest, godly subjects, and to get a pretence of power from him, to afflict those who would not submit to their insolent dominion. But there were two above all the rest, who led the van of the king's evil counsellors, and these were Laud, archbishop of Canterbury, a fellow of mean extraction and arrogant pride, and the Earl of Strafford, who as much outstripped all the rest in favour as he did in abilities, being a man of deep policy, stern resolution, and ambitious zeal to keep up the glory of his own greatness. In the beginning of this king's reign, this man had been a strong asserter of the liberties of the people, among whom he had gained himself an honourable reputation, and was dreadful to the court party; who, thereupon strewed snares in his way, and when they found a breach at his ambition, his soul was that way entered and captivated. He was advanced first to be lord president of the council in the north, to be a baron, afterwards an earl, and then deputy of Ireland; he was the nearest to a favourite of any man since the death of the Duke of Buckingham, who was raised by his first master, and kept up by the second, upon no account of personal worth or any deserving abilities in him, but only from the violent and private inclinations of the princes. But the Earl of Strafford wanted not any accomplishment that could be desired in the most serviceable minister of state: besides, he having made himself odious to the people by his revolt from their interest to that of the oppressive court, he was now obliged to keep up his own interest with his new party, by all the malicious practices that pride and revenge could inspire him with.[2]   But above

---

[1] "Quamdiù bene se gesserint," during good behaviour, as long as they act right. "Durante bene placito," during the king's good pleasure.
[2] Called by Lord Digby the grand apostate of the Commonwealth.

all these the king had another instigator of his own violent purpose, more powerful than all the rest, and that was the queen, who, grown out of her childhood, began to turn her mind from those vain extravagancies she lived in at first, to that which did less become her, and was more fatal to the kingdom; which is never in any place happy where the hands which were made only for distaffs affect the management of sceptres.—If any one object the fresh example of Queen Elizabeth, let them remember that the felicity of her reign was the effect of her submission to her masculine and wise counsellors; but wherever male princes are so effeminate as to suffer women of foreign birth and different religions to intermeddle with the affairs of state, it is always found to produce sad desolations; and it hath been observed that a French queen never brought any happiness to England. Some kind of fatality, too, the English imagined to be in her name of Marie, which, it is said, the king rather chose to have her called by than her other, Henrietta, because the land should find a blessing in that name, which had been more unfortunate; but it was not in his power, though a great prince, to control destiny. This lady being by her priests affected with the meritoriousness of advancing her own religion, whose principle it is to subvert all other, applied that way her great wit and parts, and the power her haughty spirit kept over her husband, who was enslaved in his affection only to her, though she had no more passion for him than what served to promote her designs. Those brought her into a very good correspondence with the arch-bishop and his prelatical crew, both joining in the cruel design of rooting the godly out of the land. The foolish protestants were meditating reconciliations with the church of Rome, who embraced them as far as they would go, carrying them in hand, as if there had been a possibility of bringing such a thing to pass; meanwhile they carried on their design by them, and had so ripened it, that nothing but the mercy of God prevented the utter subversion of protestantism in the three kingdoms.—But how much soever their designs were framed in the dark, God revealed them to his servants, and most miraculously ordered providences for their preservation. About the year 1639, the Scots, having the English service-book obtruded upon them violently, refused it, and took a national covenant against it, and entered

England with a great army, to bring their complaints to the king, which his unfaithful ministers did, as they supposed, much misreport. The king himself levied an army against them, wherein he was assisted by the nobility and gentry, but most of all by the prelates, insomuch that the war got the name of *bellum episcopale*, or "bishops' war;" but the commonalty of the nation, being themselves under grievous bondage, were loath to oppose a people that came only to claim their just liberties. When the king was at York, the chief of the Scotch covenanters came, under a pretence of treating with the king, but their principal intent was to disabuse the nobility of England, and to take off their edge against them, by remonstrating upon those grievances and oppressions of the prelatical innovators, which had forced them thus to defend their religion and liberties. This they did so effectually, that the hearts of the English were much moved towards them, and the king perceiving it, by their mediations, consented to a dissembled peace for that time, and returned home. But the Scots, unsatisfied in the performance of their articles, made preparation for a second return into England; whereupon the king, in his anger and necessity, was forced to have recourse to the long neglected remedy of parliaments, and assembled one at Westminster the 13th of April, 1640, which he suffered to sit but twenty-one days, and broke it up again, apprehending that if he had suffered them to sit a day longer, they would have voted against the war with Scotland, which he was violently bent to prosecute.

The bishops at that time devised as an anti-covenant, in their convocation house, that execrable oath known by the name of the *et cætera*, wherein all ministers were required to swear to uphold the government of the church of England by archbishops, deans, archdeacons, etc. After this the Scots enter England, the king makes a second expedition into the north against them, and sends part of his army to keep the passes upon the river Tyne; but the soldiers being raw and heartless in this war, and the commanders themselves inexperienced, they were vanquished, and the Scots forced their way, after they had been refused to pass quietly by, with their petitions in their hands, and thus possessed themselves of Newcastle and Durham. At that time the Scots had put forth a declaration, wherein they had affirmed their intentions not to lay down arms till the reformed religion was settled in both nations upon sure grounds, and the causers of these present troubles brought to public justice, and that in a parliament. This was so plausible to the English, that the king, finding both the hearts and hands of his people fail him on this occasion, was induced to grant the petition of twelve noble lords, who at that time interposed; and, calling together all his lords at York, agreed upon a parliament to be convened at London on the third of November following. In the meantime, a treaty was condescended to, by sixteen lords of each side, Scotch and English, who agreed upon a cessation between both armies for the present, in order to a peace, to be concluded at London with the parliament, who met, as appointed, in November.

They began with throwing down monopolies, and then impeached the Earl of Strafford of high treason, who, after a solemn trial and hot disputes on both sides, was at length attainted of treason, and the king, against his own mind, to serve his ends, gave him up to death.[1] The archbishop of Canterbury was also made prisoner upon an accusation of high treason, for which he afterwards suffered;[2] Wren, bishop of Norwich, was likewise committed to the Tower;

[1] Whoever has read the propositions delivered to his majesty by the Earl of Strafford, for bridling parliaments and increasing his revenue, which is preserved in the third volume of Ludlow's Memoirs, p. 322, ingenious, bold, and dangerous beyond example, will think him richly to have deserved his fate, but not at the hand of Charles, who herein acted so treacherously to his friends, that their very adversaries are shocked at it, and fixed on his reputation a deep and indelible stain; accordingly he seems all his life long to have borne in mind an incessant regret of this crime. As it was a thing thought of but little consequence at the time, perhaps it will ere long be forgotten that Louis the Sixteenth suffered sentence of death to be executed on a Mr. De Favras for planning to assist him, or his brother, or both to escape, but when he did really effect his escape in part, there appeared great earnestness and zeal in stopping him! Did he not merit this?

May says, that the cause of Lord Strafford's condemnation was a note produced by Sir H. Vane, proving that as a privy counsellor he had proposed to the king to bring his army from Ireland to reduce this kingdom to obedience; but Ludlow's seems the stronger reason.

[2] It may well be doubted whether it was justifiable to change the proceedings against Laud from impeachment to attainder, in order to vote his death, which the law would not have condemned him to; but certainly deposition and banishment at least were due to the man who brought ruin and disgrace upon that pure and moderate system of religion of which he was the unworthy head: that to his conduct its ruin was principally attributable may be clearly seen by the speeches preserved by Rushworth, in his fourth volume, of Lord Digby, Falkland, Fiennes, and especially Grimston. At this day there is perhaps hardly to be found a son of the church who would condescend to meddle in such base projects as this archbishop assiduously employed himself in.

several other prelatical preachers were questioned for popish
and treasonable doctrines; the Star Chamber, an unjust and
arbitrary court, was taken away, and also the High Commission Court; an act was procured for a triennial parliament,
and another for the continuation of this, that it should not
be broken up without their own consent.   There were great
necessities for money by reason of the two armies that were
then maintained in England, and the people would give the
king no money without some ease of grievances, which forced
him, against his inclination, to grant those bills, with which [1]
after he had granted, he found he had bound up his own
hands, and therefore privately encouraged plots that were in
those times contrived against the parliament.   One of them
was to have rescued the Earl of Strafford out of prison, and
put him at the head of eight thousand Irish, which the king
would not consent to disband, when the parliament had
some time before moved him to it: then the English army
in the north was to have been brought up and engaged
against the parliament itself upon a pretence of maintaining
the king's prerogative, episcopacy, and some other such
things.   This plot was managed by Percy, Germyn, Goring,
Wilmot, Ashburnham, Pollard, Suckling, O'Neale, and
others, of whom some confessed and impeached their fellows,
others fled, others were put in prison.   While this parliament
was sitting, the king would needs, contrary to their desires,
take a journey to Scotland, and passed by the two disbanding armies in his journey, where some report that he secretly
attempted to urge the Scotch army against the parliament,
which then succeeded not.   The houses had adjourned for
some time, and left a standing committee of fifty to prepare
business.   About that time a plot was discovered to them
from Scotland, against the lives of some of the greatest peers
of that kingdom; the committee, fearing the like attempts
from the same spring, placed strong guards in divers parts

[1] This act for perpetuating the parliament was, in fact, that which
gave them a clear ascendancy over the king.   The proposing this, as
it showed the ingenuity and judgment of Mr. Pierrepont, to whom
Mrs. Hutchinson attributes it, so does it the weakness of the king and
his counsellors, who having granted this, had no longer any power
of refusal left.   For extraordinary evils extraordinary remedies are
often sought; but this, as it soon proved too strong for the king, so
was it at last thought too strong for the people.   The omnipotence of
parliament would be indeed dreadful alike to both, if, instead of being
immovable, it was permanent.

of the city of London. The king's design in going to Scotland was variously conjectured; but this was a certain effect of it, that it retarded all the affairs of the government of England, which the king had put into such disorder that it was not an easy task to reform what was amiss, and redress the real grievances of the people; but yet the parliament showed such a wonderful respect to the king, that they never mentioned him, as he was the sole author of all those miscarriages, but imputed them to evil counsellors, and gave him all the submissive language that could have been used to a good prince, fixing all the guilt upon his evil counsellors and ministers of state, which flattery I fear they have to answer for: I am sure they have thereby exposed themselves to much scandal.[1] While the king was in Scotland, that cursed rebellion in Ireland broke out, wherein above 200,000 were massacred in two months' space, being surprised, and many of them most inhumanly butchered and tormented; and besides the slain, abundance of poor families stripped and sent naked away out of all their possessions; and, had not the providence of God miraculously prevented the surprise of Dublin Castle the night it should have been seized, there had not been any remnant of the protestant name left in that country. As soon at this sad news came to the parliament, they vigorously set themselves to the work of relieving them; but then the king returned from Scotland, and being sumptuously welcomed home by the city, took courage thereby against the parliament, and obstructed all its proceedings for the effectual relief of Ireland. Long was he before he could be drawn to proclaim these murderers rebels, and when he did, by special command, there were but forty proclamations printed, and care was taken that they should not be much dispersed; which courses afflicted all the good protestants in England, and confirmed them that the rebellion in Ireland received countenance from the king and queen of England.[2] The parliament, beset with so many difficulties, were forced for their own vindication to present the king

[1] This is an oversight of Mrs. Hutchinson's, of which she is seldom guilty. Good policy required then, as it does now, that the king should be held incapable of wrong, and the criminality fixed on ministers, who are amenable to the law. If the patriots of that day were the inventors of this maxim, we are highly obliged to them.

[2] It would be difficult to draw a distinction so nice as would discriminate between the countenance shown to the rebels both before and after the rebellion breaking out, and the encouraging the rebellion

with a petition and a remonstrance on the state of the kingdom, wherein they spared him as much as truth would bear,
and complained only of his ill counsellors and ministers;
but this, instead of admonishing, exasperated him, and was
answered with another declaration of his; and upon several
occasions the parliament being enforced to justify their proceedings publicly, and the king setting forth replies, these
open debates were but the prologue to the ensuing tragedy.
The city, declaring their good affections to the parliament by
a petition, gave the king distrust, and he was observed to
entertain an extraordinary guard of cavaliers, who killed and
wounded some of the poor unarmed men that passed by his
house at Whitehall; and the parliament, conceiving themselves not safe, desired a guard might be allowed them under
the command of the Earl of Essex; but he refused it, with an
assurance that he would command such a guard to wait upon
them as he would be responsible to Almighty God for, and
that the safety of all and every one of them was as dear to
him as that of his own person and children.   Yet the very
next day after this false message, he came to the House of
Commons, attended with his extraordinary guard, of about
four hundred gentlemen and soldiers, armed with swords and
pistols, and there demanded five of their members, whom not
finding there (for a great lady at court had before informed
one of them of his coming, and the house ordered them to
retire,) he returned, leaving the house under a high sense of
this breach of their privilege.[1]   At this time the people began

itself: now that passion and prejudice have subsided there are probably many more that condemn than acquit the king and queen; but
whilst the blood of the massacred protestants yet reeked, and indignation glowed, it was neither to be wondered at nor blamed that persons
the most tolerant, as the independents professed to be, and Mrs.
Hutchinson especially, should speak with enmity of the queen and
catholics, and attribute to them those principles of intolerance and
antipathy to protestants which, whether they professed or not, they
practised.   It will hereafter be seen that, when they ceased to be
dangerous, Mr. Hutchinson did not persecute, but protect them.
   [1] The force of opinion being the only real force of any prince, and the
notion of inviolability his best protection, it was a strange infatuation
in him to overthrow them both.

> Turno tempus erit magno cùm optaverit emptum
> Intactum Pallanta, et cum spolia ista diemque
> Oderit   VIRG. Æn. 10.

> *The time shall come when Turnus, but in vain,*
> *Shall wish untouched the trophies of the slain,*
> *And curse the dire remembrance of that day.*—DRYDEN.

in great numbers to bring petitions to the king and parliament, to beg a more cheerful concurrence between them for the relief of Ireland, and to encourage the parliament in their honourable endeavours for the relief of both kingdoms. The king was offended at this, and retired first to Hampton Court, then went with the queen to Canterbury, whom he sent from thence into Holland with her daughter, lately married to the Prince of Orange, under pretence of conducting her to her own court, but really to manage his business abroad, and procure arms to be employed against the parliament, by the sale of the crown jewels, which she carried over with her.

After her departure, the king, taking the prince and the Duke of York with him, went to Theobalds, whither the parliament sent a petition to him to return to his parliament and abide near London, and that he would not carry the prince away with him, and that he would grant the militia of the kingdom to be put into such hands as the parliament should recommend, and might confide in; all which he denied, and went immediately to Newmarket, and from thence to York; all this while, by many false pretences, really obstructing the relief of bleeding Ireland, and seducing many of the poor people of England into blood and ruin.

In conducting the state of England, in those days, wherein he, whose actions I am tracing, began to enter into his part in this great tragedy, I have been too long for that I intended, and too short to give a clear understanding of the righteousness of the parliament's cause;[1] which I shall desire you to

An English gentleman, who was resident in France at the time that Louis the Sixteenth sent his guards to the parliament of Paris to seize some of the members (one of whom was the famous Duval Despresmenil), and sent out decrees and manifestoes, as has been here just before related, made this remark, " He has entered upon the career of Charles the First, and he will follow it to the end."   *Il est entré dans la carriere de Charles I. et il la suivra jusqu'au bout.*   When he saw again in England, as emigrants, the same French gentlemen before whom he had made this remark, they reminded him of it; saying how little probable this had seemed to them at the period of its being spoken, a year before the holding of the states general.

[1] Probably few people will think Mrs. Hutchinson has been too prolix, many will think that she has been too concise. Mr. May's history comes down only to September, 1643, which is much to be regretted, as he may justly be called an impartial and clear historian, but is little read, probably because his history finishes before that period which was the most interesting.

inform yourselves better of by their own printed papers, and Mr. May's history, which I find to be impartially true, so far as he hath carried it on, saving some little mistakes in his own judgment, and misinformations which some vain people gave of the state, and more indulgence to the king's guilt than can justly be allowed.

To take up my discourse of Mr. Hutchinson where I left it: he was now come to his own house at Owthorpe, about the time when the Irish massacre was acted, and finding humours begin to be very stirring, he applied himself to understand the things then in dispute, and read all the public papers that came forth between the king and parliament, besides many other private treatises, both concerning the present and foregoing times. Hereby he became abundantly informed in his understanding, and convinced in conscience of the righteousness of the parliament's cause in point of civil right; and though he was satisfied of the endeavours to reduce [1] popery and subvert the true protestant religion, which indeed was apparent to every one that impartially considered it, yet he did not think that so clear a ground for the war as the defence of the just English liberties; and although he was clearly swayed by his own judgment and reason to the parliament, he, thinking he had no warrantable call at that time, to do anything more, contented himself with praying for peace. At that time Mr. Henry Ireton was in the country, and being a kinsman of Mr. Hutchinson's, and one that had received so much advantage to himself and his family in the country by Sir Thomas Hutchinson's countenance and protection, that he seemed a kind of dependent upon him, and being besides a very grave, serious, religious person, there was a great league of kindness and good-will between them.[2] Mr. Ireton being very active in

---

[1] Reduce, Latin *reducere*, to bring back, restore, revive.

[2] As it will be seen in the sequel that Mr. Hutchinson reposed a very great confidence in Ireton, and even allowed to the information he received from him such weight in forming his judgment as he did to that of no one else, it may be well to examine how far the one was deserving, and the other discerning, in this.

The question will be probably decided to general satisfaction upon the testimony of Whitelock and Ludlow, men of very different dispositions, but both of great good sense and knowledge of their subject. Whitelock, in speaking of some reforms proposed in the election and composition of the House of Commons, says, " Ireton was chiefly employed in them, having learned some grounds of law, and having a laborious and working brain and fancy." When he comes to speak of

promoting the parliament, and the godly interest in the
country, found great opposition from some projectors, and
others of corrupt interest that were in the commission of the
peace; whereupon, making complaint at the parliament, he
procured some of them to be put out of the commission, and
others, better affected, to be put in their rooms, of which Mr.
Hutchinson was one; but he then forbore to take his oath,
as not willing to launch out rashly into public employments,
while such a storm hung threatening overhead. Yet his
good affections to godliness and the interest of his country,
being a glory that could not be concealed, many of his honest
neighbours made applications to him, and endeavoured to
learn his conduct, which he at first in modesty and prudence
would not too hastily rush into.[1] The parliament had made
orders to deface the images in all churches. Within two
miles of his house there was a church, where Christ upon the
cross, the virgin, and John, had been fairly set up in a window
over the altar, and sundry other superstitious paintings, of
the priest's own ordering, were drawn upon the walls. When
the order for rasing out those relics of superstition came, the
priest only took down the heads of the images, and laid them

the reforms of the law which Ireton likewise meditated, he says, " he
was a man full of invention and industry, who had a little knowledge
of the law, which led him into the more errors." But when by his
death the jealousy lest he should bring about those reforms which
Whitelock, and most of the lawyers, were averse to, had ceased, he
says of him, page 516, " this gentleman was a person very active, industrious, and stiff in his ways and purposes; he was of good abilities
for council as well as action, made much use of his pen, and was very
forward to reform the proceedings in law, wherein his having been
bred a lawyer was a great help to him. He was stout in the field, and
wary and prudent in councils; exceedingly forward as to the business
of a commonwealth. Cromwell had a great opinion of him, and no
man could prevail so much, nor order him so far, as Ireton could."
But Ludlow, who viewed him more constantly and closely in a post of
great power and temptation, that of deputy of Ireland, being himself
next in command to him, gives the following account of his conduct in
one instance, which will render all others superfluous. " The parliament also ordered an act to be brought in for settling two thousand
per annum on the lord-deputy Ireton, the news of which being brought
over was so unacceptable to him, that he said, they had many just
debts, which he desired they would pay before they made any such
presents; that he had no need of their land, and would not have it;
and that he should be more contented to see them doing the service
of the nation, than so liberal in disposing of the public treasure."
[1] Mr. Hutchinson being born in the latter end of the year 1616, was
only about three and twenty years old at this period; when some may
think this modesty became him. It was not the fashion of those times
to arrive at the perfection of wisdom and judgment so early as in our
days!

carefully up in his closet, and would have had the church officers to have certified that the thing was done according to order; whereupon they came to Mr. Hutchinson, and desired him that he would take the pains to come and view their church, which he did, and upon discourse with the parson, persuaded him to blot out all the superstitious paintings, and break the images in the glass; which he consented to, but being ill-affected, was one of those who began to brand Mr. Hutchinson with the name of Puritan.

At that time most of the gentry of the country were disaffected to the parliament; most of the middle sort, the able substantial freeholders, and the other commons, who had not their dependence upon the malignant nobility and gentry, adhered to the parliament. These, when the king was at York, made a petition to him to return to the parliament, which, upon their earnest entreaty, Mr. Hutchinson went, with some others, and presented at York;[1] where, meeting his cousins the Byrons, they were extremely troubled to see him there on that account. After his return, Sir John Byron being likewise come to his house at Newstead, Mr. Hutchinson went to visit them there, and not finding him, returned to Nottingham, five miles short of his own house. There, going to the mayor to hear some news, he met with such as

[1] Persons of the description which now bears the name of yeomanry, seem to have been passed over by Charles and his advisers as of little consequence, and perhaps this was the real ground of the grand error they were in of supposing they had all or most of the strength of the nation with them, because they had most of the nobility and richer gentry; whereas it was found, when a general movement took place, that the great bulk of the people was against them, and, like an overwhelming tide, bore down all before it. Yet he and they had abundant warnings by this and such like petitions, and by associations which began very early to be entered into; or still earlier in the expedition against the Scots, wherein the averseness of the common soldiers to the war was so evident, that it compelled the patching up a peace. "And, astonishing as it might be (says May, p. 64), it was seen that the common people were sensible of public interest and religion, when lords and gentlemen seemed not to be." It is true that the mass of the people, having little time for contemplation, are content to let those to whom affluence gives leisure think for them; but when they do think for themselves, and strongly adopt a sentiment, he is a bold man, and ought to have astonishing resources, who contravenes it. That will be generally, if not always, found the wiser government which informs itself well as to the real bent of the public mind; and if it is misled by a faction, takes the way of candour and frankness to dispel the mist of error or prejudice, but avoids to do violence to the general opinion. The editor of this work is proud of being the first person who, two years before its adoption, suggested an appeal to the sense and spirit of the nation by the association of armed volunteers.

he expected not, for as soon as he came in, the mayor's wife told him, that the sheriff of the county was come to fetch away the magazine that belonged to the trained bands of the county, which was left in her husband's trust; and that her husband had sent for the country to acquaint them, but she feared it would be gone before they could come in. Whereupon Mr. Hutchinson, taking his brother from his lodgings along with him, presently went to the town-hall, and going up to my Lord Newark,[1] lord-lieutenant, told him, that

[1] Eldest son of the Earl of Kingston, and brother of two Mr. Pierreponts mentioned in this work; this nobleman was afterwards created Marquis of Dorchester, and will be spoken of under that title in the sequel. In the diary mentioned in the second page of the preface, the dialogue between Lord Newton and Mr. Hutchinson is set down at full length, and as it may be an object of curiosity to some of our readers, it is here inserted in smaller type.

Mr. Hutchinson asking who were above, was told that the lord-lieutenant, my Lord Newark, was there, to whom he sent his name and desired to speak with him; and being come up, found in the room, where the powder was weighing, my Lord Newark, the sheriff Sir John Digby, and two or three captains: Mr. Hutchinson, addressing himself to my lord only, spoke to him:—

H. My lord, hearing that there were some question concerning the county's powder, I am come to kiss your lordship's hands, and to beseech you that I may know what your desires and intents are concerning it?

N. Cousin, the king desires to borrow it of the country, to supply his great necessities.

H. I beseech your lordship, what commission have you to demand this?

N. Upon my honour, I have a commission from his majesty, but it is left behind me; but I will engage my honour it shall be repaid the country.

H. Your lordship's honour as an engagement, would be accepted for more than I am worth; but in such an occasion as this, the greatest man's engagement in the kingdom, cannot be a satisfaction to the country.

N. The king's intents are only to borrow it, and if the country will not lend it, he will pay for it.

H. My lord, it is not the value of the powder we endeavour to preserve, but in times of danger, as these are, those things which serve for our defence, are not valuable at any price, should you give as many barrels of gold as you take barrels of powder.

N. Upon my faith and honour, cousin, it shall be restored in ten days.

H. My lord, such is the danger of the times, that for ought we know, we may in less than four days be ruined for want of it; and I beseech your lordship to consider how sad a thing it is in these times of war, to leave a poor country and the people in it, naked and open to the injury of every passenger; for if you take our powder, you may as well take our arms, without which we are unable to make use of them, and I hope your lordship will not disarm the country.

N. Why, who should the country fear? I am their lord-lieutenant.

hearing some dispute concerning the country's powder, he was come to wait on his lordship, to know his desires and intents concerning it. My lord answered him, that the king, having great necessities, desired to borrow it of the country. Mr. Hutchinson asked my lord what commission he had from

and engaged with my life and honour to defend them! What danger are they in?

H. Danger! yes, my lord, great danger; there is a troop of horse now in the town, and it hath often happened so that they have committed great outrages and insolencies, calling divers honest men puritans and rogues, with divers other provoking terms and carriages. I myself was abused by some of them, as I passed on the road. I chanced to meet some of these gentlemen, who, as soon as I was past, inquired my name, and being told it, gave me another, saying among themselves, that I was a puritan and a traitor; as two or three honest men that came behind told me. Besides, your lordship may be far off, and we ruined before you can come to us, being unarmed, and not able to defend ourselves from anybody, and this country being a road through which, under the name of soldiers, rude people daily pass from the north to south, and terrify the country; which if they knew to be naked and unarmed, they would thereby be encouraged to greater insolencies and mischiefs.

N. The king's occasions are such, and so urgent, as I cannot dispense with it for any reasons, but must needs have it.

H. I hope your lordship will not deny that the country hath a right, interest, and property in it.

N. I do not deny it.

H. Then, my lord, I hope his majesty will not command it from them.

N. No, he doth but desire to borrow it.

H. Then, I hope, if he do but desire to borrow it, his majesty hath signified his request to those that have interest in it, under his hand.

N. Upon my honour he hath, but I left it behind me.

H. I beseech your lordship, then, that you would not take it away till you have acquainted the country with it, who only have power to lend it; and if your lordship be pleased to do this, I will engage myself that by to-morrow at twelve of the clock, that part of the country who have interest in the powder shall all wait on your lordship, and give you their resolutions.

N. The king's occasions cannot admit of that delay.

H. I beseech of your lordship, yet be pleased to consider the dangerous consequence of taking it without the country's consent, and be pleased but to stay till they can come in.

N. That time is more than his majesty's necessities can dispense withal.

With that Mr. Hutchinson went downstairs, where by that time a good company of the country were gathered together, to whom Mr. Hutchinson told what my lord had said to him, and they desired him that he would but stand to them, and they would part with every drop of blood out of their bodies before he should have it; and said besides, that they would go up and break my lord's neck and the sheriff's out of the windows; but Mr. Hutchinson desired them to stay below, till he had once more spoken to my lord, and then, taking only one or two more with him, went up and spoke to my lord.

H. My lord, I am again, at the request of the country, that are below, come to your lordship, and do once more humbly beseech you his majesty. My lord told him he had one, but he had left it behind. Mr. Hutchinson replied, that my lord's affirmation was satisfactory to him, but the country would not be willing to part with their powder in so dangerous a time, without an absolute command. My lord urged that he would restore it

to consider the business you are about, before you proceed further in it, for it may prove of dangerous consequence if you go on.

N. Cousin, I am confident it cannot, for the country will not deny this to the king.

H. It's very probable they will not, if your lordship please to have patience till they can be called in, that they may be acquainted with his majesty's desire.

N. His majesty is very well assured of the willingness and cheerfulness of the greater part of the country to it.

H. My lord, I do not know what assurance his majesty hath of it, but if you please to look out of this window (pointing to the countrymen below in the streets), you will see no inconsiderable number gathered, who, I fear, will not be willing to part with it.

N. Those are but some few factious men, not to be considered.

H. My lord, we have been happy yet, in these unhappy differences, to have had no blood shed, and I am confident your lordship is so noble and tender of your country, that it would very much trouble you to have a hand in the first man's blood that should be spent in this quarrel.

N. Cousin, it cannot come to that, fear it not (this was spoken very slightly and contemptuously), his majesty's occasions are urgent, and must be served.

(With that, the country came very fast up, which when the cavalier captains saw, they slunk down.)

H. Why then, my lord, I must plainly tell you, not one here but will lose every drop of blood in his body, before he will part with one corn of it, without your lordship can show either a command or a request for it under his Majesty's hand and seal, or that the country be called together to give their free consent to it, for we have all property and interest in it, being members of this county, and it being bought with our money, for the particular defence and safety of the same.

My lord desired to borrow part of it, but that being denied, he turned to Sir John Digby and took him to the window, where, after he had whispered with him a while, Sir John Digby laid down his pen, ink, and paper, with which he had been taking an account of the powder, match, and bullet. The countrymen desired my lord aloud, that he would not take away their powder out of the country; upon which, turning to them, he thus spoke:—

"Gentlemen,—His majesty was assured by some of the cheerfulness of this country's affections to him, which I am very sorry to see them so much failing in, and that the country should come so much short of this town, which hath cheerfully lent his majesty one barrel of powder, but it seems he can have none from you; I pray God you do not repent this carriage of yours towards his majesty, which he must be acquainted withal."

A countryman, standing forth, asked his lordship this question, "Whether, if he were to take a journey into a place where probably he might be set upon by thieves and robbers, and having a charge about him, if any friend should ask him to lend his sword, he would part with it and go himself without?" My lord, the case is ours; our wives, children, and estates, all depend upon this country's safety; and how

in ten days.   Mr. Hutchinson replied, they might have use for
it sooner, and he hoped my lord would not disarm his country
in such a time of danger.   My lord contemned the mention
of danger, and asked what they could fear while he was their
lord-lieutenant, and ready to serve them with his life.   Mr.
Hutchinson told him they had some grounds to apprehend
danger by reason of the daily passing of armed men through
the country, whereof there was now one troop in the town,

can it be safe in these dangerous times, when so many troops and companies pass through and commit outrages and abuses among us, if we
have not arms and powder wherewith to defend us?

My lord made no reply, but bade the men whom he had employed
to weigh up the powder desist; and so went down the stairs.   Mr.
Hutchinson followed him, and as he went, an ancient gentleman, who
was with my lord, whose face and name were both unknown to him,
came to him and said these words: "Stand to it; I'll warrant you,
gentlemen, it is well done."   And as they passed through a low room,
my lord took Mr. Hutchinson aside, and said,—

N. Cousin, I must acquaint the king with this!

H. My lord, it is very likely you must, being employed upon his
majesty's service, give him an account.

N. Nay, cousin (smiling), I mean not so; but I must acquaint him,
and I am sorry I must, that you are the head and ringleader of a
faction, whereby you hinder his majesty's service.

H. My lord, I do not conceive how this can be a faction, I speaking
only, out of the noble respect and honour I bear your lordship, in
private to you, to prevent a mischief, the sense of these men, who I
perceived were come to know by what authority, and why, their
powder, which is their proper goods, and only means of safety in these
times of danger, should be taken from them; and if it were a faction,
I am not the head of it; I, accidentally coming to town from Sir John
Byron's last night, and neither knowing nor imagining any of this
business, was this morning importuned to wait on your lordship, at
the town's hall, by many countrymen, who informed me you were
taking away their powder out of the country.

N. Cousin, if you can answer it I shall be glad of it; but I will assure
you I must let his majesty know.

H. If his majesty must know it, I am very happy I spoke to none
but your lordship; who, I am confident, is so noble, that you will
neither add nor diminish anything to my prejudice; and then I am
confident the justness and reasonableness of what I have said, with
my own innocency in speaking it, will bear me out.

N. I, cousin, but your name is up already.

H. It may be so, my lord; and I believe those that set it up had no
good wishes to me; and as it rose, so, in the name of God let it fall;
for I know my own clearness and innocency in anything that can be
objected against me.

N. Well, cousin, well; I am glad of your good resolution.

And so my lord left him.   The gentlemen of the country that were
there, upon consideration, what they should do with their powder,
determined to return my lord thanks for sparing it, and to lock it up
with two locks, whereof the sheriff should have one key, and the mayor
another; which accordingly was done; but Mr. Hutchinson came no
more to my lord.

and that before they could repair to my lord, they might be destroyed in his absence, and withal urged to him examples of their insolence; but my lord replied to all, the urgency of the king's occasions for it, which were such that he could not dispense with it. It was in vain to argue with him the property the country had in it, being bought with their money, and therefore not to be taken without their consent; my lord declared himself positively resolved to take it, whereupon Mr. Hutchinson left him. There were in the room with him Sir John Digby, the high sheriff of the county, who was setting down the weight of the powder and match, and two or three captains and others, that were busy weighing the powder. By the time Mr. Hutchinson came down, a good company of the country was gathered together; whom Mr. Hutchinson acquainted with what had passed between him and my lord, and they told him that if he would but please to stand by them, they would part with all their blood before he should have a corn of it; and said, moreover, they would go up and tumble my lord and the sheriff out of the windows. Mr. Hutchinson, seeing them so resolved, desired them to stay below while he went up yet once again to my lord, which they did; and he told my lord some of the country were come in, at whose request he was again come to beseech his lordship to desist from his design, which if pursued might be of dangerous consequence. My lord replied, it could not be, for the king was very well assured of the cheerful compliance of the greatest part of the country with his service. Mr. Hutchinson told him, whatever assurance his majesty might have, if his lordship pleased to look out, he might see no inconsiderable number below that would not willingly part with it. My lord replied, they were but a few factious men; whereupon Mr. Hutchinson told him, since it was yet the happiness of these unhappy times that no blood had been spilt, he should be sorry the first should be shed upon my lord's occasion, in his own country. My lord scornfully replied, Fear it not, it cannot come to that, the king's occasions are urgent and must be served. Whereupon Mr. Hutchinson, looking out at the countrymen, they came very fast up the stairs; and Mr. Hutchinson told him, however he slighted it, not one was there but would part with every drop of his blood before they would part with it, except he could show a command or request for it under the king's hand, or would stay till the country were called in to give their consent; for it was their property, and all had interest in it, as bought with their money for the particular defence of the country. Then my Lord fell to entreaties to borrow part of it, but that being also denied, he took the sheriff aside, and, after a little conference, they put up their books and left the powder; when my lord, turning to the people, said to them, "Gentlemen, his majesty was by some assured of the cheerfulness of this country's affections to him, whereof I am sorry to see so much failing, and that the county should fall so much short of the town, who have cheerfully lent his majesty one barrel of powder, but it seems he can have none from you; I pray God you do not repent this carriage of yours towards his majesty, which he must be acquainted withal." A bold countryman then stepping forth, by way of reply, asked my lord, whether, if he were to take a journey with a charge into a place where probably he should be set upon by thieves, if any friend should ask to borrow a sword he would part with it: my lord, said he, the case is ours; our lives, wives, children, and estates, all depend upon this country's safety; and how can it be safe in these dangerous times, when so many rude armed people pass daily through it, if we be altogether disarmed? My lord made no reply, but bade the men who were weighing the powder desist, and went down. Mr. Hutchinson followed him down the stairs, when an ancient gentleman, that was sitting with my lord, came and whispering him, commended his and the country's zeal, and bade them stand to it, and they would not be foiled. As they passed through a long room below, my lord told Mr. Hutchinson he was sorry to find him at the head of a faction. Mr. Hutchinson replied, he could not tell how his lordship could call that a faction which arose from the accident of his being at that time in the town; where, hearing what was in hand, and out of respect to his lordship, he only came to prevent mischief and danger, which he saw likely to ensue. My lord replied, he must inform the king, and told him his name was already up; to which Mr. Hutchinson answered, that he was glad, if the king must receive an information of him, that it must be from so honourable a person; and for his name, as it rose, so in the name of God let it fall; and so took his leave and went home. The rest of the country that were there, determined to give my lord thanks for sparing their ammunition, and locked it up with two locks, whereof the key of the one was entrusted with the mayor of Nottingham, the other with the sheriff of the county, which accordingly was done.[1]

In the meantime, at York, the king had sent the parliament a message, that he intended to go in person to Ireland, and to raise a guard for his own person, about West Chester, which he would arm out of his magazine at Hull. But the parliament, having before intercepted a letter of the Lord Digby's, sent to the queen from Middleburgh in Zealand, wherein he intimated, that, if the king would retire to some safe place, and declare himself, he should be able to wait upon him from thence, etc. Upon this letter, and other presumptions, they suspected that the chief end of the king's going northward was to seize the magazine at Hull, and arm himself from thence against them; wherefore they sent a petition, for leave to remove that magazine to the tower of London, and accordingly had sent Sir John Hotham thither to do it. Sir John prevented the Earl of Newcastle, whom the king had sent for the same purpose, to seize the magazine, and kept him out; at which the king was much incensed, and on the 23rd of April, 1642, went himself to Hull, attended with some noblemen, gentlemen, and soldiers, and demanded entrance; but the gates were shut; and Hotham, kneeling upon the wall, entreated the king not to command that which, without breach of trust, he could not obey.

In conclusion, the king not getting entrance, proclaimed Hotham a traitor, and sent a complaint of the affront to the parliament. The parliament justified Hotham. Many declarations about it were published on both sides, and many cross-commands; the parliament authorising Hotham to issue out warrants to constables and other officers, to come in armed to the defence of Hull, and the king forbidding it. The king meanwhile in the north, summoned divers of the nobility and gentry to attend him, and made speeches to them to desire a guard for his person, pretending danger from the parliament. He then began to entertain soldiers, and was much encouraged by the defection of divers lords and

[1] How my lord may have reported this matter to the king signifies little; but he probably remembered as a kindness Mr. Hutchinson's interposition between him and the more rough arguments of the countrymen; for there appears to have existed on all suitable occasions, an intercourse of friendship during the remainder of their lives.

many of the Commons' house, who forsook their trust and came to him at York; whereupon he called those who remained only a faction, a pretended parliament, and such names; but they continued still petitioning to him, and the well-affected and godly, in all countries, did the like, that he would return to his parliament. The papists all over England were high partakers with him and promoters of his designs, and all the debauched nobility and gentry, and their dependents, and the lewder rout of people; yet even of these there were some that had English hearts, who came in to the parliament; but finding afterwards that the advance of liberty and righteousness could not consist with riot and ungodliness, they forsook their party, and were content to be the king's slaves rather than divorce themselves from those lusts, which found countenance from both priests and princes on one side, and on the other were preached down by the ministers, and punished by the magistrates.[1]

Towards the end of May, the parliament sent the king word, that if he would not disband his forces, and rely upon the laws and affections of his people for his security, as all good princes before him had done, they held themselves bound in duty to God and the people's trust reposed in them, and by the fundamental laws, to employ their utmost care and power for securing the parliament and preserving the kingdom's peace. Whereupon they voted, "That it seems that the king, seduced by wicked counsel, intends a war against the parliament, etc.

"That whensoever the king makes war upon the parliament, it is a breach of the trust reposed in him by the people, contrary to his oath, and tending to the dissolution of this government.

"That whosoever shall assist him in such wars are traitors, by the fundamental laws of this kingdom, and have been so adjudged in two acts of parliament, 11 Richard II.

---

[1] Whatever may be said at this day of the hypocrisy of the religionists of those times, the most that can possibly be allowed is, that their professions might somewhat outgo their practice; but this must in some degree befall every Christian. No one can deny that, instead of captivating vulgar minds by breaking the bonds of morality, as modern demagogues have done, the forefathers of our liberties set the pattern of a religious and decent conduct, and caused the same to be observed in their armies with an exactness that surprises us, and of which rigour many striking examples are to be found in Whitelock's Memorials.

and 1 Henry IV.; and that such persons ought to suffer as traitors."

Hereupon nine of the lords, that first went to the king, were summoned to return; who, sending a letter of denial, were, by the whole house of peers, sentenced to be incapable of ever sitting again as members of that house, or of benefit or privilege of parliament, and to suffer imprisonment during pleasure. Then the lord keeper, who had appeared firm to the parliament, and voted with them, for settling the militia by ordinance of parliament, ran away to the king, after he had delivered up his seal, the day before, to one the king sent for it. The king, having this, issued out many proclamations, and among the rest, one that no man should obey the parliament's warrants about settling the militia. The parliament, on the other side, made ordinances forbidding all men to raise arms, by warrant from the king, without authority of parliament. And now they began to settle the kingdom's militia, both by land and sea, and made the Earl of Warwick admiral; which place the king had conferred upon Sir John Pennington, in the room of the Earl of Northumberland, and commanded my lord of Warwick to resign; but he chose to obey the parliament, and got the fleet at length wholly into his hands, and took a ship with ammunition coming to the king out of Holland. The parliament now, despairing of the king's return, made an ordinance for money and plate to be brought in, and for raising arms for the cause; which came in, in great abundance, upon public faith, and likewise horses and arms for the service. The king, who had received money, arms, and ammunition, which the queen had procured in Holland, by pawning the crown jewels, sent out commissions of array, to arm the people in all counties; and mocked the parliament, using their own words, wherein they invited men to arm for the defence of the protestant religion, the king's person, dignity, and authority, the laws of the land, the peace of the kingdom, and privilege of parliament; and thus he deceived many people, and got contributions of plate, money, and arms in the country. While these things were in transaction, the king made a solemn protestation before the lords, as in the presence of God, declaring that he would not engage them in any war against the parliament, but only for his necessary defence; that his desire was to maintain the protestant religion, the liberties of the subject, and privilege of parliament. But the next day he did some action, so contrary to this protestation, that two of the lords durst not stay with him, but returned to the parliament; and one of them, coming back through Nottinghamshire, acquainted Mr. Hutchinson with the sad sense he had in discovering that falsehood in the king.

Now had the king raised an army of three thousand foot and one thousand horse, with which he went to Beverley, in order to besiege Hull. When he was within two hours' march of the place, Sir John Hotham floated the country about it, and Sir John Meldrum, sallying out of the town, with five hundred townsmen, made the king's party retreat to Beverley. But, however, they beleaguered the town, into which the parliament sent a relief of five hundred men, by water, with whom Meldrum made another sally, routed the leaguer-soldiers, killed some, made others prisoners, took the magazine of arms and ammunition, which was in a barn, with their fire-balls, and fired the barn. Hereupon the king's council of war broke up the siege, from whence the king went back to York, and about the middle of August came to Nottingham, where he set up his standard royal; and hither his two nephews, Prince Rupert and Prince Maurice, came to him, and were put into commands. The king, marching through Nottingham, Derby, and Leicestershire, called together the trained bands, to attend him, disarmed those counties, and marched to Shrewsbury, and there set up a mint, and coined the plate that had been brought in to him. Here a great many men came in to him, with whom, marching into Warwickshire, he there fought his first battle at a village called Keynton;[1] it not being yet agreed who gained the victory that day.

As the king, on his part, made this progress, so the parliament, on theirs, upon the twelfth of July, voted an army to be raised, and the Earl of Essex to be general of it. Divers of the lords, and several members of the House of Commons, took commissions, and raised regiments and companies under his command, who marched with his army of about fourteen

---

[1] Commonly called Edge-hill fight. Both king and parliament claimed the victory, but our authoress shows rather more candour than either. The king's main design of marching to London was however frustrated, and therefore the parliament might be most properly termed gainers.

thousand horse and foot to his rendezvous at Northampton, whither the parliament sent a petition to him, to be delivered to the king, in a safe and honourable way; the sum of which was, to beseech him to forsake those wicked people with whom he was, and not to mix his danger with theirs, but to return to his parliament, etc. The king, intending to make Worcester a garrison, sent Prince Rupert thither; the Earl of Essex, to prevent him, sent other forces, between whom there was some skirmish, but the prince left the town at their approach. My lord of Essex left a garrison in Northampton, put others into Coventry and Warwick, and went to Worcester. Here he made some stay, till the king, marching from Shrewsbury, occasioned some apprehension of his going up to London; for which cause my lord left part of his artillery behind him, and followed the king's motions, which the king perceiving, took an opportunity, before his artillery and the foot left with it were come up to him, and resolved to give him battle, which was not declined on the other side, but fought with doubtful success, the circumstances whereof may be read at large in the stories of those things. The king's general was slain, and his standard was taken though not kept; but on the other side also there were many brave men slain and prisoners. My lord of Essex marched to Coventry; the king took up his winter quarters at Oxford, from whence Prince Rupert flew about the country with his body of horse, plundered and did many barbarous things; insomuch that London, growing into apprehensions of the king's army, the parliament called back the Earl of Essex to quarter about London; and he being returned thither, the king was advanced as far as Colebrooke, where he was presented with a petition from the parliament for accommodation, to which he answered, with a protestation to God, how much he was grieved for his subjects' sufferings, and, in order to peace, was willing to reside near London, to receive their propositions, and to treat with them. As soon as ever the commissioners were gone, the king advanced, with his horse and artillery, towards London, and, taking the advantage of a great mist, fell upon a broken regiment of Colonel Hollis's, quartered at Brentford, and killed many of them, and had destroyed them all, but that Brooke's and Hampden's regiments, by Providence, came seasonably to their rescue; and then so many forces flocked with the general, out of

London, that the king was enclosed, and the war had been ended, but that, I know not how, three thousand of the parliament's forces were called away by their procurement who designed the continuance of the war; and so the king had a way of retreat left open, by which he got back to Oxford, and the parliament's general was sent out again[1] with their army; whose proceedings I shall take up again in their due places, so far as is necessary to be remembered, for the story I most particularly intend.

Before the flame of the war broke out in the top of the chimneys, the smoke ascended in every country; the king had sent forth commissions of array, and the parliament had given out commissions for their militia, and sent off their members into all counties to put them in execution. Between these, in many places, there were fierce contests and disputes, almost to blood, even at the first; for in the progress every county had the civil war, more or less, within itself. Some counties were in the beginning so wholly for the parliament, that the king's interest appeared not in them; some so wholly for the king, that the godly, for those generally were the parliament's friends, were forced to forsake their habitations, and seek other shelters: of this sort was Nottinghamshire. All the nobility and gentry, and their dependents, were generally for the king; the chief of whose names I shall sum up here, because I shall often have occasion to mention them. The greatest family was the Earl of Newcastle's,[2] a lord once so much beloved in his country, that when the first expedition was against the Scots, the gentlemen of the country set him forth two troops, one all of gentlemen, the other of their men, who waited on him into the north at their own charges. He had, indeed, through his great estate, his liberal hospitality, and constant residence in his country, so endeared them to him, that no man was a greater prince in all that northern quarter; till a foolish ambition of glorious slavery carried him to court, where he ran himself much into debt, to purchase neglects of the king and queen, and scorns

[1] The account Mrs. Hutchinson gives of the affair of Brentford is much more clear and probable than that given by Rapin, vol. ii. p. 465. Indeed, he himself seems dissatisfied with those varying accounts he could collect of that business from Clarendon and others; but Ludlow, who was a military man and an eye-witness, gives a clear account, agreeing with that of Mrs. Hutchinson.

[2] This title was at that time in the family of **Cavendish**, of which this line ceased with the nobleman here mentioned.

of the proud courtiers. Next him was the Earl of Kingston, a man of vast estate, and no less covetous, who divided his sons between both parties, and concealed himself; till at length his fate drew him to declare himself absolutely on the king's side, wherein he behaved himself honourably, and died remarkably. His eldest son [1] was lord-lieutenant of the county, and at that time no nobleman had a greater reputation in the court for learning and generosity than he; but he was so high in the king's party, that the parliament was very much incensed against him. Lord Chesterfield, and all his family, were high in the royal party; so was the Lord Chaworth. The Earl of Clare was very often of both parties, and, I think, never advantaged either. All the popish gentry were wholly for the king, whereof one Mr. Golding, next neighbour to Mr. Hutchinson, had been a private collector of the catholics' contributions to the Irish Rebellion, and for that was, by the queen's procurement, made a knight and baronet. Sir John Byron, afterwards Lord Byron, and all his brothers, bred up in arms, and valiant men in their own persons, were all passionately the king's. Sir John Savill, a man of vast estate, was the like: so were Sir Gervas Eyre, Sir John Digby, Sir Matthew Palmer, Sir Thomas Williamson, Sir Roger Cowper, Sir W. Hickman, Sir Hugh Cartwright, Sir T. Willoughby, Sir Thomas Smith, Sir Thomas Blackwell, Markham, Perkins, Tevery, Pearce, Palme, Wood, Sanderson, Moore, Mellish, Butler, with divers others. Of the parliament men, Mr. Sutton, afterwards Lord Lexington, and Sir Gervas Clifton, forsook the parliament, went to the king, and executed his commission of array. Mr. William Stanhope left the parliament, and came home disaffected to them; whose eldest son was afterwards slain in the king's service. Mr. William Pierrepont,[2] second son of the Earl

---

[1] Lord Newark, before spoken of. In Collins's Peerage, under the title of Duke of Kingston, there are cited singular proofs of this nobleman's learning.

[2] From this gentleman the late Duke of Kingston and the present Earl Manvers are lineally descended. His wisdom as a politician is sufficiently evinced by this masterly stroke, which decided the fate of the king and the parliament. Of his moderation Whitelock speaks repeatedly. Of his eloquence there are preserved by Rushworth some specimens, from one of which is extracted this as a singular trait of candour and delicacy:—"It is pleasing to the nature of man that others should obey his will, and well-framed dispositions of princes may easily be persuaded their power is unlimited, when they are also put in mind that they have therefore more cause to do well, and for

of Kingston, was of the parliament, though he served not for his own country, to which notwithstanding he was an ornament, being one of the wisest counsellors and most excellent speakers in the house, and by him was that bill promoted and carried on which passed for the continuation of this parliament. He had a younger brother living at Nottingham, who coldly owned the parliament. Sir Thomas Hutchinson continued with the parliament, was firm to their cause, but infinitely desirous that the difference might rather have been composed by accommodation, than ended by conquest; and therefore did not improve his interest to engage the country in the quarrel, which, if he could have prevented, he would not have had come to a war. He was, however, clearly on the parliament's side, and never discouraged his two sons, who thought this prudential tardiness in their father was the declension of that vigour which they derived from him, and which better became their youth. It is true, they were the foremost in point of time and in degree, except a piece of a nobleman that was afterwards drawn in, who owned the parliament's interest in their country. Mr. Henry Ireton, their cousin, was older than they, and having had an education in the strictest way of godliness, and being a very grave and solid person, a man of good learning, great understanding, and other abilities, to which was joined a willing and zealous heart in the cause and his country, he was the chief promotor of the parliament's interest in the county; but finding it generally disaffected, all he could do, when the king approached it, was to gather a troop of those godly people which the cavaliers drove out, and with them to go into the army of my lord of Essex; which he, being a single person, could better do. Mr. Hutchinson was not willing so soon to quit his house, to which he was so lately come, if he could have been suffered to live quietly in it; but his affections to the parliament

doing well are more renowned. For the most oppressive designs we have suffered under, the pretences to his majesty have been the good of his subjects: his is the sin, who is to judge by the laws, who knows the laws are to the contrary, yet puts and confirms such thoughts in his prince. He that incites another to arbitrary government usually doth it for self-ends, and when they are compassed, hates him for taking that power he himself persuaded him unto." This will be found an elegant solution of the paradox which appears in the character given by Mrs. Hutchinson of Charles the First, " that so good a man should make so bad a prince."

being taken notice of, he became an object of envy to the other party.

Sir Thomas Hutchinson, a little before the standard was set up, had come to Nottingham, where his house was, to see his children and refresh himself; when, hearing of the king's intentions to come to the town, he, some days before his coming, went over to Owthorpe, his son's house, to remain there till he could fit himself to return to the parliament. One day, as Mr. Hutchinson was at dinner, the mayor of Nottingham sent him word that the high-sheriff had broken open the lock of the country's ammunition, which was left in his trust, and was about to take it away. Mr. Hutchinson immediately went in all haste to prevent it, but before he came to the town it was gone, and some of the king's soldiers were already come to town, and were plundering all the honest men of their arms. As one of them had taken a musket, seeing Mr. Hutchinson go by, he said he wished it loaded for his sake, and hoped the day would shortly come when all such roundheads would be fair marks for them. This name of roundhead coming so opportunely in, I shall make a little digression to tell how it came up. When puritanism grew into a faction, the zealots distinguished themselves, both men and women, by several affectations of habit, looks, and words, which, had it been a real forsaking of vanity, and an embracing of sobriety in all those things, would have been most commendable; but their quick forsaking of those things, when they had arrived at their object, showed that they either never took them up for conscience, or were corrupted by their prosperity to take up those vain things they durst not practise under persecution. Among other affected habits, few of the puritans, what degree soever they were of, wore their hair long enough to cover their ears, and the ministers and many others cut it close round their heads, with so many little peaks, as was something ridiculous to behold; whereupon Cleaveland, in his Hue and Cry after them, begins,

" With hayre in Characters and Luggs in Text," etc.

From this custom of wearing their hair, that name of roundhead became the scornful term given to the whole parliament party, whose army indeed marched out as if they had been only sent out till their hair was grown. Two or three years after, any stranger that had seen them, would have inquired the reason of that name. It was very ill applied to Mr. Hutchinson, who, having naturally a very fine thickset head of hair, kept it clean and handsome, so that it was a great ornament to him; although the godly of those days, when he embraced their party, would not allow him to be religious because his hair was not in their cut, nor his words in their phrase, nor such little formalities altogether fitted to their humour; who were, many of them, so weak as to esteem such insignificant circumstances, rather than solid wisdom, piety, and courage, which brought real aid and honour to their party. But as Mr. Hutchinson chose not them, but the God they served, and the truth and righteousness they defended, so did not their weaknesses, censures, ingratitude, or discouraging behaviour, with which he was abundantly exercised all his life, make him forsake them in anything wherein they adhered to just and honourable principles or practices; but when they apostatised from these, none cast them off with greater indignation, how shining soever the profession was that gilt, not a temple of living grace, but a tomb, which only held the carcase of religion. Instead of digressing, I shall ramble into an inextricable wilderness, if I pursue this sad remembrance: to return therefore to his actions at that time.

When he found the powder gone, and saw the soldiers taking up quarters in the town, and heard their threats and revilings, he went to his father's house in the town, where he had not been long before an uncivil fellow stepped into the house, with a carabine in his hand. Mr. Hutchinson asked what he would have; the man replied, he came to take possession of the house; Mr. Hutchinson told him, he had the possession of it, and would know on what right it was demanded from him; the man said, he came to quarter the general there; Mr. Hutchinson told him, except his father and mother, and their children, were turned out of doors, there was no room. The quarter-master, upon this, growing insolent, Mr. Hutchinson thrust him out of the house, and shut the doors upon him. Immediately my lord of Lindsey came himself, in a great chafe, and asked who it was that denied him quarter? Mr. Hutchinson told him, he that came to take it up for him deserved the usage he had, for his uncivil demeanour; and those who had quartered his lordship there had much abused him, the house being no ways fit to receive a person of his quality, which, if he pleased to take a view of it, he would soon perceive. Whereupon my lord, having seen the rooms, was very angry they had made no better provision for him, and would not have lain in the house, but they told him the town was so full that it was impossible to get him room anywhere else. Hereupon he told Mr. Hutchinson, if they would only allow him one room, he would have no more; and when he came upon terms of civility, Mr. Hutchinson was as civil to him, and my lord only employed one room, staying there, with all civility to those that were in the house. As soon as my lord was gone, Mr. Hutchinson was informed by a friend, that the man he had turned out of doors was the quarter-master general, who, upon his complaint, had procured a warrant to seize his person; whereupon Mr. Hutchinson, with his brother, went immediately home to his own house at Owthorpe. About four or five days after, a troop of cavaliers, under the command of Sir Lewis Dives, came to Stanton, near Owthorpe, and searched Mr. Needham's house, who was a noted puritan in those days, and a colonel in the parliament's service, and governor of Leicester: they found not him, for he hid himself in the gorse, and so escaped them. His house being lightly plundered, they went to Hickling, and plundered another puritan house there, and were coming to Owthorpe, of which Mr. Hutchinson having notice, went away to Leicestershire; but they, though they had orders to seize Mr. Hutchinson, came not at that time because the night grew on. But some days after he was gone, another company came and searched for him and for arms and plate, of which finding none, they took nothing else.

Two days after Mr. Hutchinson was in Leicestershire, he sent for his wife, who was then big with child, to come thither to him; where she had not been a day, but a letter was brought him from Nottingham, to give him notice that there was a warrant sent to the sheriff of Leicestershire to seize his person. Upon this he determined to go the next day into Northamptonshire, but at five of the clock that evening, the sound of their trumpets told him a troop was coming into the town. He stayed not to see them, but went out at the other end as they came in; who, by a good providence for his wife (somewhat afflicted to be so left alone in a strange place), proved to be commanded by her own brother, Sir Allen Apsley, who quartered in the next house to that where she was, till about two or three days before all the king's horse that were thereabouts marched away, being commanded upon some service to go before the rest.

Mr. Hutchinson, in the meantime, was carried by a servant that waited on him, to the house of a substantial honest yeoman, who was bailiff to the lord of the town [1] of Kelmarsh, in Northamptonshire. This man and his wife, being godly, gave Mr. Hutchinson very kind entertainment, and prevailed upon him to be acquainted with their master, who had just then made plate and horses ready to go in to the king, that had now set up his standard at Nottingham ; but Mr. Hutchinson diverted him, and persuaded him and another gentleman of quality, to carry in those aids they had provided for the king, to my lord General Essex, who was then at Northampton, where Mr. Hutchinson visited him, and would gladly at that time have engaged with him, but that he did not then find a clear call from the Lord; and therefore, intelligence being brought of the king's removal, he was now returning to his wife, when unawares he came into a town, where one of Prince Rupert's troops was; which he narrowly escaped, and returning to his former honest host, sent a letter to his wife, to acquaint her what hazard he was in by attempting to come to her, but that as soon as the horse was marched away, he would be with her. This letter was intercepted at Prince Rupert's quarters, and opened and sent her. There was with Prince Rupert, at that time, one Captain Welch, who having used to come to Captain Apsley, and seen Mrs. Hutchinson with him, made a pretence of civility to visit her that day that all the prince's horse marched away. They marched by the door of the house where she was, and all the household having gone out to see them, had left her alone in the house, with Mr. George Hutchinson, who was in her chamber when Captain Welch came in, and she went down into the parlour to receive him. He, taking occasion to tell her of her husband's letter, by way of compliment, said it was a pity she should have a husband so unworthy of her, as to enter into any faction which should make him not dare to be seen with her; whereat

[1] It is customary, in Nottinghamshire, to call every village of any size a town.

she being piqued, and thinking they were all marched away, told him he was mistaken, she had not a husband that would at any time hide himself from him, or that durst not show his face where any honest man durst appear; and to confirm you, said she, he shall now come to you. With that she called down her brother, who, upon a private hint, owned the name of husband, which she gave him, and received a compliment from Welch, that in any other place he had been obliged to make him a prisoner, but here he was in sanctuary; and so, after some little discourse, went away. When the gentleman of the house and the rest of the family, that had been seeing the march, were returned, and while they sat laughing together, at those that went to see the prince, telling how some of the neighbouring ladies were gone along with him, and Mrs. Hutchinson telling how she had abused the captain, with Mr. Hutchinson instead of her husband, the captain came back, bringing another gentleman with him; and he told Mr. Hutchinson, that his horse having lost a shoe, he must be his prisoner till the smith released him. But they had not sat long, ere a boy came in with two pistols, and whispered the captain, who desiring Mr. Hutchinson and the gentleman of the house to walk into the next room, seized Mr. George, in the name of Mr. John Hutchinson. It booted not for them both to endeavour to undeceive him, by telling him Mr. John was still at Northampton, for he would not, at least would seem not, to believe them, and carried him away, to be revenged of Mrs. Hutchinson, at whom he was vexed for having deluded him. So, full of wicked joy, to have found an innocent gentleman, whom he knew the blood-hounds were after, he went and informed the prince, and made it of such moment, as if they had taken a much more considerable person. The prince had sent back a troop of dragoons to guard him to them, which troop had beset the house and town, before Welch came in to them the second time; and, notwithstanding all informations of his error, he carried away Mr. Hutchinson, and put his sister into affright and distemper with it; which, when the women about her saw, they railed at him for his treachery and baseness, but to no purpose. As soon as he overtook the body of horse with his prisoner, there was a shout from one end to the other of the soldiers. Mr. Hutchinson, being brought to the prince, told him he was the younger brother, and not the person he sent for, which three or four of the Byrons, his cousin-germans, acknowledged to be so; yet Welch outswore them all that it was Mr. John Hutchinson. The Lord Viscount Grandison, a cousin-german of Mrs. Hutchinson's, was then in the king's army, to whom she immediately despatched a messenger, to entreat him to oblige her by the procurement of her brother's liberty, who, upon her imprudence, had been brought into that trouble. My lord sent her word, that, for the present, he could not obtain it, but he would endeavour it afterwards; and in the meantime he gave her notice that it was not safe for her husband to return, there being forty men left to lie close in the country, and watch his coming to her. So Mr. George Hutchinson was carried to Derby, and there, with some difficulty, his liberty was obtained by the interposition of my Lord Grandison and the Byrons. They would have had him give them an engagement, that he would not take arms with the parliament; but he refused, telling them that he lived peaceably at home, and should make no engagement to do anything but what his conscience led him to; that if they pleased, they might detain him, but it would be no advantage to them, nor loss to the other side; upon which considerations they were persuaded to let him go. Immediately after his release, he went to London to his father, where his elder brother was before him; for as soon as he understood from his wife that his brother suffered in his name, he took post to London to procure his release; and there they both stayed till they received assurance that the king's forces were quite withdrawn from the country, and then they together returned to Leicestershire, whe e Mrs. Hutchinson, within a few days after her brother was taken, was brought to bed of her eldest daughter; which, by reason of the mother's and the nurse's griefs and frights, in those troublesome times, was so weak a child that it lived not four years, dying afterwards in Nottingham Castle. When Mr. Hutchinson came to his wife, he carried her and her children, and his brother, back again to his house, about the time that the battle was fought at Edge Hill. After this the two brothers, going to Nottingham, met there most of the godly people, who had been driven away by the rudeness of the king's army, and plundered on account of their godliness, who now returned to their families, and were desirous to live in peace; but having, by experience, found they could not do so, unless the parliament interest was maintained, they were consulting how to raise some recruits for the Earl of Essex, to assist in which, Mr. Hutchinson had provided his plate and horses ready to send in.

About this time Sir John Gell, a Derbyshire gentleman, who had been sheriff of the county, at that time when the illegal tax of ship-money was exacted, and was so violent in the prosecution of it, that he starved Sir John Stanhope's cattle in the pound, and would not suffer any one to relieve them there, because that worthy gentleman stood out against that unjust payment; and he had by many aggravating circumstances, not only concerning his prosecution of Sir John Stanhope, but others, so highly misdemeaned himself that he looked for punishment from the parliament; to prevent it, he very early put himself into their service, and after the king was gone out of these countries, he prevented the cavalier gentry from seizing the town of Derby, and fortified it, and raised a regiment of foot. These were good, stout, fighting men, but the most licentious, ungovernable wretches, that belonged to the parliament. As regards himself, no man knew for what reason he chose that side; for he had not understanding enough to judge the equity of the cause, nor piety or holiness; being a foul adulterer all the time he served the parliament, and so unjust, that without any remorse, he suffered his men indifferently to plunder both honest men and cavaliers; so revengeful, that he pursued his malice to Sir John Stanhope, upon the forementioned account, with such barbarism after his death, that he, pretending to search for arms and plate, came into the church and defaced his monument that cost six hundred pounds, breaking off the nose and other parts of it. He dug up a garden of flowers, the only delight of his widow, upon the same pretence; and then wooed that widow, who was by all the world believed to be the most prudent and affectionate of womankind, till, being deluded by his hypocrisies, she consented to marry him, and found that was the utmost point to which he could carry his revenge, his future carriage making it apparent he sought her for nothing else but to destroy the glory of her husband and his house. This man kept the journalists [1] in pension, so that whatever was done in the

---

[1] Sir John Gell succeeded so far as to get some of his puffing intelligence introduced even into his Memorials by Whitelock; who, p. 186.

neighbouring counties, against the enemy, was attributed to him; and thus he hath indirectly purchased himself a name in story, which he never merited. He was a very bad man, to sum up all in that word, yet an instrument of service to the parliament in those parts. I thought it necessary to insert this little account of him here, because there will be often occasion to mention him in my following discourse; and because, although there never was any personal acquaintance between him and Mr. Hutchinson, yet that natural antipathy which is between good and evil, rendered him a very bad neighbour to Mr. Hutchinson's garrison, and one that, under the name of a friend and assistant, spoiled our country, as much as our enemies. He indeed gave his men leave to commit all insolences without any restraint; whereas Mr. Hutchinson took up arms to defend the country as much as was possible from being a prey to rude soldiers, and did oftentimes preserve it both from his and other rude troops,[1] which stirred up in him envy, hate, and ill-will against his neighbour. He was not wise in ordering the scouts and spies he kept out, and so had the worst intelligence in the world. Mr. Hutchinson, on the other side, employed ingenuous persons, and was better informed of the true state of things, so that oftentimes he communicated those informations to the chief commanders, which proved the falsehood of his; and that was another cause of envy. Some that knew him well, said he was not valiant, though his men once held him up, among a stand of pikes, while they obtained a glorious victory, when the Earl of Northampton was slain; certain it is he was never by his good will in a fight, but either by chance or necessity; and that which made his courage the more questioned was, the care he took, and the expense

talks of an expedition where he killed five of the enemy! He likewise gives him the honour of taking Shelford Manor, at least two years before it was really taken by Colonel Hutchinson. It is very much to be wondered at, that Mrs. Hutchinson nowhere speaks of this trial and condemnation for misprison of treason, which Whitelock notes in the year 1650, during the time of Mr. Hutchinson's being in the second council of state. He is said to have been convicted on the full evidence of Bernard and Titus. Colonel Andrews, who was condemned along with him, gave an attestation on his behalf a little before his death. Whitelock does not say what this treason consisted in, but he was pardoned by the third council, just before Cromwell's usurpation; and was among those members of parliament who opposed him boldly.

[1] To the interposition of such men as Colonel Hutchinson we must attribute the proportionably small quantity of mischief that was suffered by this nation, in so long and sharp a civil war as this was.

he was at, to get it weekly mentioned in the journals, so that when they had nothing else to renown him for, they once put in that the troops of that valiant commander, Sir John Gell, took a dragoon with a plush doublet. Mr. Hutchinson, on the other side, that did well for virtue's sake, and not for the vainglory of it, never would give anything to buy the flatteries of those scribblers; and when one of them had once, while he was in town, made mention of something done at Nottingham, with falsehood, and had given Gell the glory of an action wherein he was not concerned, Mr. Hutchinson rebuked him for it, whereupon the man begged his pardon, and told him he would write as much for him the next week; but Mr. Hutchinson told him he scorned his mercenary pen, warning him not to dare to lie in any of his concernments, whereupon the fellow was awed, and he had no more abuse of that kind.

But to turn out of this digression into another, not altogether impertinent to the story which I would carry on. In Nottinghamshire, upon the edge of Derbyshire, there dwelt a man, who was of mean birth and low fortunes, yet had kept company with the underling gentry of his neighbourhood. This man had the most factious, ambitious, vainglorious, envious, and malicious nature imaginable; but he was the greatest dissembler, flatterer, traitor, and hypocrite that ever was, and herein had a kind of wicked policy; knowing himself to be inferior to all gentlemen, he put on a vizard of godliness and humility, and courted the common people with all the plausibility and flattery that could be practised. All this while he was addicted to many lusts, especially to that of women, but practised them so secretly, that they were not vulgarly taken notice of, though God, to shame him, gave him up to marry a wench out of one of the alehouses he frequented; but to keep up a fame of godliness, he gave large contributions to puritan preachers, who had the art to stop the people's mouths from speaking ill of their benefactors. By a thousand arts this fellow became popular, and so insinuated himself into all the gentlemen that owned the parliament's party, that till he was discovered some years after, they believed him a most true-hearted, faithful, vigilant, active man for the godly interest; but he could never climb higher than a presbyterian persecutor, and in the end, fell quite off to a declared cavalier. In Sir George Booth's business, thinking he could sway the scales of the country, he raised a troop, brought them into Derby, and published a declaration of his own for the king; then ran away to Nottingham, and lost all his troop in the route there, and hid himself till the king [1] came in, when he was rewarded for his revolt with an office, which he enjoyed not many months, his wife and he, and some of his children, dying altogether in a few days of a fever little less than a plague. This man, called Charles White, at the beginning of the civil war, got a troop of dragoons, who armed and mounted themselves out of devotion to the parliament's cause, and being of his neighbourhood, marched forth in his conduct, he having procured a commission to be their captain; but they, having stocks and families, were not willing to march as far as the army, but joined themselves to those who were already in arms at Derby.

After the battle at Edgehill, Sir John Digby, the high sheriff of Nottinghamshire, returned from the king, and had a design of securing the county against the parliament; whereupon he sent out summons to all the gentlemen resident in the country to meet him at Newark. Mr. Hutchinson was at the house of Mr. Francis Pierrepont, the Earl of Kingston's third son, when the letter was delivered to him, and another of the same to Mr. Pierrepont; and while they were reading them, and considering what might be the meaning of this summons, an honest man, of the sheriff's neighbourhood, came and gave them notice, that the sheriff had some design in agitation; for he had assembled and armed about fourscore of his neighbours, to go out with him to Newark, and, as they heard, from thence to Southwell, and from thence to Nottingham, through which town many armed men marched day and night, to their great terror. Mr. Hutchinson, upon this intimation, went home, and, instead of going to meet the sheriff, sent an excuse by an intelligent person, well acquainted with all the country, who had orders to find out their design; which he did so well, that he assured Mr. Hutchinson if he and some others had gone in, they would have been made prisoners; for the sheriff came into Newark with a troop of eighty men, with

---

[1] By the king is here meant Charles the Second; the Rebellion under Sir George Booth having taken place in 1659, after the death of Cromwell.

whom he was gone to Southwell, and was to go the next day to Nottingham, to secure those places for the king. Mr. Hutchinson immediately went with his brother and acquainted them at Nottingham with his intelligence, which they had likewise received from other hands. Although the town was generally more malignant than well affected, yet they cared not much to have cavalier soldiers quarter with them, and therefore agreed to defend themselves against any force which should come against them; and being called hastily together, as the exigence required, about seven hundred listed themselves, and chose Mr. George Hutchinson for their captain, who having lived among them, was very much loved and esteemed by them. The sheriff hearing this, came not to Nottingham, but those who were now there thus became engaged to prosecute the defence of themselves, the town, and country, as far as they could. They were but few, and those not very considerable, and some of them not very hearty; but it pleased God here, as in other places, to carry on his work by weak and unworthy instruments. There were seven aldermen in the town, and of these only Alderman James, then mayor, owned the parliament. He was a very honest, bold man, but had no more than a burgher's discretion; he was yet very well assisted by his wife, a woman of great zeal and courage, and with more understanding than women of her rank usually have. All the devout people of the town were very vigorous and ready to offer their lives and families, but there was not a quarter of the town that consisted of these; the ordinary civil sort of people coldly adhered to the better, but all the debauched, and such as had lived upon the bishops' persecuting courts, and had been the lackeys of projectors and monopolisers and the like, they were all bitterly malignant; yet God awed them, that they could not at that time hinder his people, and he overruled some of their greatest enemies to assist them, such as were Chadwick and Plumptre, who, at the first, put themselves most forward in the business. Plumptre was a doctor of physic, an inhabitant of Nottingham, who had learning, natural parts, and understanding enough to discern between natural civil righteousness and injustice; but he was a horrible atheist, and had such an intolerable pride that he brooked no superiors, and having some wit, took the boldness to exercise it in the abuse of all gentlemen

wherever he came.[1]   Sir Thomas Hutchinson first brought
him into credit and practice in the country, it having pleased
God to make him instrumental in the cure of Mr. George
Hutchinson, who had in vain tried the skill of the best
doctors in England against an epileptic disease, under which
he laboured for some years.   Upon this occasion, Sir Thomas
and both his sons paid him much respect, and this cure gave
him reputation, and introduced him into practice in all the
gentlemen's houses in the country; which he soon lost again
by his most abusive tongue and other ill carriages, and was
even got out of favour with Sir Thomas Hutchinson himself,
for some abusive scoffs given out against his lady.   But Mr.
Hutchinson and his brother, in pity to him, and in remembrance of what God had done through him, still owned him,
and protected him a little against the bitter zealots, though
it was impossible for his darkness and their light long to
continue mixed.   This man had seen enough to approve the
parliament's cause, in point of civil right, and pride enough
to desire to break the bonds of slavery, whereby the king
endeavoured to chain up a free people; and upon these
scores, appearing high for the parliament's interest, he was
admitted into the consultations of those who were then
putting the country into a posture of defence.[2]   Chadwick

[1] It said of him, in Thoroton's History of Notts, "He was a person
eminent in his profession, of great note for wit and learning, as he had
formerly been for poetry, when he printed a book of epigrams;" a
species of composition which the more it pleases the reader, the less it
renders the author beloved.   This inclination to sport with the feelings
of others was not at all likely to recommend him to Mr. Hutchinson,
nor make him a good associate in weighty and serious business.

[2] Doubtless many adhered to the parliament's side merely on a civil
and political account, and these would naturally unite with the independents, as having no inclination to support the pretensions of the
presbyterians.   It is said by Clarendon, that many deists took part
with the independents; and it is not improbable that Dr. Plumptre
might have an inclination at least to scepticism, as sarcasm was his
talent, and for this he was termed an atheist by Mrs. Hutchinson, who
was a rigorist.

After the deaths of Colonel Hutchinson and Dr. Plumptre, there
began a great friendship between their families, which lasted many
generations.   Charles, the half-brother of Colonel Hutchinson, and his
successor in his estate at Owthorpe and in the borough of Nottingham,
was guardian of Dr. Plumptre's son, and is represented by Thoroton to
have executed his trust with great fidelity.

The Editor has in his possession several pieces, in verse and prose,
written by the late Dr. Charles Hutchinson, in favour of the last Mr.
Plumptre, who represented the town of Nottingham, and in vindication
of him against a party headed by Langford Collin, Esq., a lineal descendant of Colonel Hutchinson's master gunner, who will be spoken

was a fellow of a most pragmatical temper, and, to say truth, had strangely wrought himself into a station unfit for him. He was at first a boy that scraped trenchers in the house of one of the poorest justices in the county, but yet such a one as had a great deal of formality and understanding of the statute law, from whom this boy picked such ends of law, that he became first the justice's, then a lawyer's clerk. He then, I know not how, got to be a parcel-judge in Ireland, and came over to his own country swelled with the reputation of it, and set on foot a base, obsolete, arbitrary court there, which the Conqueror of old had given to one Peverel, his bastard, which this man entitling my lord Goring unto, executed the office under him, to the great abuse of the country. At the beginning of the parliament they would have prosecuted him for it, but my lord Goring begged of Sir Thomas Hutchinson to spare him, and promised to lay it down for ever; so from the beginning of the parliament he executed not that office, but having an insinuating wit and tongue, procured himself to be deputy recorder of Nottingham, my lord of Clare being chief. When the king was in town a little before, this man so insinuated himself into the court, that, coming to kiss the king's hand, the king told him he was a very honest man; yet by flatteries and dissimulations he kept up his credit with the godly, cutting his hair, and taking up a form of godliness, the better to deceive. In some of the corrupt times he had purchased the honour of a barrister, though he had neither law nor learning, but he had a voluble tongue, and was crafty; and it is almost incredible that one of his mean education and poverty should arrive to such things as he reached. He was very poor, although he got abundance of money by a thousand cheats and other base ways, wherein he exercised all his life; but he was as great a prodigal in spending as knave in getting. Among other villanies which he secretly practised, he was a libidinous goat, for which his wife, they say, paid him with making him a cuckold; yet were there not two persons to be found that pretended more sanctity than these two, she having a

of hereafter; they are all in a jocose or satirical style; but one of them, a short advertisement, which too well described Mr. Collin, was deemed libellous, and cost Dr. Hutchinson £500, which was well repaid by Mr. Plumptre's obtaining for him a king's living of £350 per annum. At this time Mr. Plumptre and Mr. Hutchinson's families were of the Whig or Hanover party, Mr. Collin of the Tory or Jacobite.

tongue no less glavering and false than his. Such baseness
he had, that all the just reproaches in the world could not
move him, but he would fawn upon any man that told him
of his villanies to his face, even at the very time. Never
was a truer Judas, since Iscariot's time, than he, for he would
kiss the man he had in his heart to kill; he naturally delighting in mischief and treachery, and was so exquisite a villain,
that he destroyed those designs he might have thriven by,
with overlaying them with fresh knaveries. I have been a
little tedious in these descriptions, yet have spoken very
little in comparison of what the truth would bear; indeed,
such assistants as these were enough to disgrace the best
cause by their owning of it; but the truth of God being
above the testimony of men, could neither receive credit from
the good, nor discredit from the worst men; but they were
not all such, who first offered themselves to carry on the
Lord's work with him of whom we chiefly treat. There was
then dwelling at Nottingham a third son of the Earl of
Kingston, a man of good natural parts, but not of education
according to his quality, who was in the main well affected to
honest men and to righteous liberty; a man of a very excellent good nature, and full of love to all men; but his goodness
received a little allay by a vain-glorious pride, which could
not well brook that any other should outstrip him in virtue
and estimation.[1] Mr. Francis Thornhagh, the eldest son of
Sir Francis Thornhagh, was a man of the most upright
faithful heart to God and his people, and to his country's
true interest, comprehended in the parliament's cause; a
man of greater valour or more noble daring, fought not for
them, nor indeed ever drew sword in any cause; he was of a
most excellent good nature to all men, and zealous for his
friend; he wanted counsel and deliberation, and was sometimes too facile to flatterers, but had judgment enough to
discern his errors when they were represented to him, and
worth enough not to persist in an injurious mistake because
he had once entertained it.[2] Mr. Pigott was a very religious,

[1] Mr. Francis Pierrepont, who will frequently be mentioned again in
the course of the story, when it will be clearly seen that Mrs. Hutchinson here speaks with candour, or rather favour of him, though he was
her husband's opponent.

[2] Colonel Thornhagh is often mentioned by other writers, and always
with praise in his military capacity, in which only he was known to the
public. Mrs. Hutchinson here delineates with a masterly hand a
frank, open, unsuspecting, amiable soldier. The family of Colonel

serious, wise gentleman, true-hearted to God and his country, of a generous and liberal nature, and who thought nothing too dear to expose, nor too difficult to undertake, for his friend; one that delighted not in the ruin of his neighbours, but could endure it, rather than the destruction of religion, law, and liberty; one that wanted not courage, yet chose rather to venture himself as a single person than as a leader in arms, and to serve his country in counsel rather than in action; no man in his nature, and his whole deportment, showed himself more of a gentleman than he.[1] There was one Mr. Widmerpoole, a man of good extraction, but reduced to a small fortune, in whom had declined all the splendour of an old house, and who had sunk into the condition of the middle men of the country, yet had a perfect honest heart to God, his country, and his friend; he had a good discretion, and though older than all the rest, was so humble as to be content to come in the rear of them all; having through the declining of his family, the slenderness of his estate, and the parsimony of his nature, less interest in the country.[2] To yoke with him, there was a very honest man, who could not be reckoned among the gentry, though he was called by the name of *Mr.* Lomax; he was in the strength and perfection of his age, a stout and an understanding man, plain and blunt, but withal godly, faithful to his country, and honest to all men. There lived at Nottingham, a man called Mr. Salisbury, who had very good abilities with his pen, upon

Thornhagh continued to flourish in the county of Nottingham so late as the year 1750, at which time one of them represented the county; they are believed to be now extinct in the male line, and their possessions to have centered in a female who was the lady of Francis Ferrand Foljambe, Esq.

[1] Mr. Pigott survived Colonel Hutchinson about five years. He was summoned to parliament by Cromwell, but it is very uncertain whether he condescended to sit or not to sit. Thoroton, in his History of Nottinghamshire, says of him that " he was a person of great parts, natural and acquired; he was sheriff of the county in 1669, and died presently after the summer assizes; at which time, being in mourning for his daughter Mary, wife of Robert, eldest son of Sir Francis Burdett, of Formark, he gave his attendants black liveries with silver trimmings, which served for his own funeral. His sobriety, ingenuity, generosity, piety, and other virtues, few of his rank will ever exceed, if any equal."
It is thought necessary to take more particular notice of what may appertain to Ireton, Colonel Thornhagh, and Mr. Pigott, because they are the three persons who enjoyed the greatest share in the friendship and esteem of Colonel Hutchinson, and made him a due return.

[2] The pedigree of the family of Widmerpoole, in Thoroton, shows him to have been of very ancient and good descent; his ancestor represented the town of Nottingham in the reign of Edward the Third.

which he was taken in to be their secretary; but he proved ambitious and froward, and being poor, when he was afterwards made treasurer, he fell into some temptation; but carried at first a fair colour of religion and honesty. These were they with whom Mr. Hutchinson was first mated, whose character it was necessary thus far to hint at, for the better carrying on of his story.

Sir John Digby having notice that they had prevented him, by getting arms in their hands before, came not to Nottingham; where they, having now taken up the sword, saw it was not safe to lay it down again, and hold a naked throat to their enemy's whetted knives. Wherefore, upon the parliament's commission for settling the militia some time before, there having been three colonels nominated, viz., Sir Francis Thornhagh, Sir Francis Molineux, and Mr. Francis Pierrepont, they propounded to them to raise their regiments. Sir Francis Molineux altogether declined; Sir Francis Thornhagh appointed his son for his lieutenant-colonel, and began to raise a regiment of horse, with whom many of the honest men that first enlisted themselves with Mr. George Hutchinson, became troopers. Mr. John Hutchinson and his brother were persuaded to be lieutenant-colonel and major to Colonel Pierrepont's regiment of foot; and accordingly Mr. George Hutchinson had immediately a very good standing company of foot, formed out of those townsmen who first came in to enlist under him. Mr. John Hutchinson had a full company of very honest, godly men, who came for love of him and the cause, out of the country. It was six weeks before the colonel could be persuaded to put on a sword, or to enlist any men, which at length he did, of substantial honest townsmen; and Mr. Poulton, a nephew of Sir Thomas Hutchinson, a stout young gentleman, who had seen some service abroad, was his captain-lieutenant. There were two companies more raised, one under Captain Lomax, and another under one Captain Scrimpshire. The first thing these gentlemen did was to call home Captain White with his dragoons, raised in Nottinghamshire, to the service of his own country; for Sir John Gell, at Derby, had received from Hull a regiment of grey coats, who were at first sent down from London, for the assistance of that place, when the king attempted it. They also sent to the Earl of Essex, to desire that Captain Ireton, with a troop of horse, which he had carried out of the country into his excellency's army, might be commanded back, for the present service of his country, till it was put into a posture of defence; which accordingly he was, and was major of the horse regiment. They sent also to the parliament, and received from them a commission, with instructions, whereby they were empowered to levy forces and to raise contributions for maintaining them; with all authority for seizing delinquents, sequestrating, and the like. The committee appointed were the parliament-men that served for the county, Mr. Francis Pierrepont, Mr. John Hutchinson, Mr. Francis Thornhagh, Mr. Gervas Pigott, Mr. Henry Ireton, Mr. George Hutchinson, Mr. Joseph Widmerpoole, Mr. Gervas Lomax, Dr. Plumptre, the mayor of Nottingham, Mr. James Chadwick, and Mr. Thomas Salisbury. Then did neighbouring counties everywhere associate for the mutual assistance of each other; and the parliament commissioned major-generals, who commanded in chief, and gave out commissions to the several commanders of the regiments. Nottinghamshire was put into the association with Leicestershire and other counties, whereof Lord Grey of Grooby, eldest son of the Earl of Stamford, was commander-in-chief, and from him the gentlemen of Nottingham took their first commissions.

The high sheriff and the malignant gentry, finding an opposition they expected not, wrote a letter to Mr. Francis Pierrepont and Mr. John Hutchinson, excusing the sheriff's force, that he brought with him, and desiring a meeting with them, to consult for the peace of the country, security of their estates, and such like fair pretences; which letter was civilly answered them again, and the treaty kept on foot some fourteen days, by letters signed by the Lord Chaworth, Sir Thomas Williamson, Mr. Sutton, Sir Gervas Eyre, Sir John Digby, Sir Roger Cooper, Mr. Palmer, Mr. John Millington. At length a meeting was appointed at a village in the country, on the forest side, where Mr. Sutton should have met Mr. John Hutchinson. Mr. Hutchinson came to the place, but found not Mr. Sutton there, only the Lord Chaworth came in and called for sack, and treated Mr. Hutchinson very kindly; when Mr. Hutchinson, telling my lord he was come according to appointment, to conclude the treaty which had been between Nottingham and Newark, my lord told him he knew nothing of it. Whereupon, Mr.

Hutchinson being informed that some of my Lord Newcastle's forces were to be in that town that night, and that Mr. Sutton was gone to meet them, and conduct them into the country, returned to Nottingham, where he received a kind of lame excuse from Mr. Sutton for his disappointing of him, and for their bringing strange soldiers into Newark, which they pretended was to save the town from the plunder of some Lincolnshire forces. But Mr. Hutchinson, seeing all their treaties were but a snare for him, would no longer amuse himself about them; but being certainly informed that Henderson, who commanded the soldiers at Newark, if he were not himself a papist, had many Irish papists in his troops, he, with the rest of the gentlemen, sent notice to all the towns about Nottingham, desiring the well-affected to come in to their assistance; which the ministers pressing them to do, upon Christmas-day, 1642, many came to them, and stayed with them till they had put themselves into some posture of defence.

As soon as these strange soldiers were come into Newark, they presently began to block up and fortify the town, as on the other side, they at Nottingham began works about that town; but neither of them being yet strong enough to assault each other, they contented themselves to stand upon their own defence. The Earl of Chesterfield had raised some horse for the king, and was in the vale of Belvoir with them, where he had plundered some houses near Mr. Hutchinson's; whereupon Mr. Hutchinson sent a troop of horse in the night, for they were not strong enough to march in the day, and fetched away his wife and children to Nottingham.

The preservation of this town was a special service to the parliament, it being a considerable pass into the north, which, if the enemy had first possessed themselves of, the parliament would have been cut off from all intercourse between the north and south; especially in the winter time, when the river Trent is not fordable, and only to be passed over by the bridges of Nottingham and Newark, and higher up at a place called Wilden Ferry, where the enemy also had a garrison.[1] The attempting to preserve this place, in the midst

[1] In the place of Wilden Ferry has been substituted in modern days a very beautiful bridge, called Cavendish Bridge, with a good and firm road of considerable length at each end to approach it; it is about midway on the high road between Loughborough and Derby. There is near to it a place called Sawley Ferry, little used, and hardly at all practicable in winter.

of so many potent enemies, was a work of no small difficulty;
and nothing but an invincible courage, and a passionate zeal
for the interest of God and his country, could have engaged
Mr. Hutchinson, who did not, through youthful inconsidera-
tion and improvidence, want a foresight of those dangers
and travails he then undertook. He knew well enough that
the town was more than half disaffected to the parliament;
that had they been all otherwise, they were not half enough
to defend it against any unequal force; that they were far
from the parliament and their armies, and could not expect
any timely relief or assistance from them; that he himself
was the forlorn hope of those who were engaged with him,
and had then the best stake among them; that the gentlemen who were on horseback, when they could no longer
defend their country, might at least save their lives by a
handsome retreat to the army; but that he must stand
victorious, or fall, tying himself to an indefensible town.
Although his colonel (Pierrepont) might seem to be in the
same hazard, yet he was wise enough to content himself with
the name, and leave Mr. Hutchinson to act in all things, the
glory of which, if they succeeded, he hoped to assume; if
they failed, he thought he had a retreat. But Mr. Hutchinson, though he knew all this, yet was he so well persuaded
in his conscience of the cause, and of God's calling him to
undertake the defence of it, that he cast by all other considerations, and cheerfully resigned up his life, and all other
particular interests, to God's disposal, though in all human
probability he was more likely to lose than to save them.

He and his brother were so suddenly called into this work,
that they had not time beforehand to consult their father;
but they sent to him to buy their armour and useful swords,
which he did, giving them no discouragement, but promoting
all their desires to the parliament very effectually.[1]

By reason of the coldness of the colonel, the affairs of the
war at Nottingham went on more tardily than otherwise
they would have done; but the gentlemen there, thinking it

---

[1] The reader is desired to bear this in mind, as it tends much to in-
validate the credibility of an assertion made by the stepmother of
these gentlemen, which will be noticed in its proper place. It is said,
in a note by Julius Hutchinson, Esq., that Sir Thomas Hutchinson
bought his two sons armour, though he knew not of their accepting
commissions against the king. What was the armour for? Was it to
serve the king against the parliament?

would be easier to prevent Newark from being made a fortified garrison, than to take it when it was so, sent over to
Lincoln and Derby, to propound the business to them. At
length, about Candlemas, it was agreed and appointed that
the forces of Nottingham and Derby should come on their
side of the town, and those of Lincoln on the other. All
the disaffected gentry of both those countries, were at that
time gone into Newark, and one Ballard, a gentleman who,
decayed in his family, and owing his education to many of
them, had been bred up in the wars abroad, was commander-
in-chief for the parliament in Lincolnshire. Much ado had
the gentlemen of that county to engage him in the design
against Newark; but when he could not divert them, he was
resolved to cast them away rather than ruin his old benefactors. He had appointed the forces of Nottingham and
Derby to come to a rendezvous within a mile of Newark,
upon Saturday, upon which day, all the persuasion the
Lincolnshire gentlemen could use, could not prevail with
him to march out, according to appointment; which those
at Newark had notice of, and had prepared an ambuscade
to have cut off all those forces if they had then come to the
place; but by providence of an extraordinary stormy season,
they marched not till the next day, and so were preserved
from that danger, which no doubt was treacherously contrived. As soon as they came, being about a thousand horse,
foot, and dragoons, the Lincolnshire commanders informed
ours of the sloth and untoward carriage of Ballard, and told
them how that day he had played his ordnance at a mile's
distance from the town; and how, when the Newark horse
came out to face them, upon the Beacon Hill, he would not
suffer a man of the Lincolnshire troops to fall upon them,
though the Lincoln horse were many more in number than
they, and in all probability might have beaten them. The
next day, notwithstanding Mr. Hutchinson went to him, to
give him an account of the forces they had brought, and to
receive orders, he could have none, but a careless answer to
stand at such a side of the town and fall on as they saw
occasion. Accordingly they did, and beat the enemy from
their works, with the loss of only four or five men, and entrenched themselves; the night coming on upon them, they
provided straw to have lodged in their trenches all the
night. On the other side of the town, Captain King, of

Lincolnshire, had taken a street, cut up a chain, and placed a drake [1] in a house; whereupon the Newark gentlemen were almost resolved to yield up the town, and some of them began to fly out of it, but Ballard would not suffer the horse to pursue them; only one captain went out without his leave and took fifty horses, and turned back Mr. Sutton and many others that were flying out of the town. At length, when he could no other way preserve his old patrons, but by betraying his friends, he ordered Captain King to retreat; whereupon the whole force of Newark fell upon the forces of Nottingham and Derby, in their trenches, where they fought very resolutely, till a Lincolnshire trooper came and bade them fly for their lives, or else they were all lost men. At this, two hundred Lincolnshire men, whom Ballard with much entreaty had sent to relieve them, first ran away, and then Sir John Gell's grey coats made their retreat after them. Major Hutchinson and Captain White all this while kept their trenches, and commanded their Nottingham men not to stir, who accordingly shot there, till all their powder was spent. The lieutenant-colonel in vain importuned Ballard to send them ammunition and relief, but could obtain neither, and so they were forced, unwillingly, to retreat, which they did in such good order, the men first, and then their captains, that they lost not a man in coming off. The town was sallying upon them, but they discharged a drake and beat them back. The next day all the captains importuned Ballard that they might fall on again, but he would neither consent nor give any reason for his denial; so that the Nottingham forces returned with great dissatisfaction, though Ballard, to stop their mouths, gave them two pieces of ordnance.

It being necessary to carry on the main story, for the better understanding the motion of those lesser wheels that moved within the great orb, I shall now name in what posture things were abroad in the kingdom, while these affairs I relate were transacted at Nottingham. After the retreat from Brainford fight, a treaty was ineffectually carried on between the king and parliament from the 31st of January, 1642, to the 17th of April, 1643; after which my Lord of Essex marched to Reading, where the king had a garrison, and besieged it. The king's horse came to relieve it, and had an encounter with my lord's army, wherein many gentlemen of quality fell

[1] Drake, a piece of cannon so called.

on the king's side, the king himself being in a place where he saw them. A few days after, Reading was yielded upon composition to the Earl of Essex, whose soldiers having been promised their pay and a gratuity to spare the plunder of the town, fell into a mutiny upon the failing of the performance, and many of them disbanded. Among those who remained there was a great mortality, occasioned by the infected air in the town of Reading; insomuch that my lord was forced to return and quarter his sick and weak army about Kingston and those towns near London. And now were all the countries in England no longer idle spectators, but several stages, whereon the tragedy of the civil war was acted; except the eastern association, where Mr. Oliver Cromwell, by his diligence, prevented the designs of the royal party; these were so successful the first year in all other places, and the parliament's condition appeared so desperate, that many of the members of both houses, ran away to Oxford to the king, and others sat among them conspiring against them. One plot, conducted by Mr. Waller, and carried on among many disaffected persons in the city, was near taking effect, to the utter subversion of the parliament and people; but that God, by his providence, brought it timely to light, and the authors were condemned, and some of them executed; but Waller, for being more a knave than the rest, and impeaching his accomplices, was permitted to buy his life for ten thousand pounds. This summer all the west was reduced by the king, the Earl of Stamford yielding up Exeter, and Colonel Fiennes Bristol. Sir William Waller had lost all his army, which had been victorious in many encounters. The king was master of all or most part of Wales, and the parliament had no army left in the field, so that had he taken the opportunity to have gone immediately to London that summer, he had accomplished his design; but being denied the town of Gloucester, and taking it in disdain, that that town, in the heart of the land, should make a resistance when the greater cities were yielded to him, he stopped his course to take in that place, where he stayed to turn the tide of his good fortune, as his general, my Lord of Newcastle did at the siege of Hull.[1] My Lord Newcastle was general of the north,

[1] The impolicy of this measure is more fully noticed and explained, and the cause of it set down by Sir Philip Warwick, in his Memoirs, p. 260. "One or the like counsel in both quarters, north and west, soon

and master of all the strong places to the very borders of
Scotland, and formidable to all the neighbouring counties.
Only the Lord Fairfax, with his son Sir Thomas, headed all
the religious, honest Englishmen they could raise in those
parts, and with a far inferior force, kept him in play, and in
several skirmishes came off conquerors.[1]   But as the fortune
of the parliament declined in other places, so those who had
not principle strong enough to hold them fast to a just,
though falling cause, sought early to secure their lives by
treasons which destroyed them.   The Earl of Newcastle's
army was judged to be about eight thousand, horse and foot;
my Lord Fairfax had not above two thousand one hundred
foot, and seven troops of horse.   After this there was a great
accession of strength to my Lord Newcastle, by the coming,
first of the Lord Goring, with many old commanders; then
of General King, with six thousand arms, from beyond the
seas; then of the queen herself, who, in February 1642,[2]
landed near Sunderland, coming out of Holland, with large
provisions of arms, ammunition, and commanders of note,
with which she was convoyed, by the Earl of Newcastle, to
York.   Thither came to her the Earl of Montrose, out of

blasted the prosperity in each place, for the king pitched upon that
fatal resolution, recommended to him by Lord Culpeper, of besieging
Gloucester, thinking it a good policy not to leave a strong town behind
him: but the counsel proved fatal, for had the king at that time resolved in himself to have struck at the proud head of London, and had
had authority enough at that time to have required the Earl of Newcastle to have joined with him, humanly speaking, he had raised such
confusion among the two houses and the Londoners, that they had
either sent him his own terms, of if they had fought him, most probably
he had been victorious.   But the king fixes on Gloucester and the Earl
of Newcastle upon Hull, upon the advice of his Lieutenant-General
King, who was suspected."

A few pages further, he reckons among the king's misfortunes the
Earl of Newcastle's too much affecting independency, which may
serve to account for some other matters which will occur; but it is
here natural to observe, that the king having, by separating himself
from his parliament, lost his acknowledged and unquestionable
authority, he retained only a very precarious one over the different
chiefs of his party: which, on many occasions, turned to the disadvantage of his cause.   After all, it is in no way certain that his march to
London would have been so effectual and so little opposed, as it is here
taken for granted it would have been.

[1] In fact, the resistance so long maintained, and frequently with
such success, by Lord Fairfax and his sons, against so superior a force,
has been always thought next to miraculous, and marked out Sir
Thomas as the fittest man in the kingdom to command the forces and
fix the fortunes of the parliament.

[2] Clarendon says February, 1643.

Scotland, with a hundred and twenty horse: then Sir Hugh Cholmly, governor of Scarborough, revolted from the parliament, whereof he was a member, and came to the queen, with three hundred men. Browne Bushell also, who was left in charge of the town, yielded it up. Then had the queen's practices wrought so upon the two Hothams, that their treason was not altogether undiscerned; but my Lord Fairfax, having only strong presumptions, and no power to secure them, while they had the strong town of Hull in their hands, all he could do was to be vigilant and silent, till God should give opportunity to secure that great danger. My Lord of Newcastle had given the papists in the north commissions to arm in the king's defence,[1] and now the queen was preparing to march up with the assistance she had gotten to the king. Those countries through which she was to pass, could not but be sensible of their danger, especially the gentlemen at Nottingham, who were but a few young men, environed with garrisons of the enemy, and scarcely firm among themselves, and hopeless of relief from above, where the parliament, struggling for life, had not leisure to bind up a cut finger. But God was with them in these difficulties, and gave an unexpected issue.

The Earl of Kingston a few months stood neuter, and would not declare himself for either party, and being a man of great wealth and dependencies, many people hung in suspense, by his example; whereupon the gentlemen of Nottingham often spoke to his son, to persuade his father to declare himself; but he told them, he knew his father's affections were firm to the parliament, that he had encouraged him to join with them, and promised him money to carry it on, and such like things, which he continually assured them; till the colonel's cold behaviour, and some other passages, made them at length, those at least who were firm to the cause, jealous both of the father and the son. Hereupon, when the danger grew more imminent, and my lord lay out a brave prey to the enemy, they sent Captain Lomax, one of

---

[1] The king pretended never to do this himself; but the Earl of Newcastle did it, as most people would in his place, and avowed it as it became him. Sir Philip Warwick recites a witticism of his on the occasion of his going to see him at the siege of Hull, where his men being very badly entrenched, he said to Sir Philip, who remarked it, "You hear us often called the popish army, but you see we trust not in our *good works*."

the committee, to understand his affections from himself, and to press him to declare for the parliament, in that so needful a season. My lord, professing himself to him as rather desirous of peace, and fully resolved not to act on either side, made a serious imprecation on himself in these words: "When," said he, "I take arms with the king against the parliament, or with the parliament against the king, let a cannon-bullet divide me between them;" which God was pleased to bring to pass a few months after; for he, going to Gainsborough, and there taking up arms for the king, was surprised by my Lord Willoughby, and, after a handsome defence of himself, yielded, and was put prisoner into a pinnace, and sent down the river to Hull; when my Lord Newcastle's army marching along the shore, shot at the pinnace, and being in danger, the Earl of Kingston went up on the deck to show himself and to prevail with them to forbear shooting;[1] but as soon as he appeared, a cannon-bullet flew from the king's army, and divided him in the middle, and thus, being then in the parliament's pinnace, he perished according to his own unhappy imprecation. His declaring himself for the king, as it enforced the royal, so it weakened the other party.

Sir Richard Byron was come to be governor of Newark. A house of my Lord Chaworth's in the vale was fortified, and some horse put into it, and another house of the Earl of Chesterfield's, both of them within a few miles of Nottingham.[2] Ashby de la Zouch, within eighteen miles of Nottingham, on the other side, was kept by Mr. Hastings. On the forest side of the country, the Earl of Newcastle's house had a garrison, and another castle of his, within a mile, was garrisoned. Sir Roger Cooper's house, at Thurgaton, was also kept; so that Nottingham, thus beleaguered with enemies, seemed very unlikely to be able either to resist the enemy or support itself.[3] Therefore the gentlemen, upon the news of my Lord Newcastle's intended approach that way, sent up Mr. John Hutchinson to acquaint the parlia-

[1] This is a most singular story, and no doubt peculiarly gratifying to a fatalist to recite; it is however assuredly true, being mentioned by several historians, with only the difference of his being said to be under, instead of on, the deck; the latter of which is by far the most probable.

[2] Wiverton-house and Shelford manor.

[3] In a letter to the king, the queen writes from Newark that " all the force the parliament had in those parts was only one thousand men in Nottingham."

ment with their condition; who so negotiated their business that he procured an order for Colonel Cromwell, Colonel Hubbard, my Lord Grey, and Sir John Gell, to unite their forces, and rendezvous at Nottingham, to prevent the queen from joining with the king, and to guard those parts against the cavaliers. Accordingly, in the Whitsun holidays, 1643, they all came, and the younger Hotham also brought some more rude troops out of Yorkshire, and joined himself to them. The forces now united at Nottingham were about five or six thousand, my Lord Grey being their commander-in-chief. Upon the urgency of the gentlemen at Nottingham, he drew them out against Wiverton-house in the vale, but, upon a groundless apprehension, quitted it, when they might in all probability have taken it, and retreated to Nottingham, where, two or three days after, the enemy's horse faced them; but they would not be prevailed upon to go out, though they were not inferior to them. Young Hotham, at that time, carried on a private treaty with the queen, and every day received and sent trumpets, of which he would give no account. Then was Nottingham more sadly distressed by their friends than by their enemies; for Hotham's and Gell's men not only lay upon free quarter, as all the rest did, but made such a havoc and plunder of friend and foe, that it was a sad thing for any one that had a generous heart to behold it. When the committee offered Hotham to assign him quarters for his men, because they were better acquainted with the country, he would tell them he was no stranger in any English ground. He had a great deal of wicked wit, and would make sport with the miseries of the poor country; and, having treason in his heart, licensed his soldiers, which were the scum of mankind, to all the villanies in the country that might make their party odious. Mr. Hutchinson was much vexed to see the country wasted, and that little part of it, which they could only hope to have contribution from, eaten up by a company of men who, instead of relieving, devoured them; and Hotham's soldiers, having taken away goods from some honest men, he went to him to desire restitution of them, and that he would restrain his soldiers from plunder; whereupon Hotham replied, " he fought for liberty, and expected it in all things." Replies followed, and they grew to high language; Hotham bidding him, if he found himself grieved, to complain to the parliament. Mr.

Hutchinson was passionately concerned, and this being in the open field, Colonel Cromwell, who had likewise had great provocations from him, began to show himself affected with the country's injuries, and the idle waste of such a considerable force, through the inexperience of the chief commander, and the disobedience and irregularities of the others. So they, at that time, being equally zealous for the public service, advised together to seek a remedy, and despatched away a post to London, who had no greater joy in the world than such employments as tended to the displacing of great persons, whether they deserved it or not; him they sent away immediately from the place, to inform the parliament of Hotham's carriages, and the strong presumptions they had of his treachery, and the ill management of their forces. This they two did, without the privity of any of the other gentlemen or commanders; some of whom were little less suspected themselves, and others, as my Lord Grey, through credulous good nature, were too great favourers of Hotham. The messenger was very diligent in his charge, and returned, as soon as it was possible, with a commitment of Hotham; who accordingly was then made prisoner in Nottingham Castle, and Sir John Meldrum was sent down to be commander-in-chief of all those united forces. When they marched away, a troop of my Lord Grey's, having the charge of guarding Hotham towards London, suffered him to escape, and thereby put the town of Hull into a great hazard; but that the father and son were there unexpectedly surprised, sent up prisoners to London, and after some time executed. Those who knew the opinion Cromwell afterwards had of Mr. Hutchinson, believed he registered this business in his mind as long as he lived, and made it his care to prevent him from being in any power or capacity to pursue him to the same punishment, when he himself deserved it; but from that time, growing into more intimate acquaintance with him, he always used to profess the most hearty affections for him, and the greatest delight in his plainness and open-heartedness imaginable.[1]

[1] Those who consider and represent Cromwell as a prodigy not only of treachery, design, ambition, and artifice, but likewise of sagacity and foreknowledge, will deem this a proof of his having thus early conceived his scheme of aggrandisement; but to those who are better satisfied with the probable than the marvellous it will seem to prove no such thing; they must well know that if he had so soon any great

As soon as Sir John Meldrum came down to his charge at Nottingham, the queen's forces came and faced the town; whereupon the cannon discharging upon them, the Duke of Vendome's son and some few others were slain. The parliament horse drew out of Nottingham to receive the queen's, but they came not on, after this execution of the cannon, for in the meantime the queen was passing by, and although the parliament horse pursued them, yet they would not engage, for it was not their business; so when they saw they had lost their design, the horse returned again to Nottingham, where the foot had stayed all the while they were out. When the Earl of Kingston declared himself for the king, he raised what forces he could, and went into Gainsborough, a town in Lincolnshire, situated upon the river Trent. There, before he was fortified, my Lord Willoughby, of Parham, surprised the town and all his soldiers, who disputed it as long as they could, but being conquered, were forced to yield; and the earl himself retreated into the strongest house, which he kept till it was all on flame round him, and then giving himself up only to my Lord Willoughby, he was immediately sent prisoner to Hull, and shot according to his own imprecation. Immediately part of my Lord Newcastle's army, with all that Newark could make, besieged my Lord Willoughby in Gainsborough; and General Essex sent a command to Sir John Meldrum to draw all the horse and foot he could out of

views, they must have been very distant and indistinct; they will find here only the first of a long series of instances, wherein will be seen the quick and clear discernment, the strong and well-poised judgment, the promptitude and firmness of decision, which enabled him to seize and convert to his advantage every opportunity that presented itself, and even the actions, thoughts, and inclinations, of other men; and they will see united to these such a command over his own thoughts and passions as permitted exactly so much, and no more of them than was convenient, to appear: these qualities, though less astonishing than the prescience and almost the power of creating events, which is attributed to him, would and did equally well answer the purpose of his progression; which he effected in such a manner as to fill with the greatest propriety all the intermediate situations through which he passed, to take as it were a firm footing at each gradation, and to arrive at the pinnacle of power without having once run any considerable risk of an overthrow in his career. Such rational observers will likewise see here, what will in the sequel still more strikingly appear, that if he must be called a traitor, he was not of that paltry treachery which sacrifices a man's party to self; he was steadily bent on procuring the triumph of his own party over their opponents, but too covetous of commanding his party himself. It may be thought there wanted but little, perhaps only the survivance of Ireton, to have made Cromwell intrinsically as well as splendidly great.

Nottingham, to relieve my lord, leaving only a garrison in the castle of Nottingham. Sir John Meldrum called the committee of Nottingham together, to consult what was to be done for the settlement of the place, which upon deliberation he had judged it not fit to leave in the hands it was, nor in Colonel Pierrepont's, who, with some appearance, lay under suspicion at that time; and therefore conceiving Mr. Hutchinson the most able to manage, and the most responsible for it, both Sir John and the whole committee ordered him to take the castle into his charge; which, though there were many causes why he should decline, yet believing that God hereby called him to the defence of his country, and would protect him in all the dangers and difficulties he led him into, he accepted it, and on the 29th June, 1643, received an order for that government from Sir John Meldrum and the whole committee. Whereunto Col. Pierrepont subscribed, though with a secret discontent in his heart; not from any ill opinion or ill affection he had to Mr. Hutchinson's person, but because he resented it as a great affront that himself should be passed by. It is true that this discontent produced some envious and malicious practices, secretly in him, against Mr. Hutchinson, who however in the end overcame him, with so many good offices, in requital of his bad ones, that he lived and died full of love, and acknowledgment of kindness to him.

The castle was built upon a rock, and nature had made it capable of very strong fortification, but the buildings were very ruinous and uninhabitable, neither affording room to lodge soldiers nor provisions. The castle stands at one end of the town, upon such an eminence as commands the chief streets of the town. There had been enlargements made to this castle after the first building of it. There was a strong tower, which they called the old tower, built upon the top of all the rock, and this was that place where Queen Isabel, the mother of King Edward the Third, was surprised with her paramour Mortimer, who, by secret windings and hollows in the rock, came up into her chamber from the meadows lying low under it, through which there ran a little rivulet, called the Line, almost under the castle rock. At the entrance of this rock there was a spring, which was called Mortimer's Well, and the cavern Mortimer's Hole. The ascent to the top is very high, and it is not without some wonder that at the top of all the rock there should be a spring of water. In the midway to the top of this tower there is a little piece of the rock, on which a dove-cote had been built, but the governor took down the roof of it, and made it a platform for two or three pieces of ordnance, which commanded some streets and all the meadows better than the higher tower. Under that tower, which was the old castle, there was a larger castle, where there had been several towers and many noble rooms, but the most of them were down; the yard of that was pretty large, and without the gate there was a very large yard that had been walled, but the walls were all down, only it was situated upon an ascent of the rock, and so stood a pretty height above the streets; and there were the ruins of an old pair of gates, with turrets on each side.

Before the castle, the town was on one side of a close, which commanded the fields approaching the town; which close the governor afterwards made a platform. Behind it was a place called the Park, that belonged to the castle, but then had neither deer nor trees in it, except one tree, growing under the castle, which was almost a prodigy, for from the root to the top, there was not a straight twig or branch in it; some said it was planted by King Richard the Third, and resembled him that set it. On the other side the castle, was the little river of Line, and beyond that, large flat meadows, bounded by the river Trent. In the whole rock there were many large caverns, where a great magazine and many hundred soldiers might have been disposed, if they had been cleansed and prepared for it; and they might have been kept secure from any danger of firing the magazines by any mortar-pieces shot against the castle. In one of these places, it is reported, that one David, a Scotch king, was kept in cruel durance, and with his nails, had scratched on the wall the story of Christ and his twelve apostles. The castle was not defended by lateral fortifications, and there were no works about it, when Mr. Hutchinson undertook it, but only a little breastwork, before the outermost gate. It was as ill provided as fortified, there being but ten barrels of powder, eleven hundred and fifty pounds of butter, and as much cheese, eleven quarters of bread corn, seven beeves, two hundred and fourteen flitches of bacon, five hundred and sixty fishes, and fifteen hogsheads of beer. As soon as the governor received his charge, he made proclamation in the town, that whatsoever honest persons desired to secure themselves or their goods in the castle, should have reception there, if they would repair their quarters; which divers well-affected men accepting, it was presently made capable of receiving 400 men commodiously.

In the beginning of July, 1643, Sir John Meldrum, with all the force that was quartered in Nottingham, marched forth to the relief of Gainsborough, leaving the town to be guarded by few more than the very townsmen.   There had been large works made about it, which would have required at least three thousand men to man and defend well, and upon these works there were about fourteen guns, which the governor, when the forces were marching away, before they went, drew up to the castle; whereupon the townsmen, especially those that were ill-affected to the parliament, made a great mutiny, threatening they would pull the castle down, but they would have their ordnance again upon their works, and wishing it on fire, and not one stone upon another. Hereupon the governor sent Alderman Drury, with fourteen more, who were heads of this mutiny, prisoners to Derby, whither Major Ireton convoyed them with his troop.   The reasons which made the governor carry the ordnance from the town-works up into the castle were:—First, That the town, being so ill-affected, the ordnance remaining in it, would but be an invitation to the enemy to come to take them away, and a booty for them if they should.   Secondly, He had often visited the guards, and found them much exposed by their carelessness, wherefore he thought it his duty to preserve them, by soldiers more under his command. Thirdly, Intelligence was brought to the committee, by a friend, then with the Earl of Newcastle, that Mr. Francis Pierrepont kept intelligence with his mother, the Countess of Kingston, carrying on a design for betraying the town to the earl; and that letters were carried between them by a woman, who often came to town to the colonel; and that two aldermen and a chief officer, employed about the ordnance, were confederates in the plot; whereupon a suspected cannonier was secured, who, as soon as he obtained his liberty, ran away to Newark.   Fourthly, When the town was full of troops, there had been several attempts to poison and betray them, which, if it should be again attempted, after the most of the forces were gone, might prove effectual.   Fifthly,

The main reason was, that if the town should be surprised or betrayed (which was then most to be feared), the ordnance would be useless; if any considerable force came against the town, it was impossible then to keep the works against them, with so few men, and it would be difficult, at such a time, to draw off the artillery; if any force they were able to deal with came, it would then be time enough, after the alarm was given, to draw them to the works, unless they were surprised.

It was not only the town malignants that murmured at the drawing up of the ordnance, but Dr. Plumptre, hearing that the forces were to march away, was raging at it; whereupon being answered, that it was more for the public interest of the cause, in great passion he replied, " What is the cause to me if my goods be lost?" The governor told him, he might prevent that hazard and secure them in the castle. He replied, " It pitied him to soil them, and he had rather the enemy had them, than they should be spoiled in removing." While this was boiling upon his spirit, he met the governor, with some other gentlemen, in the street, and began to rail at him for countenancing the godly townsmen, whom he called a company of puritanical prick-eared rascals, and said, that the worst of the malignants the governor had sent out of the town, were honester men than the best of those he favoured; and in spite of his teeth he would have three of the most eminent of them turned out of the castle. The governor telling him, he would maintain them as the most faithful friends to the cause, Plumptre replied he was as honest to the cause as the governor. " No," said the governor (who was not ignorant of his atheism), " that you cannot be, for you go not upon the same principles." The doctor told him, it was false, with such uncivil insolence, that the governor struck him, at which he departed quietly home; and after two or three days, retired with his wife and children to the house of Mr. Parkyns of Bunney, who was at that time in arms against the parliament, where he stayed till the parliament-forces were routed, and Nottingham castle summoned and preparing for a siege; and then he sent a ridiculous challenge to the governor, with all the foolish circumstances imaginable, which the governor, at that present, only answered with contempt. The pretence he made was a distress, wherein the committee had employed some of the governor's soldiers, for the levying of an assessment, which his brother would not pay, and this distress he called the governor's affront to his family. Though these passages may seem too impertinent here, yet as they have been grounds and beginnings of injurious prosecutions, wherewith the governor was afterwards much exercised, it was not altogether unnecessary to insert them; since even these little things were links in the chain of providences which measured out his life.[1]

All the horse that had been raised in Nottinghamshire, marched away with Sir John Meldrum, namely, the troops of Colonel Thornhagh, Major Ireton, Captain White, and Captain Farmer; which, together with Captain Lomax and Captain Schrimpshire's foot companies, joining with Colonel Cromwell's men, marched to Gainsborough, and engaged those that besieged it, and were victorious, killing their general, Sir Charles Cavendish, with many more commanders, and some hundreds of soldiers; and this was opportunely done, as my Lord Newcastle was hastening to come over the water and join them, and who, by a bridge of boats, passed all his army over, and came near Gainsborough, just in a season to behold the rout of all his men. The parliament's forces expected he would have fallen upon them, and drew up in a body and faced him, but he advanced not; so they contented themselves by relieving Gainsborough, and made a very honourable retreat to Lincoln; but Gainsborough not being fortified, nor provided, this relief did not much advantage them, for my Lord Newcastle again besieged it, which was rendered to him, after eight days, upon conditions honourable for the defendants, though they were not performed by the besiegers; for all my Lord Willoughby's men were disarmed contrary to articles,[2] and with them, some of the Nottingham soldiers that had gone into the town to refresh themselves, and so were shut up with them, when my lord laid siege to it; the rest had gone to Lincoln. They had behaved themselves very well in the fight, when Captain White received a wound in his hand in the forlorn hope; Colonel Thornhagh, who had fought very gallantly, was

---

[1] To some readers the recital of these bickerings and intrigues may seem little interesting, to others highly so; certain it is, that whoever refuses to read them, refuses to acquaint himself with the temper of those times, which they characterise in the most peculiar manner.

[2] Particularly noticed by Whitelock.

taken prisoner, and after he was stripped of his arms and coat, a major of the enemy's, whom the colonel had slightly wounded in the fervour of the fight, came and basely wounded the colonel, being disarmed, so that he left him for dead. But by the good providence of God, that wound, by which the enemy intended to give him death, gave him liberty; for coming to himself a little after his hurt, he crept into one of his own tenant's houses, and there had his wounds bound up, and found means to get to Lincoln, from whence all the forces that went from Nottingham dispersed into different services. Major Ireton quite left Colonel Thornhagh's regiment, and began an inseparable league with Colonel Cromwell, whose son-in-law he afterwards was. None of them could return to Nottingham, by reason of my Lord Newcastle's army, which lay between them and their home.

And now it was time for them at Nottingham to expect my Lord Newcastle, which the governor made provision for with all the diligence that it was possible under so many difficulties and obstacles, which would to any one else have been discouragements; but he had so high a resolution that nothing conquered it. The townsmen, through discontent at the drawing out of the forces, whereby their houses, families, and estates were exposed, began to envy, then to hate the castle, as grieved that anything should be preserved when all could not; and indeed those who were more concerned in private interests than in the cause itself, had some reason, because the neighbourhood of the castle, when it was too weak to defend them, would endanger them. In this hate and discontent, all the soldiers being townsmen, except some of the governor's own company, they resolved they would not go into the castle to behold the ruin of their houses; little considering that when the governor first came into Nottingham to defend them, at their earnest desire, he left a house and a considerable estate to the mercy of the enemy, rather desiring to advance the cause than to secure his own stake; but their mean and half-affected hearts were not capable of such things. The governor, perceiving this defection, set some of the most zealous honest men to find out how many there were in the town who, neglecting all private interests, would cheerfully and freely come in and venture all with him; intending, if he could not have found enough to defend the place, that he would have sent to other neighbouring garrisons to have borrowed some. Upon this inquiry, it was found that many of Colonel Pierrepont's own company were desirous to come in, but first wished to know their colonel's resolution as to how he would dispose of them; whereupon a hall was called, and the danger of the place declared to the whole town, that they might have time to provide for their goods and persons before the enemy came upon them. The colonel being present, his company asked him what he would advise them to do; to whom his answer was, " You have but three ways to choose, either leave the town and secure yourselves in some other parliament-garrisons, or list into the castle,[1] or stand on the works and have your throats cut." Two or three days after this he went to his mother's, and carried his children with part of his goods, and sent his wife to Sir Gervas Clifton's house. Notwithstanding this public resolution in the hall to his company, he told them, and many others in private, that he preferred the interest of the town above that of his life, and would expose his life for the good of it, and stand on the works of the town as long as they could be defended, and when they could no longer be kept, he would retire to some other parliament-garrison. Others he told, he scorned that his colours should serve in the castle; that if his company went up thither he would get him a new one, which should follow him wherever he went, and many more such things in private; but he openly, both to the governor and others, approved and encouraged their going into the castle. According to his advice, the townsmen, as they were diversely affected, disposed of themselves; the malignants all laid down their arms and stayed in the town, but some honest and well-affected, not bold enough to stand the hazard, went to other parliament - garrisons and served there; others secured themselves, their goods, and families in the country; some enlisted into the castle; one Alderman Nix, captain of two hundred, gave up his commission, and disbanded all his men except about forty, who came into the castle and filled up the broken companies there. At length, out of all the

[1] The particular account which has before been spoken of, has in this place a little difference of expression, which yet perhaps signifies much. There Colonel Pierrepont says, " List into the castle with *John*, for so in a jesting way he used to call Colonel Hutchinson," alluding no doubt to his frank and downright mode of speaking and acting.

four companies and the whole town, about 300 men enlisted into the castle.

The governor had procured forty barrels of powder, and two thousand weight of match from London, and had increased the store of provision as much as the present poverty of their condition would permit him. Then the committee of Nottingham, so many of them as were remaining in the town, and all the ministers of the parliament's party there, came up to the castle, and, with the officers of the garrison, ate at the governor's, to his very great charge; considering that he was so far from receiving pay at that time, that all the money he could procure of his own credit, or take up with others, he was forced to expend for the several necessities of the soldiers and garrison; yet were the soldiers then, and a long time after, kept together as long as they could live, without any pay, and afterwards paid part in victuals, and the rest run on in arrears.[1]

The townsmen who came into the castle disposed their families into several villages in the country; and at length a trumpet was sent, for a safe conduct for a gentleman, from my Lord Newcastle; and having it, Major Cartwright came from him, with a summons for the delivery of the town and castle, to which the committee for the town, and the governor for the castle, returned a civil defiance in writing, about the 10th day of August. Cartwright, having received it, and being treated with wine by the governor and the rest of the officers, grew bold in the exercise of an abusive wit he had, and told both the Mr. Hutchinsons that they were sprightly young men, but when my lord should come with his army, he would find them in other terms, beseeching my lord to spare them, as misled young men, and to suffer them to march away with a cudgel, and "then," said he, "shall I stand behind my lord's chair and laugh." At which the governor, being angry, told him he was much mistaken, for

---

[1] In all the histories of those times we read so much of the soldiers' complaints of want of pay, and of auditing their officers' accounts, which being no way reconcilable with modern practice, makes one suppose the officers fraudulent, and the soldiers mutinous; but this opinion will be corrected by observing what is here recited. Hence we shall likewise conceive a high idea of the virtue of those men, who started forth out of every rank of life to devote themselves to the service of God and their country, and persevered through such privations and difficulties; and consider their interference in the settling the constitution of their country, for which they had fought, in a far different light from the tumult and mutiny of mercenary soldiers.

he scorned ever to yield on any terms, to a papistical army led by an atheistical general.[1]   Mr. George Hutchinson told him, " If my lord would have that poor castle he must wade to it in blood." Which words they say he told his general. After these summonses were received, the governor drew all his soldiers into the castle, and committed the guard of the town to the aldermen, who were to set guards of fifty in a night, according to their wards.   Then calling together his soldiers, he once again represented to them their condition, and told them, that being religious and honest men, he could be assured no extremity would make them fail in what they found themselves strong enough to undertake; and therefore he should not fear to let them freely understand their danger, which yet they had power to shun, and therefore whatever misery might be the issue of their undertaking, they could not justly impute it to him, it being their own election.   For after this summons they must expect the enemy, and to be reduced to the utmost extremity by them that thought could reach.   It must not move them to see their houses flaming, and, if need were, themselves firing them for the public advantage, or to see the pieces of their families cruelly abused and consumed before them; they must resolve upon hard duty, fierce assaults, poor and sparing diet, perhaps famine, and the want of all comfortable accommodations. Nor was there very apparent hope of relief at last, but more than common hazard of losing their lives, either in defence of their fort or of the place; which, for want of good fortifi- cations, and through disadvantage of a neighbouring mount and building, was not, in human probability, tenable against such an army as threatened it.   All which, for his own part, he was resolved on; and if any of them found their courage failing, he only desired they would provide for their safety in time elsewhere, and not prejudice him and the public interest so highly, as they would do, to take upon them the defence of the castle, except they could be content to lay down their

---

[1] Charles the First, when accused of retaining papists, denied having any in his army, and tried to have it believed that those which the Earl of Newcastle had enlisted were unknown to him, although there is ample proof that it was done by his order; that nobleman acted in a much more ingenuous manner, and, as is before related in a quotation from Sir P. Warwick's *Memoirs*, turned the imputation into a jest; probably his indifference about the religion of his soldiers caused the epithet of *atheistical* to be applied to him, certainly without sufficient reason.

lives and all their interests in it. The soldiers were none of them terrified at the dangers which threatened their undertaking; but at the latter end of August took, upon the solemn fast-day, the national covenant, and besides it, a particular mutual covenant between them and the governor, to be faithful to each other, and to hold out the place to the death, without entertaining any parley, or accepting any terms from the enemy. This the governor was forced to do to confirm them, for he had his experience not only of the ungodly and ill-affected, but even of the godly themselves, who thought it scarcely possible for any one to continue a gentleman, and firm to a godly interest, and therefore repaid all his vigilancy and labours for them with a very unjust jealousy.[1] The governor of Newark was his cousin-german, to whom he was forced, against his nature, to be more uncivil than to any others that were governors in that place. Whether it was that the dissension of brethren is always most spitefully pursued, or that Sir Richard Byron, as it was reported, suffered under the same suspicions on his side, it is true they were to each other the most uncivil enemies that can be imagined. After this summons, my Lord Newcastle came not, according to their bravadoes, but diverted his army to Hull, to besiege my Lord Fairfax there; they of Newark having gotten him to send this summons upon confidence, knowing the condition of the place, that it would have been yielded to a piece of paper. The governor immediately set upon the fortification of his castle, made a work behind it, another on the Line side, turned the dovecote into a platform, and made a court of guard in Mortimer's Hole.

At this time Sir Thomas Hutchinson died in London,[2] and gave all his personal estate, and all that was unsettled at Mr. Hutchinson's marriage, to his second wife and her

---

[1] It passes for a saying of Charles the Second, that the presbyterian might be a very good religion, but it was not the religion of a gentleman; these good folks seem to have been of the same mind. The French have taken care not to fall short in imitating this malicious prejudice, but stamp with the hated name of Aristocrat every person at all elevated above the vulgar, though ever so generous a friend of liberty.

[2] August 18, 1643, as appeared by his tombstone, under the communion table in St. Paul's, Covent Garden, London, and that he was 55 when he died. J. H.

A marginal note, written by Julius Hutchinson, grandfather of the editor.

children; at which his two sons had not the least repining thought, but out of tender love, were very much afflicted for his loss, and procured a pass from Newark for Mr. George Hutchinson, to go to London, to visit his mother and fetch mournings, which accordingly he did; and upon a letter the committee sent up by him, he brought down an order of parliament to allow a table to the governor and committee, whom Mr. Hutchinson had till that time entertained at his own cost, with all the officers of the garrison and the ministers, which was no small charge to him; but he had a noble heart, and could not basely evade the expense, which that place necessarily drew upon him, not only by the constant entertainment of the committee, officers, and ministers, and all parliament officers, that came and went through the garrison, but by relieving the poor soldiers, who had such short pay, that they were, for the most part, thirty weeks and more behind; and when they marched out at any time, the governor would not suffer them to take a cup of drink, unpaid for, in the country, but always, wherever they took any refreshment in their marches, paid it himself. He gave them besides much from his own house, especially when any of them were sick or wounded, and lent money to those who were most necessitous. All this run him into a great private debt, besides many thousands of pounds, which he engaged himself in with other gentlemen, and took up for the supply of the garrison and carrying on of the public service. Although the allowance for his table was much envied by those mean fellows, that never knew what the expense of a table was, and although it was to him some ease, yet it did not defray the third part of his expense in the service, being but ten pounds a week allowed by the state; and his expenses all that time, in the public service only, and not at all in any particular of his own family, being, as it was kept upon account, above fifteen hundred pounds a year. As soon as his father was dead, and rents became due to him, the enemies, in the midst of whom his estate lay, fetched in his tenants and imprisoned them, and took his rents; his estate was begged and promised by the king; those who lived not upon the place, flung up his grounds, and they lay unoccupied, while the enemy prevailed in the country. He was not so cruel as others were to their tenants, who made them pay over again those rents with which the enemy forced them to redeem themselves out of prison, but lost the most part of his rents, all the while the country was under the adverse power. He had some small stock of his own plundered, and his house, by the perpetual haunting of the enemy, defaced, and for want of inhabitation, rendered almost uninhabitable. For these things he had some subscriptions,[1] but never received one penny of recompense; and his arrears of pay, which he received after all the war was done, did not half pay the debts of those services contracted. But when he undertook this engagement, it was for the defence of his country's and God's cause, and he offered himself and all he had a willing sacrifice in the service; and rather praised God for what was saved, than repined at what was spent, it being above his expectation, that deliverance which God gave him out of his enemies' hands. He might have made many advantages by the spoil of his enemies, which was often brought in, and by other encroachments upon the country, which almost all the governors, on both sides, exacted everywhere else, but his heart abhorred it: the soldiers had all the prizes, and he never shared with them; all the malignants' goods the committee disposed of; and it ever grieved his heart to see the spoil of his neighbours, how justly soever they deserved it; but he chose all loss, rather than to make up himself [2] by violence and rapine. If in a judicial way, he was forced at any time, in discharge of his trust, to sign any harsh orders against any of the gentlemen of the country, it was with grief that they should deserve that severity; but this testi-

---

[1] By subscriptions are here meant acknowledgments or certificates given by the committees, which parliament professed to make good, but many times did not. But Col. Hutchinson's disinterestedness and devotion to the cause did not suffice to exempt him from calumny, for in Walker's *History of Independency*, p. 166, *et seq.*, a list is given of members of parliament, who were unduly returned, who held commands contrary to the self-denying ordinance, or had moneys or offices given them. And Colonel Hutchinson is accused of all *three*; how absurdly and unjustly every one must perceive. He was regularly elected to parliament in place of his father deceased: he had a regiment which he raised, and in a great degree subsisted himself; he had a government, which at the time of his undertaking it, was a charge others feared to accept, and which for a long time was a loss and a detriment to him, and at the end of all he fell far short of receiving as much as he had expended. In the same place, Mr. William Pierrepont is most invidiously accused of getting £40,000,—*but how? it was the personal estate of his own father!*

[2] Make himself up, make himself whole, reimburse himself.

mony is a truth of him, that in his whole actings in this cause, he never prosecuted any private lust, either of revenge, ambition, avarice, or vain glory, under a public vizard, but was most truly public-spirited. Conscience to God, and truth and righteousness, according to the best information he could get, engaged him in that party he took; that which engaged him, carried him through all along, though he encountered no less difficulties and contradictions from those of his own party, that were not of the same spirit he was, than he did from his enemies.

The death of Sir Thomas Hutchinson made every way a great reverse in the affairs of his eldest son, who had before been looked upon as his father's heir, and reverenced as much, or rather more, upon his father's score, than his own, so that no man durst attempt to injure him, whom they looked upon as under such a powerful protection. Sir Thomas and his fathers before him had ever deserved very well of their country, and, as lovers of their country, their neighbours had an implicit faith in all their dictates and actions, insomuch that Sir Thomas Hutchinson's single authority swayed with many, more than all the greater names of the country. But he at his death having divided, all things considered, his estate between the children of his two wives, though it be true the latter deserved more than they had, yet it is as true the first deserved not to be so much lessened as they were: and Mr. Hutchinson having been known to be the most pious and obedient son, from his childhood, that ever any father was blessed with, when it came to be known that his father had given away all that was in his power to give from him, those that had a great reverence and esteem for Sir Thomas would not believe him to be so defective in justice as to do this without some secret cause; and therefore it was given out that he was displeased with his son's engagement, and for that cause disposed away so much of his estate from them. But that was not so; indeed, at the time of his death the parliament's interest was so low, that he might well look upon them as lost persons, and so what he gave away to the unengaged infant he might well look upon as all that could be preserved. Mr. Hutchinson had only an allowance from his father, while he lived, which was duly paid him; but as soon as he died all his estate was seized by the enemy, who had so much desire not to injure publicly a person so popular, that they disturbed not Sir Thomas's tenants while he lived, though he continued with the parliament, and faithful to their interest; because he was moderate, and one that applied all his endeavours to peace, which he did not out of policy, but out of conscience to his country, and by a wise foresight of the sad consequences of a conquest by either side; for he had often expressed, that accommodation was far more desirable than war, and he dreaded that the spirits of those men would become most insolent after conquest, who were so violently bent to prosecute a war; that some of them whom we have since known to be vile apostates, then professed that they abhorred accommodation. This report of Sir Thomas's dislike of his son's engagement was raised and dispersed by those who themselves were ill-affected to it; but, however, it abated all the respect men had for him, upon every account but his own. Those who had entertained a secret envy of him, now feared not to manifest it, and began to work secret mines, to blow him up on all sides; but God was with him, and disappointed all his enemies, and made his virtues more illustrious by the oppositions they encountered, and by the removal of all those props of wealth and power which are necessary to hold up weaker fabrics.[1]

[1] Here is in the original a marginal note in the following words: "The division of Sir Thomas Hutchinson's estate. Sir Thomas Hutchinson being mightily beloved in the country, and a moderate man, using all his endeavours for peace, his estate was never plundered in his lifetime; and though it is here falsely insinuated that he approved of his son's conduct in taking arms against the king, it is most true that he was extremely afflicted at it, being altogether for peace, and condemned such rash counsels as arms on both sides; and the miseries he saw his king and country involved in were certainly the occasion of his death: and though Sir Thomas Hutchinson sat longer in the house than many honest men, it was only in hopes by his moderate counsels to effect a happy peace between his king and country. All this I have heard attested by his lady and relict, my grandmother. Teste J. Hutchinson." This is that testimony of Lady Katharine Hutchinson which was spoken of in the preface, and which, in attempting to impeach the veracity of the author in a single point, contributes largely to corroborate it in all. In the very instance before us there seems much more reason for the opinion of Mrs. Hutchinson than of Lady Katharine: Sir Thomas Hutchinson had before been imprisoned for his opposition to the court; was in this parliament on all committees for the reform of religion; sat with the parliament after the war was deeply engaged in; sent his sons arms, and promoted their desires to the parliament: it is incredible that he should have any great objection to the part they took, other than the general one of regretting that arms were taken on either side. The most probable thing is that this lady, being of the same party and opinion as her

Soon after the death of his father, one Mr. Ayscough, a gentleman of the country, allied to Sir Richard, since Lord Byron, then governor of Newark, came to the governor of Nottingham, and told him that Sir Richard Byron, out of that tender, natural affection which he ever had for him, and still preserved, desired him now to consider his wife and children, and the loss of his whole estate, which was inevitable, if he persisted in the engagement he was in; that some had already been suing to the Earl of Newcastle for it; but if he would return to his obedience to the king, he might not only preserve his estate, but have what reward he pleased to propound for so doing. To which the governor telling him this was a thing he ought to scorn, Mr. Ayscough told him that Sir Richard had, only out of love and tender compassion to him, given him this employment, with many protestations how much Sir Richard desired to employ all his interest to save him, if it were possible, and therefore begged of him that if he would still persist in this party, that he would yet quit himself of this garrison, and go into my Lord of Essex's army; for there, he said, Sir Richard would find pretence to save his rents for him for the present, and his estate for the future; for, said he, he can plead, " you were an inconsiderate young man, rashly engaged, and dares assure himself of your pardon; but to keep a castle against your king is a rebellion of so high a nature, that there will be no colour left to ask favour for you." The governor told him he should deliver the same propositions, and receive his answer, before some witnesses; whereupon he carried the gentleman to two of the committee, before whom he repeated his message, and the governor bade him return Sir Richard this answer, " That except he found his own heart prone to such treachery, he might consider there was, if nothing else, so much of a Byron's blood in him, that he should very much scorn to betray or quit a trust he had undertaken; but the grounds he went on were such, that he very much despised such a thought as to sell his faith for base rewards or

brother and family, and jealous of Sir Thomas Hutchinson's children by his former wife, influenced him to their disadvantage in the making of his will, and set up these reasons to countenance it after his death. The other estates of Sir T. Hutchinson in Nottinghamshire were fully equal, if not superior, in value to that of Owthorpe. This being the only instance wherein the truth of the narrative is called in question, and this certainly invidiously, if not unjustly, we may safely say we have the testimony of an adversary in our favour to all the rest.

fears, and therefore could not consider the loss of his estate, which his wife was as willing to part with as himself in this cause, wherein he was resolved to persist, in the same place in which it had pleased God to call him [1] to the defence of it."

About this time a woman was taken, whereof the committee had before been informed that she carried intelligence between Colonel Pierrepont and his mother, the countess of Kingston. The woman was now going through Nottingham, with letters from the old countess to her daughter-in-law, the colonel's wife, who was then at Clifton, Sir Gervas Clifton's house. In this packet there was a letter drawn, which the countess advised her daughter to sign, to be sent to Colonel Stanton, one of the king's colonels, to entreat back from him some goods of her husband's, which he had plundered; wherein there were these expressions: "That though her husband was unfortunately engaged in the unhappy rebellion, she hoped ere long he would approve himself a loyal subject to his majesty." The committee having read these letters, sealed them up again, and inclosed them in another to the colonel, then at Derby, telling him, that having intercepted such letters, and not knowing whether his wife might follow her mother's advice, which if she should would prove very dishonourable to him, they had chosen rather to send the letters to him than to her. The colonel was vexed that they had opened them, but for the present took no notice of it. All the horse having been drawn out of Nottingham to the relief of Gainsborough, and the Newarkers, knowing that the garrison was utterly destitute, plundered all the country even to the walls of Nottingham; upon which some godly men offered themselves to bring in their horses, and form a troop for the defence of the country, and one Mr. Palmer, a minister, had a commission to be their captain.[2] This man had a bold, ready, earnest way of preaching, and lived holily and regularly as to outward conversation, whereby he got a great reputation among the godly; and this reputation swelled his spirit, which was very vain-glorious, covetous,

[1] Notice is taken by Whitelocke of several attempts to prevail on Colonel Hutchinson to betray his trust, and of his steady adherence to it: there will be seen other instances more remarkable than this; but here are two things extremely well worth notice; this elegant and forcible apostrophe to Sir Richard Byron; and the patriotic and disinterested devotion of Mrs. Hutchinson to the cause, at least a rare example in her sex.

[2] This, if not unique, is at least a singular trait.

contentious, and ambitious. He had so insinuated himself as to make these godly men desire him for their captain, which he had more vehement longing after than they, yet would have it believed that it was rather pressed upon him, than he pressed into it; and therefore being at that time in the castle with his family, and feeding at the governor's table, who gave him room in his own lodgings, and all imaginable respect, he came to the governor and his wife, telling them that these honest people pressed him very much to be their captain, and desiring their friendly and Christian advice whether he should accept or refuse it. They freely told him, that having entered into a charge of another kind, they thought it not fit for him to engage in this; and that he might as much advance the public service, and satisfy the men, in marching with them in the nature of a chaplain as in that of a captain. He, that asked not counsel to take any contrary to his first resolve, went away confused when he found he was not advised as he would have been, and said he would endeavour to persuade them to be content; and afterwards said, they would not be otherwise satisfied, and so he was forced to accept the commission. The governor, having only declared his own judgment when he was asked, as a Christian ought to do according to his conscience, left the captain to act according to his own, and censured him not, but entertained him with the same freedom and kindness he had done before; but the man, being guilty of the avarice and ambition of his own heart, never afterwards looked upon the governor with a clear eye, but sought to blow up all factions against him whenever he found opportunity, and in the meantime dissembled it as well as he could. And now, before his troop was well raised, Colonel Thornhagh being recovered, brought back his troop from Lincoln, and both the troops quartered in the town; which being a bait to invite the enemy, the governor gave charge to all that belonged to the castle, being about three hundred men, that they should not upon any pretence whatever be out of their quarters; but they having, many of them, wives and better accommodations in the town, by stealth disobeyed his commands, and seldom left any more in the castle than what were upon the guard.

The townsmen were every night out upon the guard of the town, according to the wards of the alderman; but the most of them being disaffected, the governor, fearing treachery, had determined to quarter the horse in those lanes which were next to the castle, and to block up the lanes for the better securing them. Just the night before these lanes should have been blocked up, Alderman Toplady, a great malignant, having the watch, the enemy was, by treachery, let into the town, and no alarm given to the castle. Though there were two muskets at the gate where they entered, both of them were surrendered without one shot to give notice; and all the horse, and about two parts of the castle soldiers, were betrayed, surprised, and seized on in their beds, but there were not above fourscore of the castle foot taken; the rest hid themselves, and privately stole away, some into the country, some by night came up to the castle and got in, in disguises, by the river side; but the cavaliers were possessed of the town, and no notice at all given to the castle. When, at the beating of reveille, some of the soldiers, that had been on the watch all night, were going down into the town to refresh themselves, they were no sooner out of the castle gates but some of the enemy's musketeers discharged upon them, and they hasting back, got in with such care that the enemy was prevented of their design of falling in with them. They brought a strong alarm into the castle, when the governor coming forth, was exceedingly vexed to find that his men were, so many of them, contrary to his command, wanting in their quarters; but it was no time to be angry, but to apply himself to do what was possible to preserve the place; wherefore he immediately despatched messengers by a private sally-port, to Leicester and Derby, to desire their assistance, either to come and help to beat the enemy out of the town, or to lend him some foot to help keep the castle, in which there were but fourscore men, and never a lieutenant nor any head officer but his brother, nor so much as a surgeon among them. As soon as the governor had despatched his messengers he went up to the towers, and from thence played his ordnance into the town, which seldom failed of execution upon the enemy; but there was an old church, called St. Nicholas Church, whose steeple so commanded the platform that the men could not play the ordnance without woolpacks before them. From this church the bullets played so thick into the outward castle-yard, that they could not pass from one gate to the other, nor relieve the guards, but with very great hazard; and one weak old man was shot the first day, who, for want of a surgeon, bled to death before they could carry him up to the governor's wife, who at that time supplied that want as well as she could; but at night the governor and his men dug a trench between the two gates, through which they afterwards better secured their passage. In the meantime the cavaliers that came from Newark, being about six hundred, fell to ransack and plunder all the honest men's houses in the town, and the cavaliers of the town, who had called them in, helped them in this work. Their prisoners they at first put into the sheep-pens in the market-place,[1] whereupon an honest townsman, seeing four or five commanders go into his own house, procured a cunning boy that came with him, while the enemy regarded more their plunder than their prisoners, to run privately up to the castle and give them notice, who presently sent a cannon bullet into the house. The cavaliers called in all the country as soon as they were in the town, and made a fort at the Trent bridges, and thither they carried down all their considerable plunder and prisoners. The next day after Sir Richard Byron had surprised the town, Mr. Hastings, since made lord of Loughborough, then governor of Ashby-de-la-Zouch, came with a body of about four hundred men; but being displeased that the plunder was begun before he came, he returned again and left the Newark gentlemen to themselves; who, as they made a fort at the bridges, threw down the half moons and bulwarks that had been raised about the town. They stayed five days, but very unquietly, for the cannon and muskets from the castle failed not of execution daily upon many of them, and they durst not in all that time go to bed. The third day Major Cartwright sent a letter, desiring the governor or his brother to come and meet him in St. Nicholas church, and promised them safe passage and return; but the governor read the letter to his soldiers, and commanded a red flag to be set upon the tower to bid them defiance, and shot three pieces of cannon at the steeple in answer to his desired parley.

Five days the enemy stayed in the town, and all that time the governor and his soldiers were none of them off from the guard, but if they slept, which they never did in the night, it

[1] It appears, by Deering's account of Nottingham, that these once occupied a considerable portion of the market-place.

was by the side of them that watched. At length, on Saturday, September 23, in the afternoon, the governor saw a great many goods and persons going over the Line bridge, and not knowing what it meant, sent some cannon bullets after them; when on the other side of the town he discerned a body of men, whom he knew not at first, whether to be friends or foes, but having at that time about eightscore men in the castle, for in that five days' space fourscore were come in by stealth, he caused them all to be drawn out in the castleyard, and perceiving that those he last saw were friends, he sent out his brother, Major Hutchinson, with all the musketeers that could be spared, to help drive the enemy out of the town. They having effected what they came for, in fortifying the bridges, had nothing more to do but to get safe off, which they endeavoured with more haste and disorder than became good and stout soldiers. When Major Hutchinson came into the town with his men, they, greedy of knowing what was become of their wives and houses, dropped so fast from behind him to make the inquiry, that they had left him at the head of only sixteen men, when Sir Richard Byron, with Captain Hacker, followed by a whole troop of horse and a company of foot, came upon him. The major commanded his men to charge them, which they did, but shot over; yet falling in with them pell-mell, they had gotten Sir Richard Byron down, and they had his hat, but he escaped, though his horse was so wounded that it fell dead in the next street.

These men that came to the governor's relief were Captain White with his troop, who were quartered at Leicester, on his return from Lincolnshire, from whence he was coming back to Nottingham; and at Leicester he met the messenger the governor had sent for assistance, which he prosecuted so well, that from the two garrisons of Leicester and Derby, with his own troop, he brought about four hundred men. As soon as they were come into the town, Sir John Gell's men, seeing the cavaliers had a mind to be gone, interrupted them not, but being as dexterous at plunder as at fight, they presently went to Toplady's house, who had betrayed the town, and plundered it and some others, while the governor's soldiers were busy in clearing the town of the enemy. When they had done this, the governor did what he could to restrain the plunder; but the truth is, Gell's men were nimble youths at that work, yet there was not very much mischief done by them. Toplady's house fared the worst, but his neighbours saved much of his goods; he himself, with several other townsmen and countrymen, who had been very active against the well-affected, at this time were brought up prisoners to the castle. There were not above five-and-twenty of the Newark soldiers taken; how many were slain at their going off, and during the time of their stay, we could not certainly tell, because they had means of carrying them off by the bridge, where they left Captain Hacker governor [1] of their new fort with fourscore men. Their prisoners and plunder they sent away in boats to Newark; many of the townsmen went with them, carrying away not only their own but their neighbours' goods; and much more had been carried away, but that the unexpected sally from the castle prevented them. Dr. Plumptre, one of the committee of Nottingham, whom they found prisoner at the marshal's house in the town, and released, went out of the town with them. This man, when he had provoked the governor to strike him, for his malicious and uncivil railings against him for the respect he showed to the godly men of the town, had retired to the house of a malignant gentleman in arms against the parliament; had received a protection from the governor of Newark, and had divers meetings with the Newark officers; yet after all this had the impudence to come into the town of Nottingham: and in all the taverns and ale-houses he came into, he belched out abominable scoffs and taunts against the governor and the committee-men, before Colonel Thornhagh's face, who commanded him out of the room for it; and upon information of these things to the governor and the committee, he was sent for by some musketeers, and the enemy's protection for himself and his goods being found about him, he was committed prisoner, but there being no good accommodation for him in the castle, the governor, in more civility than he deserved, suffered him to be in the town, whence he went with them, and afterwards

---

[1] The brother of Colonel Hacker, who was tried, condemned, and executed for attending the execution of Charles the First. This brother, who served the king during the whole war with great zeal, could not obtain the pardon of Colonel Hacker, nor prevent the confiscation of his family estate, which was granted to the Duke of York, the king's brother, from whom he was obliged to ransom it at a high rate. It lay at Colston Basset, joining to Owthorpe.

retired to Derby. At the same time, the cavaliers having taken some prisoners upon the parliament's score who lived quietly in the country, the committee had fetched in some gentlemen's sons of their party, who were left at their fathers' houses; whereof one was remaining at the marshal's house when the cavaliers came into the town, whom the governor suffered to be there upon his parole, there being no good accommodation for him in the castle. Him the cavaliers would have had to have gone away with them, but he would not; which handsome behaviour so pleased the governor, that he freely gave him his liberty without exchange.[1]

As soon as the enemy was driven out of the town, the governor brought down two pieces of ordnance to the market-place, and entreated the soldiers that were come from Leicester and Derby to march with him immediately, to assault them in their fort at the bridges, before they had time to put themselves in order, and re-collect their confused souls, after their chase; but the mayor of Derby, an old dull-headed Dutchman, said ten thousand men could not do it, and could by no means be entreated to go on, nor to stay one day longer, but to stand by, while the governor made the attempt, with his own men. He, when he saw he could not prevail, thought it not convenient, at that time, to urge his men beyond their power, after they had had a week of such sore labour, and so, much discontented that he could not effect his desire, he drew back his ordnance into the castle. Here his women, while the men were all otherwise employed, had provided him as large a supper as the time and present condition would permit, at which he entertained all the strangers, and his own officers and gentlemen.

There was a large room, which was the chapel, in the castle: this they had filled full of prisoners, besides a very bad prison, which was no better than a dungeon, called the Lion's Den; and the new Captain Palmer, and another minister, having nothing else to do, walked up and down the castle-yard, insulting and beating the poor prisoners as they were brought up. In the encounter, one of the Derby captains was slain, and five of our men hurt, who for want of

---

[1] This story resembles some of those recited in the early and virtuous times of the Roman republic. Such anecdotes serve to relieve the mind, fatigued with reading of the crimes and follies of mankind.

another surgeon, were brought to the governor's wife, and she having some excellent balsams and plasters in her closet, with the assistance of a gentleman that had some skill, dressed all their wounds, whereof some were dangerous, being all shots, with such good success, that they were all well cured in convenient time.[1] After our wounded men were dressed, as she stood at her chamber-door, seeing three of the prisoners sorely cut, and carried down bleeding into the Lion's Den, she desired the marshal to bring them in to her, and bound up and dressed their wounds also: which while she was doing, Captain Palmer came in and told her his soul abhorred to see this favour to the enemies of God; she replied, she had done nothing but what she thought was her duty, in humanity to them, as fellow-creatures, not as enemies. But he was very ill satisfied with her, and with the governor presently after, when he came into a very large room where a very great supper was prepared, and more room and meat than guests; to fill up which the governor had sent for one Mr. Mason, one of the prisoners, a man of good fashion, who had married a relation of his, and was brought up more in fury, than for any proof of guilt in him, and I know not whether two or three others, the governor had not called to meat with them; for which Captain Palmer bellowed loudly against him, as a favourer of malignants and cavaliers.[2] Who could have thought this godly, zealous man, who could scarce eat his supper for grief to see the enemies of God thus favoured, should have afterwards entered into a conspiracy, against the governor, with those very same persons, who now so much provoked his zeal? But the governor took no notice of it, though he set the very soldiers a muttering against himself and his wife, for these poor humanities.

The next day the neighbouring forces returned home. Colonel Thornhagh having lost most of his troop, went to

[1] The reader will remember that the mother of Mrs. Hutchinson had patronised and assisted Sir Walter Raleigh, when prisoner in the Tower, in his chemical experiments, and had acquired a little knowledge of medicine; whether her daughter had obtained instructions from her mother, or the mother herself was here (for she passed the latter part of her life with her daughter, and died in her house at Owthorpe), is uncertain. Mrs. Hutchinson was certainly an extraordinary woman, and this is not one of the least singular, nor least amiable instances of it.

[2] Behold a presbyterian and a sectary, a Levite and a Samaritan!

London to get another. Captain White stayed at Nottingham with his, where intelligence being given that the cavaliers intended to possess themselves of Broxtowe and Woollerton (two gentlemen's houses each within two miles of Nottingham), Captain Palmer was sent, with the remainder of his men to keep Broxtowe-house, and the governor's captain-lieutenant, with his company, to Woollerton. The governor, at Nottingham, broke up the Line Bridge to prevent the cavaliers coming suddenly by that way into the town; then he blocked up the lanes next the castle, and cut up all the hedges, that were dangerous to make approaches to the castle; and having the experience of the mischief of it, pulled down St. Nicholas's church by the advice of the committee.[1]

Presently after the cavaliers were gone out of town, some naughty people, set on by them, fired the town, but it was quenched without burning above two or three houses; yet for a fortnight together it was perpetually attempted, fire being laid to hay-barns and other combustible places, insomuch that the women were forced to walk nightly by fifties to prevent the burning;[2] which the committee perceiving to be attempted by the instigation of the Newark gentlemen, they wrote them word, that if they forbade not their instruments, if so much as one house were fired, they would fire all the cavaliers' houses near them. The gentlemen returned them a scornful letter, full of taunts and disdain, but after that no more houses were attempted with fire.

The Derby soldiers, when they returned home, being asked why they left the cavaliers at the bridges unassaulted, made answer, they would have beaten them out, but the governor would not lend them a piece of ordnance out of his castle;

[1] It is said, in Deering's *History of Nottingham*, that this church was pulled down by Colonel Hutchinson, and the bells carried to Owthorpe; which last was at that time impossible, the enemy being in possession of the Vale of Belvoir and the ways to it. And moreover, the church at Owthorpe was, as Deering in another place observes, too small to contain them. In Throsby's edition of Thoroton, he remarks that neither Deering nor Thoroton were properly acquainted with the circumstances of that affair, and mentions, that in digging near the foundation of the present tower (for the church has been rebuilt), a bell was found, evidently broken to pieces at the demolition of the church; probably by the cannon-shot which was sent in answer to Major Cartwright's message. The situation of this church was both very near to the castle, and on a parallel height.

[2] This is a curious fact, and points out a way of turning to use and profit the timorousness and watchfulness of her sex.

which false report, when the governor heard, piqued him
heartily, being so notorious a lie; for he drew down two
pieces of ordnance, and could not entreat them to do more
than stand by, while he attempted it with his own men; but
their Major Molanus, being an old soldier, discouraged our
soldiers, and told them it was a vain and impossible attempt.
For this cause, the governor resolved he would set upon it
alone, whenever it was seasonable; and watching an opportunity, he soon took it, at a time when intelligence was
brought him that all the forces Newark could send forth,
were gone upon a design into Lincolnshire. Then, on the
Lord's day, under colour of hearing a sermon at the great
church in the town, he went thither, and after sermon, from
the steeple, took a view of the fort at the bridges; no one
perceiving his design, but his engineer, who was with him,
and took a full survey of Hacker's works. Then, after
supper, he called the committee together, and communicated
his intentions to them, which they approved of. So all that
night he spent in preparations against the next morning; he
sent away orders to the horse and foot that lay at Broxtowe
to come to him in the morning by eight o'clock, with all the
pioneers they could gather up in the country; he sent into
the town, and caused all the pioneers there to be brought up,
under pretence of making a breastwork before the castle-
gates, and pretending to set them upon the platforms, caused
all the cannon-baskets to be filled, which he intended for
rolling trenches. All things, betimes in the morning, being
gotten into perfect readiness, and so discreetly ordered, that
the enemy had no notice from any of their friends in town,
nor knew anything of the design, till it was ready; the
governor, about eleven o'clock on Monday morning, marched
out, although the weather at that time, being very tempestu-
ous and rainy, seemed to have combined with his enemies to
withstand the attempt; but the soldiers were rather animated
than discouraged, thinking that difficulties, after they were
vanquished, would increase their glory. So when the ugly
storm had, for three or four hours, wasted itself in its fury on
them, it fell at their feet, and no more envious clouds obscured
the cheerful face of heaven, so long as they continued in the
field. The governor's own company marched through the
meadows, and gave the alarm to the enemy's foot, while Mr.
George Hutchinson's company went through the lanes, to

gain a nook, which was very advantageous for the approaches of our men, and of which they easily possessed themselves, and then advancing, planted their colours within musket-shot of the fort. Although they planted so many colours, the governor had but eightscore foot, and a hundred horse, in all that went with him out of the castle, but he set the pioneers fairly among them to make the better show.

When the colours were thus planted, the pioneers were set at work to cast up a breastwork; and being left in a safe posture with the inferior officers, the governor and his brother went up to the castle, to order the drawing down of the ordnance. Meanwhile the cavaliers sallied out of their fort to gain the colours, at whose approach all the pioneers ran away from their works; but the soldiers kept their ground and their colours, and beat back the enemy into their own fort, killing some of them, whereof two were left dead before our men, whom they thought it not safe to carry off. Our horse meeting the flying pioneers, brought them back again to their works, which they continued all that day, and the cavaliers attempted no more sallies. At evening the ordnance were brought down and planted within musket-shot of the fort, and then the governor despatched a messenger to Derby to tell Sir John Gell, if he pleased to send any of his men, they might come and see the fort taken. Accordingly, on Tuesday the Dutch major came, with about sixscore foot and dragoons. Hard by the fort at the bridges, and at that side which our men approached, there were two houses full of coals, into which, if the cavaliers had put any men, they might have done much mischief to the assailants; wherefore the governor sent two or three soldiers, who very boldly went almost under their works and fired them both, by the light of which, they burning all night, the governor's men wrought all that night in their trenches, and cut a trench in the meadows, some of them calling to the cavaliers in the fort, and keeping them in abusive replies, one upon another, while the pioneers carried on their works. The governor and his brother, and all the other officers, continuing all night in the trenches with them, they behaved themselves so cheerfully, that the governor gave them the next morning twenty pounds; and they had very good drink and provisions brought them out of the garrison, which much encouraged them, but the governor's presence and alacrity among them much more. When the Derby men came on Tuesday, the Dutch major came down to the trenches, and told the governor that he wondered he would attempt the fort, for it was impregnable, and therefore much dissuaded him from going on, and said that he and his men would return. The governor told him that he and the soldiers with him were resolved to leave their lives rather than their attempt; and if they failed for want of seconding by that force which was sent with him to their assistance, let the blame lie on him. When the Derby officers saw him so resolute to persist, they, after much dissuasion and dispute, determined to stay, and the officers went up with the governor to supper in the castle, and the soldiers to quarters provided for them in the town: but after supper, the governor went down again, and stayed all night in the trenches with his men, and left them not as long as they stayed there, but only to fetch down what was necessary for them. He, his brother, and all the officers, were every night with them, and made them continue their custom of railing at each other in the dark, while they carried on their approaches. There was in the Trent, a little piece of ground of which, by damming up the water, the cavaliers had made an island; and while some of the soldiers held them in talk, others on Wednesday night cut the sluice, and by break of day on Thursday morning had pitched two colours in the island, within carbine-shot of the fort, and the governor's company had as much advanced their approach on the other side. When they in the fort saw, in the morning, how the assailants had advanced, while they were kept secure in talk all the night, they were extremely mad, and swore like devils, which made the governor and his men great sport: and then it was believed they in the fort began to think of flight; which the besiegers not expecting, still continued their approaches, and that day got forty yards nearer to the island and also to the other side. Although Sir John Gell's men came but on Tuesday, on Thursday the second messenger came from him, to call them back. The governor entreated them to stay that night and keep the trenches, while his men refreshed themselves: which they did, but his men would not go out of their trenches, but slept there to fit themselves for the assault, which the governor had resolved on for the morning, and for that purpose, after he had left them with all things provided in their trenches, he went to the castle to see the fire-balls and other necessaries for the assault brought down, and at three in the morning came to them, when the soldiers told him the cavaliers in the fort had for two hours left off shooting. He sent some soldiers then to the work sides to discover what this meant; but they, perceiving the place empty, went in and found that all the garrison had stolen away, and had left behind them fourscore sheep, a hundred loads of coals, twenty quarters of oats, much hay, a great deal of plundered lead, and a fort so strong, that if they had had such courage as became men of their profession, they would never have quitted it. They left all their works standing, and only broke up two arches of the Trent bridges, to hinder the governor's men from following them. Their flight was by that means secured, the river being so out that the horse could not ford over. Mr. George Hutchinson and his company were appointed to possess and keep the fort at the bridges, which he did; and the next week the garrison kept a day of solemn thanksgiving to God, for this success and the mercy in it, whereby all their men were preserved, notwithstanding their very bold adventures, so that not one of them was slain, and but four of them wounded, whereof three were so slightly hurt, that they returned again next day into the field. To increase their thanks to God, news was brought them that the same week the forces that went out from Newark, joined with Henderson's, had received a great overthrow by Cromwell; and that my Lord Newcastle had been forced to raise his siege of Hull with great loss and dishonour. Some time after the bridge was recovered, the horse went forth and brought in some oxen of Mr. John Wood's, a justice of the county, disaffected to the parliament, but not in action against them. He, following his oxen, came to the governor, and, after he had despatched his business, told him how Mr. Sutton would have once employed him on a message, to offer the governor any terms he would ask the king, to come over to his side and deliver up the castle to his use. Mr. Wood told him (Sutton), that such a message would not obtain credit, unless he had some propositions in writing; whereupon Sutton called for pen and ink, and wrote that he should offer the governor, if he would resign his castle, not only to be received into favour, but to have what reward of honour, money, or command, he himself would propound; which

paper when Mr. Wood had received, Sir Richard Byron came
in, and Mr. Sutton told him the business; to which Sir
Richard answered, he believed it would not take effect, for
he himself had made the like offers to him, and been rejected:[1] which Mr. Wood hearing, would not undertake the
employment, but the governor made him declare the story
to two of the gentlemen of the committee.

The governor not growing secure by his successes, was but
stirred up to more active preparations for the defence of
the place he had undertaken; and having a very ingenious
person, Mr. Hooper, who was his engineer, and one that
understood all kind of operations, in almost all things imaginable, they procured some saltpetre men and other necessary
labourers, and set up the making of powder and match in the
castle, both of which they made very good; they also cast
mortar pieces in the town, and finished many other inventions for the defence of the place.   The governor also caused
a mount near the castle to be bulwarked, and made a platform for ordnance, and raised a new work before the castle-
gates, to keep off approaches, and made a new in-work in the
fort at the bridges.

Sir Thomas Fairfax, being overmastered in the north, by
the Earl of Newcastle's great army, after his father was
retired into Hull, came with those horse that were left him,
into the Vale of Belvoir, and so visited Nottingham Castle;
where he and the commanders that were with him, considering of what advantage it was to the parliament to keep that
place, by reason of the commodious situation of it, and the
pass which might be there maintained, between the north
and south, and the happy retreat it might afford to their
northern forces, very much pressed the governor and the
committee to raise all the force they could, offering arms
and commissions for them: especially he pressed the governor
to complete a regiment for himself, which at that time he
would not accept, because Colonel Pierrepont had not yet
declared what he would do with his regiment.   The colonel
was then at Derby, whither some of his officers going to him,
to know what they should do, he dismissed them; yet
coming to the town, he gave out strange envious whispers,
and behaved himself so disingenuously to the governor, that

[1] This is the second instance of attempting Colonel Hutchinson's
fidelity, but the most remarkable one will be found in the sequel.

he had just cause to have no more regard for him; and being again importuned by Sir Thomas Fairfax, he received a commission to raise a regiment of twelve hundred. He presently recruited his own companies, and began to raise more: Mr. George Hutchinson was his lieutenant-colonel, and one Mr. Widmerpoole his major; there was a company raised by one Captain Wright; there remained a broken piece of Colonel Pierrepont's company, and Captain Poulton, who had been their captain-lieutenant, being dismissed by the colonel, had a new commission under the governor for a company; and those soldiers of Colonel Pierrepont's not knowing what to do, it was determined at a council of war of strangers, whereof Sir William Fairfax was president, that they should enlist under Captain Poulton. Sir William and Sir Thomas Fairfax, both of them, when the governor made scruple of passing by Colonel Pierrepont, assured him that they had intelligence given them in the north of his intentions to deliver over Nottingham to the king.

About this time Chadwick, the deputy recorder of Nottingham, and one of the committee, came to Nottingham, from whence he had gone, when the soldiers were all drawn out, and all that were fearful went to other places to secure themselves. This fellow being sent on a message to the Lord Fairfax, general of the north, had received letters of credence from the committee; but instead of prosecuting their business, which was to have procured some force from my lord to help keep the place, when my Lord Newcastle was daily expected to come against it, he procured himself a commission for a regiment, and a joint commission for himself and Colonel Pierrepont to be governors of the town and castle. The last he kept very private; the first he bragged of as a thing, which, my lord considering his great abilities, would needs enforce upon him. In execution of this, he raised seven men, who were his menial servants, went into Staffordshire, possessed a papist's fine house, and fired it to run away by the light, when the enemy was thirty miles off from it; and he also cheated the country of pay for I know not how many hundred men: for which, if he had not stolen away in the night, he had been stoned; and as his wife passed through the towns, she was in danger of her life, the women flinging scalding water after her. But before this, he came to Nottingham at the time the governor raised his regiment, and coming up to the castle, behaving himself somewhat insolently, and casting out mysterious words of his authority; the governor set on a person to find out his meaning, to whom he showed a commission he had privately obtained some four months before, for himself and Colonel Pierrepont to be joint governors of the county, town, and castle; but neither did he now declare this to any of the committee, but only made some private brags in the town, that he would shortly come and take order for the safety of the place, and so went out of town again. The governor acquainted the committee with this, who seemed to have great indignation at it, and wrote immediately to Mr. Millington, burgess of the town of Nottingham, to have the government of the castle confirmed to Colonel Hutchinson by authority of parliament. Mr. Salisbury, their secretary, had also put in " the government of the town," but Colonel Hutchinson caused him to put it out; and the governor, being informed that Colonel Pierrepont, at London, was labouring to obtain a regiment, and to be sent down as governor of the town, he for the more speedy despatch, sent his own chaplain with the committee's letters to London, and sent other letters of his own to Sir Thomas Fairfax, to acquaint him how Chadwick had abused my lord, his father, in the surreptitious procurement of this dormant commission; which, during all the time of danger, had lain asleep in his pocket, and now was mentioned, as a thing, whereby he might, when he would, take that place out of Colonel Hutchinson's hands, which he had with so many labours and dangers preserved, by God's blessing, for the parliament's service; he therefore desired a commission for the castle only.

As soon as Mr. Allsop came to London, he was immediately despatched again to Nottingham, with an order of parliament, dated November 20, 1643, for Colonel Hutchinson to be governor both of the town and castle of Nottingham, with an acknowledgment of the good service he had done in preserving the place; and Mr. Millington said he should likewise have a commission from the Earl of Essex. At Leicester, Mr. Allsop met letters, directed to the governor, from Sir Thomas Fairfax, wherein was a commission enclosed from his father, then general of all the north, for the government of both the town and castle. These coming both together, although the general and the parliament had added the government of the town to that of the castle, as more honour to him, Colonel Hutchinson was for many reasons much troubled at it, among which these were some of his considerations. First, they were almost all malignants, there being scarcely a man left who was to be confided in, except those who had already enlisted into the castle. Secondly, they were not so much open, professed enemies, as close, hypocritical, false-hearted people; amongst whom were some leading eminent men, so subtle in their malignity, that though their actions were most prejudicial to the public service, yet did they cast such cunning, specious pretences over them of public good, that even the most upright men of the garrison were often seduced by their fair colours. Thirdly, the most religious and the best people were so pragmatical, that no act, nor scarcely word, could pass without being strictly arraigned and judged at the bar of every common soldier's discretion, and thereafter censured and exclaimed at. Fourthly, the townsmen, being such as had lived free and plentifully by themselves, could not subject themselves to government; but were so saucy, so negligent, and so mutinous, that the most honourable person in the world could expect nothing but scandal, reproach, and ingratitude, for the payment of his greatest merit; and this the worthy governor found sufficiently from them. Lastly, the few good men were so easily blown up into causeless suspicions and jealousies, and there were so many malignant whispers daily spread abroad of every one in office, that it was impossible for any man so worthily to demean himself, but that a jealous misconstruction of some inconsiderable trifle, was enough to blast the esteem of all his actions, though never so pious and deserving; and of all things in the world, nothing was so contrary to the governor's clear and generous heart, as a base and causeless jealousy of him.[1] But notwithstanding these and many other reasons, such as the unprofitable expense of his time, estate, and labours, where he should reap neither glory nor advantage to himself, he considered, that since he had rather declined than sought the enlargement of his power and command, and that the parliament and generals had, at such a distance been moved to put it, unsought, upon him, it was a work which

[1] In effect it will be seen that this gave him more uneasiness than his enemies, in the plenitude of power, were ever able to do.

God called him to, and that the Lord, who set him into the employment, would conquer all the difficulties. For the unjust thoughts or reports of men or their ungrateful returns, he was as much above the grief of that, as the vain-glory of mutable popular applause. It was in all things his endeavour to do and deserve well; and then he never regarded the praise or dispraise of men, for he knew that it was impossible to keep on a constant career of virtue and justice, and to please all. It sufficed him, for his inward peace, that he did not thrust himself into this and other employments, for any popular, ambitious, or advantageous interest of his own; but that he was called of God, to the carrying on of the interests of truth, righteousness, and holiness, and to the defence of his country, wherein he was faithful, and found the Lord's protection and glorious presence, not only in all he did, but in all he suffered for him and from him.

As soon as the governor had received his commission, he thought it his duty to put it into execution, and to arm and fortify the town; but my Lord Newcastle coming with all his forces into Nottingham and Derbyshire, the governor, by the advice of the committee, forbore to publish his new commissions, lest the enemy, perceiving an intent to enlarge the garrison, should utterly destroy the town, before they were able to defend it. At the reading of his commission in the committee chamber, Colonel Thornhagh showed much discontent and was melancholy after it; whereupon the governor told him, that as he had not sought that enlargement of command, so if any of them thought themselves abridged by it, or of any other inconvenience to the public service, he would resign it, and never make use of his commission. The colonel answered with much kindness, that he only wondered how the town came to be added, when they wrote for the castle; but he was well satisfied with it, and forced himself to a seeming content, though the truth is he had some emulation, but not malice, towards the governor; and being of a nature a little jealous and easy to be wrought upon, the wicked enemies of the cause endeavoured, all they could, by insinuations to work disaffection and division between these two gentlemen, who were the most faithful, unbiassed, and zealous champions of the public interest, in their country. But after Colonel Thornhagh had been wrought up to declare his discontent, there were many odd passages, by which others also of the committee, who durst not before reveal their envious hearts, showed themselves displeased. Whereupon, when they were all together, the governor, who hated secret heart-boilings, spoke to them, and told them that their carriages since the commission came to him, did manifest their dissatisfaction in it; and if they would deal ingenuously with him and let him know it, as he had not sought the additional government of the town, so he would never undertake it, if they had any suspicion that, unknown to them, he had procured it for himself, and closely sought after the enlargement of his own power, by the abridgment of theirs; he assured them he was much misunderstood, and that neither to Mr. Millington, nor to Sir Thomas Fairfax, had he mentioned anything more than the government of the castle. For that of the town he rejoiced not in it, but looked upon it as a great burden; yet since it was conferred as an honour upon him, he should not decline serving them who had thought him worthy of it, except it gave distaste to any of those present; which if it did, he would esteem it an obligation, if they would but declare it before he published his commission. They all unanimously replied, they were not only contented, but exceedingly well pleased in it. Then the governor told them, if they were real,[1] as they professed, he should expect their ready and free concurrence with him, in all affairs tending to the public service, and in those courses he should apply himself to, or the good of the garrison: and again earnestly desired them, if they had any dislikes, either of himself personally, or of the alteration of the town out of the hands it had been in the last year, that they would now freely declare it: for as he should take it exceedingly kindly of them, to do so at this time; so if, after he had undertaken the charge, there should be any thwarting or crossing of powers and commands between them, he should not bear it; for as he should not stand upon all punctual niceties in his command, so he would not be abridged of the just and lawful power due to him in his place. They all unanimously answered, it was very fit and just he should have it, and they would rather endeavour to uphold him in it than in any way to retrench it.

Now was my Lord Newcastle's army come into Derbyshire, and having taken some places there, nothing was ex-

[1] Real—*Fr*. Vrais—sincere.

pected at Derby and Nottingham but a siege; whereupon Captain Palmer's troop was called away from Broxtowe, and all the rest of the horse was sent away into Leicestershire, except a few left for scouts; and as soon as they were gone, my Lord Newcastle's forces came and quartered almost at the town side, and in all the near towns, and Hastings took this opportunity to make a garrison at Wilden Ferry.[1] By the mercy of God the enemy was restrained from coming up to the town, though it lay so open that they might have come in at their pleasure; and they not only miserably wasted and plundered the country all about, but one of them told a malignant, where he quartered, that it was their design in coming to those parts, to devour the country. The regiments that were quartered the nearest to Nottingham were Sir Marmaduke Langdale's and Colonel Dacre's, who had been a familiar acquaintance of Lieutenant-colonel Hutchinson's when he was in the north, and they loved each other as well as if they had been brothers. Colonel Dacre sent a trumpet to desire Lieutenant-colonel Hutchinson to send him a safe convoy, that he might come and see him, which he acquainted the committee with, and would have refused, but that the committee, thinking some good use might be made of it, persuaded him to suffer him to come; accordingly he sent him a ticket under his hand, promising him to come and go safely; so upon Thursday morning he came, with about eight more, to the top of the hill at Nottingham, and from thence sent his trumpet to the governor, as if not willing to trust himself without his leave, to know whether he would permit him and his two servants to come into his garrison to visit the lieutenant-colonel. The governor sent him a ticket for them to come in; and though usually they kept no sentinels in the town, yet he sent down

[1] Wilden Ferry was said before to be in the possession of the king's forces; but whether that was an anachronism, or that the thing now meant was an increase of the fortifications, and the placing a larger number of men there, it is clear that the garrison of this place did after this period become a greater annoyance to the parliament, and Lord Grey, of Groby, who commanded in chief the associated forces of Leicester, Nottingham, etc., attacked and took it, assisted, as White- locke says, p. 96, by Sir John Gell, who contrived to get the thanks of the parliament for his services herein, and for taking Winkfield manor and Shelford manor; although some time after, we find him besieging Winkfield manor in conjunction with Lord Denbigh, and that Shelford manor was not taken till more than two years after by Colonel Hutchin- son, acting under the command of Poyntz.

some officers and soldiers to show him a guard at his entrance. When the lieutenant-colonel came to him, he made many endearing expressions to him; how much he rejoiced when his regiment was designed for that place where he was, and how kind an affection he retained for him, notwithstanding their contrary engagements. Falling into further discourse of this kind, he said that if he could but be convinced that the king first entertained papists into his army, and that the parliament had none in theirs, he would never fight more on his side. The lieutenant-colonel told him he should easily be able to do that. " Well," said Dacre, " you and I must have some discourse in private,[1] and I shall be glad if you can satisfy me in that." Then the colonel desired some drink might be sent out to two or three gentlemen, that stayed for him upon the top of the hill; which the lieutenant-colonel hearing, sent some of his own officers and soldiers on horseback to fetch them down, who coming in all together with them, the town rose in an uproar, and came to the governor with a high complaint, that I know not how many cavaliers were come into the town, and rode up and down armed, threatening the people to their great terror. This the governor thinking to be true, was vexed at it, and sent down an angry letter to his brother, requiring him to send up the men that came last into the town. Colonel Dacre hearing this, desired the lieutenant-colonel that the gentlemen might pass as they came, and offered to go up himself and answer for the offence they had given. But the lieutenant-colonel presently carried them all out of the town, and came himself up to the castle, taking it something unkindly that his brother should write such a letter to him, and worse, that others should have suspicions of him; so that though he had made a promise to dine the Saturday following at Dacre's quarters, yet, to take away all offence and suspicions, he resolved he would have no more meetings with him, and to that end wrote him a very civil letter to excuse his not coming; and the governor wrote another to excuse the mis-

---

[1] Though this may appear somewhat improbable at a time when religious opinions have so little effect upon political ones, it was otherwise considered at that time; for nearly at this same juncture it is to be seen, in Whitelocke, page 81, that Sir E. Deering did on this very account of there being so many papists and Irish rebels entertained in the king's army, quit him and come into the parliament, who admitted him to composition, being the first.

take, whereupon the gentlemen were sent for to the castle. Dacre returned complimentary answers to them both, and wrote another to Captain Poulton, entreating very earnestly the lieutenant-colonel and Captain Poulton to come and dine with him on Wednesday, and desiring the governor he might have the honour to see him.   These letters being communicated to the committee, they would fain have had the lieutenant-colonel to have gone, but he held firm to his resolution and would not; so with their privity Captain Poulton only went to excuse it, and two of White's officers were sent along with him, with charge, if they could, to find out how the enemy lay.   When Captain Poulton came, the colonel entertained him very kindly, and expressed a great deal of trouble that the lieutenant-colonel was not come, and took him aside and told him that the governor of Nottingham and his brother had now an opportunity whereby they might much advantage themselves, and do the king excellent service.   Captain Poulton asking him how, he said, if the governor would deliver up the castle he should be received into favour, have the castle confirmed to him and his heirs, have ten thousand pounds in money, and be made the best lord in the country.   If the lieutenant-colonel would deliver up the bridges he should have three thousand pounds, and what command he would ask in the army; and offered Captain Poulton two thousand pounds to effect this.   The captain told him, for his own part, nothing should buy him to such a villainy, and he believed the same of the governor and his brother, and made no question but they had before been attempted.   The colonel told him he did not this without authority, and thereupon pulled a paper out of his pocket wherein were words to this effect: " These are to authorise Colonel Dacre to treat with Colonel Hutchinson and Lieutenant-colonel Hutchinson for the delivery of Nottingham Castle and the bridges, and to make them large promises, which shall be performed by W. Newcastle." Having shown him this warrant, the colonel was very importunate with the captain to acquaint the governor and his brother, and return their answer to him upon the Friday after, when he offered to meet him, if they would, at a place called St. Ann's Well.   Captain Poulton told the governor and his brother, and they told the committee, and showed them what very disdainful refusals they all had written to the colonel, and sent him by a drum; who was not long gone out of the garrison but another came from Colonel Dacre with a letter to Captain Poulton, excusing himself that he could not stay in his quarters for him, according to appointment, but assuring him that what he had promised should be really performed. The governor's drum, in the absence of Colonel Dacre, delivered the three letters to Langdale, who wrote them back a good civil letter, saying that he believed my Lord Newcastle and Dacre, out of familiarity and acquaintance with them, might have made these offers in kindness to them, but for his part he should otherwise pursue the king's service.[1]

After this, the weather being pretty fair, and the moon shining at that time, the governor sent out a foot company to beat up their quarters, and gave them a fierce alarm throughout, and took twelve horses out of one of their stables, which they sent home. On their return, meeting a great body of horse, they all at once discharged upon them, and killed some eight of them, as we were told in the morning. After this charge the horse immediately retreated and would not stand another, and the next day removed their quarters further from the garrison. Then the governor and committee sent for the Nottingham horse back from Leicester, and appointed them to bring five hundred muskets which were come to Leicester for the governor. They came, but left the arms behind them. Besides this, the colonel and all his regiment fell into disputes, that the governors of the parliament garrisons had no command of the horse that were quartered in their towns; and hereupon the governor was often prevented of many opportunities advantageable to the public service, and much discouraged to find such obstructions from the envious pride and humour of those who should have been his assistants; but he bore with it as long as himself only suffered by it, and was willing for quiet-

[1] This proposal for betraying the castle, together with the refusal, is mentioned by Whitelocke, p. 79. Mr. Noble, who is mentioned in the preface as having published the lives of one hundred and thirty-six regicides, makes this remark, " that Colonel Hutchinson hereby lost a fine opportunity of aggrandising himself and his family, which doubtless they must regret." That very discerning gentleman is here informed, that the Editor of this work, who is the only representative of Colonel Hutchinson in these kingdoms, is much more proud of counting amongst his ancestors so firm and faithful a patriot than the most illustrious of traitors.

ness' sake to pass by many injuries offered himself, till the public service came to be infinitely prejudiced by it. In the meantime he went on, as well as he could, through all difficulties, in the faithful and active discharge of his trust. He called a committee and council of war, where it was put to the question and voted that the town should be fortified. Then he applied himself to the thing, and called a full Hall of all the town, who declared sufficiently their disaffection to the parliament, but in such a subtle way as would have entrapped a less prudent person. But the governor over-looked many things that he saw, and made use of all the advantages they gave him; and did not manifest his resent-ment at anything which they could cloak under a specious pretence, how disadvantageously soever it might have been designed against the parliament interest. The whole town unanimously voted that the place should be fortified, except Alderman Drury, and two or three that followed him. Then the governor gave them encouraging promises of his protec-tion and care over them, and his endeavours to preserve them with his regiment, if they would assist in their own defence. The town being well satisfied, or at least seeming so (for he treated them with that dexterity that they could not for shame openly oppose him, though he was not ignorant that the cavalier party cursed him in their hearts, as the only obstacle in their greater desire of having declared themselves on the other side), with general outward cheerfulness, in Christmas week the works were begun. About this time Sir Thomas Fairfax having to march into Staffordshire, sent for some arms he had left in Nottingham castle; and by the same convoy that went with them the governor got his five hundred muskets brought home from Leicester. Sir Thomas sent orders to the governor to send him all the horse in the garrison; but when the governor acquainted them with it, they would none of them obey him and go, though Sir Thomas sent twice very earnestly for them, but they stayed in Nottingham, where they would obey no order of the governor's; and by doing things that concerned the garrison without and against his orders, they made a sad confusion and thwarting of powers, which the governor bore with in respect to Col. Thornhagh, who did things not so much out of malice in himself, as out of a little emulation, which did not destroy his kindness to the governor, and by the subtle instigation of Capt. White, who wrought upon his facility to do those things which his malice and factious ambition prompted him to wish, but he durst not himself attempt. Although the horse would not obey Sir Thomas Fairfax, it was not out of cowardice, for the men were very stout and cheerful in the service, but only had the general fault of all the parliament party, that they were not very obedient to commands, except they knew and approved their employment. They had no sooner refused Sir Thomas, but my Lord Grey, sending for two troops, they went to him to Melton, which he had begun to fortify. The governor, notwithstanding these obstacles from secret enemies and refractory friends, carried on his business with good success, and brought about many events according to his endeavours. Among the rest, his men encountering a party where Colonel Frecheville and Sir Henry Humlack were in person, fought them, killed many of their men, and took Frecheville prisoner; but his captain-lieutenant Jammot came to his rescue and freed him, though he himself was taken in his stead and brought to Nottingham. Here, after he had been some time kept, he corrupted a soldier, who disguised and led him out, and went away with him. The man being a Frenchman and a proper black man, some would needs report him to be Prince Rupert, and thereupon raised a great clamour at the governor.

But before his escape, upon the 15th of January, intelligence was brought that all the forces in Newark were marching on a design upon Sleaford in Lincolnshire. The governor, not trusting that pretence, commanded all the soldiers and townsmen to sit up that night and expect them; and the next morning, being Tuesday, two of his intelligencers came and brought him word very early that the design was against Nottingham. After them the horse scouts came in with the news of their approach, the enemy's scouts and they having fired upon each other. Hereupon a strong alarm was given throughout the garrison, and a foot company sent down from the castle to the works, and the horse were there set with them, to dispute the enemy's entrance into the town; but the horse perceiving the enemy's body to be a great one, retreated to the castle, and the foot seeing them gone, and none of the townsmen come forth to their assistance, made also an orderly retreat back to the castle, in which there was not a man lost nor wounded. The works being imperfect and quitted, were easily entered, though the cannon that played upon them from the castle took off wholly the second file of musketeers that entered the gates. The first was led up by Lieutenant-colonel Cartwright, who two days before had sent to the governor for a protection to come in and lay down his arms. The enemy being entered, possessed themselves of St. Peter's church and certain houses near the castle, from whence they shot into the castle-yard and wounded one man and killed another, which was all the hurt that was done our men that day.

The governor was very angry with the horse for coming up so suddenly, and stirred them up to such a generous shame, that they dismounted, and all took muskets to serve as foot, with which they did such very good service, that they exceedingly well regained their reputations. Having taken foot arms, the governor sent one of his own companies with part of them, and they beat the cavaliers out of the nearest lanes and houses, which they had possessed, and so made a safe way for the rest to sally out and retreat, as there should be occasion.

When this was done, which was about noon, the governor sent out all the rest of the horse and foot, to beat the enemy out of the town. Sir Charles Lucas, who was the chief commander of all the forces there, had prepared a letter to send up to the governor to demand of him the castle; or if he would not deliver it, that then he should send down the mayor and aldermen, threatening, that if they came not immediately, he would sack and burn the town. There were, at that time, above a thousand cavaliers in the town, and as many in a body without the town, to have beaten off the Derby and Leicester forces, if they should have made any attempt to come in, to the assistance of their friends in Nottingham. On the other side the Trent, were all the forces Mr. Hastings could bring out, from his own garrison and Belvoir and Wiverton to force the bridges. All the cavalier forces that were about the town, were about three thousand. When Sir Charles Lucas had written his letter, he could find none that would undertake to carry it to the castle, whereupon they took the mayor's wife, and with threats, compelled her to undertake it; but just as she went out of the house from them, she heard an outcry, that " the roundheads were sallying forth," whereupon she flung down their letter and ran away; and they ran as fast, from four hundred soldiers, who came furiously upon them out of the castle, and surprised them; while they were secure the castle would not have made so bold an attempt. But the governor's men chased them from street to street, till they had cleared the town of them, who ran away confusedly: the first that went out shot their pistols into the thatched houses to have fired them, but by the mercy of God neither that, nor other endeavours they showed to have fired the town, as they were commanded, took effect. Between thirty and forty of them were killed in the streets, fourscore were taken prisoners, and abundance of arms were gathered up, which the men flung away in haste, as they ran; but they put some fire into a hay barn and hay mows, and all other combustible things they could discern in their haste, but by God's mercy, the town, notwithstanding, was preserved from burning. While their foot marched away, their horse faced the town in a valley where their reserve stood, till towards evening, and then they all drew off. Many of them died on their return, and were found dead in the woods and in the towns they passed through. Many of them, discouraged by this service, ran away, and many of their horses were quite spoiled: for two miles they left a great track of blood, which froze as it fell upon the snow, for it was such bitter weather that the foot had waded almost to the middle in snow as they came, and were so numbed with cold when they came into the town, that they were fain to be rubbed to get life into them, and in that condition were more eager for fires and warm meat than for plunder; which, together with their feeling of security, saved many men's goods; as they did not believe that an enemy, who had unhandsomely, to speak truth, suffered them to enter the town without any dispute, would have dared, at such great odds, to have set upon driving them out. Indeed, no one can believe, but those that saw that day, what a strange ebb and flow of courage and cowardice there was in both parties on that day. The cavaliers marched in with such terror to the garrison, and such gallantry, that they startled not when one of their leading files fell before them all at once, but marched boldly over the dead bodies of their friends, under their enemies' cannon, and carried such valiant dreadfulness

about them, as made very courageous stout men recoil.
Our horse, who ran away frighted at the sight of their foes,
when they had breastworks before them, and the advantage
of freshness to beat back assailants already vanquished with
the sharpness of the cold and a killing march, within three or
four hours, as men that thought nothing too great for them,
returned fiercely upon the same men, after their refreshment, when they were entered into defensible houses. If it
were a romance, one should say, after the success, that the
heroes did it out of excess of gallantry, that they might the
better signalise their valour upon a foe who was not vanquished to their hands by the inclemency of the season: but
we are relating wonders of Providence, and must record this
as one not to be conceived of, but by those who saw and
shared in it. It was indeed a great instruction, that the best
and highest courages are but the beams of the Almighty;
and when He withholds His influence, the brave turn
cowards, fear unnerves the most mighty, makes the most
generous base, and great men to do those things they blush
to think on; when God again inspires, the fearful and the
feeble see no dangers, believe no difficulties, and carry on
attempts whose very thoughts would, at another time,
shiver their joints like agues. The events of this day
humbled the pride of many of our stout men, and made them
afterwards more carefully seek God, as well to inspire as
prosper their valour; and the governor's handsome reproaches of their faults, with showing them the way to repair
them, retrieved their straggling spirits, and animated them
to very wonderful and commendable actions.

The governor would not let his men pursue the rear, but
thought they might, in the night, have completed their
day's work, if they had fallen upon the enemy's quarters,
which he gave orders to the horse to do; but Colonel Thornhagh would not obey them, because they came from him,
and so lost a great opportunity, and contented himself with
praising God for the great deliverance of the day, wherein
there was not one townsman that came in to the assistance
of the soldiers.

The next day, the governor called the town together, and
represented to them the mercy of God and the malice of their
enemies, who, without regard of any friends they had among
them, came purposely to fire the town, which God alone pre-

served; and, having showed them their danger, he required they should be no longer slothful in their own defence, but should take arms to preserve their families and houses. He propounded to them, that if they would so do, they should choose their own captains. They, considering the just reasons and motives with which he urged them, at length resolved to join in their own defence, and chose four captains; but the captains refusing, the soldiers that day went home unenlisted, yet by the governor's dexterity in managing them, he at last brought four hundred, whereof more than half were high malignants, to enlist themselves under one Mr. Coates, a minister, an honest, godly man,[1] and Mr. Mason,[2] an attorney, a great cavalier, but a reserved, silent man, who, for an austere knit of his brow, and a grave, severe countenance, had the reputation of a wise man, but was known to be disaffected to the parliament, though cunning enough not to do anything that might expose him to sequestration. Into these men's hands he put arms, and so ordered them, that at the last they grew fiercer in the service than those who were uprightly honest.

The next month the Lord Chaworth sent a letter to the governor, acquainting him that he was sick, and desired a protection to come and remain at his own house, in order to make his peace with the parliament; which protection the governor gave him.

The governor had acquainted the parliament with the late successes, whereupon they ordered a thousand pounds to be sent to the garrison out of the sequestrations of London, and the excise of the town to go to the payment of the garrison; but through Mr. Millington's negligent prosecution, the thousand pounds never came.

The governor went on again successfully in his employment, and began to endear himself to all the town as well as to the soldiery; which awakening White's sleeping envy, he cast new plots to disturb him; and first made a motion to

[1] It appears from this that Mr. Palmer, mentioned before, and who will be mentioned more than once in the sequel, was not quite singular in taking up arms notwithstanding his function. The famous preacher, Hugh Peters, acted as an officer of horse. It was in those days common to quote the expression, that the saints should have the praises of God in their mouths, and a two-edged sword in their hands!

[2] The same whom, when put into confinement at the castle, the governor invited to his table.

[3] Mentioned by Whitelocke as *given*.

send to London for two hundred soldiers: to which the governor answered—If they were honest, there were men enough to keep the garrison; if they were not, to call in other forces was but to bait their treachery with a greater prize; and that to send for more force, while they had such slender maintenance for these, was to increase trouble without any benefit.

The same afternoon the committee sent the governor a warrant to be signed, which was before subscribed by four of them, White in the front. The warrant was to this effect:—

" *To* Mr. Hooper, *Engineer of the Garrison of Nottingham.*

"You are hereby required to make your present appearance to this committee, there to give an account of what you have done about the works of the town, and how far you have proceeded in them; how, and in what manner, and by what time you intend to finish them; and what materials are needful for the finishing of them, there being imminent danger to the garrison."

As soon as the governor received the warrant, he took the engineer with him, and went to the committee, to whom, said he, " Gentlemen, I received just now such a strange warrant from you, that I can impute it to nothing but a picked occasion for quarrel. If you desire to question anything in the fortifying of the town, I have not only brought the engineer, but am here myself to answer it: if there be money in his hands, let him give you an account of it; but concerning the fortifications, I conceive he is only to be accountable to me; therefore why this warrant should be made, I cannot tell, unless purposely to affront me; as for that imminent danger you pretend, it is utterly unknown to me, and if there be any, I ought to have been made acquainted with it, and desire now to understand it." They answered, " Were they not in daily peril? " He replied, " That was certain, but at this time none more imminent than usual that he knew of; and further desired them, if he had been negligent in those things which conduced to the safety of the town, that they would article against him, whatever they could accuse him of; if he had done nothing worthy of blame, he took it exceedingly ill, to be thus thwarted and affronted in his just and lawful command." Upon replies and debate, White said, " If Hooper did not render them an account of his works, they would clap him by the heels." Whereupon the governor, addressing him only, told him, " That from the first opening of his commission, he had manifested his discontent, and that he had taken notice of his secret endeavours to oppose him, and was glad the humour was now so ripe as to vent itself; that for the time to come, since he saw his condescensions did but encourage them to wrest all things from him, and to question all his dues, he would now expect that full observance from them all, that was due from the officers of a garrison to the governor; that he expected the horse should receive orders from him, and that he would no more put up with such affronts and neglects as he had that very day received, when, calling for a muster of the horse to have been sent out upon a very advantageous design, a whole troop, unknown to him, was by the committee sent out for hay, whereby that opportunity was lost." He told them further, " that protections charging officers and soldiers to forbear plunder, ought to be given only by him upon their certificate, and not by them; and," said he, " Gentlemen, I received that affront from you lately, which no governor in the world, but myself, would have put up with; when at a public council of war, among all the officers, enough to have caused a mutiny, it was propounded how far my command extended, and questioned whether I could command horse in the garrison? And all of you, at a council of war, ordered that the booty taken should be at the disposal of the chief officer that went out; so that if a corporal went out, he must dispose of the booty, which in all garrisons is the governor's right to do."

While they were in this dispute, the lieutenant-colonel came in, and seconded his brother; and after some smart disputes on both sides, they parted for that night.

The next morning the committee sent for the governor, who coming to them, one of them drew a paper out of his pocket, and offered some propositions to the governor; which were, first, that the dispute between them might be silenced and kept private; next, that he would join with them, in a letter to Mr. Millington, to desire him to get the question decided by the close committee, What were the several powers of a governor and a committee? And, lastly, that he would draw up what he conceived his power to be. To this the governor replied, that for silencing the thing, he was very willing to do it; for sending to the close committee, he very well understood his own power, and if they questioned it, they might send whither they pleased, to satisfy themselves; but for setting down the particulars wherein he conceived his power to consist, when he did anything, which they thought belonged not to him, let them call him to question where they pleased, and he should be ready to give an account of his actions, but he would not make himself so ridiculous as to send for satisfaction in unquestionable things; yet for their information he would go along with them, if any of them pleased, either to my Lord of Essex, or my Lord Fairfax, to have the power of a governor decided. They told him the generals understood not the power of a committee so well as the parliament, and therefore wrote a letter to Mr. Millington with extraordinary commendations of the governor, yet desiring to know the extent of his power, and showed it to him. He told them, if they believed those things they wrote of him, he wondered whence all this discontent had arisen, for he appealed to them all, whether, ever since he undertook the government, he had usurped any command over them, or done so much as the most inconsiderable act without acquainting them, and receiving their approbation; and what should ail them, he could not imagine, unless they were discontented at his being made governor; which if they were, they might thank themselves, who put it upon him, when he received nothing but trouble, expense, and danger in it. They all acknowledged his appeal true, and said they had desired his establishment in the government of the castle, as the man they esteemed most worthy of it and most fit for it. He told them, if the addition of the town grieved them, that was to be transferred to the parliament, who without his seeking had added that to him. One of them replied, they had so worthy an opinion of him, that they wished the assessing of the country too might be put into his power only. He said he should have been obliged to them had this proceeded from anything but discontent, and that if without his own seeking he should be honoured with that trust, as he was with this, he should endeavour to discharge it faithfully; but he rather desired it might continue in the hands it was, and if he were negligent to fetch in those assessments, which were given him, then let the blame lie on him; but for rating and assessing the towns, those who were acquainted with the country were fittest for it; and thus for the present it rested.

The design they prevented by sending out the troop unknown to him, was, the saving the town of Southwell from being made a garrison for the king; which, the town being unwilling to, sent word to the governor, that if he would come and assist them, they would join with him to beat out some soldiers that intended to fortify themselves there; but the horse, by reason of their employment, failing on those two days, and extraordinary ill weather coming after, that opportunity was lost: this was about the middle of February. Captain White still continued afterwards to prevent all designs whose events might in any way have conduced to the governor's honour, not weighing what hindrance it was to the public service, which was a great vexation to the governor; but his courage was above their malice, and his zeal to the service carried him vigorously on, in all things which he could accomplish by his own officers and soldiers, who were more obedient to him; and, although this exercised his patience, yet was it also a spur to his diligence, and made his fidelity more illustrious, and kept him more in waiting upon God, and more strict in his watch over all his actions, because he knew how all his enemies watched for his fall.

Upon the eleventh of February, Cornet Palmer, who had been prisoner at Newark, came home and told the governor that he had discovered in his prison a design intended about this time to surprise the bridge by Hacker's soldiers, who were to come in the habit of market people on the next Saturday. This intelligence was seconded, whereupon the governor sent his officers to command all the bridge-soldiers to keep in their quarters that day: he commanded also all the horse in the town to be ready to go out upon the first sound of the trumpet, and gave orders for all the drums in the garrison to beat betimes in the morning; the lieutenant-colonel set a guard beyond the bridge, with charge strictly to examine all passengers. About eleven o'clock on Saturday, the 17th of February, they took twelve of them [1] upon

[1] Hacker's soldiers.

the bridge, disguised like market men and women, with
pistols, long knives, hatchets, daggers, and great pieces of
iron about them; whereupon they sent and acquainted the
governor, who being himself on horseback at the works, went
immediately down to the bridge, and commanded all the
horse to come away and pursue them; but the horse commanders, being always slow in obeying his commands, came
not till the enemy's foot beyond the bridge, perceiving their
fellows were taken upon the bridge, retired and got safe off;
only nine, who were to have assassinated those at the bridge,
and had advanced forwarder than the rest for that purpose,
were overtaken, and with their captain leaped into the
Trent to have saved themselves, of whom our men plucked
four out of the water, five were drowned, and the captain
swam to shore on the other side.   The governor was in doubt
whether these men, taken in disguises, were to be released
as prisoners of war, or executed as spies and assassins by
martial law; but though he would not have cared if the
bridge-soldiers had turned them into the Trent when they
took them, he afterwards released them all upon exchange,
except one Slater, a soldier of his own that had run away to
the enemy, and this day was taken coming into the town,
with a montero [1] pulled close about his face, but denied that
he was of the design; yet after, upon trial at a court-martial,
he was condemned and executed.   The governor had sent
out some horse and foot, to drive the grounds at the enemy's
garrison at Shelford, which they did, and from under the
very works from which the enemy shot at them, brought
away many beasts and horses, that belonged to the garrison,
and brought them up into the castle-yard.   The governor
being then in the committee-chamber, told them it was fit
the soldiers should have a reward, whereupon it was ordered
to give them six pounds, and the governor told the soldiers
the committee had assigned them a reward.   But when they
came to receive it, Salisbury, the treasurer, tithed it out, and
gave the soldiers a groat a piece, and sixpence a piece to the
officers, which in all came but to forty shillings and odd
money; at which the soldiers, being mad, flung back his
money, and desired a council of war to do them right; which
the governor assented to, and the next day the business being
heard at a full council of all the officers of the garrison, it was

[1] A kind of cap so called.

determined by the unanimous vote of all but Mr. Salisbury, that as the enemy shot at them, when they took the booty, it did of right belong to the soldiers that fought for it, and so they had it.   Whereupon Salisbury flung himself away from the board in a great huff and muttering, for which the governor rebuked him, and told him such carriage ought not to be suffered in him, who, as an officer, ought to have more respect for the place and those that sat there.   After this, about eighteen of the lieutenant-colonel's men went out and met twenty-five men in arms; between them there was a brook, the bridge-men called to them, and asked of what side they were, and perceiving they were cavaliers, told them, after some little defies between them, that though the number was unequal, they would fight with them; and passing over the brook, charged them, put them to flight, killed two of them, took eight prisoners, and twelve of their horses. Upon examination they were found to be northern gentlemen, who having enlisted themselves in the prince's own troop, after the death of Sir Thomas Byron that commanded under the prince, were assigned to my Lord Wentworth, at which being discontented, they were now returning into their own country, being almost all of them gentlemen.   Sir Richard Byron, for his brother's memory, exchanged them for prisoners of Nottingham, taken when the town was first surprised.

At the end of this month, on the fast-day, the national covenant was taken, with a great solemnity, both by the soldiers and inhabitants, men and women,[1] of the garrison. This day, unexpectedly, came Sir Edward Hartup, with a thousand horse from Leicester and Derby, to which the governor added between five and six hundred; Sir Edward being appointed to command the party, should have gone with them to take Muscam Bridges, at Newark, before which place Sir John Meldrum was now come, with about seven thousand men, and had laid siege to it.   The horse of Newark, as soon as the parliament's forces came, made an escape over Muscam Bridge, which Sir Edward Hartup, having more mind to drink than to fight, lingering a day at Nottingham, and then marching to no purpose against it, lost his opportunity of taking; yet God, by a providence, gave it up with 200 men that kept it to the parliament's forces, who, had

[1] Nota bene.

they then pursued their success, might have carried the town too, but it was not God's time then to deliver the country of that pernicious enemy. The horse that were escaped out of Newark, went into all their garrisons in the Vale and Derbyshire, and gathered up all the force they could make, to about the number of two thousand, and with these they came and quartered near Nottingham; themselves and the country giving out that they were about four thousand.

There was a fast kept at Nottingham, to seek God for his presence with our armies; and before the first sermon was ended the enemy's horse came to the town side and gave a strong alarm, and continued facing the town till night, at which time they returned to their quarters, and those horse that were in the garrison following their rear, gleaned up two lieutenants and two or three other officers. The next day the body marched just by the town side, and so passed over the river at Wilden Ferry. After they were gone from about Nottingham, the governor went down to the Leaguer, at Newark, where Sir John Meldrum had made all things ready for a general assault on the town; but at a council of war that was called in the field, it was determined that it should not then be, whereupon the governor of Nottingham returned to his garrison; who, coming to take his leave of Sir John Meldrum, Sir John entreated him that he would return again and be among them as much as he could, making a sad complaint of the envyings, heart-burnings, and dissensions that were among the several commanders, so that he had much ado to hold them together, and had great need of men of moderation and prudence to assist him, and to help to mediate among them. The forces that Sir John Meldrum commanded before this town, were gathered out of several associated counties, and the commanders were so emulous of one another, and so refractory to commands, and so piquing in all punctilios of superiority, that it galled the poor old gentleman to the heart; who, having commanded abroad, and been used to deal with officers that understood the discipline of war, was confounded among those who knew not how to obey any orders, but disputed all his commands, and lost their time and honour in a fruitless expedition, through their own vain contentions; whereas, had they joined in the assault when he then would have made it, they might probably have carried the town, but missing that opportunity, they came off at last with loss and dishonour. While the governor was at the Leaguer, Sir John Meldrum told him, that Colonel Pierrepont had been with him, to get his hand to a paper, which should have testified that the government of Nottingham did of right belong to him; but Sir John answered he could not testify any such thing, for it was his own act to confer that government where now it was; with which Colonel Pierrepont seemed very well satisfied at that time. When he could not prevail in this, he desired Sir John to set his hand to another paper, which should have certified, that in all things he had approved himself most firm and faithful to the service of the parliament. Sir John said he would not injure him so much as to make any such certificate of a thing not called into question; but if there should be any doubt of it, he should be ready to do him all right. Colonel Pierrepont, moreover, went to the governor's soldiers, that had formerly been of his regiment, and giving them twenty shillings to drink, told them he was to be governor of the town, and would shortly come among them.

Sir Edward Hartup was sent with the party of horse he before had at Muscam bridge, to pursue those that were gone out of Newark, and fight with them, and hinder their joining with Prince Rupert, who was expected to come to raise the siege; and when Sir Edward came into Leicestershire the whole country rose with him, and the governor of Leicester brought out foot and cannon to assist him. His forlorn hope being of the Nottingham horse, charged the enemy's forlorn hope and routed them, and then fell into their body of foot, which they had drained out of their little garrisons, and routed them also, and if Sir Edward Hartup would have come on with his body, they had all been cut off; but the knight would not stir, but commanded the forlorn hope to retreat, who had slain and taken many prisoners of the enemy, and among them Jammot, who had lately made his escape out of Nottingham Castle. The enemy perceiving Sir Edward would not hurt them, rallied again and joined with Prince Rupert; of which, as soon as Sir Edward had intelligence, he went back to Newark with such shameful haste, that he quitted Melton with all the prisoners the forlorn hope had lately taken. The Leicester forces, discouraged at this carriage, returned to their garrisons and marched no more with him.[1]

The governor of Nottingham kept out spies upon the enemy's motions, and sent word to the Leaguer, but the gentlemen there were so over-confident, they would not believe any force could come to raise their siege. At length, the governor of Nottingham being there himself, word was brought that Prince Rupert was come to Ashby; wherefore he, fearing some attempt upon his garrison, to divert the forces at the siege, returned home with his brother to look to their charge. It was late upon Wednesday night when the governor came home, and was certainly informed that Prince Rupert had, that afternoon, marched by to raise the siege with about six thousand men. Immediately the governor sent two men, excellently well mounted upon his own horses, to carry the alarm to Sir John Meldrum, who by two o'clock on Thursday morning delivered him their letters, and he presently prepared to fight with the prince, who came about nine or ten o'clock. Sir John had drawn all his ordnance within the walls of a ruined house, called the spittle, and the horse were the first to charge the enemy. Col. Thornhagh and Major Rossiter gave them a very brave charge, routed those whom they first encountered, and took prisoners Major-general Gerrard and others, and had they been seconded by the rest of the horse, had utterly defeated the prince's army; but the Lincolnshire troops fled away before ever they charged, and left Col. Thornhagh engaged, with only his own horse, with the prince's whole body, where, they say, he charged the prince himself, and made his way and passed very gallantly through the whole army, with a great deal of honour, and two desperate wounds, one in the arm, the other in the belly. After the Lincolnshire horse were run away, Sir John Meldrum sent the Derby horse and the Nottingham foot, with two companies of Col. King's, to keep Muscam bridge, and Molanus, the Derbyshire major, to be their commander. Colonel Thornhagh

[1] In Whitelocke's Memoirs, p. 85, there is an account of this relief, or raising the siege of Newark, agreeing with Mrs. Hutchinson's, except that it is not quite so particular, and omits the account of what befell Colonel Thornhagh. Whitelocke attributes to the misconduct of Sir E. Hartup and Colonel Bingley Prince Rupert's coming with his forces entire to the place, and informs us that a court-martial was directed to decide upon their conduct, but does not state what their decision was.

was sent home in a wagon to Nottingham. Sir John himself, with the few horse and dragoons that were left from Nottingham and Derby, being about five hundred, went into the spittle to his foot. The prince lost more than Sir John in the skirmish, but as soon as ever Sir John had betaken himself to the spittle, the prince sent horse and foot between him and Muscam bridge.[1] The horse that were left there to guard the foot ran every man away, so that they had not a horse left to fetch them any provision. The major that commanded them told them that he would go to the next town to buy them some bread, and with that pretence came away and never saw them more. The enemy was endeavouring to make a passage over the river, to come on the other side of them and encompass them, which when they saw and considered that they had no order what to do, nor bread for one meal, nor bullet more than their muskets were loaded withal, and that it was impossible for them to come off if they stayed till the enemy enclosed them; and further discovering that their friends in the spittle were in parley, they conceived it their best way to come home, which they plotted so to do that the enemy might not perceive it till they were out of their reach; so leaving lighted matches and squibs laid at certain distances, to deceive the enemy, they came safe home. But within less than half an hour after they were gone the enemy came on the other side, and not missing them till morning, by reason of the squibs, they pursued them not, by which means they came safe to Nottingham; which was a very seasonable mercy, for had they stayed the choicest arms in the garrison had been lost, and the best and most confiding soldiers disarmed. For Sir John had agreed upon articles with the prince, to deliver up the spittle wherein he lay, with all the muskets, ordnance, and ammunition in it; the foot soldiers to march away with colours flying, swords and pikes, the horsemen with their horses and swords, and all the commanders with their pistols; but the

[1] Rapin gives a different account of this matter, but to those who know or observe the situation of the places, Mrs. Hutchinson's will appear to be the true one. Besides Muscam bridge there was a bridge of boats, which enabled the prince's forces to surround the guard left at Muscam bridge. This guard, instead of *deserting*, as Rapin says of it, was deserted and sacrificed for want of support; the road still lay open to Lincoln, but probably Prince Rupert was too strong and too active to let the besiegers escape any way, unless they had acted with better accord amongst themselves.

prince broke all these conditions, and pillaged them to their shirts, and sent many captains quite naked away.

The committee of Nottingham now began again to mutter at the governor, but he would not take notice of it, but applied himself to take care for the securing of his town, where the enemy now daily threatened to come. So he floated the meadows on the Line side, where there was no fortification, and raised a fort in the midst of the meadows to preserve the float, and fortified the Trent bridges more strongly; and, expecting the enemy every hour, was forced to let the work go on during the Lord's day. When, calling the captains together to consult on the best way of preparing for their defence, Mason, the new town captain, took this time to revive the old mutiny, and said the townsmen would not stand to their works except the ordnance were drawn down from the castle to the town works; the governor rebuked him for this unseasonable insolence, as he and his men were, all the time of this great exigency, so backward that they were rather an obstruction than assistance, and there was much ado to get them either to the works or to the guards. Indeed such a blow was given to the parliament interest, in all these parts, that it might well encourage the ill-affected, when even the most zealous were cast down and gave up all for lost; but the governor, who on no occasion ever let his courage fall, but, when things were at the lowest, re-collected all his force, that his own despondency might not contribute anything to his malicious fortune, at this time animated all the honest men, and expressed such vigour and cheerfulness, and such stedfast resolution, as disappointed all the malignants of their hopes. The wives, children, and servants of such as were in the enemy's garrisons and armies, he thought it not safe to suffer any longer to be in the town in such a time of danger, and therefore commanded them all to depart, not sparing even some of his own relations; but though this was done by the concurrence of the whole committee, yet some of them, who were loath the town should lose any that wished ill to the governor and his undertakings, privately, without his consent or knowledge, brought back several persons that were very dangerous to the place.

And now, upon the twenty-fifth day of March, a letter was brought to the governor from all the commissioners at Newark, telling him that the parliament's forces had quitted

Gainsborough, Lincoln, and Sleeforth; and that the prince intended to advance against Nottingham, and to fire the town, if he did not immediately throw down the works, which if he should not do, the world would then take notice of him as the only ruin of his native country. To which the governor returned them answer, that as he never engaged himself in this service, with respect to the success or actions of other places, so though the whole kingdom were quitted except this town, he would yet maintain it as long as he was able, and he trusted that God would preserve it in his hands; but if it perished, he was resolved to bury himself in the ruins of it, being confident that God would afterwards vindicate him to have been a defender, and not a destroyer of his country. A copy of the letter which the Newark commissioners sent to the governor, was sent to one Francis Cooke, a malignant inhabitant of the town, subscribed with all the commissioners' hands, and desiring him to communicate it to the whole town. The governor, having taken what care he could at home, sent immediately to the parliament and to the Earl of Essex, acquainting them with the desperate condition of the place; and desiring that they would send him seasonable relief, if the prince should besiege him, promising to employ his utmost endeavour to hold it for them, or to lose himself with it. My lord general returned a very civil encouraging letter, and now the prince, two days after the letter, was advanced within three miles of Nottingham; when it pleased God to divert him from coming against the town by letters which were brought him from Oxford, which occasioned his hasty return into the south, without any attempt upon the place, which, by God's mercy, was thus delivered from this threatening danger. However, their enemies at Newark, by the late success, were very much exalted, and by the quitting of so many parliament garrisons about them, increased in power, and were left at leisure to turn all their designs against Nottingham, which being so infirm within itself, the governor had a very difficult task to preserve; while the disaffected, who were subtle, did not clearly declare themselves, but watched all opportunities to work the governor's disturbance, by fomenting the ill-humours of the factious committee-men and priests; for they now took occasion to fall in with them, upon the governor's release of his chief cannoniers out of prison, into which he had put them, by the instigation of the ministers and of the godly people, who had animated them almost to mutiny for separating from the public worship, and keeping little conventicles in their own chambers. It was with some reluctance he had committed them, for the men, though of different judgments in matter of worship, were otherwise honest, peaceable, and very zealous and faithful to the cause; but the ministers were so unable to suffer their separation and spreading of their opinions, that the governor was forced to commit them; yet during this great danger, he thought it not prudent to keep them discontented and then employ them, and therefore set them at liberty, for which there was a great outcry against him as a favourer of separatists.[1]

[1] This being the first time that a disunion in religion among those of the parliament's party has been plainly named, it is proper here to state, that in the outset, all those sects, which have since taken so many various names, joined their forces to repel the encroachments of the *prelates*,—it would not be fair to say of the *Church of England*, whose characteristic is moderation itself,—but when they had almost crushed the episcopalians, the presbyterian ministers began to rise pre-eminent in power, and to show that though they had changed the name, they by no means intended to diminish the dominion of the hierarchy. There are preserved in Whitelocke two speeches, one of his own and one of Selden's, on this subject. To resist this usurpation there arose a very powerful party or faction, under the name of independents, under whose banner enlisted all who desired liberty of conscience, of whatever particular persuasion they might be; and, amongst others, most naturally all such as wished to see the Church of England restored to her purity, and redeemed from her servility and subserviency to the usurpations of the crown; but whose hopes would have been totally destroyed if presbytery had obtained a full and firm establishment. It is extraordinary that almost all the historians put the cause for the effect, and suggest that many members of the parliament, and at the head of them Cromwell, raised this faction to obtain their own exaltation; whereas intolerancy raised it in the nation at large, and especially in the army, and Cromwell availed himself of it when raised.—In a scarce book, called Anglia Rediviva, or the Success of the Army under Fairfax, written by Joshua Sprigge, he says, " the army was, what by example and justice, kept in good order both respectively to itself and the country: there were many of them differing in opinion, yet not in action nor business; they all agreed to preserve the kingdom; they prospered in their unity more than in uniformity, and whatever their opinions were, they plundered none with them, they betrayed none with them, nor disobeyed the state with them, and they were more visibly pious and peaceable in their opinions than many we call orthodox." Let the blame of all the misfortunes that flowed from it rest with those who gave disturbance to such men, not to those who screened them from persecution.

The chief of these cannoniers was that Langford Collin mentioned in former note, page 106. He continued at Nottingham after all the wars were over, but being persecuted on account of his religion, applied to Cromwell for protection, and was effectually screened by him from

It will not be amiss, in this place, to carry on the parliament story, that we may the better judge of things at home, when we know the condition of affairs abroad. The queen, being suffered to pass through Nottinghamshire by those forces which were sent down thither to have prevented her, joined with Prince Rupert and came to the king; and was by the parliament voted traitor for many actions, as pawning the crown-jewels in Holland, encouraging the rebellion in Ireland, heading a papistical army in England, etc.

The Earl of Essex's army lay sick about London for recruits; Sir William Waller, after many victories in the west, was at length totally routed, and returned to London, Prince Maurice and Sir Ralph Hopton having recovered and possessed almost the whole west of England for the king. The north my Lord Newcastle's army commanded so fully,

his persecutors; he lived to more than ninety years; his descendants rose to opulence, and one of them founded a very handsome hospital. This family united themselves to that of Langford, and both being molested on the score of nonconformity, were peculiarly protected by James the Second, and stood stedfastly by him at the revolution, at which time he got many sectaries to join the catholics, and made common cause against the church of England. By this turn of events and opinions, Langford Collin, Esq., before mentioned, came to be the head of the country, Jacobite, or anti-revolutionist party, while the Plumptres and Hutchinsons embraced the Hanover or Whig party, as mentioned in the note, p. 106, just spoken of.

Since the publication of the first edition, there has appeared a very candid critique of this work in the Annual Register for 1807, containing the following remark: "It may be mentioned as an additional proof of Mr. Hutchinson's rectitude, that when George Fox, the founder of the Quakers, was imprisoned at Nottingham, he protected him; thus proving that, unlike the greater number of those who were engaged in the same cause, he allowed that liberty of conscience to others which he claimed for himself."

The Editor thought it his duty, upon this suggestion, to make further inquiry, and has in pursuance of it been furnished by a respectable friend, Mr. Barker, surgeon, at Colchester, with the two following extracts, together with some others, which will appear in their proper places.—G. Fox's *Journal*, fol. ed. p. 27. "I went to the Steeple House at Nottingham, during the time of divine worship, addressed the people, and was committed to prison. When the assizes came on, there was one moved to come and offer himself up for me, body for body, yea, life also; but when I should have been brought before the judge, the sheriff's man being somewhat long in fetching me to the sessions-house, the judge was risen before I came, at which I understood he was somewhat offended. So I was returned to prison, and put into the common gaol; and the Lord's power was great among friends, but the people began to be very rude, *wherefore the governor of the castle sent down soldiers and dispersed them, and after that they were quiet.*" Sewell's *Hist. of Quakers*, fol. ed. p. 22. "Now though the people began to be very rude, *yet the governor of the castle was so very moderate, that he sent down soldiers to disperse them.*"

that they were advanced into Nottingham and Lincolnshire, and the adjacent counties. The parliament, being in this low condition, had agreed with Scotland, and entered into a solemn national league and covenant, which was taken throughout both kingdoms; and the king had made a cessation of arms with the Irish rebels, and brought over the English army, that had been honoured with so many successes against them, to serve him here. But God never blessed his affairs after they came to him,[1] though indeed before their arrival God had begun to turn the scale; for the city of Gloucester stopping, by its faithful and valiant resistance, the career of the king's victories, after Bristol and Exeter and all the west was lost, the king, disdaining to leave it behind him unvanquished, sat down before it, which employed him and his whole army, till the Earl of Essex and his recruited army, assisted with the London auxiliaries, came and relieved it, and pursued the king's army to an engagement at Newbury; where the parliament obtained a great and bloody victory, and the king for ever lost that opportunity he lately had of marching up to London, and in probability of subduing the parliament. My Lord Newcastle, by a like error, about the same time, setting down before Hull, missed the opportunity of wholly gaining all those neighbouring counties, and much wasted his great and victorious army, being forced to rise with loss and dishonour from the unyielding town. After the fight at Newbury, Sir William Waller, having gotten a new army, had divers

---

[1] The parliament and the king seem to have been equally injudicious in seeking resources from without. Rapin says, " the presbyterians seized the occasion which was offered them of establishing their system of uniformity, and that it increased the number of the king's friends; " had he not, through partiality to his sect, withheld a part of the truth, he would have said that, in pursuit of their system of intolerance, they divided the parliament and the friends of liberty, exasperated the army, and having forced them to try their strength against them, caused the subjugation of themselves, and the ruin of their whole cause and party. So much for the league and covenant.

The king, by seeking the assistance of the Irish in a manner so injurious to the true interests of England, blemished his own fame, hurt his cause, ruined his partisans in both countries, and, indeed the Irish nation in general, which has never recovered from the depopulation which took place in consequence of those convulsions.

This last fact has been controverted by one reviewer, the Critical; but it would be easy to establish it by various arguments, one only is here adduced. The custom of emigrating and entering into the service of foreign powers, which the Irish began to do at that period, and have continued almost to the present day.

successes with it, and at length totally routed all Hopton's army, about the time that Prince Rupert raised the siege at Newark, and was the occasion that called the prince so hastily out of those counties.

The Earl of Essex pursuing the war, had a design to block up Oxford, where the king was, and accordingly attempted it, he on one side, and Waller on the other; but the king, with a few light horse, escaped out of the town, and went to join with his greater armies; which being done, Essex marched further into the west, and in Cornwall was besieged where he lost all his foot, ammunition, and ordnance, and came dishonourably home to London. Waller unsuccessfully followed the king, and the parliament's affairs, all that summer, were very unprosperous in the west, south, and midland counties, but contrary in the north, where the Scotch army, under General Leven, advanced, took some towns and forts, and wasted the Earl of Newcastle's army more by their patient sufferance of the ill weather and martial toil, which the English could not so well abide, than by fighting. Sir Thomas Fairfax, having again taken the field with his father, after a miraculous victory they had gained over the Irish army [1] which the king had brought over, joined the Scots; and the Earl of Manchester, having raised a force in the associated counties, with which he made an expedition to Lincoln, having Colonel Cromwell for his lieutenant-general, marched into Yorkshire, and uniting with the other two armies, they all besieged the Earl of Newcastle in York. To raise this siege, Prince Rupert came with a great army out of the south; the besiegers rose to fight with the prince, and Newcastle drew all his force out of York to join with him, when both armies, on a great plain called Marston Moor, had a bloody encounter, and the Scots and Lord Fairfax had been wholly routed, and the battle lost, but that Cromwell, with five thousand men which he commanded, routed Prince Rupert, restored the other routed parliamentarians, and gained the most complete victory that had been obtained in the whole war.[2] The victors possessed all the prince's

[1] Commanded by Sir John Byron, or Lord Byron, near Nantwich in Cheshire.

[2] There are very various and discordant accounts given of this battle, so that Rapin says he could neither satisfy himself nor his readers with them; that given by Whitelocke is however pretty clear, and agrees with this of Mrs. Hutchinson, in ascribing the success principally to

ordnance, carriages, and baggage; whereupon the prince fled, with as many as he could save, back into the south; the Earl of Newcastle, with some of his choice friends, went into Germany, and left Sir Thomas Glenham governor of York, which he soon after surrendered, and then the three generals parted; Leven went back into the north, and took the town of Newcastle, Fairfax remained in Yorkshire, and Manchester returned into the south, taking in many small garrisons by the way as he passed through the counties.

The queen went that summer into France, to solicit foreign aid for her husband, but ineffectually; meanwhile new treaties were carried on between the king and parlia ment, but to no purpose; for the king's false dealing and disingenuity therein was so apparent that they came to nothing, but a further discovery of the king's falsehood, and favour to the Irish rebels, with whom he had now employed Ormond to treat and conclude a peace. This treaty was that at Uxbridge, where commissioners met on both sides, but effected nothing; for the parliament itself began to grow into two apparent factions of presbyterians and independents, and the king had hope, by their divisions, to obtain the accomplishment of his own ends.[1]

It was too apparent how much the whole parliament cause had been often hazarded, how many opportunities of finishing the war had been overslipped by the Earl of Essex's army; and it was believed that he himself, with his commanders, rather endeavoured to become arbiters of war and peace, than conquerors for the parliament; for it was known that he had given out such expressions. Wherefore those in the parliament, who were grieved at the prejudice of the public interest, and loath to bring those men to public shame, who had once well merited it of them, devised to new-model the army; and an ordinance was made, called the self-denying ordinance, whereby all members of parliament, of both houses, were discharged of their commands in the army. Cromwell had a particular exception, when Essex, Man-

Cromwell; and as Mrs. Hutchinson was by no means partial to Cromwell, nor does Whitelocke upon the whole seem so, we may better believe them than Hollis, who writes a philippic rather than a history.

[1] Whoever will take the pains to read the king's letters in Clarendon's State Papers, will see that this is a true representation of his sentiments; but Heylin pretends the failure of the treaty arose from the extreme pertinacity of the rigid presbyterians; we may very well allow both their share.

chester, and Denbigh, surrendered their commissions; and Sir Thomas Fairfax was made general of the new-modelled army, Cromwell lieutenant-general, and Skippon major-general. The army was reduced to twenty-one thousand, who prosecuted the war not with design of gain and making it their trade, but to obtain a righteous peace and settlement for the distracted kingdom, and accordingly it succeeded in their hands.[1]

To return to Nottingham: after the prince had marched away out of the country, the enemy without was still designing against the garrison, and the governor's enemies within were still perplexing all his affairs. Upon the eleventh of May, a letter was found by a wench in the night-time, dropped in the shoemakers' booths; which letter was directed to Sir Richard Byron, informing him that " the business between them went on with good success, and that the time drawing on, it behoved him to be very diligent, and desiring him to burn the letter;" which was subscribed, " Your careful servant, A. C.;" and a postscript written, " Fail nothing by any means, and there shall be no neglect in me." The governor took all courses that could be imagined to discover this person, but could never find him out. About this time some troopers going by a house, where one Henry Wandall, a debauched malignant apothecary had lived (but the house was now empty, and he had the key of it), they perceived a smoke to come out of it, and went in and found some kindled sticks, laid in a potsherd, just by a

[1] It is suggested by Rapin and others that this new-model and self-denying ordinance arose not from the motives here set down, but merely from intrigue; yet Whitelocke, who even spoke against it, p. 123, shows the indispensable necessity for such a new model. " Some members of the house were sent to their generals to complain of their remissness. The Earl of Manchester was under a kind of accusation, the lord-general in discontent, Waller not much otherwise, the forces not carefully ordered, and the parliament business in an unsettled condition, so that it was high time for some other course to be taken by them." Mr. Sprigge demonstrates this more fully. He says, " Cromwell was absent in the west when the exemption was voted; that he had come to Windsor over-night to kiss the general's hand, and take his leave on quitting the service, but the following morning, ere he came from his chamber, those commands, than which he thought of nothing less in all the world, came to him from the committee of both kingdoms, in obedience to which he immediately marched away." And further, " that the house did this for their own happiness, and that of their general Fairfax."

Mrs. Hutchinson was sufficiently observant of Cromwell's artifices to have accused him of it on this occasion, if he had deserved it.

rotten post, under the stair-case, with hurdles and other combustible things about it, which it was evident were put there to fire the house, but for what reason, or by whom, was not discovered.

The governor hearing of some troops of the enemy in the Vale, had a design to go thither, and acquainted the committee with it; telling them he would take out all the horse, and himself march with the body, and leave a foot company and thirty horse behind him at the bridges, so that by the time he was marched by Wiverton, which would give Shelford the alarm, the thirty horse, which were more than Shelford had to send out, should face the house on that side next Nottingham, and the foot should march a private way through the closings;[1] so that if Shelford's horse or foot should come forth against those thirty horse, the foot might get between them and home, or take any advantage that was offered. All this the committee very well approved, and so it was resolved to put it into execution the next night after, because it would take some time to provide horses for the musketeers. The governor coming out of the committee, met Captain White upon the parade in the castle-yard, and acquainted him with the design, who with a dejected countenance and a faint voice, pretended to approve it, but desired the thirty horse who were to stay some hours behind, might be of his troop; to which the governor assented to gratify his desire, though he told him, he was very loath to spare any of that troop, who were old soldiers and well acquainted with the country; but he desired him the rest might not fail to be ready. The captain promised they should, and so departed. When the governor had made ready all the horse and dragoons, and was himself just ready to march out with them, being at Colonel Thornhagh's house, White came in; the governor, not doubting of his intention to go, asked him if his troop were ready? He replied, " They are out upon service; thirty," said he, " are gone by your consent, and the rest went to fetch in a malignant at Ekering; some few odd ones remain, which you may have if you will." The governor desired him to go himself and assist him; the captain desired to be excused, for " to what purpose should he go when his troop was not there? " The governor went from thence to his own lodgings, and meeting

[1] Closings, closes, fields, vulg. Notts. *closen.*

the committee, acquainted them how White had served him, who seemed to resent it very ill at that time; and while they were discoursing of it, White's officer came up with warrants to be signed for hay for the quarters, which being offered the governor, he tore, and said he would sign no warrants for such a disorderly troop, as would do no service but what they list, whose officers knew neither how to give nor obey commands.

Notwithstanding this discouragement, to lose eighty of his best men, the governor went out with the rest, and when he had drawn them into the Trent Lanes, one of his spies came in with intelligence that at a town in the Vale, called Sierston, and at another next it, called Elston, there were two hundred horse quartered, who having come in weary and secure, might easily be surprised that night. The governor, calling the captains together, imparted the intelligence, and they were all forward to go on in the design, except Captain Pendock, who persuaded him much against it; but while they were discoursing another intelligencer came in, to second the former; whereupon the governor told the captains, that if they would go, he was resolved to do something that night, and because Captain Pendock was best acquainted with that side of the country, he appointed him to lead on the forlorn hope, which accordingly he did, but with such sloth and muttering, that in two or three miles riding, the governor was forced to send up some officers to him, to hasten him on. Yet this was not from cowardice, but only humour and faction, for the man was stout enough when he had a mind to it, but now he rode along, muttering that it was to no purpose, and when he came to Saxondale Gorse, purposely lost himself and his forlorn hope; which the governor missing, was much troubled, fearing that by some misadventure they might have been enclosed and cut off between the enemies' garrisons; but when they came to Saxondale Lane, Pendock and his forlorn hope were found safe in the rear of the body. The governor perceiving Pendock's backwardness, had sent out some parties, one troop under Captain-lieutenant Palmer, and another party with Cornet Peirson, to some near towns, to execute some of the committee's warrants, in fetching in delinquents; when the cornet came back with an alarm that two or three hundred horse were quartered at Elston and Sierston, which he must

either fight with or retreat. Captain Pendock was again
wonderfully unwilling to go on, and said it would be day
before they should come there; but the governor bade those
that would, follow him, for he would go; and accordingly
he went, and when he came to the town, drew up his men at
the town's end in a body, from which he sent in some parties,
to fall into the town, himself staying with the body between
them and Newark, to defend them from any of the enemies
that might have come upon them:[1] so they brought out two
captain-lieutenants, some cornets, and other gentlemen of
quality, thirty troopers, and many more horses and arms;
Captain Thimbleby, absolutely refusing quarter, was killed.
The governor sent into the town to command all his men
immediately away; but a lieutenant and cornet not making
haste to obey, while they stayed for some drink, were surprised by a party that came from Newark, before the corporal, whom the governor had sent to fetch them off, was
well out of the town; but with those he had taken, and all
the booty, and many horses and beasts fetched from malignants in the enemies' quarters, the governor came safe home,
to the great discontent of Captain White, who was something out of countenance at it. This may serve, instead of
many more, to show how hard a task he had to carry on the
service, with such refractory, malicious persons under him.

About this time it happened, that the engineer being by,
Captain Pendock took occasion to rail at the town-works,
and Hooper making answers which drew on replies, Pendock
struck him, whereupon the man, angry, laid his hand upon
his sword and half drew it out, but thrust it in again. The
maid ran affrighted into the kitchen, where was one Henry
Wandall, who presently called some musketeers, disarmed
Mr. Hooper, and sent him prisoner to the governor; who,
asking him upon what account he came so, he told him he
had no reason to accuse himself; if those that sent him had
anything against him he was ready to answer it. After the
governor had waited till about midnight and nothing came,
he sent for Wandall, and inquiring why and by whose
authority he committed Mr. Hooper prisoner? He answered,

[1] Whoever looks upon the map, and observes the vicinity of these
places to Newark, and their great distance from Nottingham, will see
it to have been a service of great delicacy and danger. It is mentioned
cursorily by Whitelocke, p. 89; had Sir John Gell been the commander, we should have had it better displayed.

" for drawing his sword, he, as an officer of the garrison, had sent him up." The governor asked who made him an officer? and taking it upon him, why he did not send up both parties, but only one in a quarrel? and he being able to give no answer, but such as showed it was done out of malice, the governor committed him for his insolency, who being but a common soldier, presumed to make an officer prisoner, without rendering an account to the governor, and to let the other engaged in the quarrel go free. The next day after this, Plumptre came to the Trent bridges, where, being stopped, he sent up a pass which he had procured from my lord general, to come and stay in the town during his own pleasure; which, when the governor saw he sent him word, that in regard of my lord general's pass he might stay at his own house, but bade him take heed, as he would answer it, that he meddled not to make any mutiny or commotion in the garrison; to which he sent an insolent reply, that he was glad the governor was taught manners; he was come to town for some business, and when he had occasion he would repair to the committee. The committee, hearing this, were very sensible of his insolent carriage, and drew up articles against him, which were signed by six of their hands, and were sent up to Mr. Millington to be preferred against him in the parliament, and to be showed to my lord general, as the lieutenant-colonel should see occasion; whom the governor sent immediately to the general, to acquaint him with the reason why Dr. Plumptre had been forced to procure his pass for his protection. The governor took this occasion to send to the general about his cannoniers, whom some days before he had been forced to confine as prisoners to their chamber till the general's pleasure could be known concerning them; for, at the instigation of Captain Palmer, all the ministers in town, and, to make the cry the louder, certain loose malignant priests, which they had gotten to join with them, had most violently urged, in a petition to the committee, that these men might be turned out of the town for being separatists; so that the governor was forced, against his will, to confine them to prevent mutiny, though they were otherwise honest, obedient, and peaceful. After the lieutenant-colonel was gone, with letters concerning these matters, to the general, Plumptre behaved himself most insolently and mutinously, and he and Mason entering into a confederacy, had contrived some articles against the governor for committing Wandall; but when they tried and found they could do no good with them, Mason came to the governor and was most saucily importunate for his release, which, by reason of the insolent manner of his seeking it, the governor would not grant.

The general, upon the governor's letters, sent down a letter to Plumptre, to discharge him from the garrison, and another to the governor to release the cannoniers; which he accordingly did, to the satisfaction of his own conscience, which was not satisfied in keeping men prisoners for their consciences, so long as they lived honestly and inoffensively. But it caused a great mutiny in the priests against him, and they blew up as many of their people as they could, to join in faction against the governor, not caring now what men they entered into confederacy with, nor how disaffected to the cause, so that they were but bitter enough against the separatists; which the cunning malignants perceiving, they now all became zealots, and laughed in secret to see how they brought these men to ruin their own cause and champions.

Plumptre not taking notice of the general's letters, the governor sent him word he expected he should obey them and depart. Plumptre replied, his business was done, and he would go; but in spite of his teeth he would have a guard. The lieutenant-colonel would have put in the articles into the parliament, which the committee had sent up against Plumptre, but Mr. Millington pretending all kindness and service to the governor, would needs undertake it, and desired the lieutenant-colonel to trouble none of the governor's friends in any business he had to do, but to leave it in his hands, who would employ all his powers, and serve him with all vigilance and faithfulness, against all persons whatsoever; and whereas he heard the governor had some thoughts of coming to London, he wished him not to trouble himself, but to charge him with anything he had to do. Notwithstanding all this, the governor went to London, having some occasions thither. A little before his going, he and the rest of the committee had required Mr. Salisbury, their treasurer, to give in his accounts, which he being either unwilling or unable to do, he bent his utmost endeavours to raise a high mutiny and faction against the governor; and Captain White never being backward in any mischief, these, with Plumptre and Mason, made a close confederacy, and called home

Chadwick to their assistance, having engaged the persecuting priests and all their idolaters, upon an insinuation of the governor's favour to separatists. During Colonel Thornhagh's sickness, the governor undertook the command of his horse regiment, while it was quartered in the garrison; and made the men live orderly, and march out upon designs more frequently than they used to do when their colonel was well, upon whose easiness they prevailed to do what they list; and some of them, who were great plunderers, were connived at, which the governor would by no means suffer. Wherefore these men were, by the insinuations of their officers and the wicked part of the committee, drawn into the faction, which was working in secret awhile, and at last broke into open prosecutions. They had determined that as soon as the governor was gone, White, the devil's exquisite solicitor, should also follow to London, but knew not what to do for a pretence to send him upon the public purse; when wickedness, which never long wants the opportunity it waits for, soon found one out, for the committee of both kingdoms had sent a command for all the horse in Nottingham to repair to Sir John Meldrum in Lancashire; the town was put upon a hasty petition that their horse might not go, and Captain White must carry it, who pretended to have known nothing of it half an hour before, yet he was ready, and Dr. Plumptre, too, prepared to make good his brags, and go with his convoy. Presently after he was gone, Col. Chadwick, the engine of mischief, comes to town, whom Mr. Salisbury receives with great joy and exultance, boasting, to use his own words, that they would now mump the governor. At the mayor of the town's house he was entertained with much wine, whereof Mr. Ayscough, a committee man, having taken a pretty large proportion, coming that night to supper to the castle, told the lieutenant-colonel and the governor's wife, that he would advise them to acquaint the governor there was mischief hatching against him, and that Chadwick was come to town on purpose to effect it, which, though the fellow discovered it in his drink, was true enough, and he himself was one of the conspiring wicked ones.

To fortify their party, in all haste they endeavoured to raise a new troop of dragoons, under one Will Hall, a debauched malignant fellow, and therefore one of the governor's mortal enemies; but some of the honester townsmen perceiving the design, and not yet being seduced, would not raise him any horse, so at that season the troop was not formed.

And now Captain White having come home, it was observed that after his return he would not allow the governor that name, but called him only Colonel Hutchinson, and when any one else termed him governor, would decline the acknowledgment of that name; then cajoling his fellow horse-officers and the troopers, they, through his insinuations, everywhere began to detract from the governor, and to magnify Captain White, and not only to derogate from the governor, but from all persons that were well-affected to him. At this time there was a petition drawn up to be presented to the committee of both kingdoms, desiring that Mr. Millington might be sent down to compose the differences which were in the garrison. The lieutenant-colonel and some others refusing to sign it, Captain White told them it was a pretence, which Mr. Millington desired the favour that they would make, to obtain leave for him to come down and visit his wife and children, whom he had a longing desire to see, and knew not any other way to bring it about. The gentlemen, to gratify Mr. Millington, signed it; and he himself at London, with the same pretext, obtained the governor's hand to it, while the governor, deceived by his high and fair professions of service and kindness to him, never entertained any suspicion of his integrity; and this was the greatest of the governor's defects, that through the candidness and sincerity of his own nature he was more unsuspicious of others, and more credulous of fair pretenders, than suited with the great prudence he testified in everything else. Nothing awakened jealousy in him but gross flattery, which, when he saw any one so servile as to make, he believed the soul that could descend to that baseness might be capable of falsehood; but those who were cunning attempted him not that way, but put on a face of fair, honest, plain friendship, with which he was a few times, but not often in his life, betrayed. At Mr. Millington's entreaty the governor released Wandall, but would have prosecuted the committee's petition against Plumptre, which Mr. Millington most earnestly persuaded him not to do, but desired that he would permit him to come and live quietly in his own house, upon engagement that he should not raise nor foment any mutiny nor faction in the garrison, or intermeddle with any of the affairs thereof. The governor was easily wrought to assent to this also, but Plumptre refused to enter into such an engagement for quiet behaviour, and so for that time came not to town. There was again discovered a new design by the enemy against the garrison, and a spy taken, who owned that a soldier in the major's company had enlisted himself on purpose to effect his mischief; but through careless custody the spy escaped the day that the garrison were celebrating their joy for the great victory at York. Meanwhile the governor, supposing Mr. Millington to be, as he professed himself, highly his friend and his protector, complained to him of the mutinous carriage of the horse, and his disturbance and discouragement in the public service thereby, and desired him to get a resolution in the thing, whereby his power and their duty might be defined, that he might know wherein he was to command them in his garrison, and they to obey him. Mr. Millington advised him to write a letter to him concerning this, setting down his own apprehensions, what he was to exact from them, and they to render him; which accordingly the governor did, and left it with Millington, and returned to his garrison. Mr. Millington told him, that he had showed the letter to the committee of both kingdoms, who had given their opinion of it, that he required no more of them than he ought to have. Soon after the governor, Mr. Millington came down to Nottingham, with instructions from the committee of both kingdoms, to hear and, if he could, compose the differences at Nottingham; if not, to report them to the committee of both kingdoms. Mr. Millington, coming down with these, brought Plumptre as far as Leicester with him, and begged of the governor to permit him to return to his house, engaging himself that he should not meddle with anything belonging to the garrison, nor come near the castle nor any of the forts: which engagement the governor received, and suffered the man to come home; and Millington, lest the governor should suspect his great concern for Dr. Plumptre, made strong professions to him, that he desired his re-admission into the town for nothing but to be a snare to him: for he knew the turbulency and pride of his spirit such, that he would never be quiet; but if, after this indulgence, he should, as he believed he would, return to his former courses, he would be inexcusable in the eyes of all men. Then Mr.

Millington desired the governor to draw up some heads, wherein he conceived his power to consist, which he did, reducing almost the words of his commission into eight propositions; which, when he showed first to Mr. Millington, before the committee saw them, Mr. Millington seemed very well to approve of them, and protested again to the governor the faithfulness of his heart to him, excusing his intimacy with his enemies, upon a zeal he had to do him service, by discovering their designs against him, and called himself therein, Sir Politic Wouldbe: but the governor disliking this double dealing, though it had been with his enemies, desired him rather to declare himself ingenuously as his conscience led him, though it should be against him, and told him freely he liked not this fair carriage to both. When the governor put in his propositions to the committee, they desired each of them might have a copy of them, and all a week's time to consider them; at the end of which, when the governor pressed their answer, whether they assented to them, or could object anything against them; they said, with false flattering apologies to the governor, that if such command were due to any man, they should rather the governor should employ it than any person whatsoever, by reason of his unquestioned merits; but they conceived that such a power given to a governor, would not consist with that which belonged to a committee, whereupon they produced a tedious, impertinent paper, in answer to the governor's propositions, which, when the governor read over, he flung by, saying it was a ridiculous senseless piece of stuff. Some of them taking exceptions, that he should so contemn the committee's paper; he replied, he knew not yet whose it was, not being signed by any one; if any of them would own it, he desired them to subscribe it, and then he should know what to say. Thereupon, the next day, it was again brought out, signed by Mr. Millington, Chadwick, Salisbury, White, and the mayor of the town. The sum of the paper not containing any exceptions against the governor himself, but against his power, and wholly denying that my Lord Fairfax had power to make a governor, or confer any such power on him, as his commission imported; the governor told them, it no further concerned him, but only to acquaint my Lord Fairfax, with whom he should leave it, to justify his own commission, and his authority to give one. But forasmuch as my lord was concerned in it, the gentlemen who had more respect for him disowned it, and these were the governor, the lieutenant-colonel, Mr. Pigott, Colonel Thornhagh, Major Ireton, Major Widmerpoole, Captain Lomax, and Alderman James. Then the governor told them, how he had been informed that this paper was of Chadwick's contrivance, and that when Mr. Millington saw it, he hugged Chadwick in his arms, with such congratulation as is not to be imagined they could give to a fellow of whom they had justly entertained so vile an opinion; and then before his face he declared all their thoughts of indignation and contempt, which they had formerly expressed of Colonel Chadwick, of whom he asked, with what face he could question my lord's authority to make him governor, when he had formerly used such surreptitious cheats to obtain it for himself, by the same authority? And he asked the committee, how it came to pass, they now believed my Lord Fairfax had not authority to make him governor, when they themselves at first wrote to him for the commission? And to Mr. Millington he said, that he had dealt very unfaithfully to those who trusted him to compose differences, which he had rather made than found; and very treacherously with him, making himself a party and the chief of his adversaries, when he pretended only to be a reconciler. Having at full laid them open one to another, and declared all their treachery, malice, pride, and knavery, to their faces, he went away, smiling at the confusion he had left them in, who had not virtue enough in their shame to bring them back to repentance, but having begun to persecute him, with their spite and malice, were resolved to carry on their wicked design; wherein they had now a double encouragement to animate them, Mr. Millington's sheltering them in the parliament house, and obstructing all redress the governor should there seek for, and the hopes of profit and advantage they might upon the change of things expect from the garrison, if they could wrest it out of the governor's hands, either by wearying him with unjust vexations, or by watching some advantage against him, to procure his discharge from his office by the parliament; for they, knowing him to be impatient of affronts, and of a high spirit, thought to provoke him to passion, wherein something might fall out to give them advantages; but he, perceiving their drift, showed them that he governed his anger, and suffered it not to master him, and

that he could make use of it to curb their insolency, and yet
avoid all excursions that might prejudice himself.[1] When
the governor undertook this employment, the parliament's
interest in those parts was so low, and the hazard so desperate, that these pitiful wretches, as well as others faithful-
hearted to the public cause, courted him to accept and keep
the place; and though their foul spirits hated the daylight of
his more virtuous conversation, yet were they willing enough
to let him bear the brunt of all the hazard and toil of their
defence, more willing to be secured by his indefatigable
industry and courage, than to render him the just acknowledgment of his good deserts.   This ingratitude did not at all
abate his zeal for the public service, for as he sought not
praise, so he was well enough satisfied in doing well; yet
through their envious eyes, they took in a general good
esteem of him, and sinned against their own consciences in
persecuting him, whereof he had after acknowledgments and
testimonies from many of them.   All the while of this contest, he was borne up by a good and honourable party of the
committee, and greater in number and value than the wicked
ones, whom Mr. Millington's power in the house only countenanced and animated to pursue their mischiefs.   What it
was that drew Mr. Millington into their confederacy was
afterwards apparent; they hired him with a subscription of
losses, for which they gave him public credit double to what
he really had lost;[2] and they offered him a share of the
governor's spoils, if he would help them to make him a prey,
which would have been good booty to his mean family: for
although the governor had hitherto got nothing but desperate
hazard and vast expense, yet now, this garrison began to be
in a more hopeful condition, by the late success in the north.
After York was taken, the Earl of Manchester marched into
our parts, upon whose coming Bolsover and Tickhill castles

[1] To some the recital of these municipal broils may appear rather
tedious; but Whitelocke's *Memorials* show that these, and such like,
in various parts of the kingdom required the serious and frequent
attention of the parliament.   Most readers will pity a man of Colonel
Hutchinson's exalted mind for being compelled to cope with such
despicable adversaries, but they will derive some pleasure from observing the address with which he foiled their insidious attacks.
[2] Of this custom of applying to the parliament for reparation or
compensation, and of its being granted generally at the expense of
delinquents or cavaliers, there appear many instances in Whitelocke—
no doubt many abuses crept in.   In Walker's *Hist. of Independ.*, p.
81, Mr. Millington is declared to have received in this manner £2000.

were delivered up to him, and Welbeck, the Earl of New-castle's house, which was given into Colonel Thornhagh's command, and much of the enemy's wealth, by that means, brought into Nottingham: Winkfield Manor, a strong garri-son in Derbyshire, was taken upon composition, and by this means a rich and large side of the country was laid open to help to maintain the garrison at Nottingham, and more hoped for by these gentlemen, who were now as greedy to catch at the rewards of another's labours, as unable to merit anything themselves. But when the hopes of the harvest of the whole country had tempted them to begin their wicked plots, God, seeming angry at their ill use of mercy, caused the Earl of Manchester to be called back into the south, when he was going to have besieged Newark, and so that town, with the petty garrisons at Wiverton, Shelford, and Belvoir, were still left for further exercise to Nottingham. Yet the hopes that these would in time be gained, made these gentlemen prose-cute their design against the governor, whose party they endeavoured with all subtleties to weaken: and first they attempted Colonel Thornhagh, who having by his signalised valour arrived at a great reputation, they thought if they could gain him, he would be their best lever to heave out the governor, and that prop once removed they despaired not to make him contribute to his own ruin; for they had discovered in him a facility of nature, apt to be deluded by fair pretences, and more prone to suspect the kind plain dealing of his friends, than the flattery of his enemies: but the governor, after they had displayed themselves, by his vigilancy pre-vented many of their malicious designs, and among the rest those they had upon this gentleman. During his sickness the governor took care of his regiment, and employed the troops that quartered in the garrison: but through the wicked instigations of Captain White, being very refractory, and the regiment often called out on field-service, the governor sent for a commission, and raised a troop of horse, which the lieutenant-colonel commanded, and a troop of dragoons for the peculiar service of the garrison. These cunning sowers of sedition wrought, upon this occasion, Colonel Thornhagh into a jealous belief, that Colonel Hutchinson was taking the advantage of his sickness to work himself into his com-mand. Colonel Thornhagh was grieved at it, but said nothing; but the governor discovering the thing, notwithstanding his silence, when the lieutenant-colonel went to London, procured a commission for Colonel Thornhagh to be, next under Sir Thomas Fairfax, commander-in-chief of all the parliament's horse in Nottinghamshire, at all times; which being brought to Colonel Thornhagh, when he knew nothing of it, cleared him of that suspicion.   And now, although they were more inclined to delude than openly to oppose Colonel Thornhagh, yet they, having no exceptions against the governor in his own person, but only against his authority, were forced to deny Colonel Thornhagh's command as well as the governor's, they being both derived from the same power.   The horse-captains, who were allured by fair colours of preferment, and indulged in their plunder, which they hoped to do with more freedom, if Captain White prevailed, were more obedient to Captain White and their own ambition, than to their colonel or the laws and customs of war.   The committee hoped, by thus disputing the colonel's powers, under a face of parliament authority, to weary them out, and make them cast up their commissions, when they had, by Mr. Millington, blocked up the way of their complaint, so that they feared not being turned out of the committee for the abuse of that trust: and perhaps they had succeeded but that the governor scorned to give up a good cause, either particular or public, for want of courage to defend it amidst many difficulties; and then, although he had many enemies, he had more friends, whom if he should desert, would be left to be crushed by these malicious persons; and more than all this, the country would be abandoned into the hands of persons who would only make a prey of it, and not endeavour its protection, liberty, or real advantage, which had been his chief aim in all his undertakings.

The conspirators, as I may more justly term them, than the committee, had sent Captain White to York, to my Lord Fairfax, to get the governor's power defined; which the governor understanding, the next day went thither himself, and Mr. Pigott, who from the beginning to the ending showed himself a most real and generous friend to the governor, and as cordial to his country and the great cause, went along with him, arriving a day after Captain White.   When my lord gave them a hearing together, he asked whether the governor had done anything of consequence without consulting the committee, which White could not say he had; then he asked White if he had any other misgovernment to accuse him of, which when White could not allege against him, the governor before his face told my lord all the business, whereupon White was dismissed with reproof and laughter, and letters were written to the committee, to justify the governor's power, and to entreat them to forbear disturbing him in his command, and to Mr. Millington, to desire him to come over to York to my lord; both which the governor delivered, but Mr. Millington would not go over, but, on the contrary, continued to foment and raise up the factions in the town against the governor, and by his countenance the committee every day meditated and practised new provocations, to stir up the governor to rage, or at least to weary him in his employment. The horse, without his knowledge, they frequently sent abroad; protections, tickets, and passes, they gave out; and, encroaching upon his office in all things whatsoever, wrought such a confusion in the garrison, that while all men were distracted and amazed, in doubt whose orders to obey, and who were their commanders, they obeyed none, but every man did what he listed; and by that means the public service was in all things obstructed and prejudiced. The governor, while the injury was only to himself, bore it, but when it extended almost to the destruction of the garrison, he was forced to endeavour a remedy. For about this time it happened that Salisbury, being treasurer, had given base terms and wilful delays to the soldiers who were assigned their pay, when the money was ready for them in the treasury; and when this base carriage of his had provoked them to a mutiny, the governor was sent for to appease it, which he did; but coming to the committee, told them he would no longer endure this usage of theirs, to have all things of power, honour, and command, wrested out of his hands, and all things of difficulty and danger put upon him; while they purposely stirred up occasions of rigour and punishment, and then expected he should be the executioner of it, by which he perceived they did these things only with design to render him contemptible and odious to all persons. Not long afterwards a command came for all the horse that could be spared in the garrison to go to Sir John Meldrum, to the relief of Montgomery Castle. The governor went to the committee to consult what troops should march, and they voted *none*. The governor told them, he conceived when a

command was given, they were to obey without dispute, and
that he came to advise with them what troops should be sent
forth, not whether any or none; therefore although they
voted disobedience of the command, that would not discharge him, especially the service being of great consequence,
and the troops lying here without other employment: wherefore at night he summoned a council of war, and there almost
all the captains, having no mind to march so far from home,
declared they conceived themselves to be under the command of the committee, and would only obey their orders.
Upon this the governor went to the committee and desired
them that, since unanswerable things were done, the public
service neglected, and all the transactions of the garrison
confused, they would unite with him in a petition to parliament to define their several powers; and in the meantime,
either quietly to let him execute his duty, or else to take all
upon them and discharge him.   They presently made a
motion, that he would call a muster, and put it to all the
soldiers, whether they would be governed by the committee
or the governor. The governor told them his command was
not elective, but of right belonged to him, and this way was
only the next occasion to cause a mutiny, which he could not
consent to. But they persisting in their course, he came
again to them and desired they would discontinue these
affronts in his command, and also their underminings,
whereby they endeavoured to alienate men's hearts from
him, and to raise a faction against him by close unworthy
practices. So after much debate it was on all hands agreed,
that they should not at all intermeddle with anything belonging to the soldiery, nor interrupt the governor in his command, till the house of parliament should decide it, and that
the governor and Captain White should both go to London,
to procure a speedy determination of the powers in a fair and
open way. This they all faithfully promised the governor,
and made many hypocritical professions to him, some of
them with tears; whereupon he, who was of the most reconcilable nature in the world, accepted their fair pretences, and
went to drink friendly with them in token of kindness. Yet
was all this but hypocrisy and falsehood, for even at that
very time they wearied many of the governor's officers out
of the garrison, by the continued malice wherewith they
persecuted all that had any respect for him. Among these

was Mr. Hooper the engineer, a man very faithful to the cause, and very honest, but withal rough, who having to do with hateful businesses, was made odious to the common people, the priests too having a particular spite at him, as one they esteemed a leader of the separatists; yet he was very ingenious and industrious in his office, and most faithful as well to the governor himself as to the public service. The committee, to insinuate themselves with the common people, regarded him with an evil eye, and so discouraged him, that being offered much better preferment, and invited by Colonel Cromwell into other parts, he acquainted the governor with it, offering withal that, if he might yet be protected from affronts in his employment, he would stay and serve the governor for half the salary offered elsewhere. But the governor, although he was very sorry to part with him, and the service would much miss him, yet being so much injured himself, could not undertake the protection of any of his officers, and therefore would not hinder his preferment, but suffered him to go to Cromwell. Such was the envy of the committee to him, that that very day, just as he was going, they not willing to let him depart in peace, although they knew he had justly expended all the money he had received of them, yet they called for an account, from the beginning of his employment, which they had often seen in parcels; but believing he could not so readily give it them altogether, they then demanded it. He immediately brought it forth, and got by it twelve shillings due to him upon the foot thereof, which he intended not to have asked them for, but receiving it upon the exhibition of his account, went away smiling at their malice; which yet would not let him go so, for then Henry Wandall came with a petition to the governor, that he would vindicate the honour of the Earl of Essex against Mr. Hooper, whom he accused of having spoken words against him, and done actions to his dishonour. The governor knowing this was but malice, accepted security for him, which was offered by Mr. Pigott and Major Watson, that he should answer what could be objected against him at any council of war he should be called to.[1]

[1] This Mr. Hooper was undoubtedly a person of singular abilities. Mr. Sprigge, in his *Anglia Rediviva*, mentions him as serving Sir Thomas Fairfax at the siege of Oxford and other places as engineer extraordinary, and greatly expediting all his enterprises, the rapidity and number of which were surprising: he was at the siege of Ragland

Wednesday, September the 25th, 1644, Captain White went to London, to solicit the committee's business against the governor, for they pretended to put it upon a fair debate, as was promised. The next day the governor commanded Captain Barrett's troop to convoy him towards London; but just as he was going to horse, the committee, contrary to their engagements not to meddle with any military affairs, commanded them another way, and so he was forced to go without a convoy, although the captain was afforded a whole troop to wait on him.

Two or three days before the governor went, Chadwick came privately to the governor's brother, and told him that his conscience would not suffer him to conceal the malicious designs, and that treachery, which he now discovered to be in these men's oppositions to the governor; and with many insinuations, told him they were framing articles against the governor, whereof he gave him a copy, which the governor carried to London with him, and showed the lieutenant-colonel the originals in Mason's and Plumptre's own hand-writings. Three days after the governor, Colonel Thornhagh went to London. That day the governor went, one of the presbyterian ministers, whose name was Goodhall, preached the lecture at the great church, with many invectives against governors and arbitrary power, so plainly hinting at the governor, that all the church well understood it; but of the committee he spoke fawningly, and told them he had nothing to say to them, but to go on in the good way they went. Some months afterwards, this poor man, preaching at a living the committee had put him into, was taken by the enemy, and much dejected at it, because he could not hope the governor would exchange him, after his unworthy pulpit railings at him; but the governor, who hated poor revenges when his enemy and one of his friends were both in the same prison, and he had but one exchange ready, first procured the minister's release, and let his own officer stay for the next exchange. Whereupon the man coming home, was struck with remorse, and begged the governor's pardon, with real acknowledgments both to himself and others of his sin, in

Castle, the last garrison that surrendered; he came again to Notting-ham during Colonel Hutchinson's government, and, by the list of the garrison in Deering's *Nottingham*, appears to have continued with Captain Poulton.

supporting the faction against the governor, who was told that on his death-bed, for he died before the garrison was dissolved, he expressed to some of the governor's friends his trouble for having been his enemy. But not only to him, but to many others of his enemies, the governor upon sundry occasions, when they fell into his power to have requited their mischiefs, instead of vengeance rendered them benefits; so that at last his own friends would tell him, if they could in justice and conscience forsake him, they would become his adversaries, for that was the next way to engage him to obligations. But although his friends, who had greater animosities against his unjust persecutors than he himself, would say these things in anger at his clemency, his nature was as full of kind gratitude to his friends as free from base revenges upon his enemies, who either fell down to him from their own just remorse, or were cast under his power by God's just providence.

As soon as the governor was gone, the committee took all power upon them, and had the impudence to command the lieutenant-colonel, who was deputy-governor, and absolute in his brother's absence, to draw out his troop: he went to them and told them he was sorry they broke their agreement, but he could not break his trust of his brother's authority to obey them. Then they feigned a pretence and turned out the governor's quarter-master, who, by the governor's appointment, had quartered soldiers at an ale-house Mr. Millington had given protection to, saying, that none should be quartered on account of some relation they had to him who married one of the daughters of the place. This occasioning some dispute, Cooke the quarter-master had uttered some words, for which they sent for him and cast out great threats, how they would punish him; which frighted his wife, big with child, in that manner, that her child died within her, and her own life was in great hazard. The committee then called a hall, and caused the townsmen to bring in horses for dragoons, whereof they voted a regiment to be raised, Chadwick to be the colonel, and Hall and Selby to be captains under him. They took upon them to command the soldiers, and made horrible confusion, by which they often put the garrison in great danger, if the enemy had known their advantage. Among the rest, one night after the guards were set, the captain of the guard, missing the deputy-governor to receive the word from him, gave them the same word they had before, till he had found out the governor to receive a new one. Mr. Millington coming by, half flustered, would have had the captain take a word from him, which when the captain refused, he being angry, commanded Captain Mason's drums to beat, and set a double guard. The lieutenant-colonel hearing the drums, and having no notice of his command, sent to Mason to command him to forbear drawing any men to the guard, but Mason would not obey him. Besides this, they did a thousand such like things, to provoke him to give them some colour of complaint, or some advantage against him and his brother, in order to carry on a wicked design, by which they were secretly managing to destroy them; but God, by a wonderful providence, brought it to light.

Their conspiracy was to accuse the colonel and his brother, as persons that had betrayed the town and castle, and were ready to surrender them to the enemy, which they would pretend to have discovered, and to have prevented their treachery, by a surprise of the lieutenant-colonel, the castle and the bridges, and all the officers that were faithful to the governor and his friends. Because they had not a force in town who would act this villainy, they sent to Sir John Gell, in whom they had a great interest, and a man likely enough to promote their wickedness, had they even acquainted him with it, as black as it was in the cursed forge of their own hearts: but to carry on their business closely, they sent to tell him they had cause of suspicion that the lieutenant-colonel was false to his trust, and would deliver the castle to the enemy, to prevent which they desired him to assist them with some men and ammunition; which ammunition was very secretly conveyed into the town, and the men were ready to march, and quarters taken up for them in Nottingham. The lieutenant-colonel dreamed nothing of the mischief that was hatching against him, when, just at the very time of the execution, there came into Nottingham two gentlemen, whom the parliament employed to carry intelligences between the north and the south, and who used to meet at this town.

Mr. Fleetwood, who came from the south, came immediately up to the castle, and was there familiarly and kindly treated, as he used to be, by the lieutenant-colonel. This

was upon a Saturday night, in the month of October. Mr.
Marsh, his correspondent, who came from the north, passing
through Derby, was so cautioned by Sir John Gell, that he
durst not go up to the castle, but on the Lord's day sent for
Mr. Fleetwood to meet him in the town; who coming to him,
he told him what information he had received from Sir John
Gell, and for that reason he durst not trust himself in the
castle. Mr. Fleetwood undertaking for his safety, brought
him up to the lieutenant-colonel, and finding the untruth
of their forgeries, told the lieutenant-colonel all the machinations against him; whereupon, on the Monday morning, he
went away to London, and sent Mr. Millington word, that
having understood the suspicion they had of him, he was gone
to London, where, if they had anything to accuse him of, they
might send after him, and he should be ready to answer it,
and in his absence had left Captain Lomax governor of the
garrison. The committee, very much confounded that their
wickedness was come to light, resolved to outface the thing,
and denied that they had sent to Derby for any men. They
said indeed it was true, that having formerly lent Sir John
Gell some powder, they had sent for that back; but this was
not all, for they had also persuaded the master of the magazine that was in the castle to convey, unknown to the lieutenant-colonel, two barrels of powder, with match and bullet
suitable, to such place as Chadwick should direct. This he,
not dreaming of their evil intention, had condescended to do,
and sent them to Salisbury's house; but as soon as the lieutenant-colonel was gone, they took what care they could to
shuffle up this business, and presently despatched Captain
Palmer to London and Lieutenant Chadwick to Derby, where
he so wrought with Sir John Gell, that he brought back a
counterfeit letter, pretended to have been all that was sent
from the committee of Nottingham to him, and another of
Sir John Gell's writing, wherein he disowned all that Mr.
Marsh had related of his information. But God, who would
not let them be hid, had so ordered that while matters were
thus huddling up at Derby, Sir John Gell's brother came by
chance to Nottingham, and affirmed that the committee of
Nottingham had sent to his brother for three hundred men,
to surprise Nottingham Castle; which, when the committee
heard, they sent Captain Pendock after him the next day to
charm him, that he might not discover the truth in that

particular. Also the very day that these intentions of theirs were thus providentially brought to light, one of Sir John Gell's captains was known to be in town, whom Sir John had sent to discover the state of things, and the new quartermaster had been all that day taking billets for soldiers in several houses in the town.

When the governor came to London, the committee of both kingdoms had appointed a sub-committee to hear his business, whereof young Sir Henry Vane had the chair, Mr. William Pierrepont, Mr. Solicitor St. John, Mr. Recorder, and two of the Scotch commissioners, were nominated for the committee; before whom the governor's propositions and the committee's answers had been read, and when their solicitor, Captain White, saw they were likely to be cast out as frivolous, he produced some articles, which they had formed against the governor, lieutenant-colonel, and Mr. Pigott; but they proved as frivolous as the other, and the gentlemen answered them so clearly, that they appeared to be forged out of malice and envy, only to cause delays, there being scarcely anything of moment in them if they had been true, whereas they were all false. And now after they had trodden down the fence of shame, and impudently begun with articles, there was not the least ridiculous impertinency that passed at Nottingham, but they put into a scrip of paper and presented it as an additional article to the committee; to each of whom particularly Mr. Millington had written letters, and given them such false impressions of the governor, and so prepossessed them against him, who was a stranger to them all, that they looked upon him very coldly and slightly, when he made particular addresses to them. But he that scorned to be discouraged by any men's disregard, from whom he had more reason to have expected all caresses and thankful acknowledgments of his unwearied fidelity and good services, resolved to pursue his own vindication through all their frowns and cold repulses: these he met with more from Mr. William Pierrepont than from any of the rest, till Mr. Peirrepont perceived the injustice of their prosecution, and then there was no person in the world that could demean himself with more justice, honour, and kindness than he did to the governor, whose injuries first became apparent to him, when the lieutenant-colonel came and told his brother what combinations had been discovered against him at Nottingham, which the governor resenting with great indignation, complained of them to the committee. The Solicitor White impudently denied the whole matter, or that ever the committee at Nottingham had had the least suspicion of the governor or his brother, or the least ground of any. When this had been with stiffness and impudence enough outfaced before the committee, Mr. Pierrepont, then fully convinced of their devilish malice, pulled a letter out of his pocket, wherein Mr. Millington made this suggestion to him against the governor and his brother, and desired that he might be armed with power to prevent and suppress them. This would have made others ashamed, but their solicitor was notwithstanding impudent and rudely pressing upon the committee, who though they were persons of honour, and after they discovered the governor's innocence, were not forward to oppress him; yet as they were statesmen, so they were not so ready to relieve him as they ought to have been, because they could not do it without a high reflection upon one of their own members, who encouraged all those little men in their wicked persecution of him. They were such exquisite rogues, that all the while some of them betrayed one another to the governor, and told him, under pretence of honesty and conscience, the bottom of their whole designs, showed the foul original drafts of their articles, in the men's own hands that contrived them; and told him how, not so much dislike of him, as covetousness and ambition to advance themselves upon his ruins, had engaged them thus against him, and made them contrive that villainy to accuse him and his brother of treachery, and to have seized their garrisons, under that pretence, and gotten them to be made prisoners; and then Mr. Millington undertook to have so lodged their petitions in the parliament, that they should never have been heard and relieved.[1] Colonel Thornhagh too was to have been wrought out of his command, and they had divided the spoil before they caught the lions. Millington's son was designed to be governor of the castle; the ten pounds a week allowed for the governor's table, so many of the committeemen were to share by forty shillings a man; Chadwick was to be colonel of the town regiment, and Mason major; White

[1] It is averred in the *History of Independency*, "that the active speaking men pack committees who carry all the businesses of the house as they please, and when the matter is too bad, smother it with artificial delays."

colonel of the horse regiment, and Palmer, the priest, his major; and all the governor's friends were to be turned out, and their places disposed of to creatures of their own, who, drawn on with these hopes, were very active to work the governor and his party out of the opinion of all men. They forgot the public interest in this private quarrel, taking in all the malignant and debauched people that would join with them, to destroy the governor, whom they hated for his unmoved fidelity to his trust, and his severe restriction of lewdness and vice. But because he protected and favoured godly men that were sober, although they separated from the public assemblies, this opened wide the mouths of all the priests and all their idolaters, and they were willing enough to let the children of hell cry out with them to make the louder noise; and as we have since seen the whole cause and party ruined by the same practice, so at that time the zealots for God and the parliament turned all the hate they had to the enemies of both, and called on them to assist in executing their malice upon the faithful servant and generous champion of the Lord's and his country's just cause. And now the name of cavalier was no more remembered, Castilian being the term of reproach with which they branded all the governor's friends; and lamentable it was to behold how those wretched men fell away under this temptation, not only from public spiritedness, but from sobriety and honest, moral conversation; not only conniving at and permitting the wickedness of others, but themselves conversing in taverns and brothels, till at last Millington and White were so ensnared that they married a couple of alehouse wenches, to their open shame and the conviction of the whole country of the vain lives they led, and some reflection on the parliament itself, as much as the miscarriage of a member could cast on it, when Millington, a man of sixty, professing religion, and having but lately buried a religious matronly gentlewoman, should go to an alehouse to take a flirtish girl of sixteen; yet by these noble alliances, they much strengthened their faction with all the vain, drunken rogues in the town against the governor. Now, that their first plot had, by God's providence, been detected, they fell upon others, and set on instruments everywhere, to insinuate all the lies they could, that might render the governor odious to the town and to the horse of the garrison, whom they desired to stir up to petition against him, but could not find any considerable number that would freely do it; therefore they used all the strong motives they could, and told them that the governor sought to exercise an arbitrary power over them, and to have all their booties at his own disposal, and other such like things, by which at length they prevailed with many of Col. Thornhagh's regiment to subscribe a petition that they might be under the command of the committee, and not of any other person in the garrison. This petition was sent up by Captain Palmer, and he meeting Mr. Pigott at Westminster Hall, Mr. Pigott, in private discourse with him, began to bewail the scandalous conversation of certain persons of the committee, hoping that he, being familiar with them, might be a means to persuade them to reformation.

After this the governor, Colonel Thornhagh, Mr. Pigott, and some others, being in a tavern at Westminster, where they dined, Captain Palmer came to the door, and they bade him come in. Upon discourse, the governor pulled out of his pocket the articles which the committee had put in against him, showed them to Captain Palmer, and asked him whether he thought it possible that he should, after all his toils and services, have been articled against for such things. Palmer, who had been from the beginning with the committee, and knew the falsehood of these accusations, professed he was amazed at them, and that he had not till then heard anything of them. Continuing in further discourse, the governor mentioned an unchristian-like sermon, which Mr. Goodhall had preached, with invectives against him in his absence. Palmer undertook the justification of it with such saucy provocations, that the governor told him if it had not been more in respect to his black coat than his grey, he would have beaten him out of the room, which for his own safety he advised him to leave; so he went out very angry, and going to Captain White, told him how Mr. Pigott called him a whoremaster, Mr. Millington a drunkard, and Chadwick a knave. White, meeting Mr. Pigott in the hall, challenged him of these scandals. Mr. Pigott, seeing Palmer not far off, led White to him, and told him he knew that person had been his informer, repeating all he had said to him, and added, that it was in a desire for their reformation, but he would maintain that all the things he spoke were true. Palmer further, in his rage, puts into the committee a paper of reasons why he desired to be exempted from being under the governor; whereof one was, that he had cowardly and unhandsomely behaved himself on an occasion when Palmer's troop marched out with him to Elston. The governor sent a copy of this paper down to Palmer's own troop, and the lieutenant, cornet, and all the troopers sent up a certificate, under their hands, of the falsehood of their captain's accusation. After this, Palmer came into the garrison, and made a grievous exclamation all over the town against the governor and Mr. Pigott for traducing the ministers, Mr. Millington, and the committee; adding a false report, that the governor had thrown a trencher at his head; and abused the pulpit for persuading the people to vindicate them. Among other things, he misapplied a place in Nehemiah, where Nehemiah says, "I ate not the governor's bread, because the fear of the Lord was upon me," to the governor; that his accepting a public table, was a mark of the want of the fear of God; and many other such malicious wrestings of scripture did he and his fellow priests at that time practise. The committee of Nottingham, on their side, taking this occasion, called a public hall in the town, where two orations were made by Mr. Millington and Colonel Chadwick. Millington began with a large enumeration of Chadwick's worthy actions (known to no man), whereby he merited honour of all men, especially of this town; and then mentioning his own good services for the town, told them how ungratefully they were repaid by Mr. Pigott, with the scandalous aspersion of being drunkards and knaves; and that their singular affections and endeavours for the good of the town had exposed them to this calumny, wherefore they desired the town to join in their justification. Chadwick make just such another speech, and both of them seemed to pass by their own particular, and only to desire the other's justification; Chadwick, in his speech, saying that Mr. Pigott's abuse of Mr. Millington did not only asperse the committee, but even the parliament itself. Captain Lomax, then deputy-governor of the garrison, after they had spoken, stood up, and advised the townsmen that they should forbear to entangle themselves in things they understood not, adding that Mr. Pigott, and the gentlemen at London, were persons of such honour and prudence, that they would maintain whatever they had spoken of any man. Hereupon Captain Mason, and two malignant townsmen his soldiers, began to mutiny with high insolence, and to lay violent hands on him to thrust him out of the hall, giving him most reproachful terms; but the man being very stout quieted them, and would not depart till the hall broke up. After this, without acquainting the deputy-governor, they summoned another hall; but Lomax, seeing their inclination to mutiny, forbade it. Then, at ten o'clock at night, they got a common council together, at Mr. Salisbury's house, and there Mr. Millington again desired they would join in the vindication of himself, the ministers, and the committee, and got about eight of them to subscribe a blank paper. Then the committee, with certain instruments of theirs, appointed rounds to walk the town, persuading some, and threatening others, to set their hands to a petition, which none of them that subscribed knew what it was, but they told them it was for the good of the town.

All this while these petty committee fellows had carried themselves as absolute governors, and Plumptre was now their intimate favourite, and began to vapour that he would have the castle pulled down to re-erect the church, and the fort at the bridges thrown down, and all the arms and soldiers brought into the town.

But at London, the governor being grown into acquaintance with the gentlemen of the sub-committee that were to hear his business; and they perceiving with how much wicked malice he was prosecuted, Sir Henry Vane was so honourable as to give him advice to put his business in such a way, as might take away all colour from his enemies. Whereupon he put in some propositions to the committee of both kingdoms, for the composure of these differences, wherein he was willing to decline all things of his own right, which might be done without prejudice to the public service, and to pass by all the injuries that had been done him; which condescension gave such satisfaction, that forthwith the whole business was determined at the committee of both kingdoms, and the governor sent back to his charge, with instructions drawn up for all parties, and letters written to the officers and soldiers, both of horse and foot, to be obedient; and likewise letters to the mayor of the town and to the committee. The governor returning, word was brought to Nottingham, that on Friday night he lay at Leicester, whereupon the committee, who had heard the determination of things above, got them ready to be gone, but the soldiers having notice thereof, went to the deputy-governor and entreated him to stop the treasurer; whereupon he and the major of the regiment went to them, and entreated them to stay till the governor came, merely to see what instructions he brought with him from the powers above; but when they would not be persuaded fairly, then the deputy peremptorily forbade the treasurer, as he would answer it, not to go. But he refusing to obey, the deputy told him he should pass on his sword's point if he went, and accordingly went down to set guards at the Trent bridges; which being told them, they made haste and fled out at the other end of the town. Millington, Chadwick, Ayscough, Salisbury, and Mason (whom they had added to the committee to increase their faction), were the committee men, who took with them their new marshal and another of their created officers, Palmer, two more priests, and a town captain. The governor was met on his way homewards by some of his officers, and told with what joy his garrison and regiment were preparing to entertain him, in all expressions they could possibly make, by volleys of cannon and muskets, and ringing of bells, and all such declarations as used to be made in a public and universal rejoicing; but the governor, fearing his enemies might not bear such testimonies of love to him, without grief, sent into the town to desire them to forbear their kind intentions of giving him so loud a welcome. When he was now near the town, another messenger came to acquaint him, that all those who would have been grieved at his joyful entertainment were fled, and that those who remained would be much grieved if he should not be pleased to give them leave to receive him with such demonstrations of their joy as they could make. He now permitted them to do what they pleased; which leave being obtained, every one strove to declare his gladness with all imaginable expressions of love and honour, and with all the solemnities the time and place would afford. The governor on his side received them all with a cheerful obliging courtesy, and gave a large bounty to his loving soldiers, who made that day as great a festival as if themselves and their families had been redeemed from captivity. The mayor of the town, with his brethren in their scarlets, met him, and told him if he had been guilty of any-thing prejudicial to him, he was exceedingly sorry for it, for he infinitely honoured him, and all his errors had been through ignorance or misinformation, which he should be most ready to repair. That evening White came home pining with spite and envy at the governor and the gentlemen that joined with him, viz. Colonel Thornhagh, Mr. Pigott, Lieutenant-colonel Hutchinson, Major Widmerpoole, Captain Lomax, and Alderman James; for as to the mayor of the town, notwithstanding his fair professions publicly to the governor, White had the same night again turned about that weathercock.

The next day the governor and the committee with him sent a command to all the horse in town to march to the assistance of Derby and Leicester, to fortify a house called Coleorton; which not being taken notice of, the governor and Colonel Thornhagh summoned all the horse officers, and declared to them the orders of the committee of both kingdoms, to which they cheerfully promised obedience; but White being sent for among them, insolently refused to come up to the castle, and bade the governor come down to him to the committee's chamber; yet upon second thoughts he came up, and the governor took no notice for that time. On Monday the governor sent to the mayor to call a hall, but the mayor entreated him to forbear till they saw whether the committee-men that ran away would come back, and that he might go with Captain White to persuade them; both of which the governor assented to; but the men would not return, but went from Derby to London. Then the governor called a general muster, and read to them the instructions he had brought from the committee of both kingdoms, with which all the men were exceeding well pleased. But Captain White all this while would not deliver the letters he had for the committee and the mayor of Nottingham.

Some few days afterwards word was brought the governor that the new dragoons were come for ammunition, to march out upon some design he was not acquainted with, whereupon he sent to the guards at the bridges not to suffer them to pass without his ticket. Immediately afterwards, White came along with them, and being denied to pass, gave the guards such provocative language that they were forced to send for the governor. He came down and found White in high rage, who gave him all the vile terms and opprobrious language he could invent, to provoke him to some anger upon which he might have taken his advantage; but the governor only laughed at his fogue,[1] and would not let him go till he showed a warrant from the council of war at London, and then he permitted him, after White had told him that he would not be commanded by him, and a thousand such mutinous speeches. As he went towards London he met the horse coming home from Coleorton, to whom he told such lies of the governor's usage of him, that they were frightened from coming into the garrison, but that Colonel Thornhagh prevailed with them to take his engagement, that the governor should give them no ill usage. So they came back, and that week their colonel charged the enemy's quarters with them and took eighty horse, two horse colours, a major and some other officers. The bridge troop also met with Colonel Stanhope, governor of Shelford,[2] who had two parties, each as many as they; his party where he himself was, routed, and he ran away, while the other party charged them in the rear, upon whom they turned, routed, and chased them out of the field, took Lieutenant-colonel Stanhope and his ensign, and many other prisoners, with many horse and arms. In the absence of the governor and his brother, the committee had done all they could to discourage and dissipate this troop, and would neither give them money nor provisions; yet, upon hopes of their captain's return, they kept themselves together, and when the governor came home he recruited them.

The committee of both kingdoms had sent down at this time an order for all the horse of Nottingham and Derbyshire to join with three regiments of Yorkshire, and quarter about Newark, to straiten the enemy there; and accordingly they rendezvoused at Mansfield, and from thence marched to Thurgarton, where Sir Roger Cooper had fortified his house, and lined the hedges with musketeers, who, as the troops passed by, shot and killed one Captain Heywood. Hereupon Colonel Thornhagh sent to the governor, and

---

[1] French—*Fougue,* fury or passion.

[2] Here, viz. in the end of the year 1644, Shelford clearly appears to be a garrison for the king; yet Whitelocke, p. 96, says that in July, 1644, Lord Grey of Groby, and Sir John Gell, had the thanks of the parliament for taking it. This is an evident inaccuracy of Whitelocke's, or a very successful puff of Sir John's. To put it out of doubt, Sprigge, in his *Anglia Rediviva,* counts it among the king's garrisons, May, 1645; and Colonel Hutchinson, supported by Rossiter, took it in person and by storm a year after that.

desired to borrow some foot to take the house. The governor accordingly lent him three companies, who took the house, with Sir Roger Cooper and his brother, and forty men in it, who were sent prisoners to Nottingham; where, although Sir Roger Cooper was in great dread of being put into the governor's hands, whom he had provoked before upon a private occasion, yet he received such a civil treatment from him, that he seemed to be much moved and melted with it. The foot had done all the service, and run all the hazard, in taking the house, yet the booty was all given to the horse; this they had very just reason to resent, but notwithstanding, they marched along with them to Southwell, and there were most sadly neglected, and put upon keeping outguards for the horse, and had no provisions, so that the governor was forced to send them some out of his garrison, or else they had been left to horrible distress. Hereupon they went to the governor to desire they might come home, but upon Colonel Thornhagh's entreaty and engagement that they should be better used, the governor was content to let them stay a little longer, till more horse came up, which were sent for out of Yorkshire. In the meantime, those who were there already did nothing but harass the poor country; and the horse officers were so negligent of their own duty, and so remiss in the government of their soldiers, that the service was infinitely prejudiced, and the poor country miserably distressed. The Nottingham horse, being in their own country, and having their families in and about Nottingham, were more guilty of straggling than any of the rest; and Capt. White's whole troop having presumed to be away one night when they should have been upon the guard, the Newarkers beat up our quarters, and took almost two whole troops of that regiment. White's lieutenant, without any leave from the colonel, thereupon posted up to London, and contrived a complaint against the governor, to make him appear guilty of this disorder; but soon after Newark gave them another alarm, and the parliament horse made so slender an appearance that the officers, thereupon consulting in a council of war, concluded that the design could not be prosecuted without more force, and for the present broke up their quarters.

The committee men that ran away when the governor returned had taken the treasurer away with them, and left

neither any money, nor so much as the rent rolls whereby
the governor could be instructed where to fetch in any;[1]
but by the prudence and interest of himself, and his friends,
he procured a month's pay for the foot, and twenty shillings
a man for the horse,[2] as soon as he came home; and recruited
all the stores, which the committee had purposely wasted in
his absence, and fetched in a small stock of powder they had
laid in at Salisbury's house.   While he was thus industriously
setting the things in order which they had confounded, they
at London were as maliciously active to make more confusion.   They contrived many false and frivolous articles and
petitions against him, and proceeded to that degree of
impudence in desiring alterations, and casting reflections
upon the sub-committee itself, that they grew weary of them.
Mr. Pierrepont and Sir H. Vane being now taken notice of as
leaders of the independent faction,[3] when those gentlemen
out of mere justice and honour discountenanced their envy
and malice, they applied themselves to the presbyterian
faction, and insinuating to them that the justice of those
gentlemen was partiality to the governor, because he was a
protector of the now hated separatists, they prevailed to
have Sir Philip Stapleton and Sir Gilbert Garrett, two fierce
presbyterians, added to the sub-committee, to balance the
other faction, and found this wicked invention not a little
advantageous to them: yet Mr. Hollis, who was a person
of honour, did not comply with their factious spirits, but
gave the governor all just assistance against their malice
which lay in his power.[4]   But they quitting all modesty, and
pressing the committee with false affirmations and forgeries,

---

[1] Rent rolls of sequestrated or forfeited estates.

[2] One out of many instances of Colonel Hutchinson's generous devotion to the cause, which brought on him that load of debt, so oppressive to him in the reverse of affairs.   In p. 623 and 624, of Rushworth,
Thornhagh's Nottinghamshire horse state that they had served five
years, and received barely six shillings a week in all; and that there
was £40,000 due to them.   Judge, from these two corps, Colonel
Hutchinson's being twelve hundred infantry, and two or three troops
of dragoons, Thornhagh's about six hundred horse, what was the
general state of the army as to pay!   Mr. Sprigge might well say of
the troops as he does, " it was not their pay that pacified them, for had
they not had more civility than money, things had not been so fairly
managed."

[3] Probably it was the experience these two excellent politicians had
of Colonel Hutchinson's abilities and integrity on this trial which
induced them afterwards to take him for their associate.

[4] Mrs. Hutchinson, who in other places speaks with much disap-
probation of Mr. Hollis, here most candidly gives him his due.

that all men would lay down their arms if the governor were not removed, at length prevailed, that he should be the second time sent for to London to justify himself against them. In that blank, to which they had by fraud and threats procured so many signatures, they wrote a petition, alleging that the governor was so generally detested, that if he were not removed all men would fling down their arms; and the subscriptions they thus abused were those they procured to vindicate Mr. Millington. Salisbury and one Silvester had, for their own profit, gotten a commission to set on foot the excise in the county, and joined with them one Sherwin. These two were such pragmatical knaves, that they justly became odious to all men; and although necessity might excuse the tax in other places, yet here it was such a burden that no man of any honesty or conscience could have acted in it. For when plundering troops killed all the poor countrymen's sheep and swine, and other provisions, whereby many honest families were ruined and beggared, these unmerciful people would force excise out of them for those very goods which the others had robbed them of; insomuch that the religious soldiers said they would starve before they would be employed in forcing it, or take any of it for their pay. The governor, being inclined in conscience to assist the poor country, was very active in his endeavours to relieve them from this oppression, which his enemies highly urged in their articles against him. These excisemen came very pressingly to urge the governor to enforce the payment of it in the town; he told them before he would use compulsion he would try fair means, and call a hall to see whether the townsmen would be persuaded, which accordingly he did: but when the day came the excisemen came to the governor and advised him to take a strong guard with him, telling him that the butchers had been whetting their knives, and intended mischief, and had cast out many words, intimating a dangerous design. The governor told them he should not augment his usual guard, and could fear nothing, having no intent to do anything that might provoke them to mutiny. They went again to the men and told them the governor intended to come with many armed men, to compel them to pay it: whereupon when he came to the hall he found but a very slender appearance, yet those who were there were all fully resolved not to pay it; but the governor wrought with them to represent their reasons, in a humble manner, to the committee of both kingdoms, and that there should be a fuller meeting for that purpose the next week, and that in the meantime both parties should forbear any private addresses in this matter. To this the excisemen agreed; yet, notwithstanding, the governor took a whole packet of their letters going to London, which when he discovered, he also wrote to his friends in London on behalf of the garrison. The next week at a full meeting, a petition was signed, which the governor offered the town to have carried, being himself to go up, but they in a compliment refused to give him the trouble, pitching upon Captain Coates and the town-clerk to go up with it. They accordingly went, about the time that, after seven weeks' stay in the garrison, the governor was called again up to London to justify himself against the malicious clamours of his adversaries. When Captain Coates and the other came to London they applied themselves to Mr. Millington, who, perceiving that the governor stood for the ease of the garrison, put them into a way to frustrate their own designs, and so they returned home; and at the sessions, rendering the town an account of their negotiations, they told them they found it an impossible thing to get the excise taken off. Yet the governor knew a way how to ease them, but they feared he would be discouraged in it, because at his coming up he had found their disaffections expressed against him in a petition to cast him out of his command, " which," said the clerk, " you cannot do, for he still is and must be governor; therefore, if any of you have been cheated of your hands, contrary to your intentions and desires, you would do well to testify your honesty, by disclaiming what goes under your name." Soon after, these malignants stirred up the soldiers to mutiny, and there being no governor in the garrison that could tell how to order them otherwise, they were appeased with money; upon which occasion a general muster being called, the major told the soldiers how they were injured at London by a petition, preferred in the name of the whole garrison, to cast the governor out of his command, which, if it were not their desire, he wished them to certify to the contrary. They all with one voice cried, they desired no other governor; whereupon a certificate to that purpose was drawn up; but when it came to be subscribed, certain of the committee faction went up and down persuading the companies not to subscribe; and when they found how little they prevailed, they foamed for anger, and with such malicious railing, that one of the governor's soldiers, not able to bear them longer, cried out, "Why do we suffer these fellows to vapour thus? let us clout them out of the field:" but the major hearing it, committed him; and the next morning the certificate went up, subscribed with seven hundred townsmen's hands. After all was done, the major gave some small sum to the soldiers to drink, and the malicious faction, when they saw they could not hinder this certificate, made another false one of their own, that the major had with crowns a-piece hired all these subscriptions, with other such like lies, which when they could not make good, it is said they retracted their certificate at London.

The committee at London could never finish the business by reason of the impertinent clamours of the governor's enemies, therefore at length, wearied with the continual endless papers they had daily brought in, they made an order, wherein they assigned a certain day for the determination of their power, and in the meantime commanded all matter of crimination on both sides should be forborne. At the day they both appeared, but Mr. Millington presented a petition of a most insolent nature, and fresh articles against the governor, which gave the committee much distaste. The petition was, that whereas the committee had kept them ten weeks at great charges, they desired a speedy despatch now, according to their propositions. The committee were much offended at this, and told them they did them much injury to lay their stay upon them, who five weeks before desired them to return, and only leave a solicitor for each, and then they refused it; that they had broken their first orders, and given no satisfaction either for it nor for their last, in bringing in articles against the governor. They took it very ill that they, who were plaintiffs, should prescribe to them, who were judges, how to determine the business; wherefore they ordered that the governor should return and pursue his first instructions, till he received new ones, and that the business should be reported to the house. The governor sent his brother down to take care of the garrison, and stayed himself to receive the final determination of the house, where Mr. Millington, through his interest, kept off the report, by several tricks and unjust delays, for about three or four months.

When the lieutenant-colonel came down, the captains were wonderfully obedient, and all things pretty quiet, but the governor's officers were discouraged at the countenance which was given to his enemies, and the impunity of all the crimes of that faction. He having a certain spirit of government, in an extraordinary manner, which was not given to others, carrying an awe in his presence that his enemies could not withstand, the garrison was much disordered by his absence, and in daily peril; although the lieutenant-colonel was as faithful and industrious in managing that charge as any person could be, and as excellent a person, but in a different way from his brother. Firmness and zeal to the cause, and personal valour he had equally, but that vigour of soul which made him invincible against all assaults, and overcoming all difficulties he met in his way, was proper to himself alone. The lieutenant-colonel was a man of the kindest heart and the most humble familiar deportment in the world, and lived with all his soldiers as if they had been his brothers; dispensing with that reverence which was due to him, and living cheerful and merry, and familiar with them, in such a manner that they celebrated him, and professed the highest love for him in the world, and would magnify his humility and kindness, and him for it, in a high degree above his brother. But with all this they grew so presumptuous that, when any obedience was exacted beyond their humours or apprehensions, they would often dare to fail in their duty; whereas the governor, still keeping a greater distance, though with no more pride, preserved an awe that made him to be equally feared and loved, and though they secretly repined at their subjection, yet they durst not refuse it; and, when they came to render it on great occasions, they found such wisdom and such advantage in all his dictates that, their reason being convinced of the benefit of his government, they delighted in it, and accounted it a happiness to be under his command, when any public necessity superseded the mutiny of those private lusts, whereby all men naturally, but especially vulgar spirits, would cast off their bridle, and be only their own rulers.[1]

---

[1] In the delineation of characters Mrs. Hutchinson remarkably excels. Nothing can be more amiable than that which she here draws

As the governor's absence was the occasion of many neglects in the government, not by his brother's fault, but the soldiers', who wanting their pay (which, while the committee should have been providing, they were spending in vexatious prosecutions of the governor), they were therefore discontented, and through that, careless of their duty; so, on the other side, the cavaliers, who were not ignorant of the dissensions in the garrison, took the advantage, and surprised the lieutenant-colonel's fort at the Trent bridges, while he was employed in keeping the castle. His soldiers in his absence lying out of their quarters, had not left above thirty men upon the guard, who were most of them killed, the ensign fighting it out very stoutly, after their entrance, till he died. The lieutenant-colonel was exceedingly afflicted with this loss, but presently applied himself to secure what remained. The whole town was in a sad uproar, and this happening upon a Lord's day in the morning, in May, 1645, all the people were in such a consternation that they could keep no sabbath that day. Then the lieutenant-colonel had an experiment of vulgar spirits, for even his own soldiers, who were guilty of the loss of the place by being out of their quarters, began to exclaim against him for a thousand causeless things; and although he laboured amongst them with as much courage and vigour as any man could use, to settle their spirits and regain the place, yet they slighted him most unjustly, and all cried out now to have the governor sent for, as if he himself had been their castle.

Immediately after the unhappy surprise of the bridges, the lieutenant-colonel sent away to his brother a post, who by some of the lower fords got over the water, and carried the sad news to London. A trumpet was sent to the bridges, and obtained the dead bodies of the soldiers who were slain at the surprise, and they were brought up to the town in carts and buried. There were about twenty of them, very good and stout men, though it availed them not in their last need, when a multitude had seized them unawares. All that day a body of the enemy faced the town, which, through terrors without and discouragements and discontents within, was in a very sad posture. The malignant faction against the governor improved even this occasion, and suggested to the

of Mr. George Hutchinson, and this character he will be found to sustain with increased esteem to the end of the history.

town that the castle would be the cause of their ruin; that the governor and his soldiers would secure themselves there, and leave the town undefended; and because the lieutenant-colonel was very strict that none of the castle-soldiers should lie out of their quarters, lest that place might be surprised as well as the other, the townsmen renewed their railings against the castle, and their malice to all that were in it; but the lieutenant-colonel, regarding none of their unjust railings, by God's blessing upon his vigilance, kept the town and castle till his brother's return.

As soon as the news came to the governor at London, he thought it time to throw off that patience with which he had hitherto waited at great expense, and went to the parliament-house before the house sat, and there acquainted the Speaker what had befallen at Nottingham, desiring he might be called to make a relation of it in the open house, or else he told the Speaker, though he died for it, he would press in and let them know how much the cause suffered by the indirect practices, which were partially connived at by some of their members. The Speaker seeing him so resolved, procured him, when the house was set, to be called in: and there he told them how their fort was lost, and, for ought he knew, the garrison, by that time; which was no more than what he had long expected, through the countenance that was, by one of their members, given to a malignant faction, that obstructed all the public service, disturbed all the honest soldiers and officers in their duty, and spent the public treasury, to carry on their private malice. He further told them, how dishonourable, as well as destructive to their cause, it was, that their members should be protected in such unjust prosecutions, and should make the privilege of the house their shelter, to oppress the most active and faithful of their servants. This and many other things he told them, with such boldness, that many of the guilty members had a mind to have committed him, but he spoke with such truth and convincing reason, that all those of more generous spirits, were much moved by it, and angry that he had been so injuriously treated, and desired him to take post down and to use all means to regain the place, and gave him full orders to execute his charge without disturbance.[1] From that

[1] How would a similar expostulation, made at the bar of the honourable house, be received at the present day?

time Mr. Millington so lost his credit, that he never recovered the esteem he formerly had among them; and after that time, the governor's enemies perceiving they were not able to mate[1] him, made no more public attempts, though they continued that private malice, which was the natural product of that antipathy there was between his virtues and their vices.[2] Neither was it his case alone; almost all the parliament-garrisons were infested and disturbed with like factious little people, insomuch that many worthy gentlemen were wearied out of their commands, and oppressed by a certain mean sort of people in the house, whom to distinguish from the more honourable gentlemen, they called *Worsted-stocking Men*. Some as violently curbed their committees, as the committees factiously molested them.[3] Nor were there factions only in particular garrisons, but the parliament house itself began to fall into the two great oppositions of Presbytery and Independency: and, as if discord had infected the whole English air with an epidemical heart-burning and dissension in all places, even the king's councils and garrisons were as factiously divided. The king's commissioners and the governor at Newark fell into such high discontents, that Sir Richard Byron, the governor, was changed, and Sir Richard Willis put into his place.[4] This accident of the bridges put an end to that vexatious persecution wherewith the governor had had so many sore exercises of his wisdom, patience, and courage, and so many experiences of God's mercy and goodness, supporting him in all his trials, and bearing him up against all discouragements, not only to stand without the least dejection himself, but to be able to hold up many others, who were ready to sink under the burden of unrighteousness and oppression, where they

[1] Mate, conquer; Fr. *matter*, an expression taken from the game of chess.

[2] It must almost have exhausted the patience of the reader, and certainly have excited his highest indignation, to follow through all their mazes the crafty and atrocious persecutors of Colonel Hutchinson; at the same time it must have been a great consolation to him to see integrity supported by discretion thus work out its own preservation. We may now congratulate him on emerging from these mists and intricacies, and finding himself in open field and daylight, where the colonel's nobler virtues can display themselves.

[3] These men were but the natural consequences of a state of revolution. Did these worsted-stocking men bear no likeness to the Jacobins of modern days?

[4] The same who afterwards became a spy for Cromwell; a bad substitute for the loyal Byron!

expected just thanks and rewards. It cost the governor above three hundred pounds to defend himself against their calumnies, renewed forgeries, and scandals, laid upon him; but God was with him in all in a wonderful manner, bringing truth to light through all the clouds of envy that sought to obscure it, and making his innocence and uprightness to shine forth as the noon-day, justifying him even in the eye of his enemies, and covering them with shame and confusion of face. They maintained their prosecution of him out of the public stock, and were not called to account for so misspending it. Mr. Millington perceiving how much he had lost himself by it, applied himself to seek a reconciliation by flattering letters, and professions of conviction and repentance of his unjust siding with those men. The governor, who was of a most reconcilable nature, forgave him, and ever after lived in good friendship with him.[1] Others of them also afterwards, when they saw the governor out of their power, some through fear, and others overcome with his goodness, submitted to him, who lived to see the end of them all; part of them dying before any disgrace or great sorrows overtook him, and those who survived, renouncing and apostatising from their most glorious engagements, and becoming guilty of those crimes for which they falsely accused him, while he remained firm, and dying sealed up the profession of his life; in all the future difficulties of which, he was still borne up with the experience of God's goodness and manifold protections.

The governor being dismissed from the parliament, immediately took post, and coming through Northampton, met his old engineer, Hooper, and brought him with him to Nottingham, where, by God's mercy, he arrived safe about three days after the loss of the bridges, and was welcomed as if safety and victory, and all desirable blessings, had come in his train. His presence reinforced the drooping garrison, and he immediately consulted how to go about regaining the fort. To this purpose, and to hinder the enemy from having an inlet into the town by the bridges, he made a little fort on the next bridge, and put a lieutenant and thirty men into it,

---

[1] As Mr. Millington will figure no more in this history, the reader is here informed that he finished his career, after becoming one of the judges who sentenced Charles the First, by coming in upon proclamation, making a pitiful recantation, and being sentenced to perpetual imprisonment.

thereby enclosing those in the fort the enemy had surprised, whom he resolved to assault on the town side, having thus provided that their friends should not come from the other side [1] to help them. But those of Newark understanding this, came as strong as they could one morning, and assaulted the little new fort, where Lieutenant Hall, failing of that courage which he had professed when he begged the honour of keeping it, gave it up, which the governor seeing from the other side, was exceedingly vexed at, and marched up to the bridge to assault them in that fort; but he found that they had only stormed the other little fort to make their own way to be gone, and that they had made shift to get to their friends upon the ribs of two broken arches, which, when they had served to help their passage, they pulled up, to hinder pursuit after them: and thus in a month's space God restored to the governor the fort which was lost in his absence; and he newly fortified the place and repaired the bridges, whereby the great market out of the vale was again brought into the town, to their exceeding joy and benefit.

This summer there was a much greater progress made in the war than had been before, and the new parliament army prosecuted it so much in earnest, that they made a show to block up the king in his main garrison at Oxford, but he broke out, and joining Prince Rupert's horse, came, after several attempts elsewhere, to Leicester, which he took by storm. The loss of this town was a great affliction and terror to all the neighbouring garrisons and counties, whereupon Fairfax closely attended the king's motions, came within a few days and fought with the king, and overcame him in that memorable battle at Naseby, where his coach and cabinet of letters were taken; which letters being carried to London and printed, and manifested his falsehood, how that, contrary to his professions, he had endeavoured to bring in Danes and Lorrainers, and Irish rebels, to subdue the good people here, and had given himself up to be governed by the queen in all affairs both of state and religion.[2] After this fight Fairfax

---

[1] To understand this rightly it is necessary to be informed, that in approaching Nottingham from the south there is a very wide valley, through which the Trent and the Lene run in several branches, over which are bridges united by a causeway.

[2] The public is in possession of these, they having been printed by the parliament, which some have thought a hardship, but surely without reason. It is useless here to discuss the question as to what help it was allowable for the king to call in· but it is not out of all

took again the town of Leicester, and went into the west, relieved Taunton, took Bristol, and many other garrisons. West Chester also and other places were taken that way. Meanwhile, the king, having coasted about the countries, came at last to Newark, and there his commanders falling out among themselves, he changed the governor, and put the lord Bellasis into the place, and went himself to Oxford, where he was at last blocked up.

When Sir Thomas Fairfax was made chief general, Poyntz was made major-general of the northern counties, and a committee of war was set up at York, whereof Colonel Pierrepont, by his brother's procurement, was appointed one, and was pretty well satisfied, as thinking himself again set above Colonel Hutchinson, because all the northern garrisons were to receive orders from that committee: but the governor heeding not other men's exaltations or depressions, only attended to his own duty. About the latter end of this summer, Poyntz came to Nottingham with all the horse that could be gathered in the neighbouring counties. He had before marched with them and the Nottingham regiment into Cheshire, and brought several gentlemen prisoners into the garrison of Nottingham, who had been taken in divers encounters. When he marched out, Palmer the priest, not daring to venture himself in the field, laid down his commission, when he saw that there was now no connivance to be found at disobeying commands.

By reason of the rout at Naseby, and the surrender of Carlisle and several other garrisons to the Scots, the broken forces of the cavaliers had all repaired to Newark, and that was now become the strongest and best fortified garrison the king had, and Poyntz was ordered to quarter his horse about it, till the Scots should come on the other side and besiege it. At that time also the king himself was there.[1] The governor having informed Poyntz how prejudicial it would be to his design to suffer those little garrisons in the Vale at Shelford and Wiverton to remain, it was agreed that all the forces

question that the discovery of that bitterness with which he was inclined to pursue the quarrel, and the fraudulency with which he had managed treaties, and showed that he meant to do others, cut up by the roots both compassion and confidence.

[1] Having come hither from Wales with a body of three thousand men; he stayed till fearing to be besieged by the Scots, who were approaching, he went away by night to Oxford, November 6, 1645.

should take them in their way. But the governor having obtained permission of Poyntz, through a respect he had to the family, sent a letter to Colonel Philip Stanhope, governor of Shelford, to persuade him to surrender the place he could not hold, and to offer to obtain honourable terms for him, if he would hearken to propositions. Stanhope returned a very scornful, huffing reply, in which one of his expressions was, that he should lay Nottingham castle as flat as a pancake, and such other bravadoes, which had been less amiss, if he had done anything to make them good. Hereupon the whole force marched against the place, and the several posts were assigned to the several colonels. The governor, according to his own desire, had that which seemed most difficult assigned to him, and his quarters that night were appointed in Shelford town. When he came thither, a few of the Shelford soldiers were gotten into the steeple of the church, and from thence so played upon the governor's men that they could not quietly take up their quarters. There was a trap door that led into the belfry, and they had made it fast, and drawn up the ladder and the bell-ropes, and regarded not the governor's threatening them to have no quarter if they came not down, so that he was forced to send for straw and fire it, and smother them out. Hereupon they came down, and among them there was a boy who had marched out with the governor's company, when he went first against Newark, and carried himself so stoutly, that Captain Wray begged him for a foot-boy, and when his troop was once taken by the enemy, this boy, being taken among them, became one of their soldiers. The governor making him believe he should be hanged immediately for changing his party, and for holding out to their disturbance, where he could not hope for relief, the boy begged he might be spared, and offered to lead them on to the only place where they could enter, where the palisade was unfinished. The governor, without trusting to him, considered the probability of his information, kept him under guard, and set him in the front of his men, and he accordingly proved to have told them the truth in all that he had said, and did excellent good service, behaving himself most stoutly. The governor being armed, and ready to begin the assault, when the rest were also ready, Captain White came to him, and, notwithstanding all his former malicious prosecutions, now pretended the most tender care and love that could be declared, with all imaginable flattery; and persuaded the governor not to hazard himself in so dangerous an attempt, but to consider his wife and children, and stand by among the horse, but by no means to storm the place in his own person. Notwithstanding all his false insinuations, the governor, perceiving his envy at that honour which his valour was ready to reap in this encounter, was exceedingly angry with him, and went on upon the place. This being seated on a flat, was encompassed with a very strong bulwark, and a great ditch without, in most places wet at the bottom, so that they within were very confident of being able to hold it out, there being no cannon brought against them; because also a broken regiment of the queen's, who were all papists, were come in to their assistance. A regiment of Londoners was appointed to storm on the other side, and the governor at the same time began the assault at his post. His men found many more difficulties than they expected, for after they had filled up the ditches with faggots and pitched the scaling ladders, they were twenty staves too short, and the enemy, from the top of the works, threw down logs of wood, which would sweep off a whole ladderful of men at once: the lieutenant-colonel himself was once or twice so beaten down. The governor had ordered other musketeers to beat off those men that stood upon the top of the works, which they failed to do by shooting without good aim; but the governor directed them better, and the Nottingham horse dismounting, and assailing with their pistols, and head-pieces, helped the foot to beat them all down from the top of the works, except one stout man, who stood alone, and did wonders in beating down the assailants, which the governor being angry at, fetched two of his own musketeers and made them shoot, and he immediately fell, to the great discouragement of his fellows. Then the governor himself first entered, and the rest of his men came in as fast as they could. But while this regiment was entering on this side, the Londoners were beaten off on the other side, and the main force of the garrison turned upon him. The cavaliers had half moons within, which were as good a defence to them as their first works; into these the soldiers that were of the queen's regiment were gotten, and they in the house shot from out of all the windows. The governor's men, as soon as they got in, took the stables and all their horses, but the governor

himself was fighting with the captain of the papists and some
others, who, by advantage of the half moon and the house,
might have prevailed to cut him off and those that were with
him, which were not many.   The enemy being strengthened
by the addition of those who had beaten off the assailants
on the other side, were now trying their utmost to vanquish
those that were within.   The lieutenant-colonel, seeing his
brother in hazard, made haste to open the drawbridge, that
Poyntz might come in with his horse; which he did, but
not before the governor had killed that gentleman who was
fighting with him, at whose fall his men gave way.   Poyntz
seeing them shoot from the house, and apprehending the king
might come to their relief, when he came in, ordered that no
quarter should be given.   And here the governor was in
greater danger than before, for the strangers hearing him
called governor, were advancing to have killed him, but that
the lieutenant-colonel, who was very watchful to preserve
him all that day, came in to his rescue, and scarcely could
persuade them that it was the governor of Nottingham;
because he, at the beginning of the storm, had put off a very
good suit of armour that he had, which being musket-proof,
was so heavy that it heated him, and so would not be persuaded by his friends to wear anything but his buff coat.
The governor's men, eager to complete their victory, were
forcing their entrance into the house: meanwhile Rossiter's
men come and took away all their horses, which they had
taken away when they first entered the works and won the
stables, and left in the guard of two or three, while they were
pursuing their work.   The governor of Shelford, after all
his bravadoes, came but meanly off; it is said he sat in his
chamber, wrapt up in his cloak, and came not forth that day;
but that availed him not, for how, or by whom, it is not
known, but he was wounded and stripped, and flung upon
a dunghill.   The lieutenant-colonel, after the house was
mastered, seeing the disorder by which our men were ready
to murder one another, upon the command Poyntz had
issued to give no quarter, desired Poyntz to cause the
slaughter to cease, which was presently obeyed, and about
sevenscore prisoners were saved.   While he was thus busied,
inquiring what was become of the governor, he was shown
him naked upon the dunghill; whereupon the lieutenant-
colonel called for his own cloak and cast it over him, and sent

him to a bed in his own quarters, and procured him a surgeon. Upon his desire he had a little priest, who had been his father's chaplain, and was one of the committee faction; but the man was such a pitiful comforter, that the governor, who was come to visit him, was forced to undertake that office: but though he had all the supplies they could every way give him, he died the next day.[1] The house which belonged to his father, the Earl of Chesterfield, was that night burned, none certainly knowing by what means, whether by accident or on purpose; but there was most ground to believe that the country people, who had been sorely infested by that garrison, to prevent the keeping it by those who had taken it, purposely set it on fire. If the queen's regiment had mounted their horses and stood ready upon them when our men entered, they had undoubtedly cut them all off; but they standing to the works, it pleased God to lead them into that path he had ordained for their destruction, who being papists, would not receive quarter, nor were they much offered it, being killed in the heat of the contest, so that not a man of them escaped.

The next day our party went to Wiverton, a house of the Lord Chaworth's, which, terrified with the example of the other, yielded upon terms, and was by order pulled down and rendered incapable of being any more a garrison.

Poyntz now quartered all his horse in the towns about Newark, and since he had no peculiar regiment of his own, the governor's regiment served him for his guards. The Scots also came and quartered on the other side of the town towards the north.

---

[1] Thoroton, in his *History of Nottinghamshire*, says. " Shelford House was a garrison for the king, and commanded by Colonel Philip Stanhope, son of the first Earl of Chesterfield, which being taken by a storm, he and many of his soldiers were therein slain, and the house afterwards burned; his brother Ferdinando Stanhope was slain some time before by a parliament soldier at Bridgford." This last happened in that skirmish with the bridge soldiers recited in page 213, where he is said only to have been made prisoner. Lady Catherine Hutchinson, who attested the remark to Colonel Hutchinson her son-in-law's disadvantage, page 136, was the sister of the Earl of Chesterfield, and of course aunt of Colonel Stanhope, and as she takes no exception to it, we may safely give credit to this story of the storming of Shelford with all its circumstances: a very interesting one it certainly is, and told in the most unaffected, and therefore most affecting, manner; the scene with which it finishes is surely as striking and as singular as any that story or imagination can furnish, not excepting the death of Le Fevre in the *Sentimental Journey*.

All that winter the governor lay at the Leaguer, and about Christmas time writs were sent down for new elections to fill up the parliament. There being a burgess-ship void at Nottingham, the town would needs, in a compliment, make the governor free, in order to elect him to the parliament. Mr. Francis Pierrepont hearing this, wrote to the governor to desire that he would rather come into his father's place in the county, and give him his assistance in this, as he should engage his own and all his friends' interest for him in the county. The governor, who was ever ready to requite injuries with benefits, employed his interest in the town to satisfy the gentleman's desire, and having very many in his regiment that had votes, he sent for them all home the night before the day of election; which had like to have been a very sad one, but that by the mercy of God, and the courage of Poyntz and the lieutenant-colonel and Captain Poulton, it had not so bad an event.[1] The Newarkers, hearing that so many of the regiment were away, fell upon their quarters, and most of the men being surprised, were rather endeavouring flight than resistance; when the lieutenant-colonel and Captain Poulton rallied all they could find, lined some pales with musketeers, and beat the enemy again out of their quarters, and Poyntz, mounting with as many horse as were about him, which was very few, followed them in the night up to the very works of Newark. Some loss there was in the quarters, but nothing considerable; some soldiers ran away home, and brought the governor word they were all cut off, but his brother sent a messenger to acquaint him with the contrary. Hereupon, immediately after the election, he returned back again with his men. Not long after, the elections were made for the county, who all pitched upon the governor, in his father's room. White, whose envy never died, used all the endeavours he could to have hindered it;

[1] A fair and honest acknowledgment of a considerable oversight! But this passage leads us to observe of what sort of people the parliament armies were composed, viz. the horse mostly of freeholders, the foot of burghers. It will not probably be thought beside the purpose to quote here Whitelocke's description of Cromwell's own regiment. "He had a brave regiment of his countrymen, most of them freeholders and freeholders' sons, and who upon matter of conscience engaged in this quarrel; and thus being well armed within by the satisfaction of their own consciences, and without by good iron arms, they would, as one man, stand firmly and charge desperately." These circumstances must be allowed their due weight, when we come to consider the right of the army to interfere in matters of state.

but when he saw he could do no harm, with a sad heart, under a false face, he came and took his part of a noble dinner the new knights had provided for the gentlemen of the country. Without any competition Mr. Hutchinson had the first voice in the room of his father, and Mr. Pigott the second, in the room of Mr. Sutton, now a commissioner at Newark. About the same time Colonel Thornhagh was chosen burgess for the town of Retford; but none of them went up to their places in parliament till the siege of Newark was finished.

Poyntz drew a line about the town, and made a very regular entrenchment and approaches, in such a soldier-like manner as none of them who had attempted the place before had done. Most of that winter they lay in the field, and the governor, carried on by the vigour and greatness of his mind, felt no distemper then by that service, which all his captains and the soldiers themselves endured worse than he. Besides daily and hourly providences, by which they were preserved from the enemy's cannons and sallies, there were some remarkable ones, by which God kept the governor's life in this Leaguer. Once as Poyntz and he, and another captain, were riding to view some quarter of the town, a cannon bullet came whizzing by them, as they were riding all abreast, and the captain, without any touch of it, said he was killed; Poyntz bid him get off, but he was then sliding down from his horse, slain by the wind of the bullet; they held him up till they got off from the place, but the man immediately turned black all over. Another time the governor was in his tent, and by chance called out; when he was scarcely out of it, a cannon bullet came and tore up the whole tent, and killed the sentinel at the door. But the greatest peril wherein all on the English side were, was the treachery of the Scots, which they had very good reason to apprehend might have been the cutting off of all that force. Sir Thomas Fairfax had now besieged Oxford, and the king was stolen out of the town and gone in disguise, no man knew whither, but at length he came into the Scots' army. They had before behaved themselves very oddly to the English, and been taking sundry occasions to pick quarrels, when at the last certain news was brought to the English quarters that the king was come to the Scots, and by them received at Southwell. The English could then expect nothing but that the

Scots, joining with those that were in Newark, would fall upon them, who were far inferior in number to the other, and therefore they all prepared themselves, as well as they could, to defend themselves in their trenches. The governor had then very fine horses at the Leaguer, which he sent home to the garrison; but while they were in expectation of being thus fallen upon, the king had more mind to be gone; and because the Scots knew not how to break up their quarters while the town was not taken, the king sent to my Lord Bellasis, the governor of Newark, to surrender up the place immediately, which he did upon pretty handsome terms, but was much discontented that the king should have no more regard for them who had been so constant to his service.[1] The governor with his regiment was appointed to receive the town and the arms, and to quarter in it; where he now went and had the greatest danger of all, for the town was all over sadly infected with the plague; yet it so pleased God that neither he nor any of the fresh men caught the infection, which was so raging there that it almost desolated the place.

Whether the king's ill council or his destiny led him, he was very failing in this action; for had he gone straight up to the parliament and cast himself upon them, as he did upon the Scots, he had in all probability ruined them, who were highly divided between the presbyterian and independent factions; but in putting himself into the hands of the mercenary Scotch army, rather than the parliament of England, he showed such an embittered hate to the English nation, that it turned many hearts against him. The Scots in this business were very false both to the parliament and to the king. For them to receive and carry away the king's person with them, when they were but a hired army, without either the consent or knowledge of the parliament, was a very false carriage in them; but besides that, we had *certain evidences* that they were prepared, and had an intent to have cut off the English army which beleaguered Newark,[2] but that God

[1] Among the names of those who signed the capitulation on the part of the parliament (as it appears in Rushworth) are those of Colonel Hutchinson and Colonel Twissleton.

[2] It has always been, and perhaps will always remain a mystery, what were the conditions or engagements on which the king relied in putting himself into the hands of the Scots. In Clarendon's *State Papers* there are several letters from the French ambassador, persuading him to this measure, and undertaking for the Scots to give him effectual support; and the king wrote very positively to Ormond a

changed their counsels and made them take another course, which was to carry the king to Newcastle, where they again sold him to the parliament for a sum of money.

The country being now cleared of all the enemy's garrisons, Colonel Hutchinson went up to London to attend his duty there, and to serve his country as faithfully, in the capacity of a senator, as he had before in that of a soldier. When he came there he found a very bitter spirit of discord and envy raging, and the presbyterian faction (of which were most of those lords and others that had been laid aside by the self-denying ordinance), were endeavouring a violent persecution, upon the account of conscience, against those who had in so short a time accomplished, by God's blessing, that victory which he was not pleased to bestow upon them. Their

letter, which was intercepted, and is produced by Rushworth, that the Scots had given him good security that they would join their forces to those of Montrose and the king's friends. On the other side, the general and committee of estates resident in the Scots' army wrote, that " the king came privately into their camp, and that there had been no *treaty* or *capitulation* with him by them, nor any in their names, and that the assertion of the king in his letter to Ormond was a *damnable untruth*." Heylin, in his *Hist. of Presbyterianism*, says, " The commissioners residing with the Scotch army, promised protection to the king and his friends, but broke their promise and sold him for £200,000, *as they would have done our Saviour for half the money*." In another place he says, " Lowdon ranted to some tune about the disgrace of selling the king, but however the Presbyterians on both sides concluded the sinful bargain." Not to dwell upon what is elsewhere said on either side of the question, the symptoms of treachery discerned by Colonel Hutchinson and others, before and at the time of the king's arrival, give ample reason to conclude that the Scots were aware of his coming, and that either there were two parties, one of which was devoted to the king and the other not so, and that the latter was prevalent, or else that the whole expected from the king conditions which he was unwilling to perform, and principally the signing the covenant, the refusal of which they afterwards openly resented, and this might be that " change God is said to make in their counsels."

There is much less doubt as to the justice of Mrs. Hutchinson's reflection, that, of all courses, that which he took was the worst: she, who had a truly British heart, well knew what effect ingenuous confidence would have had on the parliament, with the virtues as well as vices of which she was well acquainted. The parliament had asked him to " come to them with a royal, not martial, attendance, and promised to receive him well." The last message was passed on March 23, and in a few days after he went to the Scots' army. *Quem Deus vult perdere prius dementat.* Those whom God destines to destruction he first deprives of their understanding. Artifice, which was Charles's greatest fault, was likewise his ruin, and he fell not like a conquered prince, as *præda victoris*, a noble prize for the victor, but *pretium sceleris*, the object of a scandalous traffic, apprehended and sold as a culprit and fugitive; and forfeited as his last resource, that respect and pity which the generous reserve for the unfortunate.

directory of worship was at length sent forth for a three years' trial, and such as could not conform to it, marked out with an evil eye, hated and persecuted under the name of separatists.[1] Colonel Hutchinson, who abhorred that malicious zeal and imposing spirit which appeared in them, was soon taken notice of for one of the independent faction,[2] [whose heads were accounted Pierrepont, Vane, St. John's, and some few other grandees, being men that excelled in wisdom and utterance, and the rest were believed to adhere to them only out of faction, as if those who did not vain-gloriously lay out themselves, without necessity, but chose rather to hear and vote, had had no understanding of right and wrong but from the dictates of these great oracles.] Though, to speak the truth, they very little knew Colonel Hutchinson that could say he was of any faction; for he had a strength of judgment able to consider things himself and propound them to his conscience, which was so upright that the veneration of no man's person alive, nor the love of the dearest friend in the world, could make him do the least thing, without a full persuasion that it was his duty so to act. He very well understood men's gifts and abilities, and honoured those most whom he believed to manage them with most uprightness of soul, for God's glory and the good of his country, and was so far from envying the just renown any man acquired that he rejoiced in it. He never was any man's sectary, either in religious or civil matters, farther than he apprehended them to follow the rules of religion, honour, and virtue; nor any man's antagonist, but as he opposed that which appeared to him to be just and equal. If the greatest enemy he had in the world had propounded anything profitable to the public, he would promote it; whereas some others were to blame in that particular, and chiefly those of the presbyterian faction, who would obstruct any good, rather than that those they envied and hated

[1] Mrs. Hutchinson differs from most of those who have written on the subject respecting the rise and progress of the deadly feuds between the presbyterians and independents; but she differs not from the truth and reason. Certainly the most impartial historian is Rapin; but he, though a presbyterian, and labouring their defence, effects their condemnation. Vol. ii. p. 624, he says, "They thought themselves in slavery if themselves did not command." What need of more words?

[2] All that is contained between these two brackets had lines struck through it in the manuscript, and one of the names defaced.

should have the glory of procuring it; the sad effects of which pride grew at length to be the ruin of the most glorious cause that ever was contended for. At the first, many gentlemen, eminent in gifts and acquirements, were as eminent in zealous improvements of them, for the advantage of God's and their country's interests, whereby they obtained just glory and admiration among all good men; but while the creature was so magnified, God, who was the principal author, was not looked upon, and gave them therefore up to become their own and others' idols, and so to fall.

And now it grew to be a sad wonder, that the most zealous promoters of the cause were more spitefully carried against by their own faithful armies, by whom God had perfected their victory over their enemies, than against the vanquished foe, whose restitution they henceforth secretly endeavoured, by all the arts of treacherous, dissembling policy, in order that they might throw down those whom God had exalted in glory and power to resist their tyrannical impositions. At that time, and long after, they prevailed not, until that pious people too began to admire themselves, for what God had done by them, and to set up themselves above their brethren, and then the Lord humbled them again beneath their conquered vassals.[1]

So long as the army only resisted unjust impositions, and remained firm to their first pious engagement, Mr. Hutchinson adhered to that party, which protected them in the parliament house.[2] His attendance there changing his custom of life into a sedentary employment, less suitable to

---

[1] To those, and they are not few, who, like Colonel Hutchinson, believe the peculiar interposition of Providence, this remark of the punishment inflicted on those who abused its gifts, will appear pleasing and edifying; to those who admit only a general dispensation, the fall of each party successively by their own malversation, will seem a signal mark of justice; by both, this chain of causes and effects will be acknowledged to be drawn by the hand of a master.

[2] This history, which, as far as it relates to public affairs, is called only a summary, will nevertheless be found to redress many errors in larger histories, and to open a great field for reflection: in none, perhaps, more than in this question of the right of the army to interfere with the conduct of parliament or the business of the state: this is generally decided against them lightly and inconsiderately. The danger of admitting *armed* assemblies to *deliberate*, and the duty of a soldier to *obey*, but not *debate*, are very *boldly asserted*; and as this doctrine suits the governors of every state, it will always be favoured; but it goes on *a petitio principii*, a begging of the question that the military are the *hired servants* of the state: and military men have so

his active spirit, and more prejudicial to his health, he fell into a long and painful sickness, which many times brought him near the grave, and was not perfectly cured in four years. The doctors could not find a name for it; but at length resolved upon the running gout, and a cure, proper for that disease, being practised upon him, took effect.

The truth is, his great mind so far surmounted the frailty of his flesh, that it would never yield to the tenderness of his constitution, nor suffer him to feel those inconveniences of martial toils, which often cast down his captains, men of more able bodies and healthful complexions, while the business was in hand; but when that was finished, he found, what he had not leisure to consider before, that his body's strength was far unequal to the vigour of his soul.

After the surrender of Newark, Nottingham town and castle was continued a garrison for some time: between this and his greater employment at London, the governor divided himself. Meanwhile, upon the 15th day of July, 1646, propositions were sent to the king, then with the Scots at Newcastle, little higher than those which had been made him at

far agreed to this unjust postulate, that they have consented to accept that which is a nickname, or term of reproach, as the generic one of their whole profession; viz. soldier; which is but a translation of the Italian *soldato*, mercenary or hireling. It has been repeatedly shown how ill this term agreed with the parliament troops in general, being mostly volunteers, and freeholders or burghers, and ill, or sometimes not at all paid. Were such to be considered as mere machines, as having forfeited all right to an opinion of their own, and bound to support that of others?—If so, then those who expected to maintain our constitution by putting arms into the hands of almost all whom patriotism or the preservation of their property animated to take them up, would have bereaved it of nearly all its defenders! With good right did these men, who had taken a pious engagement to God and their country, and most manfully acquitted themselves of it, call on the parliament to complete it by a happy settlement. Their several petitions and remonstrances, preserved in Rushworth, vol. vii. p. 4, et infra, show that their views were just and rational, and such as have since in part been realised, in part are still wished for, viz. " The duration of parliaments to be limited; elections better regulated— the representation better distributed; improper privileges, and particularly that of being screened from creditors, given up; not bishops, but their coercive power and civil penalties taken away; the king restored to his rights (but with some restrictions as to appointments for ten years); the laws simplified and lessened in expense; monopolies set aside; tithes commuted, etc. But all this was interrupted by the domineering party." Who can help lamenting that there were not more found to unite with Colonel Hutchinson and this army to perfect the best system of government that ever did or will exist?

These proposals of the army are supposed to have been penned by Ireton.

Uxbridge; but he wove out delays, and would not assent to
them, hoping a greater advantage by the difference between
the two nations, and the factions in the city and parliament,
which both he and all his party employed their utmost
industry to cherish and augment. Both parliaments perceiving this, and not yet senseless of approaching destruction,
from the common enemy, began to be cemented by the king's
averseness to peace, and to consider how to settle the kingdom without him; and when they had agreed that the Scots
should deliver up the English garrisons for a certain sum of
money, it fell into debate how to dispose of the king's person;
where the debate was, not who should, but who should not
have him. At length, about January of the same year, two
hundred thousand pounds was carried down by part of the
army to Newcastle; and upon the payment of it, the Scots
delivered their garrisons, to the soldiers, and the king to
certain commissioners of both houses of parliament, who
conducted him honourably to his own manor of Holmeby,
in Northamptonshire.

During this time Sir Thomas Fairfax himself lay at Nottingham, and the governor was sick in the castle. The
general's lady was come along with him, having followed his
camp to the siege of Oxford, and lain at his quarters all
the while he abode [1] there. She was exceeding kind to her
husband's chaplains, independent ministers, till the army
returned to be nearer London, and then the presbyterian
ministers quite changed the lady into such a bitter aversion
against them, that they could not endure to come into the
general's presence while she was there; and the general had
an unquiet, unpleasant life with her, who drove away from
him many of those friends, in whose conversation he had

---

[1] Here is another of those paradoxes, with which historians have
perplexed themselves and their readers, reduced to a very plain tale.
It is generally said and believed, that Fairfax was a presbyterian, and
much wonder is expressed that he should have so faithfully (it is even
said *too faithfully*) served the independents; but it is impossible that
any one could have a more clear and certain knowledge of his religious
opinions than Colonel and Mrs. Hutchinson had, and they declare his
chaplains to have been *independent ministers ;* nor does it appear that
he ever *changed his opinion*, but only that he suffered himself to be
over-ruled by his wife. Heroes as great as he have been, both before
and since, under the same dominion; as Horace sets forth in his face-
tious ode to Xanthias Phoceus, parodied by Rowe:

Nec sit ancillæ tibi amor pudori.
Do not, most fragrant earl, disclaim.

found such sweetness. At Nottingham they had gotten a very able minister into the great church, but a bitter presbyterian; him and his brethren my Lady Fairfax caressed with so much kindness, that they grew impudent enough to preach up their faction openly in the pulpit, and to revile the others, and at length would not suffer any of the army chaplains to preach in the town. They then coming to the governor and complaining of their unkind usage, he invited them to come and preach in his house, which when it was known they did, a great concourse of people came thither to them; and the presbyterians, when they heard of it, were mad with rage, not only against them, but against the governor, who accidently gave them another occasion about the same time, a little before the general came. When formerly the presbyterian ministers had forced him, for quietness' sake, to go and break up a private meeting in the cannonier's chamber, there were found some notes concerning pædobaptism, which were brought into the governor's lodgings; and his wife having then more leisure to read than he, having perused them and compared them with the Scriptures, found not what to say against the truths they asserted, concerning the misapplication of that ordinance to infants; but being then young and modest, she thought it a kind of virtue to submit to the judgment and practice of most churches, rather than to defend a singular opinion of her own, she not being then enlightened in that great mistake of the national churches. But in this year she, happening to be with child, communicated her doubts to her husband, and desired him to endeavour her satisfaction; which while he did, he himself became as unsatisfied, or rather satisfied against it. First, therefore, he diligently searched the scriptures alone, and could find in them no ground at all for that practice; then he bought and read all the eminent treatises on both sides, which at that time came thick from the presses, and was still more satisfied of the error of the pædobaptists. After this, this wife being brought to bed, that he might, if possible, give the religious party no offence, he invited all the ministers to dinner, and propounded his doubt, and the ground thereof to them. None of them could defend their practice with any satisfactory reason, but the tradition of the church, from the primitive times, and their main buckler of federal holiness, which Tombs and Denne had so excellently overthrown. He and his wife then, professing themselves unsatisfied in the practice, desired their opinions, what they ought to do. Most answered, to conform to the general practice of other Christians, how dark soever it were to themselves; but Mr. Foxcraft, one of the assembly, said, that except they were convinced of the warrant of that practice from the word, they sinned in doing it: whereupon that infant was not baptised.[1] And now the governor and his wife, notwithstanding that they forsook not their assemblies, nor retracted their benevolences and civilities from them, yet were they reviled by them, called fanatics and anabaptists, and often glanced at in their public sermons. And not only the ministers, but all their zealous sectaries, conceived implacable malice against them upon this account; which was carried on with a spirit of envy and persecution to the last, though he, on his side, might well have said to them, as his Master said to the old Pharisees: "Many good works have I done among you; for which of these do you hate me?" Yet the generality, even of that people, had a secret conviction upon them, that he had been faithful to them, and deserved their love; and in spite of their own bitter zeal, could not but have a reverent esteem for him, whom they often railed at, for not thinking and speaking according to their opinions.

This year Sir Allen Apsley, governor of Barnstaple for the king, after the surrender of that garrison, came and retired to the governor's house, till his composition with the parliament was completed, the governor's wife being his sister, and the governor's brother having married the other sister;[2] and this was another occasion of opening the mouths of the malignants, who were ready to seize upon any one to his prejudice. Sir Allen Apsley had not his articles punctually performed, by which he suffered great expense and intolerable vexation; and the governor, no less concerned in the injustice done to him than if he had suffered it himself, endeavoured to protect him only in that which was just, and

[1] Surely this shows an unbecoming propensity to speculate in religion: the story is, however, told with candour.
[2] Amongst the discords and distraction, public and private, which must have harassed the reader's mind, it is soothing for a moment to contemplate the harmony which reigned within Colonel Hutchinson's family, and the sincere friendship between them and Sir Allen Apsley, which will re-appear on many and frequent occasions to the very close of his life.

for this was called a cavalier, and said to have changed his party, and a thousand more injuries; in which none were so forward as those who had all the while been disaffected to the whole parliament party; but after they were conquered, burying their spite against the cause in their own bosoms, suffered that secret fire to rise up in a black smoke against the most faithful assertors of it.

When the commissioners went down to fetch up the king from the Scots, one of the lords coming to visit the governor, and finding him at that time very sick, persuaded him to make use of one of the king's physicians that was with them, that was called Dr. Wilson, and was a very able physician; but he mistook the method of his cure, and made issues in both his arms, which rather wasted his strength than his disease, which when he was cured were stopped up. That spring, growing a little better for the present, he went to London, and having ineffectually tried several physicians, Sir Allen Apsley persuaded him to make use of Dr. Frazier, with whom he began a course of physic, in the midst of which the doctor came and acquainted him that he was likely to be imprisoned upon suspicion of carrying on designs against the parliament underhand, for now the Scots were threatening invasion and open war. He professed his innocency with many protestations, and desired Mr. Hutchinson to oblige him so far as to engage for him that he intended no design beyond his calling; which the colonel believing, undertook for him to the committee of Derby-house. When the false Scot having thus abused him, left a letter of lame excuse for him, and stole away out of England to the princes, then beyond the seas, leaving a blot upon Mr. Hutchinson for having undertaken for him;[1] but he, acknowledging his error in having been so abused, was thereby warned from credulity of any of that false nation any more. That summer he attended to the service of the house, being freed for a while from his distemper during the summer, till the fall of the leaf, when it returned again. In the meantime jealousies were sown between the parliament, the city of London, and the army. The presbyterian faction were earnest to have the army disbanded; the army resented the injury, and, being taught to value their own merit, petitioned the general

---

[1] This Dr. Frazier was afterwards employed by Charles the Second to negotiate with the Scots.

that they might be satisfied, not only in things relating to themselves particularly as an army, but the general concernments and liberties of the good people of the nation which they had fought for. The presbyterians were highly offended at this, and declared it with such violence as gave the army cause to increase their jealousies. The soldiers, led on to it by one Cornet Joyce, took the king from Holmeby out of the parliament commissioners' hands, and carried him about with them. The parliament voted that the king should come to Richmond, attended by the same persons that attended him at Holmeby; but the army, instead of obeying, impeached eleven members of the house of commons of high treason, and petitioned that those impeached members might be secluded the house, till they had brought in their answer to the charge; which being violently debated, they made a voluntary secession for six months. The general also entreated that the king might not be brought nearer to London than they would suffer the army to quarter. So he was carried with them to Royston, Hatfield, Reading, and at last to Woburn, till about July, 1647, when London grew into a tumult, and made a very rude violation upon the parliament house, which caused them to adjourn; when, understanding the fury to the citizens, the greatest part of the members, with the Speaker, withdrew and went to the army, among whom was Colonel Hutchinson.[1] The presbyterian members who stayed behind chose new Speakers, and made many new votes, and vigorously began to levy forces to resist the army, which were conducted by Massie and Poyntz. The parliament that was with the army made an order against the proceedings of the members at London, and advanced with the general; which, when the city heard of, their stomachs would not serve them to stand it out, but they sent commissioners, and, by the consent of the members with the general, obtained a pacification, upon condition that the city should disband all their new forces, deliver up their tower and their

---

[1] As did fourteen peers, among them the Earls of Manchester and Warwick, Lords Say and Sele and Mulgrave, and one hundred commoners, and the palsgrave, or elector palatine, visited them. It would have been very seasonable to have offered to the consideration of both parties Horace's beautiful apologue of the Horse and the Stag.

Cervus equum bello melior, etc.

The calling in foreign aid to control their antagonists proved equally destructive to both, but was begun by the presbyterians.

forts to the general, and desert the members then sitting. They daring to deny nothing, the general came triumphantly to Westminster, and brought back both the Speaker and the members, and put them again in their seats. The general had solemn thanks from both houses, and then, with all his chief officers, marched through the city, from the western parts of it to the tower, where many commands were changed, the presbyterian party depressed, and their generals, Poyntz and Massie, with all the remaining officers of that faction, forced to retire; who most of them then changed their party, and never more appeared on the parliament side. Yet there was still a presbyterian faction left in the house, of such as were moderate, and who were not by the bitterness of their zeal carried on to break their covenant with God and men, and to renew a league with the popish interest, to destroy that godly interest which they had at first so gloriously asserted. After this tumult at London was quieted, about August of that year the king was brought to one of his stately palaces at Hampton Court, near London, and the army removed to quarters about the city, their head-quarters being at Putney. The king, by reason of his daily converse with the officers, had begun tampering with them, not only then but before, and had drawn in some of them to engage to corrupt others to fall in with him; but to speak the truth of all, Cromwell was at that time so incorruptibly faithful to his trust and to the people's interest, that he could not be drawn in to practise even his own usual and natural dissimulation on this occasion. His son-in-law Ireton, who was as faithful as he, was not so fully of the opinion (till he had tried it and found to the contrary) but that the king might have been managed to comply with the public good of his people, after he could no longer uphold his own violent will; but, upon some discourses with him, the king uttering these words to him, "I shall play my game as well as I can," Ireton replied, "If your majesty have a *game* to play, you must give us also the liberty to play ours." Colonel Hutchinson privately discoursing with his cousin about the communications he had had with the king, Ireton's expressions were these: "He gave us words, and we paid him in his own coin, when we found he had no real intention to the people's good, but to prevail by our factions, to regain by art what he had lost in fight."

The king lived at Hampton Court rather in the condition of a guarded and attended prince, than as a conquered and purchased captive; all his old servants had free recourse to him; all sorts of people were admitted to come to kiss his hands and do him obeisance as a sovereign. Ashburnham and Berkley, by the parliament voted delinquents, came to him from beyond the seas, and others by permission of the army, who had hoped they might be useful to incline him to wholesome counsels; but he, on the other side, interpreting this freedom wherein he was permitted to live, not to the gentleness and reconcilableness of his parliament, who, after all his injuries, yet desired his restitution, so far as it might be without the ruin of the good people of the land, but rather believing it to proceed from their apprehension of their own declining and his re-advancing in the hearts of the people, made use of this advantage to corrupt many of their officers to revolt from them and betray them; which some time after they did, and paid the forfeiture with their lives.[1] When the king was at Hampton Court the lords who were formerly of his privy council at Oxford, also repaired to him, to be as a council attending him, but this gave so much disgust at London that they retreated again; but the Scotch lords and commissioners having free access to him, he drew that nation into the design of the second war; which broke out furiously the next summer, and was one of the highest provocations which, after the second victory, brought him to the scaffold. But I shall respite that, to return to his affairs whom I principally trace.

[1] This is one of the places where we find reason to regret Mrs. Hutchinson's being so summary in her account of public affairs. This matter of endeavouring to bring the king to reason, and his perverting the good intentions of friends as well as foes, is treated much at length by Ludlow, in his first volume, from p. 194 to 204, and he agrees with Mrs. Hutchinson in most particulars; but it seems extraordinary that he should attribute a very considerable and active part in this business to Sir Allen Apsley, and his sister should make no mention of him in it. The candour and benevolence of Ireton, who is so generally represented as a cynic, are equally apparent in both places, as likewise are the obstinacy and duplicity of the king. If Ireton is by any supposed to have been too favourably represented by Mrs. Hutchinson, it will not be thought that he is likewise favoured by Walker in his Hist. of the Independents, yet, p. 164, he reports thus. Ireton said the king had committed crimes enough to *depose and imprison him*, and crown the Duke of York, then a child, in his stead (*not to kill the king*), and that if any thought their treatment of the king severe, they would applaud their clemency to the Duke of York.

After the parliament was by the general restored to their seats, Colonel Hutchinson came down to his garrison at Nottingham, which, the war being ended, was reduced only to the castle; the works at the town and the bridges being slighted, the companies of the governor's regiment, all but two, disbanded, and he thinking, now in a time when there was no opposition, the command not worthy of himself or his brother, gave it over to his kinsman, Captain Poulton. With the assistance of his fellow parliament men he procured an order from the parliament for five thousand pounds, that had been levied for the Scotch army, but which they, departing with too much haste, had not received, to be distributed among the officers and soldiers of his regiment that were at this time disbanded, in part of their arrears; and, that it might go the farther amongst them, he himself had none of it.[1] The garrison at Nottingham being reduced, Colonel Hutchinson removed his family back to his own house at Owthorpe, but found that, having stood uninhabited, and been robbed of everything which the neighbouring garrisons of Shelford and Wiverton could carry from it, it was so ruined that it could not be repaired, to make a convenient habitation, without as much charge as would almost build another. By reason of the debt his public employment had run him into, and not being able to do this at present while all his arrears were unpaid, he made a bad shift with it for that year. At this time his distemper of rheum was very sore upon him, and he was so afflicted with pains in his head, which fell down also with violent torture upon all his joints, that he was not able to go for many weeks out of his chamber; and here we had a notable example of the victorious power of his soul over his body. One day, as he was in the saddest torture of his disease, certain horse came, somewhat insolently and injuriously, exacting quarters or moneys in the town; whom he sent for, and telling them he would not suffer such wrong to be done to his tenants, they seeing him in so weak a condition, would not be persuaded to forbear violent and unjust actions, but told him his government was expired, and they were no more under his command; with which, and some other saucy language, being provoked to be heartily angry, he felt not that he was sick, but started out of his chair and beat them out of the house

[1] Nota Bene.

and town, and returned again laughing at the wretched
fellows and at himself, wondering what was become of his
pain, and thinking how strangely his feebleness was cured in
a moment.   But while he and those about him were in this
amazement, half an hour had not expired before his spirits
cooled, and that heat and vigour they had lent his members
retired again to their noble palace, his heart; and those
efforts, which had violently employed his limbs, made them
more weak than before, and his pain returned with such re-
doubled violence, that we thought he would have died in
this fit.

While he was thus distempered at home, Major-general
Ireton sent him a letter, with a new commission in it, for the
resuming his government of Nottingham Castle: for the
principal officers of the army, foreseeing an approaching
storm, desired to place it in his hands, by whom it had before
been so prosperously and faithfully preserved: but the
colonel sent them word, that as he should not have put his
kinsman into the place, although he was assured of his
fidelity, so he would never join with those who were so forgetful of the merits of men that had behaved themselves well, as
to discourage them without a cause.   Hereupon they suffered
Captain Poulton to remain in his command; but while the
house was very busy in faction, they took no care of any of
the garrisons, especially of such as were likely to continue
firm to the cause; the presbyterian faction having a design
to weaken or corrupt them all, that they might be prepared
for the great revolt from the parliament, which was now
working in all countries.   In Nottinghamshire, Colonel
Gilbert Byron, a brother of Lord Byron's, meeting Captain
Poulton, began to insinuate into him, and tempt him to
betray Nottingham Castle; which proposition, when he
heard, he thought fit not utterly to reject, lest the castle
being then in a weak condition, and the soldiers discontented,
some of his under officers might be more ready to embrace it
and betray both the place and him.   He therefore took a
little time to consider of it, and came to Colonel Hutchinson
and acquainted him with it.   He advised him to hold his
cousin Byron on in the treaty, till he himself could go to
London and provide for the better securing of the place,
which, his distemper of health a little abating, he did: and
when the place was well provided, Captain Poulton, who was

too gentle-hearted to cut off Mr. Byron under a pretence of assenting to him, sent to him to shift for himself, which Mr. Byron accordingly did; and now the insurrection began everywhere to break out.

In the meantime, some months before, when the king had laid the design of the second war with the Scots, and had employed all his art to bring the English presbyters to a revolt, and was now full of hopes to bring about *his game*, and conquer those who had conquered him, while he was amusing the parliament with expectations of a treaty, he privily stole away from Hampton Court, by the assistance of Ashburnham and Berkley, no man knew whither; but these wise men had so ordered their business, that instead of going beyond seas, which was his first intent, he was forced to give himself up to Hammond, governor of the Isle of Wight, who immediately gave notice to the parliament, and they sent him thanks for his fidelity, and ordered that the king should be honourably attended and guarded there in Carisbrook Castle. The parliament were again sending him propositions there, when they received a letter from him, urging that he might come to a personal treaty in London. Hereupon the two houses agreed on four propositions to be sent him, to be passed as bills; upon the passing of which, they were content he should come to a personal treaty for the rest. The four propositions were: First, That a bill should be passed for the settling the militia of the kingdom. Secondly, That all oaths, declarations, etc., against the parliament and their adherents should be called in. Thirdly, That the lords made by the great seal at Oxford, should not thereby be capable of sitting in the house of peers. Fourthly, That the parliament might have power to adjourn, as the two houses think fit. The Scotch commissioners opposed the sending these bills to the king, and urged his coming to a personal treaty in London. The king, understanding their mind and the factions in London, absolutely refused to sign them. Wherefore the houses, debating upon the king's denial, these votes were at length passed by both houses, on the 17th day of January:—That they would make no more addresses nor applications to the king. That no person whatever should make address or application to him. That whoever should break this order, should incur the penalty of high treason. That they should receive no more messages

from the king, and that no person should presume to bring
any to either house, or to any other person. Upon these
votes the army put forth a declaration, promising to stand
by the houses in them, which was signed by the general and
all his officers, at Windsor, January 19, 1647. But in May
following, tumults first began in London; then the Surrey
men came with a very insolent petition, and behaved themselves so arrogantly to the parliament, killing and wounding
some of the guards, that a troop of horse was fetched from
the Mews, and was forced to kill some of them before they
could quiet them. After this, the parliament was informed
of another insurrection in Kent, coming under the face of a
petition, and sent out General Fairfax with seven regiments
to suppress them, who pursued them to Rochester. A great
company of these Kentish men were gotten together about
Gravesend, with fifteen knights, and many commanders of
the king's army to head them; who, although they were
more in number than Fairfax's men, yet durst not await his
coming. Some of them went to Dover Castle and besieged
it, but the general sent out Sir Michael Livesey, who happily
relieved that place and raised the siege; others went to
Maidstone, and a few kept together about Rochester. The
general himself went to Maidstone, where two thousand of
them were gotten into the town, and resolved to keep it;
whom the general assaulted, and with difficulty entered the
town, and fought for every street, which were barricaded
against him, and defended with cannon. Yet at length he
killed two hundred, and took fourteen hundred prisoners.
Four hundred horse broke away to an army of their friends,
bigger than Fairfax's, who saw the town taken, yet had not
the courage to engage against the general for the relief of it;
but after they saw his victory they dispersed. The Lord
Goring then having rallied about two thousand of these
Kentish men, led them to Greenwich, from whence he sent
to try the affections of the Londoners; but while he stayed
there expecting their answer, some troops of the army came,
upon the sight of whom, he and his men fled; the Kentish
men, most of them to their own houses, himself, with about
five hundred horse, getting boat, crossed the Thames into
Essex, where the Lord Capel with forces out of Hertfordshire,
and Sir Charles Lucas with a body of horse at Chelmsford,
joined him; to whom, in a short time, divers that had been

the king's soldiers, with many Londoners, and other malignants, flocked in. General Fairfax, with part of his forces
crossed the Thames at Gravesend, and sending for all the
rest out of Kent and London, pursued the enemies, and drove
them into Colchester, where he besieged them, and lay before
them three months. At last, hearing of the defeat of Duke
Hamilton and the Scots, and others of the king's partisans,
and being reduced to eating horse-flesh, without hopes of
relief, they yielded to mercy. The general shot Sir Charles
Lucas and Sir George Lisle to death upon the place, and
reserved Goring, Capel, and others, to abide the doom of the
parliament. While Fairfax was thus employed in Kent and
Essex, Langhorne, Powell, and Poyer, celebrated commanders
of the parliament side, revolted with the places in their command, and got a body of eight thousand Welshmen, whom
Colonel Horton, with three thousand, encountered, vanquished, routed, and took as many prisoners as he had
soldiers; but Langhorne and Powell escaped to Poyer, and
shut up themselves with him in Pembroke Castle, a place
so strong that they refused all treaty; and thereupon they
were besieged by Lieutenant-general Cromwell, to whom at
length, after some months' siege, it was surrendered at the
conqueror's mercy. In divers other countries, at the same
time, there were several insurrections and revolts; but those
of the parliament party, as if they had lost courage and conscience at once, could no more behave themselves with that
valour, which had before renowned them; and were slain
or taken, losing the places they had betrayed, to their old
companions, whose fidelity was crowned with success everywhere. Among the rest, Colonel Gilbert Byron had risen,
with other gentlemen of Nottinghamshire and Lincolnshire,
and had gotten together about five hundred horse; wherewith, after he had failed of his hopes of corrupting the
governor of Nottingham, they intended to go and join
themselves with others that were up in other countries; and
this was so suddenly and secretly done, that they were upon
their march before the rising was suspected. The governor
of Nottingham had not time enough to send a messenger to
be with Colonel Hutchinson at his house before them, and
therefore shot off a piece of cannon; which Colonel Hutchinson hearing as he sat at dinner, and believing some extraordinary thing to be in it, commanded horses to be made

ready, and went to Nottingham; but met the messenger
who came to give him notice of the enemies' approach. The
news being sent home in haste, his arms and writings, and
other things of value, were put in a cart and sent away;
which was not long gone before the enemy marched by the
house, and keeping their body on a hill at the town's end,
only sent a party to the house to fetch them what provisions
of meat and drink they found there; besides which, they
took nothing but a groom with two horses, who having
ridden out to air them, fell into their mouths, because he
could not be readily found when the rest of the horses were
sent away. The reason why no more mischief was done by
the cavaliers to his family, at that time, was, partly because
Colonel Gilbert Byron had commanded not to disturb them,
if he were not there, and partly because they were so closely
pursued by the Lincolnshire troops, that they could not
stay to take, nor would burden themselves with plunder,
now they saw it unlikely to get off without fighting. This
they did the next day at Willoughby within three miles of
Owthorpe, and were there totally routed, killed, and taken
by a party under Colonel Rossiter's command, by whom
Colonel Byron was carried prisoner to Belvoir Castle. Being
in distress there, although he was an enemy, and had dealt
unhandsomely with Colonel Hutchinson, in endeavouring to
corrupt one for whom he was engaged, yet the colonel sent
him a sum of money for his present relief, and afterwards
procured him a release and composition with the parliament.
The greatest of all these dangers seemed now to be in the
north, where Duke Hamilton's faction being prevalent in
Scotland, he had raised an army, and was marching into
England. Sir Marmaduke Langdale and Glenham had
already raised some men in those parts, whom Lambert, with
the assistance of some Lincolnshire forces, joined to his
Yorkshire brigade, kept in play; but they reserved themselves to join with Hamilton. Argyle and others of the
kirk party, protested against him, and many of the ministers
cursed his attempt, but were silenced for it, although God
heard them. The presbyterians in London secretly prayed
for his success, and hardly could the house of lords be brought
to join with the house of commons in voting all the English
traitors, that should join with the Scots, which yet at the
last they did.

Colonel Hutchinson having been about this time at London, and wanting a minister for the place where he lived, and for which he had procured an augmentation, repaired to some eminent ministers in London,[1] to recommend a worthy person to him for the place. They, with a great testimonial, recommended a Scotchman to him, whom the colonel brought down; but having occasion to be with the committee at Nottingham, to take order for the security of the county in these dangerous times, while he was out the man made strange prayers in the family, which were couched in dark expressions; but Mrs. Hutchinson, understanding them to be intended for the prosperous success of those who were risen against the parliament, and of his nation that were coming to invade ours, told her husband at his return, that she could not bear with nor join in his prayers. The next day, being the Lord's day, the colonel heard his sermon, which was so spiritless and so lamentable, that he was very much vexed the ministers should have sent such a man to him; withal he publicly made the same prayers he uttered in the family for the success of the Scots; whereupon, after dinner, the colonel took him aside, and told him that he had done very sinfully to undertake an office for which he was so ill gifted, and desired him to depart in peace again the next day, and to forbear any further employment in his house. The man at first was very high, and told the colonel he was there by authority of the parliament, and would not depart; the colonel then dealt high with him, and told him he would declare to them the expressions of his prayers, which so confounded the man, that he besought him to have pity, and confessed that he was fled from his own country for having been of Montrose's party; and that covetousness, against his conscience, had drawn him to dissemble himself to be of the parliament's principles, but that God had judged him for his hypocrisy, and withdrawn his Spirit from him, since he practised it; he then submitted to go quietly and silently away, even begging it as a favour of the colonel, that he would permit him so to do. He did it with such a counterfeit sorrow and conviction, that the colonel being of a most placable nature, freely forgave him, and sent him not away

[1] This entirely contradicts the opinion so generally propagated and believed, that all the independents were so fanatical as to decry and lay aside all regular ministry, and to give themselves up to the guidance of self-created teachers, pretending inspiration, *i.e.* impostors.

empty, for he had fifteen pounds for only a fortnight's
service; yet this rogue, before he went out of the country,
went to the presbyters at Nottingham, and told them his
conscience would not permit him to stay in the colonel's
house, because he and his wife were such violent sectaries,
that no orthodox man could live comfortably with them;
and this scandal those charitable priests were ready to
receive and more largely to spread. They themselves, with
divers of their zealous disciples, whom they had perverted,
among whom were Colonel Francis Pierrepont, Captains
Rosse, White, Chadwick, and many others, were watching
opportunity to break their covenant and rise against that
parliament, under which they had served and sworn to
assist, till all delinquents, as well greater as less, were brought
to condign punishment.

At London things were in a very sad posture, the two
factions of presbytery and independency being so engaged
to suppress each other, that they both ceased to regard the
public interest; insomuch, that at that time a certain sort of
public-spirited men stood up in the parliament and the army,
declaring against these factions and the ambition of the
grandees of both, and the partiality that was in these days
practised, by which great men were privileged to do those
things which meaner men were punished for, and the injustice and other crimes of particular members of parliament, were rather covered than punished, to the scandal of
the whole house. Many got shelter in the house and army
against their debts, by which others were defrauded and undone. The lords, as if it were the chief interest of nobility
to be licensed in vice, claimed many prerogatives, which set
them out of the reach of common justice, which these good-
hearted people would have equally to belong to the poorest
as well as to the mighty; and for this and such other honest
declarations, they were nicknamed levellers. Indeed, as all
virtues are mediums, and have their extremes, there rose up
afterwards with that name a people who endeavoured the
levelling of all estates and qualities; which these sober
levellers were never guilty of desiring, but were men of just
and sober principles, of honest and religious ends, and therefore hated by all the designing self-interested men of both
factions. Colonel Hutchinson had a great intimacy with
many of these; and so far as they acted according to the

just, pious, and public spirit which they professed, he owned
and protected them as far as he had power. These were
they who first began to discover the ambition of Lieutenant-
general Cromwell and his idolators, and to suspect and dislike it. About this time, he was sent down, after his victory
in Wales, to encounter Hamilton in the north. When he
went down, the chief of these levellers following him out of
the town, to take their leave of him, received such professions
from him, of a spirit bent to pursue the same just and honest
things which they desired, that they went away with great
satisfaction, till they heard that a coachful of presbyterian
priests coming after them, went away no less pleased; by
which it was apparent he dissembled with one or the other,
and by so doing lost his credit with both.

When he came to Nottingham, Colonel Hutchinson went
to see him, whom he embraced with all the expressions of
kindness that one friend could make to another, and then
retiring with him, pressed him to tell him what his friends,
the levellers,[1] thought of him. The colonel, who was the

[1] The information Mrs. Hutchinson gives us on this subject is curious
and valuable, but differs from the tradition generally received respecting the levellers; it is however well supported by Walker in his *History
of Independency*. He begins with describing two juntos of grandees,
and calls the rest the common people of the house; the former only
feigned opposition, but played into one another's hands, the latter
were sincere and earnest in it: he speaks of the *honest middlemen*, the
same as Mrs. Hutchinson calls by that name, and likewise *levellers* ;
he declares levellers and asserters of liberty to be synonymous terms:
in a variety of places they are treated as the only sincere patriots and
opposers of the selfish schemes of the grandees of both parties, peculiarly
the independents, and above all, of Cromwell; and the engrossers and
monopolisers of oligarchy, desiring to make themselves a corporation
of tyrants, are said chiefly to dread the opposition of these levellers;
but the most remarkable passage is in p. 194. " Reader, let me
admonish thee that the levellers, for so they are miscalled, only for
endeavouring to level the exorbitant usurpations of the council of
state and council of officers, are much abused by some books lately
printed and published in their names, much differing from their declared principles, tenets, and practices, but forged by Cromwell and
others to make the sheep (the people) betray the dogs that faithfully
guard them." The mode here and before taken by Colonel Hutchinson, of readily adopting a name which was intended him for a reproach,
was certainly the best way of disarming it of its sting. The principles
held by that party of the levellers which he supported, none venture
openly to oppose, but try to attach to them the absurd extreme of
those he blames; the modern philosophers who have stated that all
men have equal rights, but to unequal things, have not met with a
much more candid construction. The abuses Colonel Hutchinson
complained of, especially that of the privilege of parliament, have
since been a little diminished; but many families still continue to be

freest man in the world from concealing truth from his friend, especially when it was required of him in love and plainness, not only told him what others thought of him, but what he himself conceived; and how much it would darken all his glories, if he should become a slave to his own ambition, and be guilty of what he gave the world just cause to suspect, and therefore he begged of him to wear his heart in his face, and to scorn to delude his enemies, but to make use of his noble courage to maintain what he believed to be just, against all great opposers. Cromwell made mighty professions of a sincere heart to him, but it is certain that for this and such like plain dealing with him, he dreaded the colonel, and made it his particular business to keep him out of the army; but the colonel desiring command, not to serve himself but his country, would not use that art he detested in others, to procure himself any advantage.

At this time Colonel Thornhagh marched with Cromwell, and at his parting with Colonel Hutchinson, took such a kind leave of him, with such dear expressions of love, such brotherly embraces, and such regret for any rash jealousies he had been wrought into, that it took great impression in the colonel's kind heart, and might have been a presage to him that they should meet no more, when they parted with such extraordinary melting love; but that Colonel Hutchinson's cheerful and constant spirit never anticipated any evil with fear. His prudence wanted not foresight that it might come, yet his faith and courage entertained his hope, that God would either prevent it, or help him to bear it.

defrauded and undone by the shelter which members of parliament find from their debts, and which seems long likely to continue a defect in our legislature, and a reproach to our morals. Among a number of pamphlets published in Mr. Hutchinson's time, one was found at Owthorpe, setting forth the views and desires of these inferior levellers. They therein stated, that they were willing to acknowledge the proprietors of lands, and principally the lords of manors, as their elder brothers, and rightfully possessed of the chief inheritance; but prayed to be allowed to cultivate the wastes and commons for their support. Whether the permitting or even encouraging this under moderate reservations might not have been conducive to the public good, is a question which seems to have been decided in the affirmative by the practice of the French under the ancient government: a great share of the lands in every parish having been thus granted out, and cultivated by small proprietors, who paid what was called *champarts*, fieldings or tithes, being seven in the hundred; the industry and population this produced is felt by all Europe. The abrogating these payments to the lords, was one of the grand *incitements* to, and *crimes* of, the revolution.

This summer the revolt was not greater at land than at sea. Many of the great ships set the vice-admiral on shore, and sailed towards Holland to Prince Charles: to whom the Duke of York had come, having, by his father's advice, privately stolen away from London, where the parliament had received and treated him like a prince, ever since the surrender of Oxford. To reduce these revolted ships, and preserve the rest of the navy from the like, the Earl of Warwick was made lord high admiral of England. But at the same time his brother, the Earl of Holland, who had floated up and down with the tide of the times, rose also against the parliament, and appeared in arms, with the young Duke of Buckingham and Lord Francis Villars, his brother, and others, making about five hundred horse, at Kingston - upon - Thames. Here some of the parliament troops, assailing them before they had time to grow, totally routed and dispersed them. The Lord Francis Villars was slain; the Earl of Holland, flying with those he could rally, was fought with at St. Neots; Dalbier and others of his associates were slain, and himself taken prisoner and carried to Warwick Castle. Buckingham fled, and at last got beyond seas, with a blot of base ingratitude and treachery, which began then to appear, and hath since marked out all his life. For these two lords being pupils, and under the king's tuition, were carried with him to Oxford, where they remained till the surrender of the place; and then coming to London, as they were under age, they had all their father and mother's great estates, freely, without any sequestration or composition; and while they enjoyed them, their secret intentions of rising being discovered to the parliament, the parliament would not secure them, as some advised, but only sent a civil warning to the duke, minding him how unhandsome it would be if the information should prove true. Whereupon the duke protested he had no such intention, but utterly detested it, making all the expressions of just gratitude to them that could be; and yet, within a very few days afterwards, he openly showed himself in arms, to tell the world how perfidious a hypocrite he was; for which the parliament exempted him from pardon, and ever afterwards detested his name, as one that rose only to fall into contempt and obloquy.

And now was Cromwell advanced into Lancashire, where

Lambert, retreating from the invading Scots, joined with him and made up an army of about ten thousand; which were but few to encounter five-and-twenty thousand, led by Hamilton, Langdale, and other English joined with them. Yet near Preston, in Lancashire, they fought, and Cromwell gained an entire victory, about the end of August, and had the chase of them for twenty miles, wherein many fell, and many were taken prisoners. Hamilton himself, with a good party of horse, fled to Uttoxeter, and was there taken by the Lord Grey. But, in the beginning of this battle, the valiant Colonel Thornhagh was wounded to death. Being at the beginning of the charge on a horse as courageous as became such a master, he made such furious speed to set upon a company of Scotch lancers, that he was singly engaged and mortally wounded, before it was possible for his regiment, though as brave men as ever drew sword, and too affectionate to their colonel to be slack in following him, to come up time enough to break the fury of that body, which shamed [1] not to unite all their force against one man: who yet fell not among them, but being faint and all covered with blood, of his enemies as well as his own, was carried off by some of his own men, while the rest, enraged for the loss of their dear colonel, fought not that day like men of human race; but deaf to the cries of every coward that asked mercy, they killed all, and would not that a captive should live to see their colonel die; but said the whole kingdom of Scotland was too mean a sacrifice for that brave men. His soul was hovering to take her flight out of his body, but that an eager desire to know the success of that battle kept it within till the end of the day, when the news being brought him, he cleared his dying countenance, and said, " I now rejoice to die, since God hath let me see the overthrow of this perfidious enemy; I could not lose my life in a better cause, and I have the favour from God to see my blood avenged." So he died, with a large testimony of love to his soldiers, but more to the cause, and was by mercy removed, that the temptations of future times might not prevail to corrupt his pure soul. A man of greater courage and integrity fell not, nor fought not, in this glorious cause; he had also an excellent good nature, but easy to be wrought upon by flatterers, yet as flexible to the admonitions

[1] Shamed not, used neutrally, instead of were not ashamed, blushed not.

of his friends; and this virtue he had, that if sometimes a cunning insinuation prevailed upon his easy faith, when his error was made known to him, notwithstanding all his great courage, he was readier to acknowledge and repair, than to pursue his mistake.[1] Colonel Thornhagh's regiment, in the reducing of the garrison forces, had one Major Saunders (a Derbyshire man, who was a very godly, honest, country gentleman, but had not many things requisite for a great soldier) assigned them for their major, and with him he brought in about a troop of Derbyshire horse; but the Nottinghamshire horse, who certainly were as brave men as any that drew swords in the army, had been animated in all their service by the dear love they had to their colonel, and the glory they took in him, and their generous spirits could not take satisfaction in serving under a less man, which they all esteemed their major to be. But remembering their successes under Colonel Hutchinson, and several other things that moved them to pitch their thoughts upon him, the captains addressed themselves to Cromwell, and acquainted him with the discouragement and sorrow they had by the death of their colonel, for whom nothing could comfort them, but a successor equal to himself; which they could not hope to find so well as they might in the person of Colonel Hutchinson, with whose worth and courage they were well acquainted, and who was now out of employment. Their only difficulty was, whether he would accept the command, which they hoped to prevail on him to do, if he would oblige them by sending to Lord Fairfax, to stop all other ways that might be thought of for disposing it, till they could know whether Colonel Hutchinson would accept it, for which they had prepared a messenger to send to his house. Cromwell, with all the assentation imaginable, seemed to rejoice they had made so worthy a choice, and promised them to take care

[1] The valour of this gentleman seems to have been a favourite topic of admiration and praise among his brother warriors. In Cromwell's letter (preserved by Whitelocke), wherein he gives an account of his victory, he laments " the death of this *too brave gentleman*." Ludlow is full in his praises of him, and adds a very picturesque circumstance; " that as he lay wounded among his soldiers, he made them open to the right and left, that he might see the enemy run." But it is doubtful whether at any time the pencil or the pen has consecrated anything to the memory of a departed chief, so animated, so appropriate, as this character and description, which we may surely say Mrs. Hutchinson conceived in the very spirit in which her hero lived and flourished, fought and fell.

the regiment should not be disposed of till they received Colonel Hutchinson's answer; whereupon the captains severally wrote to Colonel Hutchinson, with most earnest entreaties that he would give them leave to procure a commission for him to conduct them, which the lieutenant-general had already promised to send for, if he pleased to accept it.

The colonel, though he had more inclination to rest at that time, by reason of the indisposition of his health, yet not knowing whether the earnest desires of his countrymen were not from a higher call, wrote them word that he preferred the satisfaction of their desires before his own, and if the commission came to him to be their leader, he would not refuse it, though he should not do anything himself to seek any command. Meanwhile Cromwell, as soon as the Nottingham-shire men had imparted their desires to him, sent for Saunders, and cajoling him, told him none was so fit as himself to command the regiment; but that all the regiment did not think so, but were designing to procure themselves another colonel, which he advised him to prevent, by sending speedily to the general, to whom Cromwell also wrote to further the request, and before the messenger came back from Owthorpe procured the commission for Saunders. When it came, he used all his art to persuade the captains to submit to it, and to excuse himself from having any hand in it; but they perceived his dissimulation, and the troops were so displeased with it, that they thought to have flung down their arms; but their captains persuaded them to rest contented until the present expedition were over. But they had not only this cheat and disappointment by Cromwell, but all the Nottingham captains were passed over, and a less deserving man made major of the regiment. The new colonel and major made it their business to discountenance and affront all that had showed any desire for Colonel Hutchinson, and to weary them out, that they might fill up their rooms with Derbyshire men; but as soon as they got to London, all that could other wise dispose of themselves, went voluntarily off; and the rest that were forced to abide, hated their commanders, and lived discontentedly under them. The reasons that induced Cromwell to this, were two: first, he found that Colonel Hutchinson understood him, and was too generous either to fear or flatter him; and he carried, though under a false face of friendship, a deep resentment of the colonel's plain dealing with him in Nottingham. He had besides a design, by insinuating himself with Colonel Saunders, to flatter him into the sale of a town of his called Ireton, which Cromwell earnestly desired to buy for Major-general Ireton, who had married his daughter; and when at last he could not obtain it, in process of time, he took the regiment away from him again.[1] Colonel Hutchinson was not at all displeased that the regiment was not given to him, but highly resented it that the men were ill used for their affections to him; and was sorry that this particular carriage of Cromwell's gave him such a proof of other things suspected of him, so destructive to the whole cause and party, as it afterwards fell out.

Sir Marmaduke Langdale, after the rout of Hamilton, came with two or three other officers to a little alehouse which was upon Colonel Hutchinson's land, and there were so circumspect, that some country fellows, who saw them by chance, suspecting they were no ordinary travellers, acquainted Mr. Widmerpoole, who lived within two or three miles, and had been major to the colonel in the first war: whereupon he came forth, with some few others, and sent down to the colonel to acquaint him that some suspicious persons were at the lodge. The colonel, hearing of it, took his servants out, and was approaching near the house, when Major Widmerpoole, being beforehand in the house, had given Langdale some jealousy that he might be surprised; thereupon one of his company went out to fetch out his horses, which were stopped for the present, and they seeing the colonel coming up towards them, rendered themselves prisoners to Major Widmerpoole, and were sent to Nottingham Castle, where they continued some months, till at last Langdale finding an opportunity, corrupted one of the guard, who furnished him with a soldier's disguise, and ran away with him. The major, who would have been baffled by these persons, if the colonel had not come in, had all the booty, which the colonel never took any share of whatever: but the major thinking the best of his spoils justly due to him, pre-

---

[1] This gentleman is mentioned in Granger's *Biography;* and there is a print of him in the hands of some curious collectors, peculiarly of John Townely, Esq. He is said to be of Ireton, in Derbyshire, but Ireton is believed to be in the Vale of Belvoir.

sented him with a case or two of very fine pistols, which he accepted.

About this time, the gentlemen that were commissioners for the king at Newark, fell into disputes one with another; nor only so, but suits were commenced in chancery upon this occasion. One Atkins, and several other rich men at Newark, when that garrison began to be fortified for the king, lent certain sums of money, for the carrying on of that work, to the commissioners of array, for which those gentlemen became bound to the Newarkers. After the taking of that town by the parliament, they, with other persons, coming in within the set time, were admitted to composition. Having been so cunning as to put out their money in other names, they ventured to leave out these sums, believing they were put into such sure hands, that it would never be discovered. Mr. Sutton, Sir Thomas Williamson, Sir John Digby, Sir Gervas Eyre, the Lord Chaworth, Sir Thomas Blackwell, Sir Roger Cowper, Sir Richard Byron, and others, had given bond for this money, which Mr. Sutton, presenting to the king, as a sum that *he* had raised to signalise his loyalty, the king, to reward him, made him a baron. The whole sum thus taken up for the king's service, was eight or ten thousand pounds; fifteen hundred of it, that was lent by Atkinson, being demanded, would have been paid, but they would not take the principal without the interest. Sir Thomas Williamson was openly arrested for it in Westminster Hall; upon which Mr. Sutton and he, being maddened, put in a bill in chancery against Atkinson and others, praying that they might set forth to what ends and uses this money was lent to the said gentlemen, etc., etc.

The parliament had made a law, that all estates of delinquents, concealed and uncompounded for, should be forfeited, one half to the state, and the other half to the discoverer, if he had any arrears due to him from the parliament, in payment of them. There were clerks and solicitors, who in those days made a trade of hunting out such discoveries, and making them known to such as had any arrears due to them. Colonel Hutchinson at that time had received no pay at all. One of the clerks of that committee, which was appointed for such discoveries, sent him word that two officers of the army were upon this chancery bill, endeavouring to make a discovery of certain concealed moneys in Nottinghamshire, which being his own country, he thought might be more proper for him. Colonel Hutchinson, who had never any mind to disadvantage any of the gentlemen of the country, demurred upon this information, and did nothing in it, till some came to him, intimating a desire of my Lord Lexington's, that the colonel would pitch upon that for the payment of his arrears, that so they might fall into the hands of a neighbour, who would use them civilly, rather than of a stranger. After the colonel was thus invited by the gentlemen themselves, to pitch upon this money, he waived all the rest, and only entered as his discovery that money which these townsmen of Newark had lent; but upon full search and hearing at the committee, the money was found to be forfeited money, and the debtors were ordered to pay it into the committee, and Colonel Hutchinson had also an order to receive his arrear from that committee of Haberdashers' Hall. Hereupon Sir Thomas Williamson and Lord Lexington, who being the men of the best estates, were principally looked upon for the debt, applied themselves to Colonel Hutchinson, begging as a favour that he would undertake the management of the order of sequestration given out upon their estates; and would also oblige them, by bringing in several other gentlemen, that were bound to bear proportionable shares. The colonel, to gratify them, got the order of sequestration, and brought them to an accommodation, wherein every man, according to his ability, agreed upon an equal proportion; and the gentlemen, especially Mr. Sutton, acknowledged a very great obligation to the colonel, who had brought it to so equal a composition among them; and then, upon their own desires, the order of sequestration was laid upon their estates, but managed by one of their own bailiffs, in order to free them from inconveniences that otherwise would have come upon them. Some of them made use of it to get in arrears of rent, which they knew no other way of getting, and for which at that time they pretended the greatest sense of gratitude and obligation imaginable. The colonel also procured them days of payment, so that whereas it should have been paid this Michaelmas, 1648, it was not paid till a year after; and for these, and many other favours on this occasion, he was then courted as their patron, though afterwards this civility had like to have been his ruin. And now, about Michaelmas, 1648, he went to attend his duty at the parliament, carrying his whole family with him, because his house had been so ruined by the war that he could no longer live in it, till it was either repaired or newly built. On coming to London, he himself fell into his old distemper of rheumatism with more violence than ever, and being weary of those physicians he had so long, with so little success, employed, he was recommended to a young doctor, son of old Dr. Rudgely, whose excellence in his art was everywhere known; and this son being a very ingenious person, and considering himself, and consulting with his father, believed that all the other physicians who had dealt with him had mistaken his disease; which he finding more truly out, in a short space perfectly cured him of the gout, and restored him, by God's blessing on his endeavours, to such a condition of health as he had not enjoyed for two years before. When he was well again to attend the house, he found the presbyterian party so prevalent there, that the victories obtained by the army displeased them; and they had grown so hot in the zeal of their faction, that they from thenceforth resolved and endeavoured to close with the common enemy, that they might thereby compass the destruction of their independent brethren. To this end, and to strengthen their faction, they got in again the late suspended members; whereof it was said, and by the consequence appeared true, that Mr. Hollis, during his secession, had been into France, and there meeting with the queen, had pieced up an ungodly accommodation with her; although he was the man that at the beginning, when some of the more sober men, who foresaw the sad issues of war and victory to either side, were labouring for an accommodation, said openly in the house, that " he abhorred that word accommodation." After these were gotten in again, and encouraged by the presbyterian ministers and the people in the city, they procured a revocation of the votes formerly made; with such convincing reasons publicly declared for the same, why they had resolved on no more addresses to be made to the king. And now nothing was agitated with more violence than a new personal treaty, with honour and freedom; and even his coming to the city, before any security given, was laboured for, but that prevailed not. Such were the heats of the two parties, that Mr. Hollis challenged Ireton, even in the house; out of which they both went to fight, but that one who sat near them overheard the wicked whisper, and prevented the execution of it.[1]

Amidst these things, at last a treaty was sent to the king, by commissioners, who went from both houses, to the Isle of Wight; and although there were some honourable persons in this commission, yet it cannot be denied, but that they were carried away by the others, and concluded, upon most dangerous terms, an agreement with the king. He would not give up bishops, but only lease out their revenues; and upon the whole, such were the terms upon which the king was to be restored, that the whole cause was evidently given up to him. Only one thing he assented to, to acknowledge himself guilty of the blood spilt in the late war, with this proviso, that if the agreement were not ratified by the house, then this concession should be of no force against him.[2] The commissioners that treated with him had been cajoled and biassed with promises of great honours and offices to every one of them, and so they brought back their treaty to be confirmed by the houses; where there was a very high dispute about them, and they sat up most part of the night: when at length it was voted to accept his concessions, the dissenting party being fewer than the other that were carrying on the faction. Colonel Hutchinson was that night among them, and being convinced in his conscience that both the cause, and all those who with an upright honest heart asserted and maintained it, were betrayed and sold for nothing, he addressed himself to those commissioners he had most honourable thoughts of; and urged his reasons and apprehensions to them, and told them that the king, after having been exasperated, vanquished, and captived, would be restored to that power which was inconsistent with the liberty of the people, who, for all their blood, treasure, and misery, would reap no fruit, but a confirmation of their bondage; and that it had been a thousand times better never to have struck one stroke in the quarrel, than, after victory, to yield up a righteous cause; whereby they should not only betray the interest of their country and the trust reposed in them, and those zealous friends who had engaged to the death

---

[1] Clarendon pretends Ireton would not fight. Surely Ludlow knew him best, and he says he would!

[2] Certainly there are many strange things to be found in the history of diplomacy, but perhaps none so strange as that an assertion should be admitted to be *provisionally true*.

for them, but be false to the convenant of their God, which was to *extirpate prelacy*, not to *lease* it.[1] They acknowledged to him that the conditions were not so secure as they ought to be; but in regard of the growing power and insolence of the army, it was best to accept them. They further said, that they who enjoyed those trusts and places, which they had secured for themselves and other honest men, should be able to curb the king's exorbitances; and such other things they said, wherewith the colonel, dissatisfied, opposed their proceedings as much as he could. When the vote was passed, he told some men of understanding, that he was not satisfied in conscience to be included with the major part in this vote, which was contrary to their former engagements to God, but he thought it fit to testify their public dissent; he and four more, therefore, entered into the house-book a protestation against that night's votes and proceedings.[2] Whether it yet remains there, or whether some others of them got it out, he knew not, but he much wondered, after the change and scrutiny into all these things, that he never heard the least mention of it.

By this violent proceeding of the presbyterians they finished the destruction of him in whose restitution they were now so fiercely engaged, for this gave heart to the vanquished cavaliers, and such courage to the captive king that it hardened him and them to their ruin. On the other side, it so frightened all the honest people, that it made them as violent in their zeal to pull down, as the others were in their madness to restore, this kingly idol; and the army, who were principally levelled and marked out as the sacrifice and peace-offering of this ungodly reconciliation, had some colour to pursue their late arrogant usurpations upon that authority which it was their duty rather to have obeyed than interrupted; but the debates of that night, which produced such destructive votes to them and all their friends, being reported to them, they the next morning came and seized about [3]

[1] There is, among Clarendon's *State Papers*, a letter from the queen to the king, assuring him that those with whom he had to deal were too penetrating to be duped by this artifice; if they were, or pretended to be, the queen was not.
[2] Ludlow says he wished to do this very thing, but could not.
[3] [A gap in the MS. here has space for two numerals.] Dugdale gives a list of the secluded members, forty-one in number, and hence we are furnished with some names which will serve to establish a peculiar fact stated at the latter end of the history of the republic.

. . . of the members as they were going to the house, and carried them to a house hard by, where they were for the present kept prisoners. Most of the presbyterian faction, disgusted at this insolence, would no more come to their seats in the house; but the gentlemen who were of the other faction, or of none at all, but looked upon themselves as called out to manage a public trust for their country, forsook not their seats while they were permitted to sit in the house.[1] Colonel Hutchinson was one of these who infinitely disliked this action of the army, and had once before been instrumental in perventing such another rash attempt, which some of the discerning and honest members having a jealousy of, sent him down to discover. When he came, going first to commissary Ireton's quarters, he found him and some of the more sober officers of the army in great discontent, for the *lieutenant-general* had given order for a sudden advance of the army to London, upon the intelligence they had had of the violent proceedings of the other party, whereupon Cromwell was then in the mind to have come and broken them up; but Colonel Hutchinson, with others, at that time persuaded him that, notwithstanding the prevalency of the presbyterian faction, there were yet many who had upright and honest hearts to the public interest, who had not deserved to be so used by them, and who could not join with them in any such irregular ways, although in all just and equitable things they should be their protectors. Whereupon at that time he was stayed;[2] but having now drawn the army nearer London, they put this insolent force upon the house. Those who

[1] Whitelocke, who was exactly in the same predicament, acted in the same manner, and gives the same reasons for it.

[2] Mrs. Hutchinson does Ireton that justice which Whitelocke refuses him who seems to consider him in the light of an *instigator*; but this is clearly decided by Ludlow, who declares that " he himself, being sensible that the presbyterian party were determined to sacrifice the common cause to the pleasure of triumphing over the independents and the army, by agreeing with the king, or by any means, went down to apprise Fairfax and Ireton, then at the siege of Colchester, of this design, and to court the interposition of the army. Fairfax readily agreed, but Ireton demurred to interfering till the king and presbyterians should have actually agreed, and the body of the nation been convinced of the iniquity of their coalition." Additional provocations and imperious circumstances afterwards constrained him, but he acted no conspicuous part in the business. In this difference of opinion respecting the interference of the army we may see the source of the dissension which more openly took place afterwards between Colonel Hutchinson and Ludlow, and caused the latter to calumniate Colonel Hutchinson as he did.

were suffered to remain, not at all approving thereof, sent out their mace to demand their members, but the soldiers would not obey. Yet the parliament thought it better to sit still and go on in their duty than give up all, in so distempered a time, into the hands of the soldiery; especially as there had been so specious a pretext for the necessity of securing the whole interest and party from the treachery of those men, who contended so earnestly to give up the victors into the hands of their vanquished enemies. Many petitions had been brought to the parliament from thousands of the well-affected of the cities of London and Westminster and borough of Southwark, and from several counties in England, and from the several regiments of the army, whereof Colonel Ingolsby's was one of the first, all urging them to perform their covenant, and bring delinquents, without partiality, to justice and condign punishment, and to make inquiry for the guilt of the blood that had been shed in the land in both wars, and to execute justice; lest the not improving the mercy of God should bring judgments in their room.

Then also a declaration to the same purpose was presented to the house from the Lord General Fairfax and his council of officers, and strange it is how men who could afterwards pretend such reluctancy and abhorrence of those things that were done, should forget that they were the effective answer to their petitions.

After the purgation of the house, upon the new debate of the treaty at the Isle of Wight, it was concluded dangerous to the realm and destructive to its better interest, and the trial of the king was determined. He was sent for to Westminster, and a commission was given forth to a court of high justice, whereof Bradshaw, serjeant-at-law, was president, and divers honourable persons of the parliament, city, and army, nominated commissioners. Among them Colonel Hutchinson was one, who, very much against his own will, was put in; but looking upon himself as called hereunto, durst not refuse it, as holding himself obliged by the covenant of God and the public trust of his country reposed in him, although he was not ignorant of the danger he run as the condition of things then was.

In January 1648,[1] the court sat, the king was brought

---

[1] Hume and Clarendon say January 1649.

to his trial, and a charge drawn up against him for levying war against the parliament and people of England, for betraying the public trust reposed in him, and for being an implacable enemy to the commonwealth. But the king refused to plead, disowning the authority of the court, and after three several days persisting in contempt thereof, he was sentenced to suffer death.[1] One thing was remarked in him by many of the court, that when the blood spilt in many of the battles where he was in his own person, and had caused it to be shed by his own command, was laid to his charge, he heard it with disdainful smiles, and looks and gestures which rather expressed sorrow that all the opposite party to him were not cut off, than that any were: and he stuck not to declare in words, that no man's blood spilt in this quarrel troubled him except one, meaning the Earl of Strafford. The gentlemen that were appointed his judges, and divers others, saw in him a disposition so bent on the ruin of all that opposed him, and of all the righteous and just things they had contended for, that it was upon the consciences of many of them, that if they did not execute justice upon him, God would require at their hands all the blood and desolation which should ensue by their suffering him to escape, when God had brought him into their hands. Although the malice of the malignant party and their apostate brethren seemed to threaten them, yet they thought they ought to cast themselves upon God, while they acted with a good conscience for him and for their country. Some of them afterwards, for excuse, belied themselves, and said they were under the awe of the army, and overpersuaded by Cromwell, and the like; but it is certain that all men herein were left to their

---

[1] Without entering into the *merits* of the question, we may safely assert that the trial of the king was *without precedent*, though many sovereigns had been deposed and put to death *without trial*. It may appear fanciful to many to suggest that the precedent set at this period could have any influence on the fate of the unfortunate Louis XVI.; but those who have well observed the proneness of the French to mimicry (*singerie*), and peculiarly at the time of their first revolution, their *Anglomania*, or aping of the English (preferably in their foibles), will not be far from believing that this precedent emboldened them to the mockery of justice which they exhibited in his trial and condemnation. It is true that many, and even most circumstances were wanting to render the cases parallel, but they were determined to come up to the height of the English revolution (*à la hauteur des Anglais*), and therefore malice and invention supplied all deficiencies.

free liberty of acting, neither persuaded nor compelled; and as there were some nominated in the commission who never sat, and others who sat at first, but durst not hold on, so all the rest might have declined it if they would, when it is apparent they would have suffered nothing by so doing. For those who then declined were afterwards, when they offered themselves, received in again, and had places of more trust and benefit than those who ran the utmost hazard; which they deserved not, for I know upon certain knowledge that many, yea the most of them, retreated, not for conscience, but from fear and worldly prudence, foreseeing that the insolency of the army might grow to that height as to ruin the cause, and reduce the kingdom into the hands of the enemy; and then those who had been most courageous in their country's cause would be given up as victims. These poor men did privately animate those who appeared most publicly, and I knew several of them in whom I lived to see that saying of Christ fulfilled, " He that will save his life shall lose it, and he that for my sake will lose his life shall save it; " when afterwards it fell out that all their prudent declensions saved not the lives of some nor the estates of others. As for Mr. Hutchinson, although he was very much confirmed in his judgment concerning the cause, yet herein being called to an extraordinary action, whereof many were of several minds, he addressed himself to God by prayer; desiring the Lord that, if through any human frailty he were led into any error or false opinion in these great transactions, he would open his eyes, and not suffer him to proceed, but that he would confirm his spirit in the truth, and lead him by a right enlightened conscience; and finding no check, but a confirmation in his conscience that it was his duty to act as he did, he, upon serious debate, both privately and in his addresses to God, and in conferences with conscientious, upright, unbiassed persons, proceeded to sign the sentence against the king. Although he did not then believe but that it might one day come to be again disputed among men, yet both he and others thought they could not refuse it without giving up the people of God, whom they had led forth and engaged themselves unto by the oath of God, into the hands of God's and their own enemies; and therefore he cast himself upon God's protection, acting according to the dictates of a conscience which he had sought the Lord to guide, and accordingly the Lord did signalise his favour afterwards to him.[1]

After the death of the king it was debated and resolved to change the form of government from a monarchy into a commonwealth, and the house of lords was voted dangerous and useless thereunto, and dissolved. A council of state was to be annually chosen for the management of affairs, accountable to the parliament, out of which, consisting of forty councillors and a president, twenty were every year to go off by lot, and twenty new ones to be supplied. It is true, that at that time almost every man was fancying a form[2] of government, and angry, when this came forth, that his invention took not place; and among these John Lilburne, a turbulent-spirited man, who never was quiet in anything, published libels; and the levellers made a disturbance with a kind of insurrection, which Cromwell soon appeased, they indeed being betrayed by their own leaders.

But how the public business went on, how Cromwell finished the conquest of Ireland, how the angry presbyterians spit fire out of their pulpits, and endeavoured to blow up the people against the parliament, how they entered into a treasonable conspiracy with Scotland, which had now received and crowned the son of the late king, who led them in hither with a great army, which the Lord of hosts discomfited; how our public ministers were assassinated and murdered in Spain and Holland; and how the Dutch, in this unsettlement of affairs, hoped to gain by making war, wherein they were beaten and brought to sue for peace,—I shall leave to the stories that were then written; and only in general

---

[1] The account here given of Colonel Hutchinson's motives in this great transaction is most ingenious, and lays his conduct fairly open to the discussion and decision of the reader, who, according to his own feelings, will determine it for himself to be *commendable*, *censurable*, or *venial*. The legislature unanimously voted it *venial*. It would be an invidious, but not a very difficult task, to point out the persons who, by their *politic declensions*, failed of saving their lives and estates; but it is worthy of notice that Fairfax, after the restoration, with that ingenuousness which belonged to him, declared (Ludlow, vol. iii. p. 10), " that if any person must be excepted from pardon for the death of the king, he knew no man that deserved it more than himself, who being general of the army, and having power sufficient to prevent the proceedings against the king, had not thought fit to use it to that end." It is needless to multiply examples, one reasoning extending to the whole.

[2] A natural consequence of great popular revolutions, in which the modern French have had the glory of outdoing all the world!

say that the hand of God was mightily seen in prospering and preserving the parliament till Cromwell's ambition unhappily interrupted them. Mr. Hutchinson was chosen into the first council of state, much against his own will; for, understanding that his cousin Ireton was one of the commissioners to nominate that council, he sent his wife to him, before he went to the house, that morning they were to be named, to desire him, upon all the scores of kindred and kindness that had been between them, that he might be left out, in regard that he had already wasted his time and his estate in the parliament's service; and having had neither recompense for his losses, nor any office of benefit, it would finish his ruin to be tied by this employment to a close and chargeable attendance, besides the inconvenience of his health, not yet thoroughly confirmed, his constitution being more suitable to an active than to a sedentary life. These and other things he privately urged upon him; but he, who was a man regardless of his own or of any man's private interest, wherever he thought the public service might be advantaged, instead of keeping him out got him in, when the colonel had prevailed with others to have indulged him with that ease he desired. Mr. Hutchinson, after he had endeavoured to decline this employment and could not, thought that herein, as in other occasions, it being put upon him without his own desire, God had called him to his service in councils as formerly in arms, and applied himself to this also, wherein he did his duty faithfully, and employed his power to relieve the oppressed and dejected, freely becoming the advocate of those who had been his late enemies, in all things that were just and charitable. Though he had now an opportunity to have enriched himself, as it is to be feared some in all times have done, by accepting rewards for even just assistances, and he wanted not many who offered them and solicited him therein, yet such was his generous nature that he abhorred the mention of anything like reward, though ever so justly merited; and although he did a thousand highly obliging kindnesses for many, both friends and enemies, he never had anything in money or presents of any man.[1] The truth is, on the contrary, he met with many

[1] The lists of the first two councils, which embraced almost the whole duration of the republic, are preserved by Whitelocke, and Colonel Hutchinson is in each of them; he went out at the formation

that had not the good manners to make so much as a civil verbal acknowledgment. Among the rest one Sir John Owen may stand for a pillar of ingratitude. This man was wholly unknown to him, and with Duke Hamilton, the Earl of Holland, the Lord Capell, and the Lord Goring, was condemned to death by a second high court of justice. Of this, though the colonel was nominated a commissioner, he would not sit, his unbloody nature desiring to spare the rest of the delinquents, after the highest had suffered, and not delighting in the death of men, when they could live without cruelty to better men. The parliament also was willing to show mercy to some of these, and to execute others for example; whereupon the whole house was diversely engaged, some for one and some for another of these lords, and striving to cast away those they were not concerned in, that they might save their friends. While there was such mighty labour and endeavour for these lords, Colonel Hutchinson observed that no man spoke for this poor knight; and, sitting next to Colonel Ireton, he expressed himself to him, and told him that it grieved him much to see that, while all were labouring to save the lords, a gentleman, that stood in the same condemnation, should not find one friend to ask his life; " and so," said he, " am I moved with compassion that, if you will second me, I am resolved to speak for him, who, I perceive, is a stranger and friendless." Ireton promised to second him, and accordingly, inquiring further of the man's condition, whether he had not a petition in any member's hand, he found that his keepers had brought one to the clerk of the house; but the man had not found any who would interest themselves for him, thinking the lords' lives of so much more concernment than this gentleman's. This the more stirred up the colonel's generous pity, and he took the petition, delivered it, spoke for him so nobly, and was so effectually seconded by Ireton, that they carried his pardon clear. Yet although one who knew the whole circumstance of the business, how Mr. Hutchinson, moved by mere compassion and generosity, had procured his life, told him, who admired his own escape, how it came about, yet he never was the man that so much as once came to give him thanks; nor was his

of the third. It is extremely to be regretted, that Mrs. Hutchinson should have been so concise in this part of her history, it being a period which naturally excites much curiosity, but of which we have only indistinct, and, generally speaking, invidious and partial accounts.

fellow-prisoner Goring, for whom the colonel had also effectually solicited, more grateful.[1]

Some of the army, being very desirous to get amongst them a person of whose fidelity and integrity to the cause they had such good experience, had moved it to the general, my Lord Fairfax; who commanded to have it inquired in what way he would choose to be employed; and when he told them that, in regard of his family, which he would not willingly be much absent from, he should rather accept the government of some town than a field employment, four governments were brought to him, to select which he would have; whereof Plymouth and Portsmouth, and one more in the west, being at a vast distance from his own country, he made choice of Hull, in the north, though it was a less beneficial charge than the other, thinking they had not offered him anything but what had fairly fallen into their disposal. Soon after this, the lieutenant-general, Cromwell, desired him to meet him one afternoon at a committee, where, when he came, a malicious accusation against the governor of Hull was violently prosecuted by a fierce faction in that town. To this the governor had sent up a very fair and honest defence, yet most of the committee, more favouring the adverse faction, were labouring to cast out the governor. Colonel Hutchinson, though he knew him not, was very earnest in his defence, whereupon Cromwell drew him aside, and asked him what he meant by contending to keep in that governor? (it was Overton.) The colonel told him, because he saw nothing proved against him worthy of being ejected. " But," said Cromwell, " we like him not." Then said the colonel, " Do it upon that account, and blemish not a man that is innocent, upon false accusations, because you like him not." " But," said Cromwell, " we would have him out, because the government is designed for you, and except you put him out you cannot have the place." At this the colonel was very angry, and with great indignation told him,

[1] This is differently represented by Whitelocke, Rapin, and Ludlow. Whitelocke simply says that he was reprieved; Rapin, that his sentence was suspended, because he should have been tried by an inferior court: and Ludlow, that Ireton moved the house in his favour, omitting Colonel Hutchinson either by negligence or design; there is some reason to think it to have been by the latter. Notwithstanding Colonel Hutchinson experienced ingratitude from many individuals, the general and collective sense of his justice and benevolence will be seen to have its full operation in his favour in the sequel.

if there was no way to bring him into their army but by casting out others unjustly, he would rather fall naked before his enemies, than so seek to put himself into a posture of defence. Then returning to the table, he so eagerly undertook the injured governor's protection, that he foiled his enemies, and the governor was confirmed in his place. This so displeased Cromwell that, as before, so much more now, he saw that as even his own interest would not bias him into any unjust faction, so he secretly laboured to frustrate the attempts of all others who, for the same reason that Cromwell laboured to keep him out, laboured as much to bring him in.

But now had the poison of ambition so ulcerated Cromwell's heart, that the effects of it became more apparent than before; and while as yet Fairfax stood an empty name, he was moulding the army to his mind, weeding out the godly and upright-hearted men, both officers and soldiers, and filling up their rooms with rascally turn-coat cavaliers, and pitiful sottish beasts of his own alliance, and other such as would swallow all things, and make no questions for conscience' sake. Yet this he did not directly nor in tumult, but by such degrees that it was unperceived by all that were not of very penetrating eyes; and those that made the loudest outcries against him lifted up their voices with such apparent envy and malice that, in that mist, they rather hid than discovered his ambitious minings. Among these, Colonel Rich and Commissary Staines and Watson had made a design even against his life, and the business was brought to the examination of the council of state. Before the hearing of it, Colonel Rich came to Colonel Hutchinson and implored his assistance with tears, affirming all the crimes of Cromwell, but not daring to justify his accusations, although the colonel advised him if they were true to stand boldly to it, if false to acknowledge his own iniquity. The latter course he took, and the council had resolved upon the just punishment of the men, when Cromwell, having only thus in a private council vindicated himself from their malice, and laid open what pitiful sneaking poor knaves they were, how ungrateful to him, and how treacherous and cowardly to themselves, became their advocate, and made it his suit that they might be no farther published or punished. This being permitted him, and they thus rendered contemptible to others, they became beasts and slaves to him, who knew how to serve himself by them without trusting them. This generosity, for indeed he carried himself with the greatest bravery that is imaginable herein, much advanced his glory, and cleared him in the eyes of superficial beholders; but others saw he creeped on, and could not stop him, while fortune itself seemed to prepare his way[1] on sundry occasions. All this while he carried to Mr. Hutchinson the most open face, and made the most obliging professions of friendship imaginable; but the colonel saw through him, and forbore not often to tell him what was suspected of his ambition, what dissimulations of his were remarked, and how dishonourable to the name of God and the profession of religion, and destructive to the most glorious cause, and dangerous in overthrowing all our triumphs, these things which were suspected of him, would be, if true. He would seem to receive these cautions and admonitions as the greatest demonstrations of integrity and friendship that could be made, and embrace the colonel in his arms, and make serious lying professions to him, and often inquire men's opinions concerning him, which the colonel never forbore to tell him plainly, although he knew he resented it not as he made show, yet it pleased him so to discharge his own thoughts.[2]

The islanders of Jersey wanting a governor, and being acquainted, through the familiarity many of their countrymen had with him, with the abilities and honour of Colonel Hutchinson, they addressed themselves to my Lord General Fairfax, and petitioned to have him for their governor, which my lord assented to: and accordingly commanded a commission to be drawn up, which was done; but the colonel made no haste to take it out. But my lord, having ordered the commission, regarded him as governor, and when the model of the castle was brought to my lord to procure orders and money for the repairing of the fortifications, he sent it to the colonel, and all other business concerning the island.

[1] By the admirers of Tacitus the development of this intrigue will be highly relished; it aids likewise to confirm the remark that Cromwell's fort lay in watching and adroitly seizing opportunities, not in creating or inventing them. By the former method a man swims with the tide of human affairs, and is assisted by it; by the latter he must stem and encounter it.

[2] Men who think superficially will instantly proclaim the simplicity of Colonel Hutchinson and the shrewdness of Cromwell; those who think deeper, will in that simplicity see wisdom, in that shrewdness a more exquisite folly. In life, in death, and in reputation, which of these two was the happier?

In the meantime, the Scots having declared open war against the parliament of England, it was concluded to send an army into Scotland, to prevent their intended advance hither. But when they were just marching out, my Lord Fairfax, persuaded by his wife and her chaplains, threw up his commission at such a time, when it could not have been done more spitefully and ruinously to the whole parliament interest. Colonel Hutchinson and other parliament men, hearing of his intentions the night before, and knowing that he would thus level the way to Cromwell's ambitious designs, went to him and laboured to dissuade him; which they would have effected, but that the presbyterian ministers wrought with him to do it. He expressed his opinion that he believed God had laid him aside, as not being worthy of more, nor of that glory which was already given him.

To speak the truth of Cromwell, whereas many said he undermined Fairfax, it was false; for in Colonel Hutchinson's presence, he most effectually importuned him to keep his commission, lest it should discourage the army and the people at that juncture of time, but could by no means prevail, although he laboured for it almost all the night with most earnest endeavours.[1] But this great man was then as immovable by his friends as pertinacious in obeying his wife;

[1] Whitelocke tells the same story nearly in the same manner, but thinks Cromwell was not sincere: yet certainly he took all the same steps with those who were unquestionably so. How little soever Cromwell might wish to succeed, there was good policy in attending this conference, as it might in some degree serve to diminish the suspicions entertained of his own ambitious views, and prevent their being urged in argument to Fairfax, which if he had been absent they most likely would have been. Be this as it may, it may be truly said,

> Ex illo fluere et retro sublapsi referri
> Res Danaum.

for the true republicans or commonwealth's men,

> From thence the tide of fortune left their shore,
> And ebbed much faster than it flowed before.

For it was only with the co-operation of a man, who to his martial talents, which certainly exceeded all of his time, added that moderation and integrity, which will distinguish Fairfax to the end of time, that the great politicians of those days could have planned and finished such schemes of representation, legislation, and administration, as would have rendered the nation great and happy, either as a commonwealth or mixed government. They had in some respects such opportunities as never can again arise; and if the presbyterians have nothing else to answer for, the perverting the judgment of this excellent man was a fault never to be forgiven; if the ruin of their own cause could expiate it, they were not long before they made atonement.

whereby he then died to all his former glory, and became the monument of his own name, which every day wore out. When his commission was given up, Cromwell was made general, and new commissions were taken out by all the officers from him. He finding that Colonel Hutchinson's commission for the island was not taken out, and that he did not address himself to him, made haste to prevent the islanders, and gave a commission for the government to one of his own creatures. At this time the Lady Dormer being dead, had left to her grandchild, the Lady Anne Somerset, a papist, daughter to the Marquess of Worcester, a manor in Leicestershire, which the lady, being more desirous of a portion in money, had a great mind to sell, and came and offered it to Colonel Hutchinson, with whom she had some alliance; but he told her he was not in a purchasing condition, whereupon she earnestly begged him, that if he would not buy it himself, he would procure of the parliament leave for her to sell it. This he moved for and was repulsed, whereupon both the lady, and one that was her priest, who negotiated for her, and other friends, most earnestly solicited Colonel Hutchinson to buy it; who urging that he had not money for such a purchase, they offered him time for payment, till he could sell his own land, and assured him it should be such a pennyworth, that he should not repent the selling his own land to buy it. He urged to them the trouble and difficulty it would be to obtain it, and that it might so fall that he must lay a weight upon it, more than the thing would be worth to him, he having never yet made any request to the house, and having reason to expect recompenses for the loss of his estate, as well as others. But my lady still importuned him, promising a pennyworth in it, that should countervail the difficulty and the trouble; whereupon, at the last, he contracted with her, upon the desire both of her and her brother, the Lord Herbert, who was her next heir, and was then at full age, and he gave a release of all claim to it, under his hand and seal; and my lady, being between nineteen and twenty years old, then passed a fine, and covenanted at her coming to full age to pass another, and absolutely bargained and sold the land to Colonel Hutchinson, who secured the price of it to the Marquess of Dorchester, whom the lady and her friends had a great hope and desire to compass for a husband, and had thoughts, that when the portion was secured in his hands, it would be easily effected. This they afterwards entrusted to Colonel Hutchinson, and desired his assistance to propound the business to my lord, as from himself, out of mutual well-wishes to both parties; but my lord would not hearken to it, though the colonel, willing to do her a kindness, endeavoured to persuade him, as much as was fitting. In the meantime the colonel could not, by all the friends and interest he had in the house, procure a composition and leave for my lady to sell her hand, because they said it would be a precedent to other papists, and some moved, that what service he had done, and what he had lost, might be some other way considered, rather than this should be suffered. But he vigorously pursuing it, and laying all the weight of all his merits and sufferings upon it, all that he could obtain at last was, to be himself admitted, in his own name, for taking off the sequestration, after he had bought it, which he did; and they took two thousand pounds of him for his composition. By the interest of Sir Henry Vane and several others of his friends, powerful in the house, this too was with much difficulty wrought out, though violently opposed by several others. Of these Major-general Harrison was one, who, when he saw that he could not prevail, but that, through particular favour to Colonel Hutchinson, it was carried out by his friends; met the colonel after the rising of the house, and embracing him, desired him not to think he had acted from any personal opposition to him, but in his own judgment he had thought it fit the spoil should be taken out of the enemy's hands, and no composition admitted from idolaters. Whatever might be for a particular advantage to him, he envied not, but rejoiced in it, only he so dearly loved him, that he desired he would not set his heart upon the augmenting of outward estate, but upon the things of the approaching kingdom of God, concerning which he made a most pious and seemingly friendly harangue, of at least an hour long, with all the demonstrations of zeal to God and love to the colonel that can be imagined. But the colonel, having reason to fear that he knew not his own spirit herein, made him only a short reply, that he thanked him for his counsel, and should endeavour to follow it, as became the duty of a Christian, and should be glad to be as effectually instructed by his example as by his admonition. For at that time the major-general, who was but a mean man's son, and of a mean education, and of no estate before the war, had gathered an estate of two thousand a year, besides engrossing great offices, and encroaching upon his under-officers; and maintained his coach and family, at a height as if they had been born to a principality.

About the same time a great ambassador from the King of Spain was to have public audience in the house, and was the first who had addressed them, owning them as a republic. The day before his audience, Colonel Hutchinson was sitting in the house, near some young men handsomely clad, among whom Mr. Charles Rich, since Earl of Warwick; and the colonel himself had on that day a habit which was pretty rich but grave, and no other than he usually wore. Harrison addressing himself particularly to him, admonished them all, that now the nations sent to them, they should labour to shine before them in wisdom, piety, righteousness, and justice, and not in gold and silver and worldly bravery, which did not become saints; and that the next day when the ambassadors came, they should not set themselves out in gorgeous habits, which were unsuitable to holy professions. The colonel, although he was not convinced of any misbecoming bravery in the suit he wore that day, which was but of sad-coloured cloth trimmed with gold, and silver points and buttons; yet because he would not appear offensive in the eyes of religious persons, the next day he went in a plain black suit, and so did all the other gentlemen; but Harrison came that day in a scarlet coat and cloak, both laden with gold and silver lace, and the coat so covered with clinquant (foil), that one scarcely could discern the ground, and in this glittering habit he set himself just under the speaker's chair; which made the other gentlemen think that his godly speeches, the day before, were but made that he alone might appear in the eyes of strangers. But this was part of his weakness, the Lord at last lifted him above these poor earthly elevations, which then and some time afterwards prevailed too much with him.[1]

After the colonel had bought my lady's land, some that were extremely vexed at her having that sum of money,

---

[1] Ludlow gives very extraordinary accounts of his devotion to that which he thought the cause of God, as well as of his readiness to suffer martyrdom for it when it was in his power to avoid that severe trial.

dealt with the colonel to permit them to sequester it into his hands, and offered him he should have it all himself; which, he told them, he would be torn to pieces before he would do, and that it was a treachery and villainy that he abhorred. Though, notwithstanding this, he was much pressed yet he would not yield, and to prevent force, which they threatened, after moving in the house, how dangerous it was to suffer such a sum of money to be in the hands of the daughter of an excepted person, especially at such a time (for now the king was crowned in Scotland, and the Scots ready to invade, and the presbyters to join with them), the colonel put the money out of his own hands, to preserve it for my lady. All that time both she and her brother, and other friends, made all the acknowledgments of obligation that was possible. Not to confound stories, I finish the memorial of this here.

After the parliament was broken up by Cromwell, and after that my lady, seeing her project of marrying with my lord Dorchester would not take, had embraced an offer of Mr. Henry Howard, second son to the Earl of Arundel, and when, in the protector's time, the papists wanted not patrons, she began to repent the selling of her land, which before she thought such a blessing, and told her husband false stories, as he alleged, though his future carriage made it justly suspicious he was as unworthy as she.[1]

The colonel, presently after he had that land, had very much improved it, to a fourth part more than it was at when he bought it, and they, envying his good bargain, desired to have it again out of his hands, nor dealt fairly and directly in the thing, but employed a cunning person, Major Wildman, who was then a great manager of papists' interests, to get the land again, which he was to have four hundred pounds for, if he could do it. Whereupon he presently got money and came to the gentleman who had a mortgage upon it for three thousand pounds taken up to pay my lady, and tendered it. But Mr. Ash, a great friend of the colonel's, was so faithful that he would not accept it, and then Wildman began a chancery suit, thinking that the colonel, being out of favour with the present powers, would be necessitated to take any composition. When he had put the colonel to a

[1] In the third vol. of Clarendon's *State Papers*, in a letter of his, dated August, 1655, he says, " Cromwell hypocritically pretends kindness to the catholics, but the levellers have real candour towards them and are implacable enemies to Cromwell."

great deal of vain charge, and found he could do no good, at last they desired to make up the business, and the lady and Mr. Howard passed a new fine to confirm the title, and the colonel was delivered from further trouble with them, till after the change and the return of the king. Then, when the parliament men began to come into question for their lives, my Lord of Portland and Mr. Howard came to Mrs. Hutchinson's lodgings three or four times, while she was out soliciting for her husband, and my lord left her a message, that he must needs speak with her, upon a business of much concernment; whereupon she sought out my lord, knowing that he had professed much kindness and obligation to her husband, and thinking he might have some design now to acknowledge it by some real assistance. But when she came to him, he told her, her husband was in danger of his life, and that if he would resign back Loseby to Mr. Howard, he would help him to a good sum of money to fly, and Mr. Howard would stand to the hazard of buying it; but she, being vexed that my lord should interrupt her with this frivolous proposition, told my lord that she would hazard it with the rest of her estate, rather than make up such desperate bargains. When Mr. Howard saw this would not do, he prepared a petition to get it excepted out of the act of oblivion, pretending that his wife being under age, the colonel had by power and fraud wrested her out of her estate. But when he showed this petition to his friends, they being informed of the falseness of the allegations, would none of them undertake either to deliver or back it. Only one Sir Richard Onslow, who was a violent man, and railed against the colonel concerning it, but he not long afterwards died by a blast of lightning. Others of his friends, when they understood that he himself had joined in the confirmation of the fine, after the colonel had retired, in the protector's reign, bade him for shame to make no more mention of his lady's being fooled or frightened to an act which she had voluntary done. Many told the colonel how unsafe it was to displease a person who had so many powerful allies that might mischief him, but the colonel would neither be frightened nor flattered to give away the estate, which when Mr. Howard found, he let fall his purpose, and made no more vain endeavours.[1]

[1] How, when, or by whom this estate at Loseby was sold again, the editor has not been able to discover, it never having come into the

And now to return to his story where I left it.   I shall not mention every particular action of his in the employment of a senator and councillor of the realms but only some which were more remarkable, to show the honour and excellency of his nature, among which this was one.   His old opponents and enemies of the Nottingham committee had entered into the presbyterian conspiracy so deeply, that had they been brought to public trial, their lives would have been forfeited to the law, and this was discovered to him, and also that Colonel Pierrepont was the chief of them; when he took care to have the business so managed, that Colonel Pierrepont was passed by in the information, and others so favourably accused, that they were only restrained from the mischief they intended, and kept prisoners till the danger was over, and afterwards, through his mediation, released, without any further punishment on their persons and estates, though Chadwick's eldest son was one of these.   For Colonel Pierrepont, he only privately admonished him, and endeavoured to reclaim him, which the man, being good-natured, was infinitely overcome with; insomuch, that ever after, to his dying day, all his envy ceased, and he professed all imaginable friendship and kindness to the colonel.   Indeed, his excellent gentleness was such, that he not only protected and saved these enemies, wherein there was some glory of passing by revenge, but was compassionately affected with the miseries of any poor women or children, who had been unfortunately, though deservedly, ruined in the civil war; and without any interest of his own in the persons, whenever any ruined family came to seek relief, when he was in power, he was as zealous in assisting all such, as far as it might be done with the safety of the commonwealth, as if they had been his brothers.   As it was a misery to be bewailed in those days, that many of the parliament party exercised cruelty, injustice, and oppression to their conquered enemies; wherever he discovered it he violently opposed it, and defended even those enemies that were by might oppressed and defrauded of the mercies of the parliament.   Upon this account he had

hands of his branch of the family, which purchased Owthorpe.   One of the estates sold by Colonel Hutchinson in his lifetime was that of Ratcliffe on Soar, which is spoken of in a note as given to Sir Thomas Hutchinson by his uncle Sacheverell;   the purchaser was Alderman Ireton, and it was, in all probability, sold to enable him jointly with the money borrowed of Mr. Ash to purchase this estate.

contests with some good men, who were weak in these things, some through too factious a zeal, and others blinded with their own or their friends' interests. Among these Colonel Hacker's father, having married my Lady Byron's mother, was made a trustee for the estate of her son, which she had by Strelley her first husband. He had about £1,800 of the estate of young Strelley in his hands, which, he dying, his eldest son and heir, Colonel Francis Hacker, was liable and justly ought to pay. Young Strelley died in France, and left his estate to his half-brother, the son of Sir Richard Byron, who, all the time of the first war, was at school in Colonel Hutchinson's garrison at Nottingham, and afterwards was sent into France. Being there, an infant, when this estate fell to him, he returned and chose Colonel Hutchinson for his guardian, who overcame Colonel Hacker in the right of his pupil, and recovered that money out of his hands, which he would not have paid, if the infant had not found a friend that was heartily zealous to obtain his just right. Sir Arthur Haslerig was a great patron of Colonel Hacker's, and laboured to bear him out against justice and the infant's right in this thing; and when the colonel had overcome him, they were both displeased; for Hacker, on the other side, was such a creature of Sir Arthur's, that, without questioning justice or honesty, he was more diligent in obeying Sir Arthur's than God's commands. Sir Allen Apsley had articles at the surrender of Barnstaple, whereof he was governor; and contrary to these he was put to vast expense and horrible vexation by several persons, but especially by one wicked woman, who had the worst and the smoothest tongue that ever her sex made use of to mischief. She was handsome in her youth, and had very pretty girls for her daughters, whom, when they grew up, she prostituted for her revenge and malice against Sir Allen Apsley, which was so venomous and devilish, that she stuck not at inventing false accusations, and hiring witnesses to swear to them, and a thousand other practices as enormous. In those days there was a committee set up, for relief of such as had any violation of their articles, and of this Bradshaw was president; into whose easy faith this woman, pretending herself religious, and of the parliament's party, had so insinuated herself, that Sir Allen's way of relief was obstructed. Colonel Hutchinson, labouring mightily in his protection, and often foiling this

vile woman, and bringing to light her devilish practices, turned the woman's spite into as violent a tumult against himself; and Bradshaw was so hot in abetting her, that he grew cool in his kindness to the colonel, yet broke it not quite: but the colonel was very much grieved that a friend should engage in so unjust an opposition. At last it was manifest how much they were mistaken who would have assisted this woman upon a score of her being on the parliament's side, for she was all this while a spy for the king, and after his return, Sir Allen Apsley met her in the king's chamber waiting for recompense for that service. The thing she sued Sir Allen Apsley for, was for a house of hers in the garrison of Barnstaple, which was pulled down to fortify the town for the king, before he was governor of the place. Yet would she have had his articles violated to make her a recompense out of his estate, treble and more than the value of the house; pretending she was of the parliament's party, and that Sir Allen, in malice thereunto, had without necessity pulled down her house. All which were horrible lies, but so maliciously and so wickedly affirmed and sworn to by her mercenary witnesses, that they at first found faith, and it was hard for truth afterwards to overcome that prepossession.

The colonel, prosecuting the defence of truth and justice in these and many more things, and abhorring all councils for securing the young commonwealth by cruelty and oppression of the vanquished, who had not laid down their hate, in delivering up their arms, and were, therefore, by some cowards, judged unworthy of the mercy extended to them, —the colonel, I say, disdaining such thoughts, displeased many of his own party, who in the main, we hope, might have been honest, although through divers temptations they were guilty of horrible slips, which did more offend the colonel's pure zeal, who more detested these sins in brethren than in enemies.

Now was Cromwell sole general, and marched into Scotland, and the Scots were ready to invade, and the presbyters to assist them in it. The army being small, there was a necessity for recruits, and the council of state, soliciting all the parliament-men that had interest to improve it in this exigence of time, gave Colonel Hutchinson a commission for a regiment of horse. He immediately got up three troops,

well armed and mounted, of his own old soldiers, that
thirsted to be again employed under him, and was preparing
the rest of the regiment to bring them up himself; when he
was informed, that as soon as his troops came into Scotland,
Cromwell very readily received them, but would not let them
march together, but dispersed them, to fill up the regiments
of those who were more his creatures. The colonel hearing
this, would not carry him any more, but rather employed
himself in securing, as much as was necessary, his own
country, for which he was sent down by the council of state,
who at that time were very much surprised at hearing that
the king of Scots was passed by Cromwell, and had entered
with a great army into England. Bradshaw himself, stout-
hearted as he was, privately could not conceal his fear; some
raged and uttered sad discontents against Cromwell, and
suspicions of his fidelity; they all considered that Cromwell
was behind, of whom I think they scarce had any account,
or of his intention, or how this error came about, to suffer
the enemy to enter here, where there was no army to encounter him. Both the city and country (by the angry
presbyters, wavering in their constancy to them and the
liberties they had purchased) were all amazed, and doubtful
of their own and the commonwealth's safety. Some could
not hide very pale and unmanly fears, and were in such
distraction of spirit, that it much disturbed their councils.
Colonel Hutchinson, who ever had most vigour and cheerfulness when there was most danger, encouraged them, as
they were one day in a private council raging and crying out
on Cromwell's miscarriages, to apply themselves to councils
of safety, and not to lose time in accusing others, while they
might yet provide to save the endangered realm; or at least
to fall nobly in defence of it, and not to yield to fear and
despair. These and such like things being urged, they at
length re-collected themselves, and every man that had
courage and interest in their counties, went down to look to
them.[1] Colonel Hutchinson came down into Nottingham-

---

[1] The trepidation of the council of state, and the zeal with which they
were supported, is well described by Whitelocke. Whether Cromwell
suffered the king to pass by him designedly or otherwise, is uncertain;
but it is very likely that he did it by design, as knowing that those who
did not like, for the same reason as Colonel Hutchinson, to send forces
to him, would, for their own sakes, bring them forward to oppose the
king. Either his fortune or his judgment was great.

shire, and secured those who were suspected as likely to make
any commotion, and put the country into such a posture of
defence as the time would permit. But it was not long
before the king chose another way, and went to Worcester.
Cromwell following swiftly after with his army, and more
forces meeting him from several other parts, they fought
with the king and his Scots, totally routed and subdued
them, and he, with difficulty, after concealment in an oak,
and many other shifts, stole away into France.

When the colonel heard how Cromwell used his troops,
he was confirmed that he and his associates in the army were
carrying on designs of private ambition, and resolved that
none should share with them in the commands of the army
or forts of the nation, but such as would be beasts, and be
ridden upon by the proud chiefs. Disdaining, therefore,
that what he had preserved, for the liberty of his country,
should be a curb upon them, and foreseeing that some of
Cromwell's creatures would at length be put in, to exercise
him with continual affronts, and to hinder any man from
standing up for the deliverance of the country, if the insolence
of the army (which he too sadly foresaw) should put them
upon it; for this reason, in Cromwell's absence, he procured
an order for the removal of the garrison at Nottingham,
which was commanded by his kinsman Major Poulton, into
the marching army, and for the demolishing of the place;
which accordingly was speedily executed.

When Major Poulton, who had all along been very faithful and active in the cause, brought his men to the army,
he was entertained with such affronts and neglects by the
general, that he voluntarily quitted his command, and retired
to the ruined place, where the castle was which he had bought
with his arrears.[1] When Cromwell came back through the

---

[1] The machinations of Cromwell are spoken of in general terms by
Rapin, Whitelocke, and others; but are nowhere so well detailed as
here. Of all things the most necessary to Cromwell was to obtain
soldiers and subaltern officers perfectly subservient to his own purposes. but this he could hope to effect *then* and *then only*, when he had
deprived them of such superior officers as would have preserved them
from deception, and have kept them faithful to their country. The
present and similar occurrences furnished him with the means so to do,
which he employed most assiduously. Ludlow, vol. iii. p. 21. "And
thus the troops of the parliament, which were not raised out of the
meanest of the people and without distinction, as other armies had
been, but consisted of such as had engaged themselves from a spirit of
liberty in the defence of their rights and religion, were corrupted by

country and saw the castle pulled down, he was heartily vexed at it, and told Colonel Hutchinson, that if he had been there when it was voted, he should not have suffered it. The colonel replied, that he had procured it to be done, and believed it to be his duty to ease the people of the charge, when there was no more need of it.

When Cromwell came to London, there wanted not some little creatures of his, in the house, who had taken notice of all that had been said of him when he let the king slip by; how some stuck not in their fear and rage to call him traitor, and to threaten his head. These reports added spurs to his ambition, but his son-in-law, Ireton, deputy of Ireland, would not be wrought to serve him, but hearing of his machinations, determined to come over to England to endeavour to divert him from such destructive courses.[1] But God cut him short by death, and whether his body or an empty coffin was brought into England, something in his name came to London, and was to be, by Cromwell's procurement, magnificently buried among the kings at Westminster. Colonel Hutchinson was, after his brother, one of the nearest kinsmen he had, but Cromwell, who of late studied to give him neglects, passed him by, and neither sent him mourning, nor particular invitation to the funeral, only the Speaker gave public notice in the house, that all the members were desired to attend it; and such was the flattery of many pitiful lords and other gentlemen, parasites, that they put them-

him, kept as a standing force against the people, taught to forget their first engagements, and rendered as mercenary as other troops are accustomed to be." From about this period then we may date the change of sentiment of the army in general, and of course the change of opinion respecting them, in the minds of Colonel Hutchinson and others who before had sided with them.

[1] If this intention of Ireton is mentioned by any other person, it has escaped the search of the editor, it may have been known *with certainty* by Mr. Hutchinson alone; but something of the kind seems to have been in the *contemplation* of Whitelocke when he regrets his death, on account of the influence he had over the mind of Cromwell, which has been remarked in a former note; as likewise the probability that the prolongation of his life might have made a great difference in the conduct of Cromwell. What is said of his funeral well agrees with what is said by Ludlow, who adds, that " Ireton would have despised these pomps, having erected for himself a more glorious monument in the hearts of good men, by his affection to his country, his abilities of mind, his impartial justice, his diligence in the public service, and his other virtues, which were a far greater honour to his memory than a dormitory among the ashes of kings; who, for the most part, as they had governed others by their passions, so were they as much governed by them." For the rest, Colonel Hutchinson's reproof of Cromwell was a pithy one.

selves into deep mourning; but Colonel Hutchinson that day put on a scarlet cloak, very richly laced, such as he usually wore, and coming into the room where the members were, seeing some of the lords in mourning, he went to them to inquire the cause, who told him they had put it on to honour the general; and asked again, why he, that was a kinsman, was in such a different colour? He told them, that because the general had neglected sending to him, when he had sent to many who had no alliance, only to make up the train, he was resolved he would not flatter so much as to buy for himself, although he was a true mourner in his heart for his cousin, whom he had ever loved, and would therefore go and take his place among his mourners. This he did, and went into the room where the close mourners were; who seeing him come in, as different from mourning as he could make himself, the alderman came to him, making a great apology that they mistook and thought he was out of town, and had much injured themselves thereby, to whom it would have been one of their greatest honours to have had his assistance in the befitting habit, as now it was their shame to have neglected him. But Cromwell, who had ordered all things, was piqued horribly at it, though he dissembled his resentment at that time, and joined in excusing the neglect; but he very well understood that the colonel neither out of ignorance nor niggardness came in that habit, but publicly to reproach their neglects.

After the death of Ireton, Lambert was voted deputy of Ireland, and commander-in-chief there, who being at that time in the north, was exceedingly elevated with the honour, and courted all Fairfax's old commanders, and other gentlemen; who, upon his promises of preferment, quitted their places, and many of them came to London and made him up there a very proud train, which still more exalted him, so that too soon he put on the prince, immediately laying out five thousand pounds for his own particular equipage, and looking upon all the parliament-men, who had conferred this honour on him, as underlings, and scarcely worth such a great man's nod. This untimely declaration of his pride gave great offence to the parliament, who having only given him a commission for six months for his deputyship, made a vote that, after the expiration of that time, the presidency of the civil and military power of that nation should no more be in his nor in any one man's hands again. This vote was upon Cromwell's procurement, who hereby designed to make way for his new son-in-law, Colonel Fleetwood, who had married the widow of the late deputy Ireton. There went a story that as my Lady Ireton was walking in St. James's park, the Lady Lambert, as proud as her husband, came by where she was, and as the present princess always hath precedency of the relict of the dead prince, so she put my Lady Ireton below; who, notwithstanding her piety and humility, was a little grieved at the affront. Colonel Fleetwood being then present, in mourning for his wife, who died at the same time her lord did, took occasion to introduce himself, and was immediately accepted by the lady and her father, who designed thus to restore his daughter to the honour she had fallen from. Cromwell's plot took as well as he himself could wish; for Lambert, who saw himself thus cut off from half his exaltation, sent the house an insolent message, " that if they found him so unworthy of the honour they had given him as so soon to repent it, he would not retard their remedy for six months, but was ready to surrender their commission before he entered into his office." They took him at his word, and made Fleetwood deputy, and Ludlow commander of the horse; whereupon Lambert, with a heart full of spite, malice, and revenge, retreated to his palace at Wimbledon, and sat there watching an opportunity to destroy the parliament.

Cromwell, although he chiefly wrought this business in the house, yet flattered Lambert, and, having another ambitious scheme in his breast, helped to inflame Lambert against those of the parliament who were not his creatures, and cast the odium of his disgrace upon them, and professed his own clearness of it, and pity for him, that he should be drawn into such an inconvenience as the charge of putting himself into equipage, and the loss of all that provision; which Cromwell, pretending generosity, took all upon his own account, and delivered him from the debt. Lambert dissembled again on his part, and insinuated himself into Cromwell, fomenting his ambition to take the administration of all the conquered nations into his own hands; but finding themselves not strong enough alone, they took to them Major-general Harrison, who had a great interest both in the army and the church; and these, pretending to be piously troubled that there were such delays in the administration of justice, and such perverting of right, endeavoured to bring all good men into dislike of the parliament, pretending that they would perpetuate themselves in their honours and offices, and had no care to bring in those glorious things for which they had so many years contended in blood and toil. The parliament, on the other side, had now, by the blessing of God, restored the commonwealth to such a happy, rich, and plentiful condition, that it was not so flourishing before the war, and although the taxes that were paid were great, yet the people were rich and able to pay them: they (*the parliament*) were in a way of paying all the soldiers' arrears, had some hundred thousand pounds in their purses, and were free from enemies in arms within and without, except the Dutch, whom they had beaten and brought to seek peace upon terms honourable to the English: and now they thought it was time to sweeten the people, and deliver them from their burdens. This could not be but by disbanding the unnecessary officers and soldiers, and when things were thus settled, they had prepared a bill to put a period to their own sitting, and provide for new successors. But when the great officers understood that they were to resign their honours, and no more triumph in the burdens of the people, they easily induced the inferior officers and soldiers to set up for themselves with them; and while these things were passing, Cromwell with an armed force, assisted by Lambert and Harrison, came into the house and dissolved the parliament, pulling out the members, foaming and raging, and calling them undeserved and base names; and when the Speaker refused to come out of his chair, Harrison plucked him out. These gentlemen having done this, took to themselves the administration of all things; a few slaves of the house consulted with them and would have truckled under them, but not many. Meanwhile they and their soldiers could no way palliate their rebellion, but by making false criminations of the parliament-men, as that they meant to perpetuate themselves in honour and office, that they had gotten vast estates, and perverted justice for gain, and were imposing upon men for conscience, and a thousand such like things, which time manifested to be false, and truth retorted all upon themselves that they had injuriously cast at the others.[1]

[1] Almost all the historical writers who have treated of these times concur in deprecating this parliament, and represent them as a small

At the time that the parliament was broken up Colonel Hutchinson was in the country, where, since his going in his course out of the council of state, he had for about a year's time applied himself, when the parliament could dispense with his absence, to the administration of justice in the country, and to the putting in execution those wholesome laws and statutes of the land provided for the orderly regulation of the people.   And it was wonderful how, in a short space, he reformed several abuses and customary neglects in that part of the country where he lived, which being a rich fruitful vale, drew abundance of vagrant people to come and exercise the idle trade of wandering and begging; but he took such courses that there was very suddenly not a beggar left in the country, and all the poor in every town were so maintained and provided for, that they were never so liberally maintained and relieved before or since.   He procured unnecessary alehouses to be put down in all the towns, and if any one that he heard of suffered any disorder or debauchery in his house, he would not suffer him to brew any more.   He was a little severe against drunkenness, for which the drunkards would sometimes rail at him; but so much were all the children of darkness convinced by his light, that they

number or junto whose principal view was to perpetuate themselves in the enjoyment of power and honours. Those readers who desire to form a true judgment of this matter will be materially assisted by comparing the passages here before them with Whitelocke, and more particularly with the first twenty pages of the second volume of Ludlow; they will find that sort of consonance which is the best mark of truth, viz. the recital of different circumstances tending to establish one and the same principal fact. They will then be convinced that the great men who were at that time at the head of affairs had conducted them in a manner worthy of themselves, and had brought the nation to a state of prosperity which nothing less than a miracle can ever again bring it to, and which Mrs. Hutchinson describes in few and simple, but impressive words; *the people rich, the revenue great, debts paid, money in their purses, free from enemies within and without.* They had concluded with reforming the abuses of the law, and providing for their being succeeded by a fair and equal representation of the people, which all confess still to be the grand desideratum of our constitution.   And it was the very circumstance of the act being on the anvil, ready to receive the finishing stroke, that obliged Cromwell to act with such precipitation as staggered his confederates.

From all which will arise these corollaries or deductions; that a state, however great, may be governed by a republican form, and every department properly filled and administered.   But that no sufficient barrier has yet been found against a military chief, who has popularity, address, and ambition, to become the tyrant of it.   And in the end, recourse must be had to hereditary succession, from whence they at first departed.

were more in awe of his virtue than his authority. In this time he had made himself a convenient house,[1] whereof he

[1] Pained and disgusted as the mind of the reader must be with the tumults, anarchy, and crimes, it has witnessed, how welcome is the contemplation of this ease and leisure, devoted to elegant studies, virtuous pursuits, useful occupations, gentlemanlike amusements, rational converse, and conciliating hospitality! How difficult will it be to him to believe that this *otium cum dignitate* is the honourable retreat of one of those *gloomy fanatics* whose tyranny, Rapin says, had become intolerable to the nation!

About thirty years ago it was the fate of the editor to visit this mansion of his ancestors, in order to bring away a few pictures and some books, all that remained to him of those possessions, where they had lived with so much merited love and honour. Although he had not then read these memoirs, yet having heard Colonel Hutchinson spoken of as an extraordinary person, and that he had built, planted, and formed, all that was to be seen there; the country adjoining being a dreary waste, many thousand acres together being entirely overrun with gorse or furze; he viewed the whole with the utmost attention. He found there a house, of which he has the drawing, large, handsome, lofty, and convenient, and though but little ornamented, possessing all the grace that size and symmetry could give it. The entrance was by a flight of handsome steps into a large hall, occupying entirely the centre of the house, lighted at the entrance by two large windows, but at the further end by one much larger, in the expanse of which was carried up a staircase that seemed to be perfectly in the air. On one side of the hall was a long table, on the other a large fireplace; both suited to ancient hospitality. On the right hand side of this hall were three handsome rooms for the entertainment of guests. The sides of the staircase and gallery were hung with pictures, and both served as an orchestra either to the hall or to a large room over part of it, which was a ball room. To the left of the hall were the rooms commonly occupied by the family. All parts were built so substantially, and so well secured, that neither fire nor thieves could penetrate from room to room, nor from one flight of stairs to another, if ever so little resisted.

The house stood on a little eminence in the vale of Belvoir, at a small distance from the foot of those hills along which the Roman fosse-way from Leicester runs. The western side of the house was covered by the offices, a small village, and a church, interspersed with many trees. The south, which was the front of entrance, looked over a large extent of grass grounds which were the demesne, and were bounded by hills covered with wood which Colonel Hutchinson had planted. On the eastern side, the entertaining rooms opened on to a terrace, which encircled a very large bowling-green or level lawn; next to this had been a flower-garden, and next to that a shrubbery, now become a wood, through which vistas were cut to let in a view of Langar, the seat of Lord Howe, at two miles', and of Belvoir Castle, at seven miles' distance, which, as the afternoon sun sat full upon it, made a glorious object: at the further end of this small wood was a spot (of about ten acres) which appeared to have been a morass, and through which ran a rivulet: this spot Colonel Hutchinson had dug into a great number of canals, and planted the ground between them, leaving room for walks, so that the whole formed at once a wilderness or bower, reservoirs for fish, and a decoy for wild fowl. To the north, at some hundred yards' distance, was a lake of water, which, filling the space between two quarters of wood land, appeared, as viewed from the large window of the hall, like a moderate river, and beyond this the was the best ornament, and an example of virtue so prevailing, as metamorphosed many evil people, while they were under his roof, into another appearance of sobriety and holiness.

He was going up to attend the business of his country above, when news met him upon the road, near London, that Cromwell had broken the parliament. Notwithstanding, he went on and found divers of the members there, resolved to submit to this providence of God, and to wait till he should clear their integrity, and to disprove those people who had taxed them of ambition, by sitting still, when they had friends enough in the army, city, and country, to have disputed the matter, and probably to have vanquished these usurpers. They thought that if they should vex the land by war among themselves, the late subdued enemies, royalists and presbyterians, would have an opportunity to prevail on their dissensions, to the ruin of both: if these should govern well, and righteously, and moderately, they would enjoy the benefit of their good government, and not envy them the honourable toil; if they did otherwise, they should be ready to assist and vindicate their oppressed country, when the ungrateful people were made sensible of their true champions and protectors. Colonel Hutchinson, in his own particular, was very glad of

eye rested on the wolds or high wilds which accompany the fosse-way towards Newark. The whole had been deserted near forty years, but resisted the ravages of time so well as to discover the masterly hand by which it had been planned and executed. But the most extraordinary and gratifying circumstance was the veneration for the family which still subsisted, and which, at the period when the last possessor had by his will ordered this and all his estates in Nottinghamshire to be sold, and the produce given to *strangers*, induced the tenants to offer a large advance of their rents, and a good share of the money necessary for purchasing the estates, in order to enable the remains of the family to come and reside again among them. It was too late! the steward had contracted with the executors, and resold the most desirable part, whereof the timber of Colonel Hutchinson's planting was valued at many thousand pounds! The Editor could only retire repeating Virgil's first Eclogue.

Nos patriæ fines, nos dulcia linquimus arva.

*   *   *   *

Impius hæc tam culta novalia miles habebit?
Barbarus has segetes? En, quo discordia cives
Perduxit miseros! en, queis consevimus agros.

Round the wide world in banishment we roam,
Forced from our pleasing fields and native home:
Did we for these barbarians plant and sow,
On these, on these our happy fields bestow?
Good heavens! what dire effects from civil discord flow!

DRYDEN.

this release from that employment, which he managed with fidelity and uprightness, but not only without delight, but with a great deal of trouble and expense, in the contest for truth and righteousness upon all occasions.

The only recreation he had during his residence at London was in seeking out all the rare artists he could hear of, and in considering their works in paintings, sculptures, gravings, and all other such curiosities, insomuch that he became a great virtuoso and patron of ingenuity. Being loth that the land should be disfurnished of all the rarities that were in it, whereof many were set for sale from the king's and divers noblemen's collections, he laid out about two thousand pounds in the choicest pieces of painting, most of which were bought out of the king's goods, which had been given to his servants to pay their wages: to them the colonel gave ready money, and bought such good pennyworths, that they were valued at much more than they cost.[1] These he brought down into the country, intending a very neat cabinet for them; and these, with the surveying of his buildings, and improving by inclosure the place he lived in, employed him at home, and, for a little time, his hawks employed him abroad; but when a very sober fellow, that never was guilty of the usual vices of that generation of men, rage and swearing, died, he gave over his hawks, and pleased himself with music, and again fell to the practice of his viol, on which he played excellently well, and entertaining tutors for the diversion and education of his children in all sorts of music, he pleased himself with these innocent recreations during Oliver's mutable reign. As he had great delight, so he had great judgment, in music, and advanced his children's practice more than their tutors: he also was a great supervisor of their learning, and indeed was himself a tutor to them all, besides all those tutors whom he liberally entertained in his house for them. He spared not any cost for the education of both his sons and daughters in languages, sciences, music, dancing, and all other qualities befitting their father's house. He was himself their instructor

[1] That the conduct of Colonel Hutchinson differed from that of most other men in power at that time, and brought a seasonable relief to the king's servants and creditors, appears from two passages in the *History of Independency*, p. 146 and 184. " The king's servants and creditors starve for want of their own, while the members appropriate his furniture to their own use instead of selling it to pay debts." " The king's servants and creditors may gape long enough before they sell the king's goods to pay debts."

in humility, sobriety, and in all godliness and virtue, which he rather strove to make them exercise with love and delight than by constraint. As other things were his delight, this only he made his business, to attend to the education of his children, and the government of his own house and town. This he performed so well that never was any man more feared and loved than he by all his domestics, tenants, and hired workmen. He was loved with such a fear and reverence as restrained all rude familiarity and insolent presumptions in those who were under him, and he was feared with so much love that they all delighted to do his pleasure.

As he maintained his authority in all relations, so he endeavoured to make their subjection pleasant to them, and rather to convince them by reason than compel them to obedience, and would give way even to the lowest of his family to make them enjoy their lives in sober cheerfulness, and not to find their duties burdensome.

As for the public business of the country, he would not act in any office under the protector's power, and therefore confined himself to his own, which the whole country about him were grieved at, and would rather come to him for counsel as a private neighbour than to any of the men in power for greater help.

He being now reduced into an absolutely private condition, was very much courted and visited by those of all parties, and while the grand quarrel slept, and both the victors and vanquished were equal slaves under the new usurpers, there was a very kind correspondence between him and all his countrymen. As he was very hospitable, and his conversation no less desirable and pleasant, than instructive and advantageous, his house was much resorted to, and as kindly open to those who had in public contests been his enemies, as to his continued friends; for there never lived a man that had less malice and revenge, nor more reconcilableness and kindness and generosity in his nature, than he.

In the interim Cromwell and his army grew wanton with their power, and invented a thousand tricks of government, which, when nobody opposed, they themselves fell to dislike and vary every day. First he calls a parliament out of his own pocket, himself naming a sort of godly men for every county, who meeting and not agreeing, a part of them, in the name of the people, gave up the sovereignty to him. Shortly after he makes up several sorts of mock parliaments, but not finding one of them absolutely to his turn, turned them off again. He soon quitted himself of his triumvirs, and first thrust out Harrison, then took away Lambert's commission, and would have been king but for fear of quitting his generalship. He weeded, in a few months' time, above a hundred and fifty godly officers out of the army, with whom many of the religious soldiers went off, and in their room abundance of the king's dissolute soldiers were entertained; and the army was almost changed from that godly religious army, whose valour God had crowned with triumph, into the dissolute army they had beaten, bearing yet a better name. His wife and children were setting up for principality, which suited no better with any of them than scarlet on the ape; only, to speak the truth of himself, he had much natural greatness, and well became the place he had usurped. His daughter Fleetwood was humbled, and not exalted with these things, but the rest were insolent fools. Claypole, who married his daughter, and his son Henry, were two debauched, ungodly cavaliers. Richard was a peasant in his nature, yet gentle and virtuous, but became not greatness. His court was full of sin and vanity, and the more abominable, because they had not yet quite cast away the name of God, but profaned it by taking it in vain upon them. True religion was now almost lost, even among the religious party, and hypocrisy became an epidemical disease, to the sad grief of Colonel Hutchinson, and all true-hearted Christians and Englishmen. Almost all the ministers everywhere fell in and worshipped this beast, and courted and made addresses to him. So did the city of London, and many of the degenerate lords of the land, with the poor-spirited gentry. The cavaliers, in policy, who saw that while Cromwell reduced all by the exercise of tyrannical power under another name, there was a door opened for the restoring of their party, fell much in with Cromwell, and heightened all his disorders. He at last exercised such an arbitrary power, that the whole land grew weary of him, while he set up a company of silly, mean fellows, called major-generals, as governors in every country. These ruled according to their wills, by no law but what seemed good in their own eyes, imprisoning men, obstructing the course of justice between man and man, perverting right through partiality, acquitting some that were guilty, and punishing some that were innocent as guilty. Then he exercised another project to raise money, by decimation of the estates of all the king's party, of which action it is said Lambert was the instigator. At last he took upon himself to make lords and knights, and wanted not many fools, both of the army and gentry, to accept of, and strut in, his mock titles.[1] Then the Earl of Warwick's grandchild and the Lord Falconbridge married his two daughters; such pitiful slaves were the nobles of those days. At last Lambert, perceiving himself to have been all this while deluded with hopes and promises of succession, and seeing that Cromwell now intended to confirm the government in his own family, fell off from him; but behaved himself very pitifully and meanly, was turned out of all his places, and returned again to plot new vengeance at his house at Wimbledon, where he fell to dress his flowers in his garden, and work at the needle with his wife and his maids, while he was watching an opportunity to serve again his ambition, which had this difference from the protector's; the one was gallant and great, the other had nothing but an unworthy pride, most insolent in prosperity, and as abject and base in adversity.[2]

[1] The description given of the usurpations of Cromwell and his myrmidons, concise and contemptuous as it is, will be found perfectly just. With all his professions he did little else but deteriorate that state of things in which the parliament had left them: he patched up a much worse peace with the Dutch than the parliament would have made: to gratify or serve his personal views, he assisted the French against the Spaniards, and for ever weakened that power which would now have supported this nation against so dangerous a neighbour. Ireland he depopulated by encouraging the cavalier chiefs to emigrate with their adherents into foreign services. At home he rendered the very names of religion and liberty contemptible, and paved the way for the return of the Stuarts. Mrs. Hutchinson mentions nothing of a circumstance which perhaps she did not know, or if she did, passed it over as beneath notice. The following letter shows the nature of it:—
Thurloe's *State Papers*, vol. iv. p. 299, Major-general Whalley writes to the protector: "For the town of Nottingham, I have a great influence upon it; they will not choose any without my advice. The honest part of the county have of late, which I much wonder at, nominated Colonel Hutchinson to me, as not knowing upon whom better to pitch, to make up the fourth man, he having satisfied some of them concerning his judgment of the present government; but I hope what I have hinted to them will cause them to think upon some other."
[2] A *Life of Lambert* has been very obligingly put into the hands of the editor, together with some other scarce tracts relating to those times by Mr. White, jun., of Lincoln's Inn, who had collected them in the north of England, where Lambert resided. He seems to have

The cavaliers, seeing their victors thus beyond their hopes falling into their hands, had not patience to stay till things ripened of themselves, but were every day forming designs, and plotting for the murder of Cromwell, and other insurrections, which being contrived in drink, and managed by false and cowardly fellows, were still revealed to Cromwell, who had most excellent intelligence of all things that passed, even in the king's closet; and by these unsuccessful plots they were only the obstructors of what they sought to advance, while, to speak truth, the Cromwell's personal courage and magnanimity upheld him against all enemies and malcontents. His own army disliked him, and once when sevenscore officers had combined to cross him in something he was pursuing, and engaged one to another, Lambert being the chief, with solemn promises and invocations to God, the protector hearing of it, overawed them all, and told them, " it was not they who upheld him, but he them," and rated them, and made them understand what pitiful fellows they were; whereupon, they all, like rated dogs, clapped their tails between their legs, and begged his pardon, and left Lambert to fall alone, none daring to own him publicly, though many in their hearts wished him the sovereignty. Some of the Lambertonians had at that time a plot to come with a petition to Cromwell, and, while he was reading it, certain of them had undertaken to cast him out of a window at Whitehall that looked upon the Thames, where others would be ready to catch him up in a blanket if he escaped breaking his neck, and carrying him away in a boat prepared for the purpose, to kill or keep him alive, as they saw occasion, and then to set up Lambert. This was so carried on that it was near its execution before the protector knew anything of it. Colonel Hutchinson being at that time at London, by chance came to know all the plot. Certain of the conspirators coming into a place where he was, and not being so cautious of their whispers to each other before him, but that he apprehended something; by making use of which to others of the confederates, he at last found out the whole matter, without having it committed to him as a matter of trust, but which, carelessly thrown down in pieces before him,

enjoyed a better reputation among his countrymen: bis horticulture is therein much spoken of, and he is said to have *painted* flowers, not to have *embroidered* them.

he gathered together, and became perfectly acquainted with the whole design; and weighing it, and judging that Lambert would be the worst tyrant of the two, he determined to prevent it, without being the author of any man's punishment. Hereupon, having occasion to see Fleetwood (for he had never seen the protector since his usurpation, but publicly declared his testimony against it to all the tyrants' minions), he bade Fleetwood wish him to have a care of petitioners, by whom he apprehended danger to his life. Fleetwood desired more particular information, but the colonel was resolved he would give him no more than to prevent that enterprise which he disliked. For indeed those who were deeply engaged rather waited to see the cavaliers in arms against him, which they thought would be the best time to arm for their own defence, and either to make a new conquest, or fall with swords in their hands. Therefore, they all connived at the cavaliers' attempts, and although they joined not with them, would not have been sorry to have seen them up upon equal terms with the protector, that then a third party, which was to be ready both with arms and men, when there was an opportunity, might have fallen in and capitulated, with swords in their hands, for the settlement of the rights and liberties of the good people: but God had otherwise determined things; and now men began so to flatter with this tyrant, so to apostatise from all faith, honesty, religion, and English liberty, and there was such a devilish practice of trepanning grown in fashion, that it was not safe to speak to any man in those treacherous days.

After Colonel Hutchinson had given Fleetwood that caution, he was going into the country, when the protector sent to search him out with all the earnestness and haste that could possibly be, and the colonel went to him; who met him in one of the galleries, and received him with open arms and the kindest embraces that could be given, and complained that the colonel should be so unkind as never to give him a visit, professing how welcome he should have been, the most welcome person in the land, and with these smooth insinuations led him along to a private place, giving him thanks for the advertisement he had received from Fleetwood, and using all his art to get out of the colonel the knowledge of the persons engaged in the conspiracy against him. But none of his cunning, nor promises, nor flatteries, could prevail with the colonel to inform him more than he thought necessary to prevent the execution of the design, which when the protector perceived, he gave him most infinite thanks for what he had told him, and acknowledged it opened to him some mysteries that had perplexed him, and agreed so with other intelligence he had, that he must owe his preservation to him: " But," says he, " dear colonel, why will not you come in and act among us? " The colonel told him plainly, because he liked not any of his ways since he broke up the parliament, being those which would lead to certain and unavoidable destruction, not only of themselves, but of the whole parliament party and cause; and thereupon took occasion, with his usual freedom, to tell him into what a sad hazard all things were placed, and how apparent a way was made for the restitution of all former tyranny and bondage. Cromwell seemed to receive this honest plainness with the greatest affection that could be, and acknowledged his precipitateness in some things, and with tears complained how Lambert had put him upon all those violent actions, for which he now accused him and sought his ruin. He expressed an earnest desire to restore the people's liberties, and to take and pursue more safe and sober councils, and wound up all with a very fair courtship of the colonel to engage with him, offering him anything he would account worthy of him. The colonel told him, he could not be forward to make his own advantage, by serving to the enslaving of his country. The other told him, he intended nothing more than the restoring and confirming the liberties of the good people, in order to which he would employ such men of honour and interest as the people would rejoice in, and he should not refuse to be one of them. And after he had endeavoured, with all his arts, to excuse his public actions, and to draw in the colonel, who again had taken the opportunity to tell him freely his own and all good men's discontents and dissatisfactions, he dismissed the colonel with such expressions as were publicly taken notice of by all his little courtiers then about him, when he went to the end of the gallery with the colonel, and there, embracing him, said aloud to him, " Well, colonel, satisfied or dissatisfied, you shall be one of us, for we can no longer exempt a person so able and faithful from the public service, and you shall be satisfied in all honest things." The colonel left him with that respect that became the place he was in; when immediately the same courtiers, who had some of them passed by him without knowing him when he came in, although they had once been of his familiar acquaintance, and the rest, who had looked upon him with such disdainful neglect as little people use to those who are not of their faction, now flocked about him, striving who should express most respect, and, by an extraordinary officiousness, redeem their late slightings. Some of them desired he would command their service in any business he had with their lord, and a thousand such frivolous compliments, which the colonel smiled at, and quitting himself of them as soon as he could, made haste to return to the country. There he had not been long before he was informed, that notwithstanding all these fair shows, the protector, finding him too constant to be wrought upon to serve his tyranny, had resolved to secure his person, lest he should head the people, who now grew very weary of his bondage. But though it was certainly confirmed to the colonel how much he was afraid of his honesty and freedom, and that he was resolved not to let him be any longer at liberty, yet before his guards apprehended the colonel, death imprisoned himself, and confined all his vast ambition and all his cruel designs into the narrow compass of a grave. His army and court substituted his eldest son, Richard, in his room, who was a meek, temperate, and quiet man, but had not a spirit fit to succeed his father, or to manage such a perplexed government.

The people, being vexed with the pocket-parliaments and the major-generals of the counties, who behaved like bashaws, were now all muttering to have a free parliament, after the old manner of elections, without pledging those that were chosen to any terms. Those at Richard's court, that knew his father's counsels to prevent Colonel Hutchinson from being chosen in his own country, advised Richard to prick him for sheriff of the county of Nottingham, which as soon as the colonel understood, he wrote him a letter, declaring his resentment in such a civil manner as became the person. Richard returned a very obliging answer, denying any intention in himself to show the least disfavour to him for former dissents, but rather a desire to engage his kindness. And soon after, when the colonel went himself to London and went to the young protector, he told him, that since God had called him to the government, it was his desire to make men of uprightness and interest his associates, to rule by their counsels and assistance, and not to enslave the nation to an army; and that if by them he had been put upon anything prejudicial or disobliging to the colonel in pricking him for sheriff, he should endeavour to take it off, or to serve him any other way, as soon as he had disentangled himself from the officers of the army, who at present constrained him in many things; and therefore if the colonel would please, without unkindness, to exercise this office, he should receive it as an obligation, and seek one more acceptable to him afterwards. The colonel, seeing him herein good-natured enough, was persuaded by a very wise friend of his to take it upon him, and returned well enough satisfied with the courteous usage of the protector. This gentleman who had thus counselled the colonel, was as considerable and as wise a person as any in England, who did not openly appear among Richard's adherents or counsellors, but privately advised him, and had a very honourable design of bringing the nation into freedom under this young man; who was so flexible to good counsels, that there was nothing desirable in a prince which might not have been hoped for in him, but a great spirit and a just title: the first of which sometimes doth more hurt than good in a sovereign; the latter would have been supplied by the people's deserved approbation. This person was very free in imparting to the colonel all the designs of settling the state under this single person, and the hopes of felicity in such an establishment. The colonel, debating this with him, told him, that if ever it were once fixed in a single person, and the army taken off, which could not consist with the liberty of the people, it could not be prevented from returning to the late ejected family; and that on whatever terms they returned, it was folly to expect the people's cause, which, with such blood and expense, had been asserted, would not be utterly overthrown. To this the gentleman gave many strong reasons, why that family could not be restored, without the ruin of the people's liberty and of all their champions; and thought that these carried so much force with them, that it would never be attempted, even by any royalist that retained any love to his country; and that the establishing this single person (Richard) would satisfy that faction, and compose all the differences, bringing in all those of all parties that were men of interest and love to their country. Although the business was very speciously laid, and the man such a one whose authority was sufficient to sway in any state, the colonel was not much opiniated of the things he propounded, but willing to wait the event; being in himself more persuaded that the people's freedom would be best maintained in a free republic, delivered from the shackles of their encroaching slaves in the army.[1] This was now not merely muttered, but openly asserted by all but the army: although of those who contended for it, there were two sorts; some that really thought it the most conducible to the people's good and freedom; others, who by this pretence, hoped to pull down the army and the protectorian faction, and then restore the old family. It is believed that Richard himself was compounded with, to have resigned the place that was too great for him; certain it is that his poor spirit was likely enough to do any such thing. The army, perceiving they had set up a wretch who durst not reign, and that there was a convention met, by their own assent, who were ready, with a seeming face of authority of parliament, to restore the Stewarts, they were greatly distressed; finding also that the whole nation was bent against them, and would not bear their yoke, and having therefore no refuge to save themselves from being torn in pieces by the people, or to deliver themselves from their own puppets who had sold and betrayed them, they found out some of the members of that glorious parliament which they had violently driven from their seats with a thousand slanderous criminations and untruths. To these they counterfeited repentance, and that God had opened their eyes to see into what a manifest hazard of ruin they had put the interest and people of God in these nations, so that it was almost irrecoverable; but if any hope were left, it was that God would sign it, with his wonted favour, into those hands out of which they had injuriously

[1] The mention of this political discussion without the name of the principal speaker in it, naturally awakens curiosity and excites to conjecture. The judicious writer of the critique on this work in the *Annual Review* combines this with a passage at p. 305, and supposes the secret there referred to, and which endeavours were in vain used to draw from Mrs. Hutchinson, to be the same thing as is here hinted at: it is highly probable that it is so; and as no evil could now result from a discovery, the editor has taken pains to effect one, he believes with success—though when the grounds of his conjecture are laid before the reader, he will judge for himself.

taken it. Hereupon they opened the house doors for them; and the Speaker, with some few members, as many as made a house, were too hasty to return into their seats, upon capitulation with those traitors who had brought the commonwealth into such a sad confusion. But after they were met, they immediately sent summons to all the members throughout England, among whom the colonel was called up,[1] and much perplexed, for now he thought his conscience, life, and fortunes were again engaged with men of mixed and different interests and principles; yet in regard of the trust formerly reposed in him, he returned into his place, infinitely dissatisfied that any condescension had been made to the army's proposals, whose necessity rather than honesty had moved them to counterfeit repentance and ingenuity. This they did by a public declaration, stating how they had been seduced and done wickedly in interrupting the parliament, and that God had never since that time owned them and their counsels as before, and that they desired to humble themselves before God and man for the same, and to return to their duty in defending the parliament in the discharge of their remaining trust. According to this declaration, the army kept a day of solemn humiliation before the Lord; yet all this, as the event afterwards manifested, in hypocrisy.[2]

Now the parliament were sat, and were no sooner assembled but they were invaded by several enemies. The presbyterians had long since espoused the royal interest, and forsaken God and the people's cause, when they could not obtain the reins of government in their own hands, and exercise dominion over all their brethren.[3] It was treason,

[1] By this passage, that error which has become general, and which is to be found in Rapin, vol. ii. p. 605, is rendered palpable. He says they met in parliament to the number of forty-two; and again, p. 607, calls it a parliament of forty persons, but takes no notice of their sending summonses to all the members throughout England; but in the addition or suppression of this circumstance lies the total difference between truth and falsehood. Ludlow, who was one of them, says, vol. ii. p. 645, "That they amounted to a hundred and sixty, who had sat in the house since the seclusion of members in 1648."

[2] There are copies of this declaration extant, signed by Lambert, Fleetwood, etc., one particularly in the hands of John Townley, Esq., as likewise pamphlets written at that time, calling on the army to make the only amends they could to the nation, by restoring the parliament.

[3] Rapin, in a parallel passage, vol. ii. p. 611, says, that "the presbyterians, seeing no hopes of recovering the ground they had lost, agreed with the king's party to deliver the nation from the servitude to which

by the law of those men in power, to talk of restoring the king; therefore the presbyterians must face the design, and accordingly all the members ejected in 1648, now came to claim their seats in the house, whom Colonel Pride, that then guarded the parliament, turned back, and thereupon there was some heat in the lobby between them and the other members. Particularly Sir George Booth uttered some threats, and immediately they went into their several counties, and had laid a design all over England, wherein all the royalists were engaged, and many of the old parliament officers; and this was so dexterously, secretly, and unanimously carried on, that before the parliament had the least intimation of it, the flame was everywhere kindled, and small parties attempting insurrections in all places; but their main strength was with Sir George Booth in Cheshire, who there appeared the chief head of the rebellion. The city, at that time, was very wavering and false to the parliament, yet the usual presence of God, that was with them in former times, never appeared so eminent as now, miraculously bringing to light all the plots against them, and scattering their enemies before the wind, making them fly when there was none to pursue them; although even in the parliament-house there wanted not many close traitors and abettors of this conspiracy. It was presently voted to send an army down into Cheshire; but then it fell into debate who should lead. Fleetwood, upon the deposing his brother Richard (wherein he was most unworthily assistant), was made general, but not thought a person of courage enough for this enterprise; whereupon many of Lambert's friends propounded him to the house, and undertook for his integrity and hearty repentance for having been formerly assistant to the protector. Colonel Hutchinson was utterly against receiving him again into employment; but it was the general vote of the house, and accordingly he was brought in to receive his commission from the Speaker; who, intending to

it was reduced by an independent parliament, and an army whose officers were mostly fanatics. The particulars and terms of this union are not known, because the historians who speak of it, being all royalists, have not thought fit to do so much honour to the presbyterians. But it cannot be concealed, that from this time they not only ceased to be the king's enemies, but very much promoted his restoration." Behold the honour he asks for them granted by their greatest enemy, an independent! As was their motive such was their reward; beginning in rage and folly, it ended in disgrace and ruin.

accept the humble submission he then falsely made, with high professions of fidelity, and to return him an encouragement in declaring the confidence the house had in him,—through mistake made such a speech to him, as afterwards proved a true prophecy of his perfidiousness. Many of the house took notice of it then only to laugh, but afterwards thought that some hidden impulse, the man was not then sensible of, led his tongue into those mistakes. However, Lambert went forth, and through the cowardice of the enemy obtained a very cheap victory, and returned. In Nottinghamshire Colonel White rose, only to show his apostacy, and run away. The Lord Byron also lost himself and his companions in the forest, being chased by a piece of the county troop. And Mr. Robert Pierrepont, the son of the late colonel, went out to make up the rout, and ran away, and cast away some good arms into the bushes to make his flight more easy.

During the late protectors' times Colonel Hutchinson, who thought them greater usurpers on the people's liberties than the former kings, believed himself wholly disengaged from all ties, but those which God and nature, or rather God by nature obliges every man of honour and honesty in to his country, which is to defend or relieve it from invading tyrants, as far as he may by a lawful call and means, and to suffer patiently that yoke which God submits him to, till the Lord shall take it off; and upon these principles, he seeing that authority, to which he was in duty bound, so seemingly taken quite away, thought he was free to fall in or oppose all things, as prudence should guide him, upon general rules of conscience. These would not permit him in any way to assist any tyrant or invader of the people's rights, nor to rise up against them without a manifest call from God; therefore he stayed at home, and busied himself in his own domestic employments, having a very liberal heart, and a house open to all worthy persons of all parties. Among these the Lord Byron, who, thinking that no gentleman ought to be unprovided with arms, in such an uncertain time, had provided himself with a trunk of pistols, which were brought down from London; but some suspicion of it having reached the protector's officers, he durst not fetch the trunk from the carrier's himself, but entreated the colonel to send for them to his house, and secure them there. This the colonel did; but afterwards, when my Lord Byron had entered into a conspiracy with the enemies of the parliament, he knew that Colonel Hutchinson was not to be attempted against them, and was in great care how to get his arms out of the colonel's house. The colonel, being of a very compassionate and charitable nature, had entertained into his service some poor people who on the enemy's side had been ruined, and were reduced from good estates to seek that refuge; and who counterfeited, so long as their party was down, such sobriety, love, and gratitude, and sense of their sins and miscarriages whilst on the other side, that he hoped they had been converts, but could not believe they would have proved such detestable, unthankful traitors, as afterwards they did. Among these, Lord Byron corrupted a gentleman who then waited on the colonel, as the man afterwards alleged; my lord said he offered himself. However it was, the plot was laid that fifty men, near the colonel's house, should be raised for him, and he with them should first come to the colonel's house, and take away my lord's arms, with all the rest of the colonel's that they could find. To raise him these men, certain neighbours, who used to come to the house, were very busy, and especially two parsons, he of Plumptre and he of Bingham; this one had an active, proud, pragmatical curate, who used to come to this traitor in the colonel's house and help to manage the treason, and the chaplain, the waiting woman, and two servants more, were drawn into the confederacy. The colonel was then at the parliament-house, and only his wife and children at home, when, the night before the insurrection, Ivie (that was the gentleman's name) came to a singing-boy who kept the colonel's clothes, and commanded him to deliver him the colonel's own arms and buff coat.

The boy was fearful, and did not readily obey him, whereupon he threatened immediately to pistol him, if he made the least resistance or discovery of the business; so the boy fetched him the arms, and he put them on, and took one of the best horses and went out at midnight, telling the boy he was a fool to fear, for the next night, before that time, there would come fifty men to fetch away all the arms in the house.

As soon as the boy saw him quite gone, his mistress being then in bed, he went to the chaplain and acquainted him; but the chaplain cursed him for breaking his sleep: then he went to the waiting gentlewoman, but she said she thought it

would be unfit to disturb her mistress; so the boy rested till
next day, when Ivie, having failed of his men, was come
back again. Then the boy, finding an opportunity after
dinner, told his mistress, that though he had been bred a
cavalier he abhorred to betray or be unfaithful to those he
served; and that he had reason to suspect there was some
vile conspiracy in hand, wherein Ivie was engaged against
them, and told her his grounds. When Mrs. Hutchinson had
heard that, she bade him keep it private, and called immediately a servant that had been a cornet of the parliament's
party, and bade him go to the county troop's captain, and
desire him to send her a guard for her husband's house, for
she had intelligence that the cavaliers intended some attempt
against it. Mrs. Hutchinson, ashamed to complain of her
own family, thought of this way of security, till she could
discharge herself of the traitor, not knowing at that time how
many more such were about her. Then calling her gentlewoman, whom she thought she might trust, upon her solemn
protestations of fidelity, she took her to assist her in hiding
her plate and jewels, and what she had of value, and scrupled
not to let her see the *secret places in her house*, while the
false and base dissembler went smiling up and down at her
mistress's simplicity. Meantime, the man that was sent for
soldiers came back, bringing news that the cavaliers had
risen and were beaten, and that the county troop was in
pursuit of them. Then also the coachman, who finding himself not well, had borrowed a horse to go to Nottingham to be
let blood, came home, bringing with him a cravat and other
spoils of the enemy, which he had gotten. For when he
came to the town, hearing the cavaliers were up, he got a
case of pistols, and thought more of shedding than losing
blood, and meeting the cavaliers in the rout, it is said, he
killed one of them; although this rogue had engaged to
Ivie to have gone on the other side with him. Mrs. Hutchinson not being willing, for all this, to take such notice of Ivie's
treason as to cast him into prison, took him immediately to
London with her, and said nothing till he came there. Then
she told him how base and treacherous he had been; but to
save her own shame for having entertained so false a person,
and for her mother's sake whom he had formerly served,
she was willing to dismiss him privately, without acquainting
the colonel, who, if he knew, must punish him. So she gave

him something and turned him away, and told her husband she came only to acquaint him with the insurrection, and her own fears of staying in the country without him. He, being very indulgent, went immediately back with her, having informed the parliament, and received their order for going down to look after the securing of the country. His wife, as soon as she came down, having learned that the chaplain had been Ivie's confederate, told him privately of it, and desired him to find a pretence to take his leave of the colonel, that she might not be necessitated to complain, and procure him the punishment his treason deserved. He went away thus, but so far from being wrought upon, that he hated her to the death for her kindness.

The colonel having set things in order in the country, intended to have carried his family that winter with him to London; when just in that week he was going, news was brought that Lambert had once more turned out the parliament, and the colonel rejoiced in his good fortune that he was not present.

Lambert was exceedingly puffed up with his cheap victory, and cajoled his soldiers; and, before he returned to London, set on foot among them their old insolent way of prescribing to the parliament by way of petition.

The parliament, after the submission of the army, had voted that there should no more be a general over them, but to keep that power in their own hands, all the officers should take their commissions immediately from the Speaker.[1] The conspiracy of the army, to get a leader in their rebellion, was laid, that they should petition for generals and such like things as might facilitate their intents. Among others who were taken in arms against the parliament, Lord Castleton was one of the chief heads of the insurrection. Him Lambert brought along with him in his coach, not now as a prisoner, but unguarded, as one that was to be honoured. The parliament hearing of this, sent and fetched him out of his

[1] It was a great oversight that they had not taken this course from the beginning: for although it is very difficult for a republic, which has need of considerable armies, to maintain its independence, which is for ever liable to be invaded by those who have the sword in their hands, yet the best chance it has lies in keeping the military under the direction of the civil power. This method succeeded a good while with the French republic, and might have done still longer if some of the members of the executive power had not leagued with some of the military commanders.

company and committed him to prison, and then the army's saucy petition was delivered, and, upon the insolent carriage of nine colonels, they were by vote disbanded. Lambert being one of them, came in a hostile manner and plucked the members out of the house; Fleetwood, whom they trusted to guard them, having confederated with Lambert and betrayed them. After that, setting up their army court at Wallingford-house, they began their arbitrary reign, to the joy of all the vanquished enemies of the parliament, and to the amazement and terror of all men that had any honest interest: and now they were all devising governments; and some honourable members, I know not through what fatality of the times, fell in with them.[1] When Colonel Hutchinson came into the country some time before Lambert's revolt, Mr. Robert Pierrepont, the son of the late Colonel Francis Pierrepont, sent friends to entreat the colonel to receive him into his protection. Upon the entreaty of his uncle he took him into his own house, and entertained him civilly there, whilst he wrote to the Speaker, urging his youth, his surrender of himself, and all he could in favour of him, desiring to know how they would please to dispose of him. Before the letters were answered Lambert had broken the parliament, and the colonel told him he was free again to do what he pleased; but the young gentleman begged of the colonel that he might continue under his sanctuary till these things came to some issue. This the colonel very freely admitted, and entertained him till the second return of the parliament, not without much trouble to his house, himself, and his servants, so contrary to the sobriety and holiness the colonel delighted in, yet for his father's and his uncle's sakes he endured it about six months.

[1] This was that committee of safety, or council of the *Stratocracy*, among the principal members of which were Sir Henry Vane, Ludlow, and Whitelocke, as mentioned by Whitelocke, p. 685. He there says that he took his share in it reluctantly, and that all three were censured for it by the parliament at their return. Ludlow was accused of treason; Vane made an ingenious excuse, but was banished to one of his country seats. Colonel Hutchinson evidently divided from Sir H. Vane on this occasion, and, as Ludlow says, urged on the censure against him, which he considers as inconsistent with Colonel Hutchinson's judgment passed on the king, and as a proof of his treachery and underhand agreement with Monk. But no conclusion can be more unwarranted than this: it was Colonel Hutchinson's anxiety to keep the king out, or at least to prevent his coming in with a high hand and without limitation, that caused him so strenuously to oppose these rash steps which made all wish for the king's return, to deliver them from greater evils.

Some of Lambert's officers, while he marched near Notting-hamshire, having formerly served under the colonel's command, came to his house at Owthorpe and told him of the petition that was set on foot in Lambert's brigade, and consulted whether they should sign it or not. The colonel advised them by no means to do it, yet notwithstanding, they did, which made the colonel exceeding angry with them, thinking they rather came to see how he stood affected, than really to ask his counsel. When Lambert had broken up the house, the colonel made a short journey to London to inform himself how things were, and found some of the members exceedingly sensible of the sad estate the kingdom was reduced unto by the rash ambition of these men, and resolving that there was no way but for every man that abhorred it to improve their interest in their countries, and to suppress these usurpers and rebels. Hereupon the colonel took measures to have some arms bought and sent him, and had prepared a thousand honest men, whenever he should call for their assistance; intending to improve his posse comitatus when occasion should be offered. To provoke him more particularly to this, several accidents fell out. Among the rest, six of Lambert's troopers came to gather money, laid upon the country by an assessment of parliament, whom the colonel telling that in regard it was levied by that authority, he had paid it, but otherwise would not; two of them only who were in the room with the colonel, the rest being on horseback in the court, gave him such insolent terms, with such insufferable reproaches of the parliament, that the colonel drew a sword which was in the room to have chastised them. While a minister that was by held the colonel's arm, his wife, not willing to have them killed in her presence, opened the door and let them out, who presently ran and fetched in their companions in the yard with cocked pistols. Upon the bustle, while the colonel having disengaged himself from those that held him, had run after them with the sword drawn, his brother came out of another room, upon whom, the soldiers pressing against a door that went into the great hall, the door flew open, and about fifty or sixty men appeared in the hall,[1] who were there upon another business.

---

[1] The description of the house, contained in a former note, will give a just idea of the position of all the parties, and of the striking scene here described.

For Owthorpe, Kinolton, and Hicklin, had a contest about a cripple that was sent from one to the other, but at last, out of some respect they had for the colonel, the chief men of the several towns were come to him, to make some accommodation, till the law should be again in force. When the colonel heard the soldiers were come, he left them shut up in his great hall, who by accident thus appearing, put the soldiers into a dreadful fright. When the colonel saw how pale they looked, he encouraged them to take heart, and calmly admonished them for their insolence, and they being changed and very humble through their fear, he called for wine for them, and sent them away. To the most insolent of them he said, " These carriages would bring back the Stewarts." The man, laying his hand upon his sword, said, " Never while he wore that." Among other things they said to the colonel, when he demanded by what authority they came, they showed their swords, and said, " That was their authority." After they were dismissed, the colonel, not willing to appear because he was sheriff of the county, and had many of their papers sent him to publish, concealed himself in his house, and caused his wife to write a letter to Fleetwood, to complain of the affronts had been offered him, and to tell him that he was thereupon retired, till he could dwell safely at home.[1] To this Fleetwood returned a civil answer, and withal sent a protection, to forbid all soldiers from coming to his house, and a command to Swallow, who was the colonel of these men, to examine and punish them. Mrs. Hutchinson had sent before to Swallow, who was then quartered at Leicester, the next day after it was done, to inform him, who sent a letter utterly disowning their actions, and promising to punish them. This, Mrs. Hutchinson sent to show the soldiers who then lay abusing the country at Colson; but when they saw their officer's letter they laughed at him, and tore it in pieces. Some days after he, in a civil

[1] Probably this circumstance of Colonel Hutchinson concealing himself in his own home came at that time to be known at Nottingham, and gave rise to a tradition which is to be found in Throsby's edition of Thoroton, that he concealed himself in this manner after the restoration, but was taken in his return from church; both of which were untrue, as probably were some other tales, resembling the legends of romance, which the Editor heard of him at Owthorpe. But that there was an apartment so adapted for concealment, security, and convenience, as that he might have made a long residence in it without being discovered, the Editor had ocular demonstration.

manner, sent a captain with them and other soldiers to Owthorpe, to inquire into their misdemeanours before their faces; which being confirmed to him, and he beginning to rebuke them, they set him at light, even before Mrs. Hutchinson's face, and made the poor man retire sneaped to his colonel; while these six rogues, in one week's space, besides the assessments assigned them to gather up within the compass of five miles, took away violently from the country, for their own expense, above five-and-twenty pounds. Notwithstanding all this pretended civility, Fleetwood and his counsellors were afraid of the colonel, and the protection was but sent to draw him thither, that they might by that means get him into their custody. But he, having intimation of it, withdrew, while men and arms were preparing, that he might appear publicly in the defence of the country, when he was strong enough to drive out the soldiers that were left in those parts. Three hundred of them were one night drawn out of Nottingham to come to Owthorpe for him, but some of the party gave him notice, and he being then at home, immediately went out of the house. Neither wanted they their spies, who gave them notice that he was gone again, so that they turned off upon the wolds and went to Hickling; and the next day Major Grove, their commander, sent to Mrs. Hutchinson to desire permission for himself only to come down, which she gave, and so with only five or six of his party he came. With him Mrs. Hutchinson so easily dealt, that, after she had represented the state of things to him, he began to apologise that he had only taken this command upon himself to preserve the country, and should be ready to submit to any lawful authority; and he and his men were not come for any other intent but to prevent disturbance of the peace and gatherings together of men, who, they were informed, intended to rise in these parts. Mrs. Hutchinson smiling, told him it was necessary for him to keep a good guard, for all the whole country would shortly be weary of their yoke, and, no question, would find some authority to shelter them. At last he went so far as to desire her to let the colonel know he intended him no mischief, but he and all his men should be at her command to defend her from the insolencies of any others. She heard him without faith, for she knew the good will they pretended to her husband proceeded only from their fear. It is true that at that time the colonel had met with Colonel Hacker, and several other gentlemen of Northampton and Warwickshire, and at the same time Major Beque was to have reduced Coventry, and another colonel Warwick Castle. Two regiments of horse should have marched to a place within seven miles of Colonel Hutchinson's house, where his men should have rendezvoused, and the town of Nottingham at the same time to have seized all the soldiers there, and they of Leicester the like. These people had, through the spies that were about the colonel, gotten some little inkling of his rendezvous, but not right, neither could they have prevented it, had they desired.[1] But just before it should have been put into execution the parliament were restored to their seats, Lambert was deserted by his men and fled, and Monk was marching on southwards, pretending to restore and confirm the parliament; insomuch that Colonel Hutchinson, instead of raising his country, was called up to his seat in parliament. Here there were so many favourers of Lambert, Fleetwood, and their partakers, that the colonel, who used to be very silent, could not now forbear high opposition to them; in whose favour things were carried with such a stream, that the colonel then began to lose all hopes of settling this poor land on any righteous foundation.

It was the 26th of December, 1659, that the parliament met again. The manner of it, and the contest and treaty in the north between Monk and Lambert, are too well known to be repeated; the dissimulations and false protestations that Monk made are too public; yet the colonel and others suspected him, but knew not how to hinder him; for this insolent usurpation of Lambert's had so turned the hearts of all men, that the whole nation began to set their eyes upon the king beyond the sea, and think a bad settlement under him better than none at all, or than being under the arbitrary power of such proud rebels as Lambert. The whole house was divided

---

[1] Perhaps this crisis was the most favourable to the cause of liberty of any that had occurred; for the genuine assertors of it would, at this moment, have found all the different factions weakened, and the body of the nation so tired of tumult and anarchy, that, had they now stood forth in any force, the voice of reason would in all probability have prevailed. But the fluctuations of power and party were at this time so frequent and sudden as hardly to leave sufficient interval for any enterprise that required combination. Moreover it is to be considered that the march of patriotism is impeded by reserves and restraints which ambition overleaps in its career; and after all it is perhaps justly observed, that Colonel Hutchinson was *too unambitious* for his own glory or the public good.

into miserable factions, among whom some would then have violently set up an oath of renunciation of the king and his family. The colonel, thinking it a ridiculous thing to *swear out* a man, when they had no power to defend themselves against him, vehemently opposed that oath, and carried it against Sir Ar. Haslerig and others, who as violently pressed it; urging very truly that those oaths that had been formerly imposed had but multiplied the sins of the nation by perjuries; instancing how Sir Arthur and others, in Oliver's time, coming into the house, swore on their entrance they would attempt nothing in the change of that government, which, as soon as ever they were entered, they laboured to throw down. Many other arguments he used, whereupon many honest men, who thought till then he had followed a faction in all things, and not his own judgment, began to meet often with him, and to consult what to do in these difficulties, out of which their prudence and honesty would have found a way to extricate themselves; but that the end of our prosperity was come, hastened on partly by the mad rash violence of some that, without strength, opposed the tide of the discontented tumultuous people, partly by the detestable treachery of those who had sold themselves to do mischief, but chiefly by the general stream of the people, who were as eager for their own destruction as the Israelites of old for their quails.[1]

One observation of the colonel's I cannot omit, that the secluded members whom Monk brought in were, many of them, so brought over to a commonwealth that, if Sir Ar. Haslerig and his party had not forsaken their places because they would not sit with them, they would have made the strongest party in the house, but which by reason of their going off were afterwards outvoted in all things.[2]

[1] A frank acknowledgment that the independent parliament, however good the intentions of many of them might be, had become unpopular; but with the general mass of mankind the escape from any present evil is paramount to all future considerations. Perhaps this reflux of the *public mind* was the most effectual cause of the counter revolution, without which Monk might have *plotted* in vain. And thus perhaps in this, as in so many other instances, Mrs. Hutchinson's natural and rational way of tracing and unfolding the causes of great events will be found to bring us much nearer to the truth than all the subtleties employed by others!

[2] We do not know this circumstance to have been noticed by any other historian; but it appears much more probable than that the secluded members should have been *unanimous*, and that in measures of such transcendant import as were now to be decided upon. For this

Sir Anthony Ashley Cooper at that time insinuated himself into a particular friendship with the colonel, and made him all the honourable pretences that can be imagined; called him his *dear friend*, and caressed him with such embraces as none but a traitor as vile as himself could have suspected; yet was he the most intimate of Monk's confidants. Whereupon some few days before the rising of that house, when it began to be too apparent which way Monk inclined, the colonel, upon the confidence of his friendship, entreated him to tell him what were Monk's intentions, that he and others might consider their safety, who were likely to be given up as a public sacrifice. Cooper denied to the death any intention besides a commonwealth; "but," said he, with the greatest semblance of reality that could be put on, "if the violence of the people should bring the king upon us, let me

secession Whitelocke blames and Ludlow commends Sir Arthur Haslerig and his friends; their total ruin, which ensued, decides the question.

In support of the opinions and statements contained in this and the two next following pages, are adduced the following out of many extracts that might be made from the third volume of Clarendon's *State Papers*. Page 687, Broderick to Hyde, Dec. 30, 1659, ridicules the idea of its being possible to establish the Rump; says Vane, Salway, and Whitelocke sit without blush or excuse; Haslerig must ruin them or be ruined. A. A. Cooper desires to establish these people. Haslerig would admit the secluded members provided they would renounce a single person and the line of the Stuarts.

Page 696, Do. to Do. March 9, 1659-60. "Of Monk I have much more reason to hope better than you apprehend, and would lose the hand with which I pay you this duty, that Mr. Edmondson (the king) had inclosed an answer to Howard by this conveyance, time being very precious, and what a day may produce known only to the prescience of Almighty God. All the progress that can be made without is carefully pursued, nor shall anything be wanting any care can supply. The last night's conference between the officers of the army and the members is so variously reported, even by themselves (with several of whom I have this morning discoursed), that it is hard to give a narrative of particulars; the main they agree in, viz. that the demands were, indemnity for all past actions, confirmation of all purchases, sale of what remains to the state in the king's houses, forests, etc., towards the payment of arrears; with some sharp reflections on the militia of several counties put into disaffected hands.

"Sir William Lewis" (one of the secluded members, as appears by Dugdale's list, and who evidently had joined Colonel Hutchinson's party since his return), "Arthur Annesley, and Colonel Hutchinson, endeavoured their satisfaction by repeating the acts already passed in their favour, justifying many persons so chosen, promises of arrears, with whatever else they thought reasonable to urge against the intrusion of military stipendiaries upon the privilege of parliament. Haslerig and some of his faction abetted the soldiery, but all ended fairly, though far from satisfaction. The general had indeed before declared that he expected their obedience to the supreme authority, be dammed, body and soul, if ever I see a hair of any man's head touched, or a penny of any man's estate, upon this quarrel." This he backed with so many and such deep protestations of that kind, as made the colonel, after his treachery was apparent, detest him of all mankind, and think himself obliged, if ever he had opportunity, to procure exemplary justice on him, who was so vile a wretch as to sit himself and sentence some of those that died. And although this man joined with those who laboured for the colonel's particular deliverance, yet the colonel, to his dying day, abhorred the mention of his name, and held him to be a more execrable traitor than Monk himself. At this time the colonel, as before, was by many of his friends tempted every way to fall in with the king's interest, and often offered both pardon and preferment, if he could be wrought off from his party, whose danger was now laid before him: but they could in no way move him.[1] A gentleman that had been employed to tamper with him told me, that he found him so unmovable, that one time he and a certain lord being in the colonel's company, and having begun their vain insinuations, he, to decline them, seeing Cooper, went away with him; upon which this lord, that had some tenderness for the colonel, said to this gentleman, "The colonel is a ruined man; he believes that traitor,

not their usurpation of it; adding that it would be easier to find officers in the room of those that remained obstinate, than for them to find regiments if the house should deny pay. Upon the whole, I am commanded to tell you that we suffered nothing in the conference. Haslerig concluded there was no other basis to build on than the parliament. Colonels Rich, Scott, and the rest who hitherto refrained, now enter the house with faint hopes of opposing the general current. We make no doubt of success everywhere. All the people cry out, the king! the king! some indeed add, he must come in on terms; and why doth he not prevent the imposition by a fair offer published authentically, to release fears, settle their minds, and render his entrance facile."

The same to the king, March 10, 1659-60, says, "Monk declared he would acquiesce in the judgment of the parliament both as to king and lords. Another day he would spend the last drop of his blood rather than the Stuarts should ever come into England; but he is in good temper again the same night."

[1] It was hard for him, after this, to be accused by Ludlow of treachery and connivance with the king's friends; but Ludlow was at this time engaged in a different party, perhaps envious of him for escaping with impunity, when himself despaired of doing so, and went into voluntary exile: and besides Sir A. Ashley Cooper may have stipulated for Colonel Hutchinson's indemnity *gratuitously;* while most people suppose that some conditions were imposed. His moderation in a time of phrenzy was surely a sufficient argument, and was probably that which Cooper used in support of the man whom he was forced to esteem, though he did not choose to imitate him.

who will ruin him." When they could not work upon him one way, some, that were most kindly concerned in him, persuaded him to absent himself and not act for the parliament, and undertook with their lives to secure him, but he would not. He foresaw the mischief, and resolved to stay in his duty, waiting upon God, who accordingly was good to him. Some, when they saw Monk had betrayed them, would have fallen in with Lambert, but the colonel thought any destruction was to be chosen before the sin of joining with such a wretch.[1]

Now was that glorious parliament come to a period, not more fatal to itself than to the three nations, whose sun of liberty then set, and all their glory gave place to the foulest mists that ever overspread a miserable people.[2]   A new

[1] This was the point whereupon the heads of the republican party divided, but probably at this day the warmest friends of the liberties of the people will think that it was better to return to a monarchy, though not sufficiently limited and defined, than to fall under a stratocracy, or government of the army, which this would have been more completely than even that which existed under Cromwell: indeed it is not easy to see which way it would have differed from that of Algiers. Accordingly we do not find Mrs. Hutchinson ever to have repined that the king had been restored in preference to the establishment of such a power; but there were many other modes which might have been adopted, without flying to either of these extremes, had not their passions overpowered the reason of some of the great men of that day. In page 705 of the third volume of Clarendon's *State Papers*, a spy of Charles II. says to the Lords Bedford and Manchester, that Pierrepont, Popham, Waller, and St. John, made a junto to treat with the king before his restitution. But the most obvious method for obtaining a better settlement was that proposed by Whitelocke to Fleetwood, of an offer of their services to the king upon reasonable conditions: this opportunity was lost by hesitation, and an easy triumph left to Monk, whose determined conduct gave efficacy to the small force he possessed.

[2] If the change in politics was great, the change in morals was much greater: statutes have since retrieved the errors committed in the former; it is doubtful whether the national character in taste and morals has ever freed itself from the taint it then received.

Under the patronage and example of the king, wit put decency to flight; religion and patriotism, veneration of God and the love of our country, the two noblest affections of the mind, were dragged through the mire of doggrel rhymes, under the pretence of deriding hypocrisy; under the notion of gaiety and good fellowship, profligacy and sensuality gained a footing which they have never quitted, but still maintain their ground, by the dangerous secret then taught them of reducing all by invidious surmises and unjust depreciations nearly to the level of their own baseness.

The plays and other writings of those days are tinctured with an air of rakishness which often appears affected and misplaced; it was the polite ridicule of the Spectators which put this folly out of countenance and practice. Some modern wits have attempted to revive it, and but for the general turn to philosophical inquiry they would probably have succeeded. Those who *reason* cannot but see that shameless depravity is a very bad substitute for even simulated virtue.

parliament was to be chosen, and the county of Nottingham had yet such respect for Colonel Hutchinson, that they fixed their eyes on him to be their knight, but Mr. William Pierrepont having a great desire to bring in his son-in-law, the Lord Haughton, to be his fellow knight, the colonel would not come into the town until the election was passed; which if he had, he had been chosen without desiring it; for many people came, and when they saw he would not stand, returned and voted for none, among whom were fifty freeholders of the town of Newark.

Some time before the writs for the new elections came, the town of Nottingham, as almost all the rest of the island, began to grow mad, and to declare themselves so, in their desires of the king. The boys, set on by their fathers and masters, got drums and colours, and marched up and down the town, and trained themselves in a military posture, and offered many affronts to the soldiers of the army that were quartered there, which were two troops of Colonel Hacker's regiment. Insomuch that one night there were about forty of the soldiers hurt and wounded with stones, upon the occasion of taking away the drums, when the youths were gathering together to make bonfires to burn the Rump,[1] as was the custom in those mad days. The soldiers, provoked to rage, shot again, and killed in the scuffle two presbyterians, whereof one was an elder, and an old professor; and one that had been a great zealot for the cause, and master of the magazine of Nottingham Castle. He was only standing at his own door, and whether shot by chance or on purpose, or by whom, it is not certain; but true it is, that at that time the presbyterians were more inveterately bitter against the fanatics than even the cavaliers themselves, and they set on these boys. But upon the killing of this man they were hugely enraged, and prayed very seditiously in their pulpits, and began openly to desire the king; not for good will to him, but only for destruction to all the fanatics. One of the ministers, who were great leaders of the people, had been firmly engaged in Booth's rebellion, and led on very many of the godly, who, by the timely suppression of those who

[1] The number of the members of the long parliament having been, by seclusion, death, etc., very much reduced, the remainder was compared to the rump of a fowl which was left, all the rest being eaten; and this coarse emblem was burnt in derision by the mob, to hail and flatter the rising power of the cavaliers.

began the insurrection in Nottingham, were prevented from declaring themselves openly. Colonel Hutchinson was as merciful as he could safely be, in not setting on too strict inquisition; but privately admonished such as were not passed hopes of becoming good commonwealth's men, if it were possible that the labouring state might outlive the present storm. Upon this bustle in the town of Nottingham the soldiers were horribly incensed, and the townsmen ready to take part with the boys; whereupon the soldiers drew into the meadows near the town, and sent for the regiment, resolving to execute their vengeance on the town, and the townsmen again were mustering to encounter them. Mrs. Hutchinson by chance coming into the town, and being acquainted with the captains, persuaded them to do nothing in a tumultuary way, however provoked, but to complain to the general, and let him decide the business.

The men, at her entreaty, were content so to do, the townsmen also consented to restrain their children and servants, and keep the public peace; while it was agreed that both of them should send up together a true information to the general concerning the late quarrel. But one of the officers, more enraged than the rest, went away immediately to Monk, and complained to him of the malice of the presbyterians and cavaliers against the soldiers. He, without asking more on the other side, signed a warrant to Colonel Hacker, to let loose the fury of his regiment upon the town, and plunder all they judged guilty; with which the officer immediately went away. Colonel Hutchinson being at that time at the general's lodging, my Lord Howard told him what order against the town of Nottingham had just been sent down. The colonel, who had been by his wife informed of the disorders there, went to the general, and prevailed with him for a countermand of all hostility against the town, till he should hear and determine the business; which countermand the colonel sent immediately by one of the townsmen, who, though he rode post, came not till Colonel Hacker, with all his regiment, were come into the town before him, and the soldiers were in some of the houses beginning to rifle them. Wherefore the countermand coming so seasonably from Colonel Hutchinson, they could not but look upon him as their deliverer; and this being done a very few days before the election for the next parliament, when the colonel came to town and had waived the county, they generally pitched upon him for the town. But then Dr. Plumptre laboured all he could to get the burgess-ship for himself, and to put by the colonel, with the basest scandals he and two or three of his associates could raise. Mr. Arthur Stanhope, in whose house the soldiers were entered to plunder, being pitched upon for the other burgess, and having a great party in the town, was dealt with to desert the colonel, and offered all Plumptre's party; but he, on the other side, laboured more for the colonel than for himself, and at length, when the election day came, Mr. Stanhope and the colonel were clearly chosen.[1]

The colonel and Mr. Stanhope went up to the parliament, which began on the 25th day of April, 1660; to whom the king sending a declaration from Breda, which promised, or at least intimated, liberty of conscience, remission of all offences, enjoyment of liberties and estates; they voted to send commissioners to invite him.[2] And almost all the gentry of all parties went, some to fetch him over, some to meet him at the sea side, some to fetch him into London, into which he entered on the 29th day of May, with a universal joy and triumph, even to his own amazement; who, when he saw all the nobility and gentry of the land flowing in to him, asked where were his enemies. For he saw nothing but prostrates, expressing all the love that could make a prince happy. Indeed it was a wonder in that day to see the mutability of some, and the hypocrisy of others, and the servile flattery of all. Monk, like his better genius, conducted him, and was adored like one that had brought all the glory and felicity of mankind home with this prince.

The officers of the army had made themselves as fine as

[1] Both Whitelocke and Ludlow assure us, that there were great solicitations in all parts to get to be parliament-men; and Rapin says, that almost all the elections were in favour of the presbyterians and royalists, peculiarly the former. This circumstance renders Colonel Hutchinson's popularity and personal merit so much the more conspicuous.

[2] That the parliament, and this, as Rapin calls it, a *presbyterian* parliament, should thus simply and unconditionally have invited the king, has always been matter of astonishment. The first to find out the error into which their precipitancy had led them were the royalists, and of them the *best*, the Earl of Southampton, who by Burnet, p. 89, is said to have laid the chief blame on Chancellor Hyde. But was it not equally in the power of the parliament *after* the king's arrival to have imposed any reasonable conditions, at least before they established for him such an income as to render him independent?

the courtiers, and all hoped in this change to change their condition, and disowned all things they before had advised. Every ballad singer sang up and down the streets ribald rhymes, made in reproach of the late commonwealth, and of all those worthies that therein endeavoured the people's freedom and happiness.

The presbyterians[1] were now the white boys, and according to their nature fell a thirsting, and then hunting after blood, urging that God's blessing could not be upon the land, till justice had cleansed it from the late king's blood. First that fact was disowned, then all the acts made after it rendered void, then an inquisition made after those that were guilty thereof, but only seven were nominated of those that sat in judgment on that prince, for exemplary justice, and a proclamation sent for the rest to come in, upon penalty of losing their estates.

While these things were debating in the house, at the first, divers persons concerned in that business sat there, and when the business came into question, every one of them spoke of it according to their present sense. But Mr. Lenthall, son to the late Speaker of that parliament, when the presbyterians first called that business into question, though not at all concerned in it himself, stood up and made such a handsome and honourable speech in defence of them all, as deserves eternal honour. But the presbyterians called him to the bar for it, where, though he mitigated some expressions, which might be ill taken of the house, yet he spoke so generously, that it will never be forgotten of him. Herein he behaved himself with so much courage and honour as was not matched at that time in England, for which he was looked on with an evil eye, and, upon a pretence of treason, put in prison; from whence his father's money, and the lieutenant of the tower's jealousy, delivered him. When it came to Ingoldsby's

---

[1] It has been pretty generally reported and believed of the king, that he was more inclined to confirm and augment than disturb or diminish the extent of the amnesty he had proffered at Breda; and there are upon record very honourable instances of many of the royalists exhibiting a spirit of forgiveness and reconciliation; perhaps the most rational way of accounting for the chief of the presbyterian party showing rigour, is to suppose that they did it in order to remove from themselves the odium of those violences of which they had been the original and remote cause, and to cast it on those who were the immediate and proximate ones. Be the cause or reasoning what it may, the fact is well established by the trials of the regicides.

turn, he, with many tears, professed his repentance for that murder, and told a false tale, how Cromwell held his hand, and forced him to subscribe the sentence, and made a most whining recantation, after which he retired; and another had almost ended, when Colonel Hutchinson, who was not there at the beginning, came in, and was told what they were about, and that it would be expected he should say something. He was surprised with a thing he expected not, yet neither then, nor in any like occasion, did he ever fail himself, but told them, " That for his actings in those days, if he had erred, it was the inexperience of his age, and the defect of his judgment, and not the malice of his heart, which had ever prompted him to pursue the general advantage of his country more than his own; and if the sacrifice of him might conduce to the public peace and settlement, he should freely submit his life and fortunes to their disposal; that the vain expense of his age, and the great debts his public employments had run him into, as they were testimonies that neither avarice nor any other interest had carried him on, so they yielded him just cause to repent that he ever forsook his own blessed quiet, to embark in such a troubled sea, where he had made shipwreck of all things but a good conscience; and as to that particular action of the king, he desired them to believe he had that sense of it that befitted an Englishman, a Christian, and a gentleman." [1] What he expressed was to this effect, but so very handsomely delivered, that it took generally the whole house; only one gentleman stood up and said, he had expressed himself as one that was much more sorry for the events and consequences than the actions; but another replied, that when a man's words might admit of two interpretations, it befitted gentlemen always to receive that which might be most favourable. As soon as the colonel had spoken, he retired into a room where Ingoldsby was with his eyes yet red, who had called up a little spite to succeed his whinings, and embracing Colonel Hutchinson, " O colonel," said he, " did I ever imagine we could be brought to this? Could I have suspected it, when I brought them Lambert in

---

[1] This speech will probably be considered as a specimen of art carried as far as a man of honour would permit himself to go, and managed with as much refinement and dexterity as the longest premeditation could have produced; accordingly it furnished his friends with a topic for his defence, without giving his adversaries grounds for reproaching him with tergiversation.

the other day, this sword should have redeemed us from being dealt with as criminals, by that people for whom we had so gloriously exposed ourselves." The colonel told him he had foreseen, ever since those usurpers thrust out the lawful authority of the land to enthrone themselves, it could end in nothing else; but the integrity of his heart, in all he had done, made him as cheerfully ready to suffer as to triumph in a good cause. The result of the house that day was to suspend Colonel Hutchinson and the rest from sitting in the house. Monk, after all his great professions, now sat still, and had not one word to interpose for any person, but was as forward to set vengeance on foot as any man.

Mrs. Hutchinson, whom to keep quiet, her husband had hitherto persuaded that no man would lose or suffer by this change, at this beginning was awakened, and saw that he was ambitious of being a public sacrifice, and therefore, herein only in her whole life, resolved to disobey him, and to improve all the affection he had to her for his safety, and prevailed with him to retire; for she said, she would not live to see him a prisoner. With her unquietness, she drove him out of her own lodgings into the custody of a friend, in order to his further retreat, if occasion should be, and then made it her business to solicit all her friends for his safety. Meanwhile, it was first resolved in the house, that mercy should be shown to some, and exemplary justice to others; then the number was defined, and voted it should not exceed seven; then upon the king's own solicitation, that his subjects should be put out of their fears, those seven were named, and after that a proclamation was sent for the rest to come in. Colonel Hutchinson not being of the number of those seven, was advised by all his friends to surrender himself, in order to secure his estate, and he was very earnest to do it, when Mrs. Hutchinson would by no means hear of it: but being exceedingly urged by his friends, that she would hereby obstinately lose all their estate, she would not yet consent that the colonel should give himself into custody, and she had wrought him to a strong engagement, that he would not dispose of himself without her. At length, being accused of obstinacy, in not giving him up, she devised a way to try the house, and wrote a letter in his name to the Speaker, to urge what might be in his favour, and to let him know, that by reason of some inconveniency it might be to him, he desired not to come under custody, and yet should be ready to appear at their call; and if they intended any mercy to him, he begged they would begin it in permitting him his liberty upon his parole, till they should finally determine of him. This letter she conceived would try the temper of the house; if they granted this, she had her end, for he was still free; if they denied it, she might be satisfied in keeping him from surrendering himself.

Having contrived and written this letter, before she carried it to the colonel, a friend came to her out of the house, near which her lodgings then were, and told her that if they had but any ground to begin, the house was that day in a most excellent temper towards her husband; whereupon she wrote her husband's name to the letter, and ventured to send it in, being used sometimes to write the letters he dictated, and her character not much differing from his. These gentlemen who were moved to try this opportunity, were not the friends she relied on; but God, to show that it was he, not they, sent two common friends, who had such good success that the letter was very well received; and upon that occasion all of all parties spoke so kindly and effectually for him, that he had not only what he desired, but was voted to be free without any engagement; and his punishment was only that he should be discharged from the present parliament, and from all offices, military or civil, in the state for ever; and upon his petition of thanks for this, his estate also was voted to be free from all mulcts and confiscations. Many providential circumstances concurred in this thing. That which put the house into so good a humour towards the colonel that day, was, that having taken the business of the king's trial into consideration, certain committees were found to be appointed to order the preparation of the court, the chairs and cushions, and other formalities, wherein Colonel Hutchinson had nothing to do; [1] but when they had passed their votes for his absolute discharge and came to the sitting of the court, he was found not to have been one day away. A rogue that had been one of their clerks had brought in all

[1] In Nelson's *Trial of Charles I.*, it appears, that on Friday, January 12, when a committee was appointed for ordering the trial, and many minute particulars agreed to for the management of it, Colonel Hutchinson was absent, but attended most other days. On January 25, however, when the sentence was suggested, he was absent, but was present at the signing, and himself signed the warrant for execution

these informations; and above all, poor Mrs. Hacker, thinking to save her husband, had brought up the warrant for execution, with all their hands and seals.[1]

Sir Allen Apsley too, who, with all the kindest zeal of friendship that can be imagined, endeavoured to bring off the colonel, and used some artifice in engaging his friends for him. There was a young gentleman, a kinsman of his, who thirstily aspired after preferment, and Sir Allen had given him hopes, upon his effectual endeavours for the colonel, to introduce him; who being a person that had understanding enough, made no conscience of truth, when an officious lie might serve his turn. This man, although he owed his life to the colonel, and had a thousand obligations to Mrs. Hutchinson's parents, yet not for their sakes, nor for virtue, nor for gratitude, but for his own hopes, which he had of Sir Allen Apsley, told some of the leading men among the court party, that it was the king's desire to have favour shown to the colonel; whereupon Mr. Palmer, since Castlemain,[2] was the first man that spoke for the colonel, whom Finch most eloquently seconded. Then Sir George Booth and his party all appeared for the colonel, in gratitude for his civility to them. For when the parliament had passed by the rebellion of Lambert and Fleetwood, and those who joined with them, and would not make their offences capital, he had told the house, they could not without great partiality punish these, and had moved much in their favour. Mr. Pierrepont, and all the old sage parliament men, out of very hearty kindness, spoke and laboured very effectually to bring him clear off; and there was not at that day any man that received a more general testimony of love and good esteem from all parties than he did, not one of the most violent hunters of blood opposing favour, and divers most worthy persons giving a true and honourable testimony of

---

[1] To those who have not read or not remembered the trials of the regicides, it may be useful to remark, that Colonel Hacker was tried for superintending the execution of the king in his military capacity, for which it seems this warrant was expected to prove a sufficient justification: and perhaps it ought to have been so considered: but it is extraordinary that his wife, before she gave up an instrument which seemed so precious to those who were seeking revenge, had not stipulated for her husband's pardon.

[2] This Mr. Palmer was the husband of the celebrated Mrs. Palmer, mistress to Charles II., afterwards created Lady Castlemain and Duchess of Cleveland. See *Grammont's Memoirs.*

him. Although they knew his principles to be contrary to
theirs, yet they so justified his clear and upright carriage,
according to his own persuasion, that it was a record much
advancing his honour, and such as no man else in that day
received.[1]

Yet though he very well deserved it, I cannot so much
attribute that universal concurrence that was in the whole
house to express esteem for him and desire to save him,
to their justice and gratitude, as to an overruling power of
Him that orders all men's hearts, who was then pleased to
reserve his servant, even by the good and true testimony of
some that afterwards hated him and sought his ruin, for the
perseverance in that goodness, which then forced them to be
his advocates; for even the worst and basest men have a
secret conviction of worth and virtue, which they never dare
to persecute in its own name. The colonel being thus discharged the house, retired to a lodging further from Westminster, and lay very private in the town, not coming into
any company of one sort or other, waiting till the act of
oblivion were perfected, to go down again into the country;
but when the act came to be passed in the house, then the
Lord Lexington set divers friends at work in the commons'
house to get a proviso inserted, that the Newarkers' money,
which he paid into the committee of Haberdashers' Hall,
and was by that committee paid to the colonel for his pay,
might, with all the use of it, be paid out of the colonel's
estate. He forged many false pretences to obtain this; but
it was rejected in the commons' house, and the bill going up
to the lords, it was passed without any provisoes. Only the
gentlemen who were the late king's judges, and who were
decoyed to surrender themselves to custody by the house's
proclamation, after they had voted only seven to suffer, were
now given up to trial, both for their lives and estates, and put
into close prison; where they were miserably kept, brought
shortly after to trial, condemned, and all their estates con-
fiscated and taken away, themselves kept in miserable bondage under that inhuman, bloody jailor, the lieutenant of the
Tower, who stifled some of them to death for want of air;
and when they had not one penny, but what was given them

---

[1] Mr. Lassels (probably Lascelles) enjoyed exactly a similar exemption, the peculiar reasons for it are not accurately known, but it is
natural to suppose they were similar.

to feed themselves and their families, exacted abominable
rates for bare, unfurnished prisons; of some forty pounds
for one miserable chamber; of others double, besides undue
and unjust fees, which their poor wives were forced to beg
and engage their jointures and make miserable shifts for;
and yet this rogue had all this while three pounds a week
paid out of the exchequer for every one of them. At last,
when this would not kill them fast enough, and when some
alms were thus privately stolen into them, they were sent
away to remote and dismal islands, where relief could not
reach them, nor any of their relations take care of them: in
this they were a thousand times more miserable than those
that died, who were thereby prevented from the eternal infamy and remorse, which hope of life and estate made these
poor men bring upon themselves, by base and false recantations of their own judgments, against their consciences;
which they wounded for no advantage, but lived ever afterwards in misery themselves, augmented by seeing the misery
of their wretched families, and in the daily apprehension of
death, which, without any more formality, they are to expect
whenever the tyrant gives the word. And these are the
"*tender* MERCIES *of the wicked !*" [1] Among which I cannot
forget one passage that I saw. Monk and his wife, before
they were removed to the Tower, while they were yet prisoners at Lambeth House, came one evening to the garden
and caused them to be brought down only to stare at them,
—which was such a barbarism, for that man, who had be-

[1] Almost all who have written any account of the transactions of
those days show a desire to gratify the faction which then prevailed,
and have endeavoured to establish a notion that great lenity was shown
to all the regicides who were not of the seven excepted: what it was
we here learn.

The English nation have long dealt on the hackneyed theme of
French oppression, lettres de cachet, bastilles, etc., and have affected
an ignorance of what has passed here, in full sight of a British parliament. Those who have viewed the matter near at hand know very
well that *these* superlative powers were not at all more dangerous, nor
so much abused in France as here, nor the treatment near so rigorous.
The prisons of state there were always under the command of noblemen and military officers, who were little likely to practise the jailor's
arts. The more any office is despised, the more vile hands will it fall
into, and the more atrociously will it be executed; this reasoning
sufficiently establishes the necessity of watching with a jealous eye the
conduct of these ministers of justice, if such they should be called, in a
country like this. A more desolating picture of misery long drawn
out can hardly be imagined. We shall again have to notice the conduct of this lieutenant of the Tower.

trayed so many poor men to death and misery that never
hurt him, but who had honoured him, and had trusted their
lives and interest with him, to glut his bloody eyes with
beholding them in their bondage, that no story can parallel
this inhumanity.

Colonel Scrope, who had been cleared by vote as the
colonel was, was afterwards rased out for nothing, and had
the honour to die a noble martyr.

Although the colonel was cleared both for life and estate in
the house of commons, yet he not answering the court expectations in public recantations and dissembled repentance, and
applause of their cruelty to his fellows, the chancellor was
cruelly exasperated against him, and there were very great
endeavours to have rased him out of the act of oblivion. But
then Sir Allen Apsley solicited all his friends, as if it had
been for his own life, and divers honourable persons drew up a
certificate, with all the advantage they could, to procure him
favour; who in all things that were not against the interest of
the state had ever pitied and protected them in their dis-
tresses.[1] The Countess of Rochester wrote a very effectual
letter to the Earl of Manchester, making her request that the
favour to him might be confirmed as an obligation to her,
to quit some that she, and, as she supposed, her lord had
received from him. This letter was read in the house, and
Sir Allen Apsley's candidate for preferment again made no
conscience of deceiving several lords, that the preserving of
the colonel would be acceptable to the king and the chancellor, who he now knew hated his life. Many lords also of the
colonel's relations and acquaintance, out of kindness and
gratitude (for there was not one of them whom he had not
in his day more or less obliged), used very hearty endeavours
for him. Yet Sir Allen Apsley's interest and most fervent
endeavours for him, was that only which turned the scales,
and the colonel was not excepted in the act of oblivion to
anything but offices.

[1] The Countess of Rochester was the wife of Wilmot, general of the
horse for the king, who upon disgust quitted his service, and, receiving
a passport, went abroad; his wife expressed *loyalty to*, and received
much favour from, the parliament, as Whitelocke informs us; very
likely by the procurement of Colonel Hutchinson. The passage before
us (and many others such like) may serve as a useful memento to those
who are engaged in civil broils, to maintain all they can of private
kindness, consistently with what they think their public duty. For
the honour of human nature let due notice be taken of the steady
friendship of Sir Allen Apsley.

The provisoes to the act of oblivion were all cut off, and it was determined that those things should pass in particular acts; when the Lord Lexington got one for that Newark money to be repaid out of the colonel's estate, with all the interest for fourteen years. This act was committed, and the colonel had counsel to plead against it, and the Marquis Dorchester[1] having the chair, was wonderfully civil to the colonel. The adverse counsel, having been men that practised under the parliament, thought they could no way ingratiate themselves so well as by making invectives against those they formerly clawed with, and when, quite beside their matter, they fell into railings against the injustice of the former times and scandals of the colonel, the marquis checked them severely, and bade them mind their cause: but Mr. Finch, one of the colonel's counsel, after a lawyer had made a long railing speech, which held them a tedious while, he replied, " My lord, this gentleman hath taken up a great deal of time to tell your lordship how unjust that parliament was, how their committees perverted judgment and right, which he sets forth with all his power of language to make them odious, and in conclusion would persuade your lordship therefore to do the same things." After the hearing at the committee, a report was made so favourable for the colonel that the bill was cast aside, and the house being then ready to adjourn, most of the colonel's friends went out of town, which opportunity Lexington taking notice of, the very last day in a huddle got the bill past the lords' house.[2]

Then the colonel went down into the country, and found it necessary to reduce and change his family, which were many of them people he took in for charity, when they could no where else be received; and they had been more humble

[1] The same whom, when Viscount Newark, Colonel Hutchinson rescued from the violence of the countrymen at Nottingham; to whom afterwards the colonel made, at the request of her friends, the offer of the hand and fortune of Lady Anne Somerset, and who so handsomely now evinces his candour and gratitude. His character is well contrasted with that of Lord Lexington, who in the first place obtained a peerage for the sacrifice of this very money; next refused payment of it to the Newarkers, of whom he had borrowed it; then, upon being compelled to pay it, procured easy terms by the colonel's interference; and now attempts to plunder his benefactor of the whole!

[2] The practice of parliament at that time must have differed from what it now is, for such a bill to originate in the house of lords: we shall presently see it miscarry in the commons.

and dutiful while they were under hatches, but now that they might find better preferments, they were not to be confided in; yet he dismissed not any of them without bountiful rewards, and such kind dismissions as none but that false generation would not have been obliged by. But some of them soon afterwards betrayed him as much as was in their power, whose prudence had so lived with them, that they knew nothing that could hurt his person.

When the colonel saw how the other poor gentlemen were trepanned that were brought in by proclamation, and how the whole cause itself, from the beginning to the ending, was betrayed and condemned, notwithstanding that he himself, by a wonderfully overruling providence of God, in that day was preserved; yet he looked upon himself as judged in their judgment, and executed in their execution; and although he was most thankful to God, yet he was not very well satisfied in himself for accepting the deliverance. His wife, who thought she had never deserved so well of him, as in the endeavours and labours she exercised to bring him off, never displeased him more in her life, and had much ado to persuade him to be contented with his deliverance; which, as it was eminently wrought by God, he acknowledged it with thankfulness. But while he saw others suffer, he suffered with them in his mind, and, had not his wife persuaded him, he had offered himself a voluntary sacrifice; but being by her convinced that God's eminent appearance seemed to have singled him out for preservation, he with thanks acquiesced in that thing; and further remembering that he was but young at the time when he entered into this engagement, and that many who had preached and led the people into it, and many of that parliament who had declared it to be treason not to advance and promote that cause, were all now apostatised, and as much preached against it, and called it rebellion and murder, and sat on the tribunal to judge it; he again reflected seriously upon all that was past, and begged humbly of God to enlighten him and show him his sin if ignorance or misunderstanding had led him into error. But the more he examined the cause from the first, the more he became confirmed in it, and from that time set himself to a more diligent study of the scriptures, whereby he attained confirmation in many principles he had before, and daily greater enlightenings concerning the free grace and love of God in Jesus Christ, and the spiritual worship under the gospel, and the gospel liberty, which ought not to be subjected to the wills and ordinances of men in the service of God. This made him rejoice in all he had done in the Lord's cause, and he would often say, the Lord had not thus eminently preserved him for nothing, but that he was yet kept for some eminent service or suffering in this cause; although having been freely pardoned by the present powers, he resolved not to do anything against the king, but thought himself obliged to sit still and wish his prosperity in all things that were not destructive to the interest of Christ and his members on earth; yet as he could not wish well to any ill way, so he believed that God had set him aside, and that therefore he ought to mourn in silence and retiredness, while he lay under this obligation.

He had not been long at home before a pursuivant from the council was sent to fetch him from his house at Owthorpe, who carried him to the attorney-general. He, with all preparatory insinuations, how much he would express his gratitude to the king and his repentance for his error, if he would now deal ingenuously, in bearing testimony to what he should be examined, sifted him very thoroughly; but the colonel, who was piqued at heart that they should thus use him, to reserve him with an imagination that he would serve their turns in witnessing to the destruction of the rest, composed himself as well as he could, and resolved upon another testimony than they expected, if they had really called him to any. But the attorney-general was so ill-satisfied with his private examination that he would not venture a public one. He dealt with him with all the art and flatteries that could be, to make him but appear, in the least thing, to have deserted his own and embraced the king's party; and he brought the warrant of execution to the colonel, and would fain have persuaded him to own some of the hands, and to have imparted some circumstances of the sealing, because himself was present. But the colonel answered him, that in a business transacted so many years ago, wherein life was concerned, he durst not bear a testimony, having at that time been so little an observer, that he could not remember the least tittle of that most eminent circumstance, of Cromwell's forcing Colonel Ingoldsby to set his unwilling hand, which, if his life had depended on that circumstance, he could not have

affirmed. " And then, Sir," said he, " if I have lost so great
a thing as that, it cannot be expected less eminent passages
remain with me." Then being shown the gentlemen's hands,
he told him he was not well acquainted with them, as having
had commerce with but few of them by letters; and those
he could own, he could only say they resembled the writings
which he was acquainted with; among these he only picked
out Cromwell's, Ireton's, and my Lord Grey's. The attorney-
general, very ill-satisfied with his private examination, dismissed him; yet was he served with a writ to appear in the
court the next day. The colonel had been told that, when
they were in distress for witnesses to make up their formality,
Colonel Ingoldsby had put them upon sending for him,
which made him give that instance to the attorney.[1] The
next day the court sat, and the colonel was fetched in and
made to pass before the prisoners' faces, but examined in
nothing; which he much waited for, for the sight of the
prisoners, with whom he believed himself to stand at the bar;
and the sight of their judges, among whom was that *vile
traitor* who had sold the men that trusted him; and he that
openly said he abhorred the word *accommodation*, when
moderate men would have prevented the war; and the
colonel's own *dear friend*, who had wished damnation to his
soul if he ever suffered penny of any man's estate, or hair of
any man's head, to be touched;—the sight of these [2] had so
provoked his spirit that, if he had been called to speak, he
was resolved to have borne testimony to the cause and
against the court; but they asking him nothing, he went to
his lodging, and so out of town, and would not come any
more into their court, but sent the attorney-general word he
could witness nothing, and was sick with being kept in the
crowd and in the press, and therefore desired to be excused
from coming any more thither. The attorney made a very
malicious report of him to the chancellor and to the king,

[1] *Risum teneatis.* The subject is too serious for laughter, but an
involuntary smile will be excited by this sarcasm, so well pointed. It
is no wonder the attorney-general did not wish to examine him further!
[2] Monk, Ashley Cooper, and Hollis. Does not every one feel his
indignation roused at this wanton outrage upon decency? Perhaps
Colonel Hutchinson's appearance in court may have been misconstrued
by many, as they might be ignorant that it was involuntary, and no
one but himself could know that he meant to give evidence contrary
to what was desired of him.

insomuch that his ruin was then determined, and an opportunity only was watched to effect it.[1]

When Sir A. Apsley came to the chancellor he was in a great rage and passion, and fell upon him with much vehemence. "O Nall," said he, "what have you done? you have saved a man that would be ready, if he had opportunity, to mischief us as much as ever he did." Sir Allen was forced to stop his mouth, and tell him, that he believed his brother a less dangerous person than those he had brought into the king's council, meaning Maynard and Glynne;[2] but the truth is, from that time, all kindness that any one expressed to the colonel was ill resented, and the Countess of Rochester was also severely rebuked for having appeared so kind to the colonel.

When the parliament sat again, the colonel sent up his wife to solicit his business in the house, that the Lord Lexington's bill might not pass the lower house. At her first coming to town a parliament-man, a creature of Worcester-house, being in his coach, she out of hers called to him, who was her kinsman, and desired his vigilance to prevent her injury. "I could wish," said he, "it had been finished last time, for your husband hath lately behaved himself so ill, that it will pass against him." She answered, "I pray let my friends but do their endeavours for me, and then let it be as God will." He, smiling at her, replied, "*It is not now as God will,*[3] *but as we will.*" However, notwithstanding many other discouragements, she waited upon the business every day, when her adversaries as diligently solicited against her. One day a friend came out of the house and told her that they were that day so engaged that she might go home and rest secure that nothing would be done; and that day most of her friends were away, and her opposites took this opportunity to bring it into the house, which was now much alienated, especially all the court party, from the colonel; but God, to

[1] The king intimated to the lords, when there were disputes on foot respecting the exceptions to the bill of indemnity, that "*other ways* might be found to meet with those of turbulent and factious spirits:" thereby showing that he had, like the rest of his family, secret reserves for rendering insignificant his public acts.

[2] Maynard and Glynne had chimed in not only with the parliament but with Cromwell, under whom both held offices. The chancellor will hereafter find them dangerous inmates;—in pushing the affair of his accusation and exile.

[3] This well marks the change of style that had taken place.

show that not friends, nor diligence, preserved our estates, stirred up the hearts of strangers to do us justice, and the bill was thrown out when we had scarce one of those friends we relied on in the house.

Presently after Mrs. Hutchinson came to town, a kinsman of hers, fallen into the wicked counsels of the court, came to visit her one evening, and had been so freely drinking as to unlock his bosom, when he told her that the king had been lately among them where he was, and told them that they had saved a man, meaning Colonel Hutchinson, who would do the same thing for him that he had done for his father; for he was still unchanged in his principles, and readier to protect than to accuse any of his associates, and would not discover any counsels or designs, or any party, though he was known to have hated them.[1]   Then this gentleman told her how contemptuous a carriage it was, that he would only own to the signatures of those who were dead, and how they were resolved his pardon should never pass the seal, and what a desperate condition he was reduced to.   Having thus affrighted her, then, to draw her in by examples, he told her how the late statesmen's wives came and offered them all the informations they had gathered from their husbands, and how she could not but know more than any of them; and if yet she would impart anything that might show her gratitude, she might redeem her family from ruin; and then he particularly told her how her husband had been intimate with Vane, Pierrepont, and St. John, whose counsels they knew had gone far in this matter, and that if she would prevent others in the declaring them, she might much advantage herself. But she told him, she perceived that any safety one could buy of them was not worth the price of honour and conscience; that she knew nothing of state managements, or if she did, she would not establish herself upon any man's blood and ruin.   Then he employed all his wits to circumvent her in discourse, and to have gotten something out of her concerning some persons they aimed at, which, if he could, I believe it

[1] The king's satirical favourite, Rochester, reports of him that he never said a foolish thing; but surely this was not a very wise one! How could he have faith in any such sudden changes?   What he did not mean to do he did, which was to establish Colonel Hutchinson's steadiness and consistency beyond question.   We know from this history that Colonel Hutchinson's sense of honour was a complete safeguard against him; but this was a principle of which Charles felt not, and affected to disbelieve, the existence.

would have been beneficial to him: but she discerned his drift, and scorned to become an informer, and made him believe she was ignorant, though she could have enlightened him in the very thing he sought for; which they are now never likely to know much of, it being locked up in the grave, and they that survive not knowing that their secrets are removed into another cabinet.[1] After all, natural affection working at that time with the gentleman, he in great kindness advised her that her husband should leave England. She told him he could not conveniently, and the act of

[1] Any who are delighted with the discovery of a secret will be disappointed that Mrs. Hutchinson did not even here reveal hers, but resisted the bewitching vanity of showing the confidence that had been reposed in her by betraying it. She might perhaps, with great propriety, think it not prudent to commit it to writing, though it was to be read only by her own family. Of the persons here named, Sir H. Vane, it is well known, was sacrificed to the manes of Lord Strafford, whose attainder he was supposed in a great measure to have procured; but there seems not to have been any pretence for excepting him out of the amnesty. He viewed his fate, and the king who sentenced him to it, with equal contempt; and the passage before us is a proof of the fidelity he maintained towards his associates. St. John was excluded from all offices; but Pierrepont escaped untouched in all respects, and represented the county of Nottingham in the short parliament which restored the king, but appears not to have been re-chosen in that which succeeded it. That he who was so *deeply engaged* should have come off so well, is matter of wonder, and the more so when we take into consideration the following particulars.

The ingenious writer of the critique of this work in the *Annual Review* conjectures that the secret which this friend of Mrs. Hutchinson endeavoured to extort from her was, *the name of that considerable person who had formed the design of settling the state under Richard Cromwell*, as mentioned in p. 301: this is highly probable, and still more so that this person was Mr. William Pierrepont, and that the royalists aimed peculiarly at his destruction, as will appear from many passages that are to be found in the third volume of Clarendon's *State Papers*. In one part the good will of Pierrepont to Richard Cromwell and Richard's respect for him is spoken of: in another Hyde instructs his spies to " gain Thurloe, whom he thinks considerable, and he would gain St. John and Pierrepont," adding significantly, " they have manifested that they have no inveterate objection to a *single person*, and the right heir is the best person." In another place it is said by one of the spies that " St. John, Pierrepont, and Thurloe, continue to cabal and press the general (Monk); *three such evil beasts do not exist*." But when Pierrepont is reported to be ill, the most eager wishes are expressed for his death. No doubt but the *virtuous ministers* of Charles II. dreaded his abilities and integrity as they coveted his property: but supported by such connexions he as was, they could not venture to attack him without some clear and strong information against him. That these harpies were disappointed in their project of extinguishing this eminent patriot and his family, and pouncing on their possessions, may then most likely be attributed to the constancy and discretion of Mrs. Hutchinson.

oblivion being passed, she knew not why he should fear, who was resolved to do nothing that might forfeit the grace he had found. But he told her it was determined that, if there was the least pretence in the world, the colonel would be imprisoned, and never be again let loose, which warning, though others of her friends said it was but an effect of his wine, the consequence proved it but too true.

She advertised the colonel and persuaded him, being also advised to the same by other friends, to go out of England, but he would not: he said this was the place where God had set him, and protected him hitherto, and it would be in him an ungrateful distrust of God to forsake it.[1] At this time he would have sold part of his estate to pay his debts, but the purchasers scrupled, desiring to see his pardon, which he not having, was fain to break off the treaty; and though all his friends laboured for it, the chancellor utterly refused it. There was a thousand pounds offered to one person to procure it, but it was tried several times and could not be passed, by reason of which he lost the opportunity then of settling his estate; yet a year afterwards a little solicitor shuffled it in among many others, and managed it so dexterously that it passed all the seals. The colonel's estate being in mortgage with a peevish alderman, who designed to have bought it for little or nothing, he had a great trouble with him; for having procured him his money, he would not assign the mortgage, and the others would not lend the money without assignment from him, so that it put the colonel to many inconveniences and great expense.

This parliament being risen, another was called by the king's writ, wherein the act of oblivion was again confirmed, not without some convassing and opposition; and here again another act about that money of the Lord Lexington's was prepared and twice read in the house, through divers abominable untruths which they had forged and possessed the members withal. The colonel himself solicited his own defence, and had all the injustice and foul play imaginable at the committee appointed to examine it, and it was so

[1] This is a pregnant instance of Colonel Hutchinson's strong belief in the decrees of providence, and at the same time of his sincere conformity to them: it is much to be regretted that he adhered so minutely and literally to it, instead of making use of his own and his friends' discretion. He might well have lived to see the happy Revolution, and have returned and benefited his native country again by his spirit, wisdom, and experience.

desperate that all his friends persuaded him to compound it; but he would not, though his enemies offered it, but he said he would either be cleared by a just, or ruined by an unjust sentence, and, pursuing it with his usual alacrity and vigour in all things, he at last removed that prepossession that some of the gentlemen had against him; and clearing himself to some that were most violent, it pleased God to turn the hearts of the house at last to do him justice, and to throw out the bill for evermore, which was a great mercy to him and his family, for it was to have thrown him out of possession of all the estates he had, and to have put them into his enemies' hands till they had satisfied themselves. But the defending himself was very chargeable to him, and not only so, but this rumour of trouble upon his estate, and the brags of his enemies, and the cloud he lay under, hindered him both from letting and selling, and improving his estate, so that it very much augmented his debt.

Before this time, in December, 1660, Captain Cooper sent one Broughton, a lieutenant, and Andrews, a cornet, with a company of soldiers, who plundered his house at Owthorpe, while he was absent, of all the weapons they found in it, to his very wearing-swords, and his own armour for himself, although at that time there was no prohibition of any person whatsoever to have or wear arms. The colonel was not then at home, and the arms were laid up in a closet within his chamber, which they searched, and all the house over, to see if they could have found plate or anything else; but when they could not, they carried these away, which one of his servants, whom he had dismissed with a good reward, betrayed to them. His eldest son went to the Marquis of Newcastle, lord lieutenant of the county, and complained of the violence of the soldiers, and my lord gave him an order to have the swords and other things back, and some pistols which were the Lord Byron's, but Mr. Cooper contemned my lord's order, and would not obey it. The arms were worth near £100.

Also an order came down from the secretary, commanding certain pictures and other things the colonel had bought out of the late king's collection, which had cost him in ready money between £1000 and £1500, and were of more value; and these, notwithstanding the act of oblivion, were all taken from him.

After these troubles were over from without, the colonel lived with all imaginable retiredness at home, and because his active spirit could not be idle nor very sordidly employed, he took up his time in opening springs, and planting trees, and dressing his plantations; and these were his recreations, wherein he relieved many poor labourers when they wanted work, which was a very comfortable charity to them and their families: with these he would entertain himself, giving them such encouragement in their honest labours, so that they delighted to be employed by him. His business was serious revolving the law of God, wherein he laboured to instruct his children and servants, and enjoyed himself with much patience and comfort, not envying the glories and honours of the court, nor the prosperity of the wicked; but only grieved that the straitness of his own revenues would not supply his large heart to the poor people in affliction. Some little troubles he had in his own house. His son, unknown to him, married a very worthy person,[1] but with the manner of which he was so discontented that he once resolved to have banished them for ever, but his good nature was soon overcome, and he received them into his bosom; and for the short time he enjoyed her, he had no less love for her than for any of his own children. And indeed she was worthy of it, applying herself with such humble dutifulness and kindness to repair her fault, and to please him in all things he delighted in, that he was ravished with the joy of her, who loved the place not as his own wife did, only because she was placed in it, but with a natural affection, which encouraged him in all the pains he took to adorn it, when he had one to leave it to that would esteem it. She was besides naturalised into his house and interests, as if she had had no other regard in the world; she was pious and cheerful, liberal and thrifty, complaisant and kind to all the family, and the freest from humour of any woman; loving home, without melancholy or sullenness, observant of her father and mother, not with regret, but with delight, and the most submissive, affectionate wife that ever was. But she, and all the joy of her sweet, saint-like conversation, ended in a lamented grave, about a year after her marriage, when she died in childbirth, and left the sweetest babe behind her that ever was beheld, whose face promised all its mother's

[1] The daughter of Sir Alexander Ratcliffe, of the Royalist party.

graces, but death within eight weeks after her birth, ravished this sweet blossom, whose fall opened fresh the wounds of sorrow for her mother, thus doubly lost. While the mother lived, which was ten days after her delivery, the colonel and his wife employed all imaginable pains and cares for her recovery, whereof they had often hopes, but in the end all was in vain; she died, and left the whole house in very sensible affliction, which continued upon the colonel and his wife till new strokes awakened them out of the silent sorrow of this funeral. Her husband having no joy in the world after she was gone, for some months shut himself up with his grief in his chamber, out of which he was hardly persuaded to go, and when he did, every place about home so much renewed his remembrance of her, that he could not think of her but with deep affliction; so, being invited by his friends abroad to divert his melancholy,[1] he grew a little out of love with home, which was a great damping to the pleasures his father took in the place: but he, how eager soever he was in the love of any worldly thing, had that moderation of spirit that he submitted his will always to God, and endeavoured to give him thanks in all things.

This winter, about October and the following months, the papists began to be very high, and some strangers were come into Nottingham, who were observed to distinguish themselves by scarlet ribbons in their hats; and one night, in a drunken humour, a papist fired a hay barn in a wood-yard in Nottingham, which, if not discovered and prevented by many providences, might have endangered much of the town: but it did £200 worth of mischief; but the matter was shuffled up and compounded, although on the same night several other towns were attempted to be fired. A great papist, at Eastwold, was known to assemble two hundred men in arms in the night, and some of the Lord Carrington's tenants, who went to Arundel House to speak with their landlord, observed very strange suspicious signs of some great business on foot among the papists, who, both in Nottinghamshire and Leicestershire, were so exalted, that the very country people everywhere apprehended some insurrection. Among the rest, there was a light-headed, debauched young knight, living in the next town to Owthorpe, who vapoured beyond all

---

[1] Mr. Thomas Hutchinson did not marry again, but died without issue.

bounds, and had twelve pair of holsters for pistols at one time of the colonel's saddler, and rode at that time with half a dozen men armed, up and down the country, and sent them, and went himself, to several men who had been soldiers in the army, to offer them brave terms to enlist under him, telling them, that they, meaning the papists, should have a day for it. Besides, he, with the parson of the parish, and some other men, at an alehouse, began a health to the confusion of all the protestants in England; and one of the colonel's maids going to Colson, to have a sore eye cured by a woman in the town, heard there that he had vapoured that the papists should shortly have their day, and that he would not leave one alive in the colonel's house. He sent to the preacher of Cotgrove, to forbid him to preach on gunpowder treason-day, threatening to kill him if he did, insomuch that the town were forced to keep a guard all that day upon the steeple.

The men whom the papists had endeavoured to enlist acquainted the colonel with it, whereof some being in Leicestershire, the colonel sent his son to Sir George Villiers, one of the deputy-lieutenants of that county, to acquaint him with it; but he slighted the matter, although at that time it could have been proved that Golding brought a whole coach laden with pistols, as many as they could stuff under the seats and in the boots, to the house of one Smith, a papist, dwelling at Quineborough, in Leicestershire. The colonel also sent to the deputy-lieutenants of our county to acquaint them with the public danger, and how he himself was threatened; and, by reason that his house had been disarmed, desired that he might have leave to procure some arms necessary to defend it; but they sent him word that the insurrection of the papists was but a fanatic jealousy, and if he were afraid, they would send him a guard, but durst not allow him to arm his house. He, disdaining their security who would not trust him with his own, would have taken a house at Nottingham for his wife to lie in, who being then big with child, was near her account; but although she was fearful, yet when she found him resolved to stay in his own house, she would not go; whereupon he made strong shutters to all his low windows with iron bars; and that very night that they sat up, the house was attempted to be broken in, and the glass of one of the great casements broken, and the little iron bars of it crashed asunder. Mrs. Hutchinson being up late, heard the noise, and thought somebody had been forcing the doors, but, as we since heard, it was Golding who made the attempt. The common people, everywhere falling into suspicion of the papists, began to be highly offended at their insolence, and to mutter strange words; whether it was this, or what else we know not, but their design proceeded no further; yet there is nothing more certain than that at that time they had a design of rising generally all over England in arms. But the colonel lived so retired that he never understood how it was taken up, and how it fell off, yet, although they would not take the alarm from him, even the gentlemen of the county after-wards believed they were hatching some mischief, and feared it.

The colonel continued his usual retirement all that winter and the next summer, about the end of which he dreamt one night that he saw certain men in a boat upon the Thames, labouring against wind and tide, to bring their boat, which stuck in the sands, to shore; at which he, being in the boat, was angry with them, and told them they toiled in vain, and would never effect their purpose; but, said he, let it alone and let me try; whereupon he laid himself down in the boat, and applying his breast to the head of it, gently shoved it along, till he came to land on the Southwark side, and there, going out of the boat, he walked into the most pleasant lovely fields, so green and flourishing, and so embellished with the cheer-ful sun that shone upon them, that he never saw anything so delightful, and there he met his father, who gave him certain leaves of laurel which had many words written on them which he could not read. The colonel was never super-stitious of dreams, but this stuck a little in his mind, and we were therefore seeking applications of it, which proved to be nothing in the event, but that having afforded one, I know not whether the dream might not have been inspired. The boat represented the commonwealth, which several unquiet people sought to enfranchise, by vain endeavours against wind and tide, paralleling the plots and designs some im-patient people then carried on without strength, or council, or unity among themselves; his lying down and shoving it with his breast, might signify the advancement of the cause by the patient suffering of the martyrs, among which his own was to be eminent; and on the other side of the river his landing, into walks of everlasting pleasure, he dying on that shore, and his father's giving him these laurel leaves with unintelligible characters, foretold him those triumphs which he could not read in his mortal estate. But to let dreams pass,—

I cannot here omit one story, though not altogether so much of the colonel's concern, yet happening this summer, is not unworthy of mention. Mr. Palmer, a certain non-conformist preacher, was taken at his own house in Nottingham, by the mayor of the town, for preaching upon the Lord's day, and some others with him (whereof one was formerly a servant of the colonel's, and had married one of his maids), and put into the town's gaol, where they continued about two or three months. There being a grated window in the prison, which was almost even with the ground, and looked into the street, all people coming by might see these poor people, kept in a damp, ill-favoured room, where they patiently exhorted and cheered one another. One Lord's day, after sermon time, the prisoners were singing a psalm, and the people as they passed up and down, when they came to the prison, stood still, till there were a great many gathered about the window at which Mr. Palmer was preaching; whereupon the mayor, one Toplady, who had formerly been a parliament officer, but was now a renegade, came violently with his officers, and beat the people, and thrust some into prison that were but passing the street, kicked and pinched the men's wives in his rage, and was but the more exasperated, when some of them told him, how ill his fury became him who had once been one of them. The next day, or a few days after, having given order that the prisoners should every Lord's day after be locked in the coal-house, he went to London and made information, I heard on oath, to the council, that a thousand of the country came into the town armed, and marched to the prison window to hear the prisoner preach; whereupon he procured an order for a troop of horse to be sent down to quarter at Nottingham to keep the fanatics in awe. But one who had a relation to the town, being then at court, and knowing this to be false, certified to the contrary and prevented the troop. After the mayor came down, he was one night taken with a vomiting of blood, and being ill, called his man and his maid, who also at the same time fell a bleeding, and were all ready to be choked in their own blood, which at last stopping, they came to assist him; but after that he never lifted up his head, but languished for a few months and died.

While these poor people were in prison, the colonel sent them some money, and as soon as their time was expired, Mr. Palmer came to Owthorpe to give him thanks, and preached there one Lord's day.[1] Whether this was taken notice of is not evident, but within a short time after, upon the Lord's day, the 11th of October, 1663, the colonel having that day finished the expounding of the Epistle to the Romans to his household, and the servants being gone off out of the parlour from him, one of them came in and told him soldiers were come into the house. He was not at all surprised, but stayed in the room till they came in, who were conducted by Atkinson, one of those Newark men, who had so violently before prosecuted him at the parliament, and he told the colonel he must go along with them, after they had searched the house; for which the colonel required their commission, which at the first they said they need not show, but afterwards they showed him an order from Mr. Francis Leke, one of the deputy-lieutenants, forthwith to repair to his house, to search for and bring away what arms they could

[1] This transaction is seemingly of small note; but will be found of the last importance to the parties concerned. By the declaration from Breda,—" Liberty was granted to tender consciences, and none were to be questioned for difference of opinion in matters of religion, which do not disturb the peace of the kingdom." But the parliament which was chosen after the restoration, and which consisted in a great degree of tories and high churchmen, encouraged and led on by the chancellor, passed several severe acts against all dissenters indiscriminately. Particularly one called the Act of Uniformity, and this they followed up with an act forbidding nonconformists to frequent conventicles, under which probably Mr. Palmer was seized. As it had been declared that those who differed from the church could not fail to be enemies to the state, and that the fanatics as they called them, resorted to these means under pretence of religion, but in reality to form and ripen plots and seditions, and that principally for this reason these acts were framed, this renegade very aptly introduced his thousand men in arms.

How far it was discreet in Colonel Hutchinson at such a juncture to let this man preach at Owthorpe, on whom a mark had been set, is doubtful; it seems that in general he confined his religious opinions and worship to his own house, and was of course inoffensive even to the captious government under which he lived.

The manner, time, and place of his being seized, demonstrate the falsehood of the legend contained in Throsby's edition of Thoroton's *Nottinghamshire*, of his long concealment in his own house, and at last being taken *coming home from church*.

find, and to seize his person. All which they did, and found
no arms in the house but four birding-guns, that hung open
in the kitchen, which being the young gentleman's, they left
at that time. It was after sunset when they came, and they
were at least two hours searching every corner and all about
the house, and the colonel was not at that time very well
in health, and not having been on horseback for six months
before, had neither horses nor saddles at that time in the
house; the coachman was also gone away, and the coach-
horses turned out, and it was as bitter a stormy, pitchy, dark,
black, rainy night as any that year; all which considered,
the colonel desired that they would but stay for the morning
light, that he might accommodate himself; but they would
not, but forced him to go along with them then, his eldest
son lending him a horse, and also voluntarily accompanying
him to Newark, where, about four o'clock in the morning,
he was brought into the Talbot, and put into a most vile
room, and two soldiers kept guard upon him in that room.

And now what they ailed we knew not, but they were all
seized with a panic fear, and the whole country fiercely
alarmed, and kept at Newark many days at intolerable
charges, and I think they never yet knew what they were
sent for in to do, but to guard Colonel Hutchinson; who
being at first put into a room that looked into the street,
was afterwards removed into a back room, worse, if worse
could be, and so bad that they would not let the Duke of
Buckingham's footmen lodge in it; and here he continued,
no man coming to him nor letting him know why he was
brought in. The next day Mrs. Hutchinson sent him some
linen, and as soon as the man came, Tomson, the host of the
inn, would not suffer him to see his master, but seized him
and kept him prisoner two days. Mr. Thomas Hutchinson
had a mare which the innkeeper had a desire to buy, and his
father persuaded him to let him have her though worth more
money, who thereupon agreed on the price, only Tomson
desired him to let him try the mare six miles, which he condescended to, upon condition that if Tomson rode the mare above
six miles he should pay the money for her, and furnish Mr.
Hutchinson with a horse home, or to my Lord of Newcastle's,
or for any other occasion he had while he was at Newark.
Upon this bargain Tomson had the mare, but instead of
going but six miles, he led a greater party of horse than

those who had first seized the colonel, to Owthorpe, and coming in after sunset, to the affright of Mrs. Hutchinson and her children, again searched their house more narrowly if possible than at first, with much more insolent behaviour, although they found no more than at first; but they took away the birding-guns they had left before, and from Owthorpe went to Nottingham, where they took one Captain Wright and Lieutenant Frank, who had been Lambert's adjutant-general, and brought the poor men to Newark, where they are yet prisoners, and to this day know not why.[1] Several others were taken prisoners, among the rest one Whittington, a lieutenant, who, being carried to prison, "Colonel Hutchinson," said he, "hath betrayed us all;" such were the base jealousies of our own party over him, who, because he was not hanged at first, imagined and spoke among themselves all the scandals that could be devised of him, as one that had deserted the cause, and lay private here in the country to trepan all the party, and to gather and transmit all intelligence to the court, and a thousand such things, giving each other warning to take heed of coming near him. Those who began to render him thus odious among his own party were the Lambertonians, in malice because he had openly opposed their rebellious insolencies against the parliament. Frank, Whittington, etc., were of these, but the colonel would not hazard himself to rectify their unjust thoughts, and had no resort of his own friends, the more sober and honest men of the party; only, as much as the straits that were upon him would allow, he would send them relief when any of them were in distress. Hereupon some, convinced of the injuries they did him, about this time sought to do him right, in some meeting where one of the Buckingham's trepans was, and said he was unchanged in his principles, which was all that ever I could hear was informed against him, but anything would serve for those who sought a pretence.[2]

---

[1] This shows that the confinement of these persons lasted still longer than Colonel Hutchinson's, and likewise that this history was written while the events were still recent and fresh in the memory.

[2] The whole history of the reign of Charles the Second is filled with plots, real or imaginary, but mostly the latter. Of all the engines of state the most nefarious is that at this time much employed, of sham or pretended fomenters of sedition or *trepans*, who drew unwary persons either into some confederacy or expression of discontent, and

While the colonel was at Newark, Golding, the papist, was a very busy fellow in spying and watching his house at Owthorpe, and sending in frivolous stories, which amounted to nothing, but declaring his pitiful malice, as they that received them afterwards told the colonel.

When Tomson came back, Mr. Hutchinson, out of the window, spied his own gun, which some of the men brought in, and soon understood that this rogue had made use of his own horse to plunder him. At night Tomson, the host, came up into the colonel's chamber, and behaved himself most insolently, whereupon the colonel snatched up a candlestick and laid him over the chaps with it; whereupon Mr. Leke, being in the house, and hearing the bustle, with others, came in with drawn swords, and the colonel took that opportunity to tell him that he stood upon his justification, and desired to know his crime and his accusers, and that till then he was content to be kept as safe as they would have him, but desired to be delivered out of the hands of that insolent fellow, and to have accommodation fit for a gentleman; which when they saw he would not be without, for he would eat no more meat in that house, two days after they removed him to the next inn, where he was civilly treated, with guards still remaining upon him.

It was not passion which made the colonel do this, for he was not at all angry, but despised all the malice of his enemies; but he having been now four days in Newark, Mr. Leke came every day to the house where he was kept by Leke's warrant, and never vouchsafed so much as to look on him, but put him into the hands of a drunken insolent host, who daily affronted him; which, if he would have suffered, he saw would be continued upon him, therefore knowing that Leke was then in the house, he took that occasion to oblige him come to him, and thereupon obtained a removal to an accommodation more befitting a gentleman.

While he was at the other inn, several gentlemen of the king's party came to him, some whom he had known, and some whom he had never seen, complimenting him, as if he had not been a prisoner: which he very much wondered at, and yet could never understand, for by his former usage he

---

then gave information, probably heightened by invention. Many have thought the information given against Lord Russell and Algernon Sidney, whereon they were tried and condemned, was no better.

saw it was not their good nature: but whether this carriage of his had made them believe innocence was the ground of his confidence, or whether the appearance of his great spirit had made them willing to oblige him, or whether even his virtue had stricken them with a guilty dread of him, though a prisoner, certain it is, that some who had been his greatest enemies began to flatter him; whereupon, in a Bible he carried in his pocket, and marked upon all occasions, he marked that place, Prov. xvi. 7, " When a man's ways please the Lord, he maketh his enemies to be at peace with him."

The 19th of October, Mr. Leke, with a party of horse, carried the colonel to the Marquis of Newcastle's, who treated him very honourably; and then falling into discourse with him, " Colonel," saith he, " they say you desire to know your accusers, which is more than I know." And thereupon very freely showed him the Duke of Buckingham's letter, commanding him to imprison the colonel, and others, upon suspicion of a plot; which my lord was so fully satisfied the colonel was innocent of, that he dismissed him without a guard to his own house, only engaging him to stay there one week, till he gave account to the council, upon which he was confident of his liberty.[1] The colonel thus dismissed, came

[1] Here shines out the genuine spirit of a noble Briton! This was the same man, who, commanding a host, against which the forces Colonel Hutchinson had to defend Nottingham Castle with were but as a dwarf before a giant, yet, saw his fidelity to be proof both against danger, and the temptation of great rewards, and had generosity enough to see and value virtue in an adversary; he well knew that such a person as the colonel was safer in the keeping of his own honour than of all the guards or prisons of his enemies. Who can fail to regret that such a man should have been so long the dupe of his loyalty to the Stuarts, and above all that he should have to receive mandates from the infamous sycophants of Charles the Second? If a man were inevitably to be persecuted, it made much for his honour, and somewhat for his satisfaction, to have two men of such opposite characters as Newcastle and Buckingham, the one for his protector, the other for his persecutor.

Of Buckingham we shall again have occasion to speak.

As we shall not again see anything more of this *truly noble* man, the Marquis of Newcastle, we take this opportunity to cite, from a tradition preserved by Deering in his *History of Nottingham*, that at the time of the great revolution, another Cavendish, Earl, and afterwards Duke of Devonshire, together with Lord Delamere, son of that Sir George Booth whose life and fortunes Colonel Hutchinson preserved, together with Colonel Hutchinson's half-brother, and others of that country, set up their standard at Nottingham; there waked again the soul of liberty and patriotism, which had slept ever since Colonel Hutchinson's days, and causing the trumpet to sound to arms, and telling the inhabitants a Stuart was at hand with all his army, saw the

home, and upon the 22nd day of October a party of horse,
sent only with a wretched corporal, came about eleven o'clock
with a warrant from Mr. Leke, and fetched him back to
Newark, to the inn where he was before, Mr. Twentyman's,
who being still civil to him, whispered him as soon as he
alighted, that it was determined he should be close prisoner;
whereupon the colonel said he would no more pay any sentinels that they set upon him, yet they set two hired soldiers,
having now dismissed the county, but the colonel forbade
the inn to give them any drink, or anything else upon his
account. The next day, being the 23rd, Mr. Leke came to
him and showed him a letter from my Lord Newcastle,
wherein my lord wrote that he was sorry he could not pursue
that kindness he intended the colonel, believing him innocent, for that he had received a command from Buckingham
to keep him a close prisoner, without pen, ink, or paper;
and to show the reality of this, with the order he sent a copy
of the duke's letter, which was also shown the colonel; and
in it was this expression, " *that though he could not make it out
as yet, he hoped he should bring Mr. Hutchinson into the plot.*"
Mr. Leke having communicated these orders to Mr. Hutchinson, told him he was to go to London, and should leave him
in the charge of the mayor of Newark.

Because here is so much noise of a plot, it is necessary to
tell what it hath since appeared. The Duke of Buckingham
set at work one Gore, sheriff of Yorkshire, and others, who
sent out trepanners among the discontented people, to stir
them up to insurrection to restore the old parliament, gospel
ministry, and English liberty; which specious things found
very many ready to entertain them, and abundance of simple
people were caught in the net; whereof some lost their lives,
and others fled.[1] But the colonel had no hand in it, holding
himself obliged at that time to be quiet. It is true he still

whole people fly to arms, some on horseback, some on foot, with all
the various weapons they could find, march all as one man to meet
him, and take their determined stand at that pass of the Trent where
their old governor had repeatedly fought and conquered, and whose
spirit they imagined to hover over and inspire them with its wonted
energy. Having thus tried their temper, he committed to the guard
of these true-born sons of freedom, that princess (Anne) who was to
carry the British name to its highest pitch of glory.

[1] Rapin speaks slightly and cursorily of this, under the name of the
Northern Plot; but plainly shows that some of the principal persons
whom it was pretended had been concerned in it, neither were nor
could be.

suspected insurrections of the papists, and had secured his house and his yards, better than it was the winter before, against any sudden night assaults.

After Mr. Leke was gone, the mayor, one Herring, of Newark, a rich, but simple fellow, sent the jailor to Mr. Hutchinson, to tell him he must go to his house; which the colonel refusing to do voluntarily, without a mittimus from some magistrate, the mayor sent five constables and two soldiers, who by violence both forced the colonel out of his quarters, and into the gaol without any legal commitment, although the colonel warned both the jailor and the men of the danger of the law, by this illegal imprisonment. The colonel would not advance at all into the prison, into which the men would fain have entreated him; but when they saw they could not persuade, they violently thrust him in, where the jailor afterwards used him pretty civilly: but the room being unfit for him, he got cold and fell very sick, when, upon the 27th of October, Mr. Leke, with the marquis's secretary, came to him, and found him so, and acquainted him that the marquis had received express orders from the king, to send him up in safe custody to London. Mr. Leke finding him so ill, was so civil as to permit him to go by his own house, which was as near a road, that he might there take accommodations for his journey, and be carried up at more ease in his own coach; Mr. Leke himself went away before, being necessitated to make more haste than he could have done if he had stayed for the party that was to guard the colonel, and left his orders for sending him away with Mr. Atkinson, who first seized him. The same 27th day, at night, his house at Owthorpe was again searched, and he and his wife being abroad, all their boxes and cabinets were broken open, and all their papers rifled, but yet for all this they could find nothing to colour their injustice to him.

Having been falsely and illegally imprisoned, from six o'clock on Friday night, the 23rd of October, till ten o'clock in the morning, October 28, he was then, in order to his going to London, brought by Beek, the jailor, to Twentyman's inn, from whence he was hailed, to stay there till a commanded party of the county horse came to guard him to London. But one division of the county who had warrants sent them, not coming in, Atkinson sent into that part where the colonel lived, and his own neighbours coming slowly and unwillingly to that service, he was forced to stay there all that day till night in the custody of the jailor. At night, when he was in bed, the mayor being drunk, commanded him to be carried back to the jail, but the jailor, weary of his drunken commands, sat up with two soldiers, and guarded him in the inn.

The next day, the party not being come in, one Corporal Wilson, a mean fellow, who was appointed to command the colonel's guard, came and told him that he must not go by his own house, nor have the privilege of his coach, but be carried up another way; whereupon the colonel sent to Atkinson, to desire him he might not be denied that civility Mr. Leke had allowed him; but he was so peevish and obstinate that the colonel was sending his son post to the Marquis of Newcastle's to complain of his malicious inhumanity, who would have forced him on horseback without any accommodation, when he was so taken ill that he could not have ridden one stage without manifest hazard of his life: and yet Mr. Cecil Cooper and Mr. Whally, though justices and deputy lieutenants, could not prevail with him, till he saw the colonel as resolute as himself: and then at last, by their mediation (wherein Mr. Cecil Cooper did something to redeem his former causeless hatred, which made him plunder the house, and detain the plunder when it was ordered back), the colonel, about sunset, was sent out of Newark, with those horse that were come in, to stay for the rest at his own house. Being driven in the night by an unskilful coachman, the coach was overturned and broken; but about twelve o'clock at night they came safe home. Thus the colonel took his last leave of Newark, which being a place he had formerly subdued, and replete with so many malicious enemies to the whole party, and more particularly to him, upon no other account but that he had been the most formidable protector of the other party in this country, he expected far worse treatment from the generality of the town; who were so far from joining in joy of his captivity, that when he was forced through their streets, they gave him very civil respect, and when he came away, civil farewells, and all muttered exceedingly at their mayor, and said he would undo their town by such simple illegal proceedings. The colonel regarded all these civilities from the town, who were generally much concerned in his injuries, and from Cooper and others, not as of themselves, but as from God, who at that time overawed the hearts of his enemies, as once he did Laban's and Esau's; and he was much confirmed in the favour of God thereby, and nothing at all daunted at the malice of his prosecutors, but went as cheerfully into captivity as another would have come out of it.

They were forced to stay a day at Owthorpe, for the mending of the coach and the coming in of the soldiers, where the colonel had the opportunity to take leave of his poor labourers, who all wept bitterly when he paid them off; but he comforted them and smiled, and without any regret went away from his bitterly weeping children, and servants, and tenants, his wife and his eldest son and daughter going with him, upon Saturday, the 31st of October.

Golding, the night before he went, had sent him a pot of marmalade to eat in the coach, and a letter to desire all grudges might be forgotten, and high flattering stuff, by his man who was to be one of the guard, whom, he said, he had chosen out from the best he had, and his best horse, and if he did not pay him all respect, he would turn him away; and as the colonel came by his door, he came out with wine, and would fain have brought him into the house to eat oysters, but the colonel only drank with him, and bid him friendly farewell, and went on, not guarded as a prisoner, but waited on by his neighbours. Mrs. Hutchinson was exceedingly sad, but he encouraged and kindly chid her out of it, and told her it would blemish his innocence for her to appear afflicted, and told her if she had but patience to wait the event, she would see it was all for the best, and bade her be thankful for the mercy that she was permitted this comfort to accompany him in the journey; and he with divers excellent exhortations cheered her who was not wholly abandoned to sorrow, while he was with her, who, to divert her, made himself sport with his guards, and deceived the way, till upon the 3rd of November he was brought to the Crown, in Holborn. From thence, the next day, he was carried by Mr. Leke to the Tower, and committed there close prisoner, by warrant, signed by Secretary Bennett, the 20th of October, whereby he stood committed for treasonable practices, though he had never yet been examined by any magistrate, one or another. His wife, by his command, restrained herself as much as she could from showing her sadness, whom he bade to remember how often he had told her that God never preserved him so extraordinarily at first, but for some great work he had further for him to do or to suffer in this cause; and bade her be thankful for the mercy by which they had so long in peace enjoyed one another, since this eminent change; and bade her trust God with him, whose faith and cheerfulness were so encouraging that it a little upheld her; but, alas! her divining heart was not to be comforted: she remembered what had been told her of the cruel resolutions taken against him, and saw now the execution of them.

On Friday, November the 6th, he was sent for by Secretary Bennett, to his lodgings at Whitehall, which was the first time he was examined, and the questions he asked him were: First. "Where he had lived this four or five months?" To which he answered, "Constantly at home, at his own house in Nottinghamshire." Second. "What company used to resort to his house?" He told him, "None, not so much as his nearest relations, who scarcely ever saw him." Third. "What company he frequented?" He told him, "None; and that he never stirred out of his own house to visit any." Bennett said, "That was very much." Fourth. "Whether he knew Mr. Henry Nevill?" He answered, "Very well." Fifth. "When he saw him?" He said, "To his best remembrance never since the king came in." Sixth. "When he wrote to him?" He said, "Never in his life." Seventh. "When Mr. Nevill wrote to him?" He said, "Never." Eighth. "Whether any messages had past between them?" He said, "None at all." Ninth. "Whether none had moved anything to him concerning a republic?" He answered, "He knew none so indiscreet." Tenth. "What children he had?" He said, "Four sons and four daughters." Eleventh. "How old his sons were?" He said, "Two were at men's estate, and two little children." Twelfth. "Whether his sons had not done anything to injure him?" He replied, "Never that he knew of, and he was confident they had not." Thirteenth. "Where he went to church to hear divine service, common prayer?" He said, "No where, for he never stirred out of his own house." Fourteenth. "Whether he heard it not read there?" He answered, "To speak ingenuously, no." Fifteenth. "How he then did for his soul's comfort?" He replied, "Sir, I hope you leave me that to account between God and my own soul." Then Bennett told him his answers to these had cut him off of many questions he should have asked, and he might return. So he was carried back to the Tower with only two of the warders which brought him thither.[1]

Not long afterwards one Waters was brought prisoner out of Yorkshire, a fellow of a timorous spirit, who, being taken, was in so great a fear, that he accused many, guilty and not guilty, to save himself; and caused his own wife to be put in prison, and hanged the dearest friend he had in the world, and brought his wife's brother into the same danger; some say through fear, others that he was a trepanner from the beginning, for he drew in all the people whom he accused. Whatever he was, he was so utter a stranger to Colonel Hutchinson, that he never saw his face; yet the day he was examined at Whitehall, Colonel Hutchinson was in great haste fetched away from his dinner at the Tower, and told he should be examined in the king's own hearing; which he was very glad of, and, with great haste, and formality, and strictness he was carried by the deputy lieutenant and a strong guard by water from the Tower to Whitehall; and when he came to land at Whitehall Stairs, one Andrews, an officer, with two files of musketeers, was ready to receive him, and led him to Bennett's lodgings, where he observed a great deal of care to place the guard at the outward door in the court, and to keep the chamber door continually shut, that none might peep in, but a few gentlemen who were admitted to come

---

[1] What will the reader think of this examination when he is reminded, or, if he knew it not before, is informed, that this gentleman who is so anxious for the welfare of Colonel Hutchinson's soul, and so earnest for his frequenting the church, was himself a concealed papist, and privy to the king's being so too! It is necessary to be here observed, that upon the publication of the act of uniformity a very great number of the parochial clergy quitted their benefices, and were replaced by others; it is highly probable this would be the case at Owthorpe, and it was a very natural consequence of it that Colonel Hutchinson should absent himself from his church, where, although he had heretofore taken much pains to get a good minister established and his salary augmented, he had now to expect, instead of spiritual comfort, such pulpit railings as he had been assailed with at Nottingham. Accordingly he performed the worship of God in his own family, much as a protestant father of a family would have done in a catholic country. And the history informs us he was so occupied when the soldiers came to seize him: but it was prudent to say nothing of this to the *secretary confessor!*

Mr. Nevill, whom he speaks of, made a considerable figure in the latter times of the long parliament, as a staunch republican, a man of strict integrity, and a steady opposer of all the usurpations.

now and then and stare him in the face at the door, but none were in the room for a long space but Andrews and himself, till at the last the keeper thrust himself in. The colonel, having stayed two hours, concluded that he should now be confronted by some accuser, or at least have an examination more tending to treasonable practices than his first seemed to do, especially understanding that Mr. Waters had been many hours before in the house, and was yet there. But at last, *parturiunt montes !* and out comes Secretary Bennett! who, taking him to a window apart from Mr. Andrews and the keeper, most formally begins thus: " Mr. Hutchinson, you have now been some days in prison, have you recollected yourself to say any more than when I last spoke to you? " Mr. Hutchinson answered, " He had nothing to recollect, nor more to say." " Are you sure of that? " said the secretary. " Very sure," said Mr. Hutchinson. " Then," said Bennett, " you must return to prison." And accordingly he was carried by the same guard back again to the Tower, where he was kept with a great deal of strictness, and some weeks passed before his wife was admitted to see him; for whom, at the last, Sir Allen Apsley procured an order that she might visit him, but they limited it that it might not be but in the presence of his keeper. The lieutenant, in hopes of a fee, gave leave that her son and daughter might go into the room with her, who else must have stood without doors; but he would not permit her to take lodgings in the Tower, which, being in a sharp winter season, put her to great toil and inconvenience, besides excessive charge of providing his meat at the Tower, and her company in another place: meanwhile he was kept a close prisoner, and had no air allowed him, but a pair of leads over his chamber, which were so high and cold, that he had no benefit from them; and every night he had three doors shut upon him, and a sentinel at the outmost. His chamber was a room where it is said the two young princes, King Edward the Fifth and his brother, were murdered in former days, and the room that led to it was a dark great room, that had no window in it, where the portcullis to one of the inward Tower gates was drawn up and let down, under which there sat every night a court of guard. There is a tradition, that in this room the Duke of Clarence was drowned in a butt of malmsey; from which murder this room, and that joining it, where Mr. Hutchinson lay, was called the Bloody Tower. Between Mr. Hutchinson's chamber and the dark room there was a door, which Mr. Hutchinson desired the lieutenant might be left open in the night, because it left a little necessary house open to the chamber, which he and his man had occasion of in the night, having gotten fluxes with their bad accommodations and diet: but the lieutenant would not allow it him, although, when that was open, there were two doors more shut upon him, and he could not have any way attempted any escape, but he must, if it had been possible to work through the walls, have fallen upon a court of guard.

Notwithstanding all this strictness, which was also exercised on most of the other prisoners, yet their own sentinels hated the lieutenant, and his Cerberus, Cresset, because they cheated them, and had nothing of generosity or bounty to engage the hearts of their soldiers, who, seeing so much of their wickedness, abhorred them, and pitied the poor gentlemen that were so barbarously used by them; and whether out of humanity, or necessity, or villainy, I know not, but they would offer the prisoners many courtesies, and convey letters between them. Mr. Hutchinson was never so imprudent to trust any of them with his, having within an hour of his imprisonment been instructed by another prisoner a safer and more convenient way; yet was it their interest to use courteously all those who offered themselves to do them service. Among the rest, as he was one day sitting by the fire, the sentinel at the door peeped in his head and called to him: "Sir," said he, "God bless you! I have sometimes guarded you in another manner at the parliament house, and am grieved to see the change of your condition, and only take this employment now, to be more able to serve you, still hoping to see you restored to what I have seen you." The colonel, not turning his head, told the man that language suited not the coat he wore, bade him mind his present duty, and told him he had no employment of his service. "Well," said the soldier, "I perceive, sir, you dare not trust me, but my Lady Vane and my Lady Lambert know me, and if you have any service to command me to them, I will bring you a testimony from them." The colonel took no more notice of him, but the fellow, officious, or hoping to get money, went to my Lady Lambert's house, and told her that he had formerly been her husband's soldier, and that he wished his restitution, and that he used sometimes to guard the prisoners, and would carry her letters to any of them, and that he had lately been sentinel at Colonel Hutchinson's chamber, and would carry anything she would send to him. She only bade him remember her service to him, and tell him she wished him liberty; and the fellow flattering her with professing his love to her lord, she expressed some pleasure with his speeches, and gave him some money; which her daughter considering, as soon as he was gone out told her that she had done unwarily to open herself so much to one of the soldiers in present employment, whom she did not know but he might be set on purpose to trepan her. My lady, to prevent any inconvenience of her error, thought it the best way to go immediately and complain that one of the soldiers had come to her to trepan her, under colour of a message from Colonel Hutchinson, which she had not entertained; and desired they might not be allowed to do any such thing, protesting her own loyalty and readiness to discover any that were false to them. This was extremely well represented of her at the court, and as ill of Colonel Hutchinson, that he had not done the like; and Colonel Leg, whose company it was that then had the guard of the tower, was commanded to find out and punish this soldier, who, as it proved afterwards, was a good honest fellow, and was the only protestant in that company, the rest being most of them Irish and papists, and some rebels. This poor fellow, having been a parliament soldier, enlisted among them to get a living, but was very tender-hearted to the prisoners, and had a desire to do them kindness. Hereupon he came to the colonel's man, and desired his master would not own him, and that he would send to my Lady Lambert to do the same, which the colonel did; but when she was sent to by him, she sent a maid to see all the soldiers, who owned the man, and he was put in prison, and cashiered and undone, for nothing but offering his service to have done the prisoners slight services. And Colonel Hutchinson was ill thought of at the court, because when Colonel Leg brought his men under the window of his prison, and came up to Mr. Hutchinson and desired him to view them all, he would not accuse any of them; which if he had, he would not only have cut off his own, but all the other prisoners' ways of sending to their friends abroad; yet he never made use of this fellow, nor any of them, in any business of trust, although he thought it not good to discourage any that appeared to wish them well, among so many bloody murderers as they were given up to.

The colonel endured his prison patiently till the trial of those they called conspirators in Yorkshire was over; but when he had lain from November till Candlemas term in prison, he sent his wife to Secretary Bennett to desire that such persons as had business with him might have liberty to come to him. She had before been with some of the privy council who were her husband's friends and allies, to complain of his unjust imprisonment, and his harsh usage also, contrary to all law from the beginning to the ending, even their own laws; and they had told her that they were sensible of it, but that they only stood for cyphers, while the chancellor and Bennett managed all things without their privity, in most oppressive and illegal ways.[1]   She, as she was advised,

[1] It was thought better to bring together here several observations relating to Hyde, Earl of Clarendon, and chancellor Bennett, Earl of Arlington, and secretary, and Villiers, second Duke of Buckingham. The first is well known from his history and letters to have been an unreasonable enemy to presbytery and presbyterians; which prejudice induced him to persuade his royal master, whose confidence for a great length of time he almost entirely engrossed, to violate all his promises to them, though gratitude as well as honour should have made him keep them.   About this time his credit began to diminish by the introduction of Bennett to be secretary of state instead of Nicholas, who was the particular friend of Hyde.   But at the period here spoken of, this had taken effect but partially, and not enough to furnish for those who were oppressed by the one, a succour in the opposition of the other; nor did there appear much reason to hope for moderation in either.   Who it was of the privy council that gave Mrs. Hutchinson her information cannot be conjectured; but there is no doubt that the too great ascendancy of the chancellor did, no long time after, cause him to be impeached in parliament, and accused of all the misconduct of many years.   It was in vain that he endeavoured, in the written defence he sent to the parliament, to distribute the odium among the council in general; the information here given to Mrs. Hutchinson obtained general belief; he was condemned, and died in banishment. He very justly, in the same writing, attributes a good deal of the hatred and bitterness which prevailed against him to his many refusals of setting the seal to pardons and other indulgences.   When, among the speakers against him, we see the names of Maynard, St. John, Hampden, and Prynn,[1] we may well conclude that these men, though they had a little temporised, were glad to assist in the downfall of the man who had persecuted the more zealous of their former associates, and pleased to see him sue for that clemency which his own former severity gave him good reason to despair of.   Bennett was several years after impeached together with Buckingham, the same who first entrapped and caused Colonel Hutchinson to be seized, and whose infamous letter

went therefore to Bennett and told him that, by reason of some engagements for money her husband had upon his estate, this very close imprisonment had been infinitely prejudicial to him, both his tenants and his creditors taking advantage of his incapacity (by reason of his close restraint) to defend himself, or to speak with lawyers or others about affairs that nearly concerned his estate; besides the neglect of all his business, and the intolerable charge and inconvenience of his disordered family, dispersed into three several places, which would suddenly bring ruin upon his whole family, besides the destruction of his health. Bennett told her, her husband was a very unfortunate person in regard to his former crimes. She told him she had rather hoped he had been happy in being comprised in the act of oblivion, which allowed him not to be remembered as a criminal; and that she had chosen to make her addresses to him on this occasion, because some of the council had told her the king left all the management of these things to him. He was

the Marquis of Newcastle showed the colonel. On this occasion he employed his usual treachery, and criminated the earl, who was fain to save himself from the indignation of the parliament by a total change of conduct; by practising the hypocrisy he had recommended to Colonel Hutchinson, of frequenting the communion of a church he was averse to, and persecuting the papists, whom he had protected, and wished to protect. On account of his conduct a strict inquiry was made by the commons concerning the commitment of persons by order of council, and amendments were made in the Habeas Corpus Act, which, if they had existed in the Colonel's time, would have preserved him from his long and unjust imprisonment. Buckingham, after bringing the family of Fairfax to extinction by marrying and slighting his daughter, heightening and exposing his master's vices, and passing his whole life in playing, by countless alternations, the parts of traitor and sycophant, died in disgrace and beggary, and, to sum all up in that which to him would be the greatest suffering, his memory remains hung up to ridicule in the chains of never-dying satire by Pope, in some of the best lines he has written.

To those who believe in the peculiar interposition of God in human affairs, as our author did, it must be very striking, and to her, if she lived to witness it, highly gratifying, to observe this course of events. Mr. Hutchinson's three great enemies, Buckingham, Clarendon, and Arlington, ruin each other, and two of them, Clarendon and Arlington, without the design of doing anything so good, laid the foundations of an alliance which furnished the assertors of British liberty and toleration with a champion who overthrew, it is hoped never to rise again despotism in church and state; for Clarendon recommended Charles the Second to constrain his brother to marry his daughter, whom he had dishonoured; she brought him the Princesses Mary and Anne, successively queens of England; and Bennett, Earl of Arlington, to gain himself popularity in a moment of need, first proposed the match between Mary and the Prince of Orange, afterwards William the Third!

very urgent with her to know who it was that informed her that he was the sole actor in these businesses; but she desired to be excused from naming any author in that thing, which she had not mentioned but that she thought it his honour to own; but he told her he would not move for any more liberty for her husband than he had, unless he could be assured it might be done with more safety to his majesty than he could apprehend from it. "But," said he, "Mrs. Hutchinson, I have some papers of yours which I would show, not to examine you, but to see whether you will inform me anything of them." She told him she had curiosity enough to see anything that passed under her name; whereupon he called forth his man, who brought out a great bundle of papers, called examinations, taken at Grantham, of passages between Mrs. Hutchinson and Mrs. Vane. First he showed her a character which contained cyphers for the names of many gentlemen and women who were not very distant neighbours, with others whom she knew not at all. She told him she understood nothing at all of that paper; then he turned down the rest, and showed her a letter, beginning, "My dear Amaranta;" which she told him she knew not at all. "But," said he, "you will yet own your own hand;" and showed her among these papers the copy of the letter that was sent to the house of parliament in her husband's name, written in her hand, which when she saw she was a little confounded, wondering how it should come into his hands; but she told him that she could not absolutely say that was her writing, though it had some resemblance. So when she had again urged the business she came for, and could obtain nothing from him, she went away, and left in the room with the secretary, Sir Robert Byron, a cousin-german of her husband's, who had by chance come in thither upon some business of his own, and had stood by while she urged to the secretary the mischief and ruin her husband's imprisonment had brought upon his family and estate. As soon as she was gone, the secretary told Sir Robert that he had heard Mrs. Hutchinson relate the sad condition of her husband and his house; "and," said he, "you may here take notice how the justice of God pursues those murderers, that, though the king pardoned both his life and estate, yet by the hand of divine justice they were now likely to come to ruin for that crime;" which words being told Mr. Hutchinson, he laughed much at the simple folly of the man, who could call his own illegal persecutions and oppressions of innocence the judgments of God. The papers which he showed Mrs. Hutchinson she afterwards learned to have been some letters between Mrs. Vane, one of Sir Henry Vane's daughters, and one Mrs. Hutchinson, a gentlewoman who used to come thither, filled with such frivolous intelligence of private amours and intrigues as young people used to communicate to their confidants, and such as any wise statesman would have believed himself affronted to have had brought to him, and not made such politic inquiries, and imprisoned those with whom they were found, about so unconcerning a matter.

Mr. Henry Nevill and Mr. Salloway had been put into the Tower upon the same suspicion which they had of Mr. Hutchinson—a northern plot, for which there was a peculiar assizes, and some men were executed; and the judges, at their return, said that their confessions almost amounted to treason; but that almost served their turns. As soon as those assizes were past, Mr. Hutchinson sent to Mr. Nevill and Mr. Salloway, that he thought it now time for them to endeavour their liberty, and therefore desired to know what course they intended to proceed in, that they might all take one way. They both sent Mr. Hutchinson word that they looked upon him as the best befriended, and they were resolved to see first what success he had, and to make him their leading card. Hereupon he, fearful of doing anything which they could not, sat still deliberating, while they, without giving him the least notice, wrought their own liberties secretly, Mr. Nevill desiring to travel, and Mr. Salloway making such a false, flattering petition, that no honest man could make such another, and a less after his would have but more exasperated. It took so, that immediately he had his liberty, both of them taking some oaths to confirm their loyalty, which were given them by the clerk of the Tower.[1] They had a mind at court that Mr. Hutchinson should have made such another petition, and therefore Salloway's was shown to a friend of his; the words of which were, " That since God by his miraculous providence had set his majesty

---

[1] Mr. Nevill, as just before mentioned, had acted with steadiness and integrity; Mr. Salloway had been more valuable, and had been successively of the council of state, of the Rump parliament, of the committee of safety, and council of officers.

over us, he had acquiesced thankfully under it, and never, not so much as in thought, made a wish against it;" and promises of the like nature: which perhaps were no truer than his professions, for they were utterly false; for at his first coming into the Tower no man had muttered more than he, who scarce refrained even from blasphemies against God himself for bringing him into bondage. After his release he went to their common prayer, and pleased them so well that it was said they would give him an office. But when they found that, notwithstanding their hint, Mr. Hutchinson would not follow his example, their malice grew very bitter against him at the court, insomuch that a gentleman having treated with Mrs. Hutchinson for a niece of his, to whom he was guardian, that would have been a convenient fortune for her son, the Chancellor sent for the gentleman and peremptorily forbade him to proceed in the affair,[1] and openly said, " *he must keep their family down.*"

Mr. Hutchinson was not at all dismayed, but wonderfully pleased with all these things, and told his wife this captivity was the happiest release in the world for him; for before, although he had made no express engagement, yet, in regard that his life and estate had been freely left him when they took away others, he thought himself obliged to sit still all the while this king reigned, whatever opportunity he might have; but now he thought this usage had utterly disobliged him from all ties either of honour or conscience, and that he was free to act as prudence should hereafter lead him, and that he thought not his liberty out of prison worth purchasing by any future engagement, which would again fetter him in obligations to such persons as every day more and more manifested themselves to be enemies to all just and godly interests. He therefore charged his wife that she should not make applications to any person whatsoever, and made it his earnest request to Sir Allen Apsley to let him stand and fall by his own innocency, and to undertake nothing for him, which, if he did, he told him he would disown. Mrs. Hutchinson, remembering how much she had displeased him in saving him before, submitted now to suffer with him, according to

---

[1] What base and atrocious malice! yet this was the virtuous Lord Clarendon! This method of alternately persecuting those whom they suspect, and suspecting those they persecute, has for ever been the practice of bad ministers, and has for ever created rebels, and will for ever continue to create new ones in the place of those they destroy.

his own will,[1] who, as he would do nothing that might entangle him for his freedom, so he patiently suffered their unjust bondage, and had no guilt found in him; yet was he cruelly and maliciously persecuted and hated; and criminals, with threats and promises, were tried in all ways to see if they could bring out any accusation against him, but all they could arrive at was only that he was an unchanged person, yet they kept him still as close a prisoner as at the first. After Salloway was released, Sir Allen Apsley asking the Chancellor why his brother was not let out as well as Salloway; " What," said the Chancellor, " make you no difference between your brother and Salloway ? " Sir Allen replied, he thought his brother as innocent. " Surely," said the Chancellor, " there is a great difference; Salloway conforms to the government, and goes to church, but your brother is the most unchanged person of the party."

The colonel, at last, with some other prisoners were deliberating to sue out a habeas corpus, and in order thereunto sent to the lieutenant of the Tower to desire a copy of the warrant whereby he stood committed, which indeed was so imperfect, that he could not legally be kept upon that, for there was neither his Christian name nor any place of residence mentioned in it, so that any other Hutchinson might as well have been kept upon it as he; but the lieutenant refused to give him a copy, and his jailor told the prisoner it was altered after they had kept him four or five months in prison: then the colonel wrote to Bennett, but neither from him could he obtain any copy of his commitment.

After this a friend gave him notice that they had a design to transport him to some island or plantation; whereupon he wrote a narrative of his imprisonment, and procured it to be secretly printed, to have left behind him, if he had been sent away, to acquaint the parliament, which was then shortly to assemble, and to leave with his friends; but he kept it in the meantime privately.[2]

[1] There does not appear reason for supposing that Colonel Hutchinson had any distinct prospect of manifesting his sentiments with effect, nor can these declarations be accounted for upon any principle but that of general disdain. The complete and generous attachment of Mrs. Hutchinson deserves a higher term; if our language would admit of it, as the French does *dévouement*, we should call it *devotion*.

[2] At the time of Colonel Hutchinson's imprisonment the parliament were so devoted to the views of the court, that they might very likely have taken little notice of his representations. Many years elapsed

At length, through the lies that the lieutenant of the Tower told of his prisoners, and the malice of their wicked persecutors, who envied even the bread which charity sent in to feed some of the men whose estates were wholly taken away, warrants were signed for carrying away most of the prisoners, some to Tangiers, and some to other barbarous and distant places: among the rest Colonel Hutchinson was destined to the Isle of Man, which Sir Allen Apsley hearing of, told the king he had some private business of trusts with the colonel concerning his own estate, for which he obtained a respite for him for three months, with liberty for lawyers to come to him. But when the colonel heard of it, he was more displeased with this petty favour than with all their rigour, and had resolved to have done something to reverse it, but that his wife persuaded him to rest till she made a short voyage into the country to fetch him supplies, which he did.

As soon as she was gone, the lieutenant of the Tower sent his jailer, Mr. Edward Cresset, early in the morning, upon the 16th day of April, 1664, to fetch Mr. Hutchinson to his lodgings, whither being come, Cresset withdrew, and the lieutenant told Mr. Hutchinson that he had been civil to him in permitting his children to come to him with their mother, and yet he had not paid him his fees and dues, although that warrant which allowed the access of his wife did not mention his children, and therefore he now demanded his dues. Mr. Hutchinson told him, "At his departure out of the Tower he should not be behind hand with him for the civility of suffering his children to come to him." Robinson replied, " That signified nothing, he expected his dues, and would have them." Mr. Hutchinson answered, " His was not every prisoner's condition, for he had been now twenty-four weeks kept close prisoner, and yet never knew accuser nor accusation against him, and therefore he should desire to consider before he parted with his money; but for any civilities he should repay them." Robinson said, " He meddled with no man's crimes, but whether guilty or not guilty, he expected his dues, which he could recover by law if they were refused."

before they animadverted as they ought upon such arbitrary and unjust proceedings. Probably the time will never arrive when parliaments will become sensible of the solecism of making good laws and then dispensing with the execution of them. The fact is, that *governors* and *makers of laws* seldom feel the effects of them in their own persons: to the *governed*, any variableness destroys the benefit of all law.

Mr. Hutchinson asking, "What they were?" He said, "Fifty pounds." Further demanding, "By what law they were due, whereby he could recover them?" Robinson answered, "By custom." Mr. Hutchinson told him, "He was confident that pretence would not recover them; and if he thought it would, he would go to a civil and fair trial with him the next term; yet due or not due, what civilities he either had or should afford him, he would recompense at parting." Robinson answered, "He stood upon his right, and he would make Mr. Hutchinson, or somebody else, pay it." Mr. Hutchinson told him, "He knew not whom he meant by somebody else, but if his liberty were taken from him without any reason that he knew of, he would not so part with his money, if he could help it." He then, in anger, said, "he would lock him up close, and let nobody come to him." Mr. Hutchinson told him, "He could be locked no closer than he had been all this time, and he hoped he would not forbid those coming to him who had warrant from the secretary; for the rest he might use his pleasure." He, in fury, commanded Mr. Hutchinson to be taken away, and locked him up, so that no person could come to him; and he gave order at the Tower Gates to keep out his children and all his relations that should come to inquire for him; and he sent word to Serjeant Fountaine who had an order to come in, that he should not be admitted, although his business was of great concernment to others, and not to Colonel Hutchinson, who being a trustee for some of his relations, was to have made some settlements in their affairs; which could not be done, but they, to their prejudice, were forced to go without it.[1] Although his commands were executed to the full,

[1] The same respectable friend who, proceeding upon an intimation contained in the *Annual Review*, communicated to the editor the particulars of the deliverance of George Fox, given in page 201, has upon a similar intimation pointed out several passages in the life of William Penn, demonstrating the officious readiness of this same Sir John Robinson to act as the minister of oppression and persecution. He first sends a serjeant from the Tower to watch Penn; the serjeant finds him preaching to *friends*, seizes him, drags him away to the Tower, and sends to Whitehall for Robinson—Robinson comes, sits as magistrate, overrules the just and legal objections of Penn, and commits him to gaol. Penn, whilst in prison, writes a very sensible and moderate letter to Bennett, Earl of Arlington, complaining of coarse treatment in prison, although the secretary had pretended to give orders for his decent accommodation. At the trial of Penn, Sir John Robinson sits as assessor to the recorder, and at the same time obtrudes himself upon the court as an evidence, interferes to influence

yet Mr Hutchinson's eldest son found means to steal into the Tower, and to inform his father of a malicious lie which the lieutenant had made of him at court, on that day that he fell out with him; which was this.—Robinson told the king, that when Mr. Henningham and others were carried out of the Tower to be shipped away, Mr. Hutchinson, looking out of his window, bade them take courage, for they should yet have a day for it. This lie coming to Mr. Hutchinson's knowledge on the 19th of April, moved him more than all his other base usage; whereupon he wrote a letter to Robinson, to tell him he should have taken care of provoking his prisoners to speak, who had so much exposed himself to every one of them; and to let him know what he himself had observed and could prove, he drew it up under certain heads, which he told him, if he continued his vile usage of him, he would publish. The articles were:—

First. That Robinson had affirmed that the king gave no allowance to his prisoners, not so much as to those who had all their estates taken from them; and accordingly he gave them none, but converted what the king allowed them to his own use, and threatened some of the prisoners with death if they offered to demand it; and suffered others, at twelve o'clock at night, to make such a miserable outcry for bread, that it was heard in some parts of the city, and one was absolutely starved to death for want of relief; although the king at that time told a prisoner, that he took more care for the prisoners than for his own table.

Second. That he set down to the king seven pounds a week for one prisoner, for whom he never laid out above twenty-seven or thirty shillings a week at the most.

Third. That he not only kept back the prisoners' allowances, but exacted of them excessive rents for bare prison lodgings, and empty warders' houses, unfurnished; and if they had not punctually paid him, would have stifled them up by close imprisonment, without any order, although he knew

the jury against the prisoner, and abuses the foreman because he will not suffer himself to be browbeaten nor biassed. At last, when a verdict could not be obtained conformable to the views of the judges, they fine the jury for that which they have given, and Penn for contempt of the court. To enumerate, from the *Histories of the Sufferings of the Quakers* the instances of his oppression and cruelty, would fill a volume. Suffice it to hold him up here to infamy as lasting as the fame of those two virtuous men, in the hope of deterring other ministers of injustice from doing the like.

they had not a penny to buy bread, but what came from the charity of good people.

Fourth. That he received salary of the king for forty warders, and had not near so many, but filled up the list with false names, and took the pay to himself.

Fifth. That when he had received money for those warders he kept, he had detained it many months, to his own use, while the poor men were thereby in miserable wants.

Sixth. That he sold the warders' places, and let them houses at a dear rate, and yet took the most considerable prisoners, which ought to have been committed to them, into his own house, and made them pay him excessive rates for bed-rooms, and set his man, Cresset, over them, making them pay him for attendance, which the warders should have had.

Seventh. That he made many false musters in his own company belonging to the Tower, and though he had received the soldiers' money, yet it was run in arrears to them five or six pounds a man; at which they cruelly murmured, because by this means their maintenance was straitened, and their duty brought more frequently upon them.

Eighth. That notwithstanding all his defrauding, oppressive, and exacting ways of raising money, he had ungratefully complained of the king's scanty recompense of his service.

Ninth. That after the starving of the poor prisoners and their miserable outcry, when shame forced him to allow about a dozen poor tradesmen ten shillings a piece,[1] though at that time he received forty from the king for each of them, he and his man, Cresset, denied the king's allowance, and said it was his own charity.

Tenth. That he was frequently drunk, out of the Tower till twelve, one, and two o'clock, and threatened one of the warders, who came one night to fetch him home, with Newgate, and spited him ever after.

All these things being notoriously true, this letter put him into a great rage, and a no less dread that the colonel, as he had threatened him, would publish it; whereupon, as soon as these things were laid to his charge, within ten days he paid his soldiers fifteen months' pay out of twenty-two due to

---

[1] It hence appears that many more in number, and persons of a different description from what other accounts mention, were made prisoners of state at this time.

them when the letter was written, he having all that while kept back eighteen pence a week out of every soldier's pay; and the soldiers, understanding that Colonel Hutchinson's observations of his fraud had procured them this satisfaction, used to give him thanks when they came to stand sentinels at his door.

Presently after he received the letter, he went to Sir Allen Apsley and complained to him that the colonel had sent him a vile letter, but did not show it to Sir Allen, as he sent word to the colonel he would; whereupon Sir Allen Apsley sent Mr. George Hutchinson with a letter to Sir John Robinson, to tell him that if he would let him go to his brother, he doubted not but it would be a good means to persuade the colonel to pay him his fees, and to reconcile the differences between them. Sir John, upon the 21st of April, went along with Mr. George Hutchinson to his brother, and at his entrance, in a passion began to quarrel at the colonel's sour looks; who told him, if he had known they would not have pleased him, and had had notice of his coming, he would have set them in a glass for him. Then Robinson told him, in a rage, he had written him a libel. Mr. Hutchinson answered it was no libel, for he had set his name to it, and they were truths, which if he put him to it, he could prove by sufficient testimonies. Whereupon he fell into horrible railing and cruel language, but by Mr. George Hutchinson's interposition at length all was pacified, and he was fairly going out of the room, with Mr. George Hutchinson, when his man Cresset, reminding him that the colonel had a foul copy of his letter, which he had said he would send to Sir Allen, who had desired to see it; Robinson resolved to take that draught away from him; but the colonel, foreseeing that, had sent copies of it long before out of the Tower, which Robinson's dull head not dreaming of, came back and insolently commanded the colonel to give him the first draught of the letter. The colonel desired to be excused, whereupon Robinson said he would have his pockets searched, and accordingly bade Cresset feel in them. The colonel, a little moved, took a bottle in his hand, and bade Cresset forbear, if he loved his head, and told Sir John if he had any warrant to search him from the king or council, he would submit to it, but otherwise he would not suffer it, especially for a paper which was only of private concernment between

them; for all this, when Sir John saw that Cresset durst not
approach the colonel, he commanded one Wale, a warder,
to search his pockets, who coming with entreaties to the
colonel to permit it, he suffered him. And then the lieutenant caused a little dressing box which the colonel had to
be opened, and took away all the papers he found in it, among
which there was one wherein the colonel had written a verse
out of the 43rd Psalm; it was the first verse, to be joined
with the narrative of his imprisonment, that he had provided to leave behind him for the satisfaction of his friends.
This paper Robinson carried to court, and said, that by the
deceitful and unjust man the colonel intended the king,
although the application was of his own making. In the
meantime, while they were ransacking his box and pockets
Robinson fell a railing at the colonel, giving him the base
terms of rebel and murderer, and such language as none
could have learned, but such as had been conversant with
the civil society of Picked-hatch, Turnbull-street, and Billings-
gate, near which last place the hero had his education.[1]
When the colonel patiently told him he transgressed the act
of oblivion, he said he knew that well enough, and bade him
sue out his remedy; then in fury and rage he turned the
colonel's servant out of his chamber, who had been locked
up with him all the time of his imprisonment, and left him
altogether unattended, which having never been before in
his whole life, put him into a cold and a flux, with a feverish
distemper: but the greatness of his mind was not broken
by the feebleness of his constitution, nor by the barbarous
inhumanity of his jailers, which he received with disdain,
and laughed at, but lost not anger on them.

[1] In a former note we remarked that the evils of imprisonment were
considerably enhanced by the custody of prisons, and peculiarly prisons
of state, being committed to persons of low education and sordid mind;
it is here strongly exemplified, and doubly painful must it have been
to Mrs. Hutchinson to witness the unworthy treatment her husband
now received, and to compare it with that which the persons confined
in this same place had experienced from her father, a man of liberal
and noble mind. Considering the prejudice which reigns against
prisons and prisoners, and therefore how few visit them, and how few
prisoners dare make observations or remonstrances, it is to be feared
many abuses pass unknown and uncorrected; it is but once, in ages,
that there appears a Howard! These considerations ought to render
the guardians of the public welfare extremely tender of the liberty of
individuals: but if such things as state prisons be at all necessary, then
careful to provide for their being superintended by gentlemen, and
men of liberal and benevolent minds.

After these things, Mrs. Hutchinson coming out of the country was, by the lieutenant's order, denied to see her husband, but at her lodgings she found letters from him conveyed to her every day, in spite of all his guards; and thereupon she wrote to Robinson to desire to know whether the secretary had countermanded his first order for her to see her husband, or whether he denied obedience to it; whereupon Robinson sent to her to come to him the next day, but when she came he was gone forth, and she was not admitted within the gates, and thereupon she went back to her lodgings and wrote him a smart letter, and sent him with it a copy of her husband's letter, which she told him she would publish, and not suffer him to be murdered to extort undue money from him. The next day, being the Lord's day, he sent one of the warders to entreat her to come to her husband, and the blood-hound Cresset met her at the gate, and led her to her husband, and left her all the day alone with him, which they had never done before during all the time of his imprisonment, and in the evening Sir John Robinson sent for her, and partly expostulated with and partly flattered her, and told her that her husband would have been sent to the Isle of Man,[1] but that he in kindness had procured a better place for him, and that he was not covetous, but since her husband would not pay him his fees, he might use his pleasure, and she and his children and relations might freely go to him. She received this as befitted her, being in his hands, and knowing that not good nature, but fear she would put him in print, moved him to this gentler course; and this she understood, both by the inquiries his servants made of the colonel's warder concerning her intentions, and by Robinson's continuing, notwithstanding all his dissimulation, to make a thousand false insinuations against the colonel everywhere, and to do him all ill offices at court; even if there were not a more abominable wickedness than all this practised, namely, a lingering poison given him, which, though we had not wickedness enough to suspect then, the events

[1] An exile, for the second time, to the Isle of Man is mentioned. Had the colonel, or his friends, been properly informed, they would not have wished to exchange it for the flat coast of Kent. In our times, when it has become the retreat of the gay and imprudent, it must seem strange to hear it spoken of as a spot to be dreaded. Had he been sent there he would very likely have lived to see the downfall of his enemies, and have returned to shine in the autumn of his life as an evening sun, when his virtues would have been recognised and revered.

that have since ensued make a little doubtful. It is certain that Cresset did make that attempt upon Sir Henry Vane and others, and two or three days before the colonel was sent away, he brought into his chamber, when he came to lock him up at night, a bottle of excellent wine, under pretence of kindness, which he, the colonel, and the warder drank together, and the warder and the colonel both died within four months; the colonel presently after fell sick, but was very unsuspicious, and we must leave it to the great day, when all crimes, how secret soever, will be made manifest, whether they added poison to all their other iniquity, whereby they certainly murdered this guiltless servant of God.

A few days after, at nine o'clock at night, after his wife was gone from him, Cresset brought the colonel a warrant, to tell him that he must, the next morning tide, go down to Sandown Castle, in Kent; which he was not surprised at, it being the barbarous custom of that place to send away the prisoners, when they had no knowledge of, nor time to accommodate themselves for their journey. But instead of putting him into a boat at the morning tide, about eight o'clock Sir Henry Wroth came with a party of horse to receive him of the lieutenant, and finding him sick, and not well able to endure riding in the heat of the day, he was so civil as to let him go by water in the evening tide to Gravesend, with a guard of soldiers in boats hired at his own charge, where the horse guard met him. By these means he got opportunity to take leave of his children which were in town, and about four o'clock he was sent out of the Tower, with one Gregory, designed to be his fellow prisoner; who, going over the drawbridge, turned back to the lieutenant, and told him he would have accepted it as a greater mercy if the king had commanded him to have been shot to death there, rather than have sent him to a distant place to be starved, he having nothing but his trade to maintain him, and his friends would now be so far removed from him, that he could expect nothing.[1] The lieutenant in scorn told him, he went with a charitable man who would not suffer him to starve, whereby he exposed the malice of their intentions to the colonel; who thought it not enough to send him to a far prison not much differing from

[1] This Gregory seems to have been a low man, but had probably commanded a company in some of the city regiments during the latter times of the parliament.

exile, but to charge him with a companion, whom however his kindness might have rendered him charitable to, yet they ought not to have put upon him; neither would the colonel take notice of their imposition, though he designed kindness to the man, had he been worthy of it.

The colonel's wife and children got a boat and followed him to Gravesend, whither also Gregory's wife, and one that called him brother, went; and that night all the company and all the guards supped at the colonel's charge, and many of the guards lay in the chamber with him, who, with the refreshment of the evening air, and the content he felt in being out of Robinson's claws, found himself, or through the liveliness of his spirit fancied himself, something better than he was in the Tower. The next morning, very early, his guards hurried him away on horseback; but, to speak the truth, they were civil to him. His son went along with him to see the place he was sent to, and Sir Allen Apsley had procured an order for his servant to continue with him in the prison; his wife went back to London, to stay there to provide him such accommodation as she could hear he had need of.

When he came to the castle, he found it a lamentable old ruined place, almost a mile distant from the town, the rooms all out of repair, not weather proof, no kind of accommodation either for lodging or diet, or any conveniency of life. Before he came, there were not above half a dozen soldiers in it, and a poor lieutenant with his wife and children, and two or three cannoniers, and a few guns almost dismounted, upon rotten carriages; but at the colonel's coming thither, a company of foot besides were sent from Dover to help to guard the place, pitiful weak fellows, half-starved and eaten up with vermin, whom the governor of Dover cheated of half their pay, and the other half they spent in drink. These had no beds, but a nasty court of guard, where a sutler lived, within a partition made of boards, with his wife and family, and this was all the accommodation the colonel had for his victuals, which were bought at a dear rate in the town, and most horribly dressed at the sutler's. For beds he was forced to send to an inn in the town, and at a most unconscionable rate hire three, for himself, his man, and Captain Gregory; he had to get his chamber glazed, which was a thoroughfare room, having five doors in it, one of which opened upon a platform, that had nothing but the bleak air of the sea, whilst every tide washed the foot of the castle walls. This air made the chamber so unwholesome and damp, that even in the summer time the colonel's hat-case and trunks, and everything of leather, would be every day all covered over with mould,— wipe them as clean as you could one morning, by the next they would be mouldy again; and though the walls were four yards thick, yet it rained in through the cracks in them, and then one might sweep a peck of saltpetre off of them every day, which stood in a perpetual sweat upon them. Notwithstanding all this, the colonel was very cheerful, and made the best shifts he could, with things as he found them; when the lieutenant's wife, seeing his stomach could not well bear his food, offered to board him, and so he and his man dieted with her for twenty shillings a week, he finding wine besides, and linen, etc. Whilst the sutler provided his meat, Gregory ate with him; but when he tabled with the captain, Gregory's son coming to him, he had his meat from the town, and soon after a woman came down who left not the man destitute and comfortless. The worst part of the colonel's sufferings in this prison, was the company of this fellow, who being a fellow prisoner, and poor, and the colonel having no particular retreat, he could not wholly decline his company; and he being a carnal person, without any fear of God, or any good, but rather scandalous conversation, he could take no pleasure in him; meanwhile, many of his friends gave caution to his wife concerning him, as suspecting him to be a trepanner, which we had afterwards some cause to fear.

The captain of the castle, one Freeman, had all this while a chamber which was a little warmer, and had a bed in it, but this he reserved, intending to set a rate upon it, and this too was so dark that one could not have read by the fire or the bedside without a candle at noon day.

When the colonel's wife understood her husband's bad accommodation, she made all the means she could through her friends to procure liberty that she might be in the castle with him, but that was absolutely denied; whereupon she and her son and daughter went to Deal, and there took lodgings, from whence they walked every day on foot to dinner and back again at night, with horrible toil and inconvenience; and though they procured the captain's wife to diet them with the colonel, when they had meat good enough, yet through the poverty of the people, and their want of all necessaries, and the faculty of ordering things as they should be, it was very inconvenient to them; yet the colonel endured it so cheerfully that he was never more pleasant and contented in his whole life. When no other recreations were left him, he diverted himself with sorting and shadowing cockle-shells, which his wife and daughter gathered for him, with as much delight as he used to take in the richest agates and onyxes he could compass, with the most artificial engravings, which were things, when he recreated himself from more serious studies, he as much delighted in as any piece of art. But his fancy showed itself so excellent in sorting and dressing these shells, that none of us could imitate it, and the cockles began to be admired by several persons who saw them. These were but his trifling diversions, his business and continual study was the Scripture, which the more he conversed in, the more it delighted him; insomuch that his wife having brought down some books to entertain him in his solitude, he thanked her, and told her that if he should continue as long as he lived in prison, he would read nothing there but his bible. His wife bore all her own toils joyfully enough for the love of him, but could not but be very sad at the sight of his undeserved sufferings; and he would very sweetly and kindly chide her for it, and tell her that if she were but cheerful, he should think this suffering the happiest thing that ever befell him; he would also bid her consider what reason she had to rejoice that the Lord supported him, and how much more intolerable it would have been if the Lord had suffered his spirits to have sunk, or his patience to have been lost under this. One day when she was weeping, after he had said many things to comfort her, he gave her reasons why she should hope and be assured that this cause would revive, because the interest of God was so much involved in it that he was entitled to it.[1] She told him she did not

[1] The notion of the revival of The Cause, and of the advancement of it by their sufferings, seems to have been very prevalent with those who fell in these times; accordingly they supported their fate with the true spirit of martyrs. The speech of Colonel Okey at the time of his execution, preserved in the *Trials of the Regicides*, maintains the style of prophetic eloquence with so much dignity and firmness, as almost to captivate the imagination of the coolest reasoner. These sentences following are extracted from it:—

" And truly, as to the Cause, I am as confident, even as I am of my resurrection, that that cause which we first took up the sword for, which was for righteousness and justice, and for the advancement of a godly magistracy and a good ministry (however some men turned doubt but the cause would revive; but, said she, notwithstanding all your resolution, I know this will conquer the weakness of your constitution, and you will die in prison. He replied, I think I shall not, if but I do, my blood will be so innocent, I shall advance the cause more by my death hastening the vengeance of God upon my unjust enemies, than I could do by all the actions of my life. Another time, when she was telling him she feared they had but placed him on the sea-shore in order to transport him to Tangier, he told her, if they had, God was the same God at Tangier as at Owthorpe; prithee, said he, trust God with me, if he carry me away, he will bring me back again.

Sometimes when he would not be persuaded to do things wherein he had a liberty, for fear of putting a snare and stumbling-block before others that had not so, and when she would expostulate with him, why he should make himself a martyr for people who had been so censorious of him, and so unthankful and insensible of all his merits, he would say, he did it not for them, but for the cause they owned. When many ill usages he had received from godly people have been urged to him, he would say, that if they were truly the people of God, all their failings were to be borne; that if God had a people in the land, as he was confident he had, it was among them, and not among the cavaliers, and therefore although he should ever be severe against their miscarriages in any person in whomsoever he found them, yet he would adhere to them that owned God, how unkindly soever they dealt with him. Sometimes he would say, that if ever he should live to see the parliament power up again, he would never meddle any more either in councils or in armies; and then sometimes again, when he saw or heard of any of the debaucheries of the times, he would say, he would act only as a justice of the peace in the country, and be severe against drunkards, and suffer none in his neighbourhood. Oftentimes he would say, that if ever he were at liberty in the world,

about for their own ends), shall yet revive again. I am confident, I say, that cause for which so much blood hath been shed, will have another resurrection, and that you will have a blessed fruit of those many thousands that have been killed in the late war. I would say to all good men, rather to suffer than take any indirect means to deliver themselves; and God, when it shall make most for his own glory and the good of his people, will deliver, and that in such a way that himself shall have glory in, and the gospel have no reproach by."

he would flee the conversation of the cavaliers, and would write upon his doors,

Procul hinc, procul este, profani!

and that, though he had in his former conversation with them never had any communication with their manners nor vices, yet henceforth he would never, in one kind or other, have any commerce at all with them; and indeed it was a resolution he would oftener repeat than any other, telling us that he was convinced there was a serpentine seed in them. Yet he had many apprehensions of the rash, hot-heated spirits of many of our party, and fears that their pride and self-conceit of their own abilities would again bring us into confusion, if they should ever have the reins again in their hands; and therefore he would bid us advise his son, and would himself advise him, if ever we lived to see a change, not to fall in with the first, how fair soever their pretences were; but to wait to see how their practices suited them. For he would say, that a hot-spirited people would first get up and put all into confusion, and then a sober party must settle things; and he would say, let my son stay to fall in with these. He foresaw that the courses which the king and his party took to establish themselves would be their ruin, and would say, that whenever the king had an army it would be his destruction.[1] Once when his wife was lamenting his condition, having said many things to comfort her, he told her he could not have been without this affliction, for if he had flourished while all the people of God were corrected, he should have feared he had not been accounted among his children, as he had not shared their lot. Then would he with thankfulness repeat the kind and gentle dealings of the Lord at all times toward him, and erect a firm and mighty hope upon it, and wonderfully encourage her to bear it patiently, not only by words, but by his own admirable example.

After Mr. Hutchinson had been some time prisoner at Sandown, the governor of the Castle came over, and would fain have let him his chamber for 20s. a week, which Mr.

[1] Is it permissible to extend this prediction to the time when James the Second mustered his army near Salisbury, and in their almost general defection received his irrevocable doom? If it is, it will appear a very signal instance of foresight. The king then reigning, Charles II. never made but one, and that a very short-lived attempt to raise an army, which was speedily disbanded.

Hutchinson told him he would give him, if his wife might come there to him; but the governor refused that without an express order, which was endeavoured but could not be obtained. Then Freeman demanded a mark a week of the colonel for fees, but the colonel told him, except he could show how it was due by any known law, he would not pay it. Some time after, the governor of Dover came over, with the governor of Sandown and one Mr. Masters, and Freeman consulting his master of Dover how he should get money of the colonel, the governor of Dover advised him to put him into a dungeon, but the fellow durst not attempt it. Yet some time afterwards he came to the castle, and passing into his own chamber, through Mr. Hutchinson's, who was there, —as he went by with his lieutenant, Moyle, at his heels, he called out to Mr. Hutchinson's man, and bade him desire Hutchinson to come to him, without the addition of so much as the title of a gentleman. Mrs. Hutchinson being then in the room with her husband, desired that she might go in with him and answer the captain's insolency, and that he would take no notice of it; upon which he told her that he would not, neither should she, and so they both went into the captain's chamber, who had also called Gregory. When they were both there, the captain, turning to Moyle, said, "Captain Moyle, I ordain you to quarter Hutchinson and Gregory together in the next room; and if Hutchinson will make a partition at his own charge, he may have that part of the chamber which has the chimney, and for this you must expect a mark a week of Hutchinson, and a noble of Gregory; and if they will have any enlargement besides, they must pay for it."[1] Mr. Hutchinson laughed at him, and bade his wife report his usage of him to the secretary at London, to whom she immediately wrote an account of it, and sent it to Sir Allen Apsley, desiring him either to procure an order for removal, or else for better accommodation, and she showed this letter to Gregory before it went, representing equally his condition with her husband's. Seeing she could not get

[1] In speaking of the persons who had command of the castle, and the custody of the prisoners, there seems in some parts of the narrative to be a little perplexity; but this passage shows clearly that Freeman was captain, but did not reside at it; and that Moyle was his lieutenant, and did reside at it. The former was the person who, on this and some other occasions, attempted to extort money from Colonel Hutchinson and his family; the latter was the person whose wife boarded and accommodated them.

admission into the castle, she took a house in the town, to which she intended to have brought her children for the winter, had not God prevented it.

Not [1] long after, the colonel's brother, Mr. George Hutchinson, came down, and brought with him an order, signed by the secretary Bennett, to allow the colonel leave to walk by the sea-side with a keeper, which order Sir Allen Apsley and his lady had at length procured with some difficulty and sent him; wherewith he was so well satisfied, that now he thought not his prison insupportable; neither indeed was it so to him before, for his patience and faith wonderfully carried him through all his sufferings. As it now drew nigh to the latter end of the year, Mrs. Hutchinson, having prepared the house, was necessitated to go to Owthorpe to fetch her children, and other supplies for her husband; whom, when the time of her departure came, she left with a very sad and ill-presaging heart, rather dreading that while he lay so ready on the sea-coast, he might some time or other be shipped away to some barbarous place in her absence, than that which afterwards ensued. The colonel comforted her all he could, and on the morning she went away said, " Now I myself begin to be loth to part with thee." But yet, according to his usual cheerfulness, he encouraged himself and her, and sent his son along with her. His daughter and his brother stayed at Deal, who, coming to him every day, he walked out with them by the sea-side, and would discourse of the public concernments, and say that the ill-management of the state would cause

[1] We now hasten to the conclusion of our tragedy, and accordingly here are all the principal characters in their proper places and attitudes; our hero suffering with fortitude, calmness, and dignity; the kind-hearted brother, the idolising devoted wife, the observant son and daughter, soothing him with their assiduities, and the constant friend procuring and sending alleviations. Evils so endured, so consoled, almost begin to partake of the nature of enjoyments; but even this state of things will prove very transient, and like the last gleams of departing day, and we must speedily descend into the vale of tears; those who solicited this exile as a mitigation of oppression, and this licence of walking on the shore as a relief, little knew or thought of the effect this situation on this low shore would have on the constitution of a person tenderly brought up, and who had lived all his time in the centre of the kingdom; or that walks by the sea-side, in the decline of the day and of the year, would add considerably to the danger. Those who are acquainted with these parts are well aware of it, and probably so were those who granted both.

Timeo Danaos et dona ferentes.

Trust not the fraudful present of a foe.

discontented wild parties to mutiny and rise against the present powers, but that they would only put things in confusion; it must be a sober party that must then arise and settle them. He would often say to his son and his wife, as he did now to his brother, " Let not my son, how fairly soever they pretend, too rashly engage with the first, but stay to see what they make good, and engage with those who are for settlement, who will have need of men of interest to assist them; let him keep clear and take heed of too rash attempts, and he will be courted if he behave himself piously and prudently, and keep free of all faction, making the public interest only his own." He would sometimes in discourse say, that when these people once had an army, which they seemed to aim at, that army would be their destruction, for he was very confident God would bring them down; he would often say they could not stand, and that whoever had anything to do with them could not prosper. He once used this expression, " Although," said he, " I am free from any truckling with them, yet even that consenting submission which I had, hath brought this suffering upon me." And he would often say, he would never have so much as a civil correspondence with any of them again; yet when he mentioned Sir Allen Apsley, he would say, he would never serve any that would not for his sake serve the person that had preserved him. When his wife went away he was exceeding well and cheerful, and so confident of seeing Owthorpe, that he gave her directions in a paper for planting trees, and for many other things belonging to the house and gardens. " You give me," said she, " these orders, as if you were to see that place again." " If I do not," said he, " I thank God I can cheerfully forego it, but I will not distrust that God will bring me back again, and therefore I will take care to keep it while I have it."

On the third of September, being Saturday, he had been walking by the sea-side, and coming home found himself aguish, with a kind of shivering and pain in his bones, and going to bed did sweat exceedingly: the next day he was a little better, and came down; but on the Monday, expecting another fit, which came upon him, he lay in bed all day, and rose again the next day, but went not down; and after that he slept no more till his last sleep came upon him, but continued in a feverish distemper, with violent sweatings, after which he used to rise out of his bed to refresh him, and when he was up used to read much in his bible. He had directed his wife, when she went away, to send him the *Dutch Annotations on the Bible*, and she had sent it down with some other things; which he presently caused to be brought him, though he was in his bed, and some places in the Epistle to the Romans read, which having heard, " these annotations," said he, " are short; " and then looking over some notes upon that Epistle, which his wife had gathered from him, and had written in a book; " I have," said he, " discovered much more of the mystery of truth in that Epistle, and when my wife returns I will make her set it down; for," said he, " I will no more observe their cross humours, but when her children are near, I will have her in my chamber with me, and they shall not pluck her out of my arms; and then, in the winter nights, she shall collect several observations I have made of this Epistle since I came into prison." The continual study of the Scriptures did infinitely ravish and refine his soul, and take it off from all lower exercise, and he continued it in his sickness even to the last, desiring his brother, when he was in bed and could not read himself, to read it to him. He found himself every day growing weaker, yet was not exceeding sick, only he could not sleep at all, day nor night. There was a country physician at Deal, who had formerly belonged to the army, and had some gifts, and used to exercise them among godly people in their meetings; but having been taken there once by the persecutors, and being married to a wicked unquiet woman, she and the love of the world had perverted him to forsake all religious meetings; yet the man continued civil and fair-conditioned, and was much employed thereabouts. He being sent for to Mr. Hutchinson, found that on Friday his mouth grew very sore, whereupon he told Mr. George Hutchinson that he distrusted his own skill in looking to it, and apprehending some danger, advised him to send for a very famous physician who was at Canterbury, which they did, and he came on Saturday. As he came along he inquired of the messenger that fetched him what kind of person the colonel was, and how he had lived; and what he had been accustomed to, and which chamber of the castle he was now lodged in? Which when the man had told him, he said his journey would be to no purpose, for that chamber had killed him. Accordingly, when he came, he told the colonel's brother, on Saturday night, that he apprehended danger, and appointed some remedies, and some applications to his temples, and a cordial to procure rest, but it had no effect. There was a nurse watching in his chamber, and she told them after his death, that she heard him pray in the night, with the deepest sighs that ever she heard. The next morning, before the doctor and his daughter, and brother and servants came to him, the gentlewoman of the castle came up and asked him how he did? He told her, incomparably well, and full of faith.

Some time after, when the doctor came, he told his brother that the fever had seized his head, and that he believed he should soon fall into ravings and die, and therefore wished him, if he had anything to say to him, to speak while he was in his perfect senses. So Mr. George Hutchinson came to him, and told him he believed he could not live, and therefore desired him if he had anything to do, to despatch it, for he believed his end was approaching. The colonel, without the least dejection or amazement, replied, very composedly and cheerfully, " The will of the Lord be done: I am ready for it." And then he told them that he did now confirm the will he wrote in the Tower as his last will and testament, and all others were to be void. The doctor, who had, when religion was in fashion, been a pretender to it, came to him and asked him if his peace was made with God; to which he replied, " I hope you do not think me so ill a Christian, to have been thus long in prison, and have that to do now! " The doctor asked him concerning the ground of his hope; to which he answered, " There's none but Christ, none but Christ, in whom I have unspeakable joy, more than I can express; yet I should utter more, but that the soreness of my mouth makes it difficult for me to speak." Then they asked him where he would be buried? He told them, in his vault at Owthorpe; his brother told him it would be a long way to carry him: he answered, " Let my wife order the manner of it as she will, only I would lie there." He left a kind message to his wife, " Let her," said he, " as she is above other women, show herself, in this occasion, a good Christian, and above the pitch of ordinary women." [1] He commanded his daughter

[1] This is that command of her husband which Mrs. Hutchinson speaks of at the beginning of her narrative, where she says she has determined to employ her thoughts upon the preservation of his memory, not the fruitless bewailing of it.

who was present to tell the rest, that he would have them all guided by her counsels; and left with his brother the same message to his eldest son, "I would," said he, "have spoken to my wife and son, but it is not the will of God;" then, as he was going to utter something, "here's none but friends;" his brother reminded him that the doctor was present; "Oh, I thank you," said he; and such was their amazement in their sorrow, that they did not think of speaking to the doctor to retire, but lost what he would have said, which I am confident was some advice to his son how to demean himself in public concernments. He lay all the day very sensible and very cheerful, to the admiration both of the doctors and of all that saw him; and as his daughter sat weeping by him, "Fie, Bab," said he, "do you mourn for me as for one without hope? There is hope." He desired his brother to remember him to Sir Allen Apsley, and tell him that he hoped God would reward his labour of love to him. While he was thus speaking to them, his spirits decayed exceedingly fast, and his pulse grew very low, and his head was already earth in the upper part; yet he raised himself in his bed, "And now," said he to the doctor, "I would fain know your reason why you fancy me dying; I feel nothing in myself, my head is well, my heart is well, and I have no pain nor sickness anywhere." The doctor, seeing this, was amazed; "Sir," said he, "I would be glad to be deceived;" and being at a stand, he told Mr. George Hutchinson he was surprised, and knew not what to think, to see him so cheerful and undisturbed, when his pulse was gone; which if it were not death, must be some strange working of the spleen, and therefore advised him to send away for Dr. Ridgely, which he would before have done, but that the doctor told him he feared it would be in vain, and that he would be dead before the doctor could come. While they were preparing to write, the colonel spoke only these words: "'Tis as I would have it: 'tis where I would have it:" and spoke no more, for convulsions wrought his mouth, yet did his sense remain perfect to his last breath; for when some named Mrs. Hutchinson, and said, "Alas, how will she be surprised!" he fetched a sigh, and within a little while departed; his countenance settling so amiably and cheerfully after death, that he looked after he was dead as he used to do when best pleased in life. It was observable that at the same hour, and the same day of the month, and the same day of the week, that the wicked soldiers fetched him out of his own rest and quiet condition at home, eleven months before, the Lord of hosts sent his holy angels to fetch him out of their cruel hands up to his everlasting and blessed rest above; this being the Lord's day, about seven o'clock at night, the eleventh day of September, 1664; that, the same day and hour, the eleventh of October, 1663.

The two doctors, though mere strangers to him, were so moved that they both wept as if he had been their brother; and he of Canterbury said, he had been with many eminent persons, but he never in his whole life saw any one receive death with more Christian courage, constancy of mind, and stedfastness of faith, than the colonel had expressed from the first to the last; so that, considering the height of his fever, and his want of rest, there was an evidence of a divine assistance that overruled all the powers and operations of nature. This doctor, who was called Dr. Jachin, had most curiously and strictly observed all his motions. I know not by what impulse, but he afterwards said that, on account of the colonel's former engagements, he knew he should be examined of all these circumstances, and therefore was resolved diligently to observe them; and as he guessed, it afterwards fell out, for the gentlemen of the country, being of the royal party, were busy in their inquiries, which the doctor answered with such truth and clearness as made them ready to burst with envy at the peace and joy the Lord was pleased to give his servant, in taking him out of this wicked world. I am apt to think that it was not tenderness of nature alone, but conviction of their own disturbed peace, which drew those tears from the doctors, when they saw in him that blessed peace and joy which crowns the Lord's constant martyrs: whatever it was, the men were faithful in divulging the glory of the Lord's wonderful presence with his servant.

As soon as the colonel was dead, his brother sent away a messenger to carry the sad news to his house, and caused his body to be embalmed in order to his funeral, as he had thrice ordered. When he was disembowelled, all his inwards were found exceeding sound, and no taint in any part, only two or three purple spots on his lungs: his gall, the doctor said, was the largest that ever he saw in any man, and observed it to be a miracle of grace that he had been so patient as he had seen him.

Some two or three days before the colonel fell sick, Freeman, the captain of the castle, had sent down a very strict order that the colonel should carry nothing out of the castle; in pursuance of which the soldiers would not suffer them to take out his beds, furniture, or clothes, which Mr. Hutchinson forbore till an order came for them.

As soon as the news came to Owthorpe, the colonel's two eldest sons and all his household servants went up to London with his horses, and made ready a hearse, tricked with escutcheons and six horses in mourning, with a mourning coach and six horses to wait on it, and came down to Deal with an order from the secretary for the body; but when they came thither, Captain Freeman, in spite, would not deliver it, because Mrs. Hutchinson herself was not come to fetch it; so they were forced, at an intolerable expense, to keep all this equipage at Deal, while they sent to the secretary for another order, which they got directed to the lieutenant in the absence of the captain, and as soon as it came they delivered it to him, who immediately suffered them to take away the body, which they did at that very hour, though it was night, fearing a further dispute with Freeman. For he, after the body had been ten days embalmed, said he would have a jury empanelled, and a coroner to sit upon it, to see whether he died a natural death. Mr. Hutchinson asked him why he urged that, when it lay on their side to have sought satisfaction. He said he must do it to clear the king's garrison. Mr. Hutchinson told him he had slipped his time; it should have been done at the first, before the embalming. He said he would have it unlapped, and accordingly he sent for a coroner and a jury, who, when they came, would not unlap the body, but called those persons who had been about him, and examined them as to the occasion of his death. They made affidavit, which remains yet upon record, that the doctor said *that the place had killed him,* and, satisfied with this, they did not unlap the body. As it came into Deal, Freeman met it, and said, if he had been in the castle they should not have had it till they had paid the money he demanded; which, when he could not justify any right to it by any law, he began to beg most basely and unworthily, but had nothing given him for that. However, though the secretary had also ordered that the colonel should have his things out, yet he detained all he found in the castle, his trunks, and beds, and furniture, which could never be gotten out of his hands. Although this spite of his put the colonel's family to an excessive charge in staying so long in that cut-throat town of Deal, yet there was a providence of the Lord in it; for the colonel's daughter who was there, through grief had contracted a violent sickness, which took her with great severity, and wrought off of her stomach in black vomits, which made her for the present desperately ill, and the doctor that was with her said that if she had then been on her journey, as she would have been had they not been delayed by Freeman's cruel spite, she could not have lived.

The next day after they had gotten out the body, they brought it with a handsome private equipage to Canterbury, and so forwards towards London, meeting no affronts in their way but at one town, where there was a fair, the priest of which place came out, with his clerk in his fool's coat, to offer them burial, and they laid hold of the horses to stop their hearse; but the attendants putting them by, the wicked rout at the fair took part with them, and set upon the horsemen; but they broke several of their heads, and made their way clear, having beaten off all the town and the fair, and came on to London. They passed through Southwark, over the bridge, and through the whole heart of the city, in the day time, to their lodging in Holborn, and had not one reviling word or indignity offered them all the way, but several people were very much moved at that sad witness of the murderous cruelty of the men then in power.

From London he was brought down to Owthorpe, very seriously bewailed all the way he came along by all those who had been better acquainted with his worth than the strangers were among whom he died; and he was brought home with honour to his grave through the dominions of his murderers, who were ashamed of his glories, which all their tyrannies could not extinguish with his life.

APPENDIX

APPENDIX

1. THE ORIGINAL ENDING
OF THE MEMOIRS

Julius Hutchinson's 1806 edition concluded with a sentence from the original manuscript which he omitted in the 1808 edition, on which the Bohn text (used for Everyman's Library) was based. This is the sentence which followed '. . . with his life', on p. 383 of the present edition. The sentence was included in the Dryden House Memoirs edition (H. Child, 1904).

So was he brought lamented home and layd in his owne vault which he thrice before his death ordered he should be brought to.

Julius Hutchinson omitted completely from his editions Lucy Hutchinson's original ending of the manuscript. It is here printed in its entirety.

IT WAS not a little wonder to us that he should so positively appoynt his body to be carried thither when in all his life time before he had usd to say that wherever he died he would there be buried, and sometime would give it charge to his wife if she survived him to enterre him in the place he died. But att his death he very earnestly enjoynd them to carry him home, though it was about eight score miles distant from the place where he died. What moovd him to it he declared not, but I am apt to believe one thing was because he would not have any of those superstitions exercisd about him, being dead, for the opposing of which he lost his liberty and life. Neither did wee looke upon it as any kindnesse or civillity in his enemies that they permitted us so undisturbedly to fulfill his desire, but a hand of God that overruld their barbarous nature. They could doe no otherwise for they envied all those things God would not suffer them to hinder, as was apparent upon severall proofes. Among the rest, one of the King's servants that had mourning sent him was absolutely forbidden to wear it for him though providence, in a few dayes after, put them in mourning too. Then they raysd a false report and spread it from the Court that impatient of his prison he had poysond himselfe. And many other testimonies there were of their mallace, rage and madnesse, att that peace and joy and glory with which the Lord had crownd his dying servant and seald an answer of his owne prayers in his death, who usd to say that if the Lord would give him his desire he would not die in raging distemper nor in torturing payne. And so the Lord, wonderfully against the nature of the disease, kept him in perfect understanding and quiet without the least deliration though the feaver had seized his head and he had not any reliefe from sleepe, and he felt not any other pang in death but was translated with such joy and tranquillity of soule as was a manifect seale of God's favour. In the want of all things that he, who had had a comfortable house of his owne, attendants, and all things that any gentleman of his quallity could require from his infancy till his imprisonment, should come to die in a vile chamber, untrimd and unhung, in a poore wretched bed without his wife children and servants and relations about him and all his former enjoyments taken from him—these thoughts extended were enough to melt away tender bowells. But then to consider on the other side that the Lord provided his dearest brother and daughters to assist him to the last and had sent him mony to defray all charges which he wanted before, and likewise ordered it so that some which should have bene payd half a yeere before he was detaind sent in now to bring him home, and above all that the Lord not only bore up his spirit to part with all things without regrett but filld him full of joy and thankfullnesse and curbd the power of his disease and chaind up Sathan that he could not torture him in mind or body. It was an admirable and unspeakable flood of mercy which may helpe to comfort us in the losse of him.

Not long after the Collonell, the warder that was his keeper in the Tower died of a raging feaver which struck Mrs. Hutchinson into an apprehension of that which many circumstances made not alltogether unsuspicious, that the Collonell was poysond, for that was not a strange practise with them in the Tower and both the Lieftenant and his man Cresset did mortally hate this warder. After that Robinson had turned out the Collonell's men from him some few nights before he was sent away, Cresset when he came to lock up the Collonell brought with him under a shew of kindnesse a bottle of excellent wine which he drunke with the Collonell and his warder. It is true that the Collonell was ill and had a flux when he want away from the Tower which stayd upon his journey but wee thought then it might rather have bene

occasiond by some cold he gott being by the state's Bar-
barisme deprived of the assistance of his servant to wait on
him att his rising and going to bed, which was a thing he had
never bene without in his life. But there were some circumstances that did give ground to a suspicion of poyson—the
Captain's sending expresse order while he was well that none
of his things should goe out of the Castle and that but ten
dayes before he died. Then his sending unreasonably for a
Coroner to examine the cause of his death to cleare as he sayd
the King's garrison. Then the false report that was raysd att
Court, and when Mr. George Hutchinson had related the
manner of his death and sicknesse to Doctor Cox he sayd
those sweates were a symptome of poyson, but afterwards
when Mrs. Hutchinson would have urged his opinion againe
he was wise and reserved, though at first he himselfe had
enquird of her whither she did not suspect it. Alsoe Captaine
Taverner that had some little skill in Astrologie seeing Mr.
George Hutchinson come sad from his brother the night
before he died, sayd nothing but went up into his closett and
after a while came downe againe very melancholly and the
next day, just at that time the Collonell laid speechless, came
to the roome and saw him expire and after was present att his
embalming and very inquisitive of the man that did it
whether he found no signes of poyson but that man sayd not.
Yet the Captaine that had bene present at the opening of
Sindercomb who was poysond in the Tower sayd he saw some
such purple spotts upon the Collonell's lungs as he had
observed in that prisoner's and was the more induced to
believe his signe because he had some confidence in his art,
which I reject as vaine and foolish, but when he went up to his
closet from Mr. Hutchinson he sett his figure, and his starres,
he sayd, told him that the Collonell should die the next day
att that hower which he after came in and saw him expire and
that he was poysond. The Castle had bene sayd to be often
disturbd with evill spirites before the Collonell came but in all
the 4 months that he was there there was not aniething seene
or heard till about a fortnight before his death when allmost
every night the souldiers that were on the guard and the
people in the Castle (all but the Collonell) heard att midnight
in the kitchen greate noyses and preparations for getting
meate, pumping water, and winding up the jack and washing
the kitchen when the maid was in bed and nobody there, but

the Collonell never heard any of this. Only one Lord's day at evening, his chamber being over the kitchen and his wife and children and his brother with him, wee did certainly all thinke we heard the jack wound up when we were after assured there was no such thing done, nobodie being then in the kitchen and this was the Lord's day before Mrs Hutchinson went. But after he was dead those noyses ceast and nothing more was heard, but the spring after there came an apparition of a gentlewoman in mourning in such a habitt as Mrs. Hutchinson usd to weare there, and affrighted the guards mightily at the first but after a while grew familiar to them and was often seene walking in the Collonell's chamber and on the plat-formes and came sometimes into the guard among them, which is certainly true but we knew not how to interpret it. Neither can we believe that he was poysond although we know his enemies had mallice and wickednesse enough to doe it and at the same time did make as bad attempts against the lives of others and did effect their murther upon Mr. Lish in France. But if they did not that way dispatch the Collonell, it is certaine their unjust and barbarous usage of him did occasion his death, whose murther the Lord will not forget when he makes inquisition for the blood of his saints. But what they intended for his destruction, the Lord turnd to his advantage who dying in and for the Lord is translated into happiness and blessed rest from those labours which employ the living saints, whose soules are grieved with the iniquitie of the times they live in. Lett us blesse the Lord for him and for the signall and eminent mercy shewd unto him which made him in life and death victorious over the Lord's and his enemies.

2. VERSES WRITTEN BY MRS HUTCHINSON

In the small book containing her own life, and most probably composed by her during her husband's retirement from public business to his seat at Owthorpe.

ALL sorts of men through various labours press
To the same end, contented quietness;
Great princes vex their labouring thoughts to be
Possessed of an unbounded sovereignty;
The hardy soldier doth all toils sustain
That he may conquer first, and after reign;
Th' industrious merchant ploughs the angry seas
That he may bring home wealth, and live at ease.
These none of them attain: for sweet repose
But seldom to the splendid palace goes;
A troop of restless passions wander there,
And only private lives are free from care.
Sleep to the cottage bringeth happy nights,
But to the court hung round with flaring lights,
Which th' office of the vanished day supply,
His image only comes to close the eye,
But gives the troubled mind no ease of care,
While country slumbers undisturbed are;
Where, if the active fancy dreams present,
They bring no horrors to the innocent.
Ambition doth incessantly aspire,
And each advance leads on to new desire;
Nor yet can riches av'rice satisfy,
For want and wealth together multiply:
Nor can voluptuous men more fulness find,
For enjoyed pleasures leave their stings behind.
He's only rich who knows no want; he reigns
Whose will no severe tyranny constrains;
And he alone possesseth true delight
Whose spotless soul no guilty fears affright.
This freedom in the country life is found,

Where innocence and safe delights abound.
Here man's a prince; his subjects ne'er repine
When on his back their wealthy fleeces shine:
If for his appetite the fattest die,
Those who survive will raise no mutiny:
His table is with home-got dainties crowned,
With friends, not flatterers, encompassed round;
No spies nor traitors on his trencher wait,
Nor is his mirth confined to rules of state;
An armed guard he neither hath nor needs,
Nor fears a poisoned morsel when he feeds;
Bright constellations hang above his head,
Beneath his feet are flow'ry carpets spread;
The merry birds delight him with their songs,
And healthful air his happy life prolongs;
At harvest merrily his flocks he shears,
And in cold weather their warm fleeces wears;
Unto his ease he fashions all his clothes;
His cup with uninfected liquor flows:
The vulgar breath doth not his thoughts elate,
Nor can he be o'erwhelmed by their hate.
Yet, if ambitiously he seeks for fame,
One village feast shall gain a greater name
Than his who wears the imperial diadem,
Whom the rude multitude do still condemn.
Sweet peace and joy his blest companions are;
Fear, sorrow, envy, lust, revenge, and care,
And all that troop which breeds the world's offence,
With pomp and majesty, are banish'd thence.
What court then can such liberty afford?
Or where is man so uncontroll'd a lord?

3. INSCRIPTION

This inscription on the monument of Colonel Hutchinson, at Owthorpe, is supposed to have been written by Lucy Hutchinson.

Quousque Domine !

In a vault under this wall lieth the body of

JOHN HUTCHINSON,

Of Owthorpe, in the county of Nottingham, Esq.,
Eldest sonne and heire of Sir Thomas Hutchinson, by his first wife, the Lady Margaret, daughter of Sir John Biron, of Newsted, in the said county.

This monument doth not commemorate
Vaine ayrie glorious titles, birth, and state;
But sacred is to free, illustrious grace,
Conducting happily a mortal's race;
To end in triumph over death and hell,
When, like the prophet's cloake, the fraile flesh fell,
Forsaken as a dull impediment,
Whilst love's swift fiery chariot climb'd th' ascent.
Nor are the reliques lost, but only torn,
To be new made, and in more lustre worn.
Full of this ioy he mounted, he lay downe,
Threw off his ashes, and took up his crowne.
    Those who lost all their splendor in his grave,
Ev'n there yet no inglorious period have.

He married Lucy, the daughter of Sir Allen Apsley, lieutenant of the Tower of London, by his third wife, the Lady Lucy, daughter of Sir John St. John, of Lidiard Tregos, in the county of Wilts, who dying at Owthorpe, October 11, 1659, lieth buried in the same vault.

He left surviving by the sayd Lucy 4 sons; Thomas, who married Jane, the daughter of Sir Alexander Radcliffe, buried in the same vault: and Edward, Lucius, and John: and 4 daughters; Barbara, Lucy, Margaret, and Adeliza; which last lies buried in the same vault.

He died at Sandowne Castle, in Kent, after 11 months' harsh and strict imprisonment,—without crime or accusation,—upon the 11th day of Sept. 1664, in the 49th yeare of his age, full of joy, in assured hope of a glorious resurrection.

INDEX